The Golden Conquistadores

The Golden

Conquistadores

Introductions and Commentaries by
IRWIN R. BLACKER

Texts edited by
HARRY M. ROSEN

THE **BOBBS-MERRILL** COMPANY, INC.
A SUBSIDIARY OF HOWARD W. SAMS & CO., INC.
1720 EAST 38TH STREET · INDIANAPOLIS 6. INDIANA

OTHER BOOKS BY IRWIN R. BLACKER:

Irregulars, Partisans, Guerrillas

Westering

Taos

The Kilroy Gambit

Maps by ANITA S. ROGOFF

*To my parents and the
     memory of my brother*   I. R. B.

*To my wife Irma—
     in appreciation*   H. M. R.

What a troublesome thing it is to go
and discover new lands; and the riches
we took is hardly possible to exaggerate.

BERNAL DÍAZ DEL CASTILLO

Contents

Maps

Preface

THE CONQUISTADOR. He was the last remnant of the great crusades. He was a member of a small group of men at arms— adventurers, if you will—who fought for the glory of Spain and of God. He was avaricious and pious. He believed that what his arms could take belonged to him and his king, and he believed in the Church Militant.

He crossed unknown mountain ranges, freezing in the unfamiliar heights, abandoning his equipment over the torturous route, but prepared at the end to test his courage and faith against that of empires exotic and overwhelmingly large. He trailed his pike through uncharted jungles, saw strange beasts and stranger flora, buried his dead in rivers or left them face up for the carrion birds because he lacked the strength to dig a grave, but at the end of his march he fought and won. He could build a ship with nails forged from his own armor and sail it across an unknown sea. He could find his way into the great blank spaces on the map and find his way back out again.

He was a complex individual spawned of the Catholic Counter Reformation, of the long wars against the Moors, of the unknown vastness of the new world. He lied, he abused, he cheated, he plundered, he murdered, he raped, he profaned foreign gods, he destroyed whole civilizations and committed every crime known to man. But he brought his religion to a new-found land because he believed in that religion. He organized governments where none had existed, he brought in new plants, new tools, handwriting in places where there had been none. He abolished crimes of sex and human sacrifice, he built hospitals and schools, and he was even prepared to debate the rights and wrongs of a just war when the conquest was done and there was time for talking.

He was always loyal to his king and his church. He abhorred the

13

coward and the man without honor as he understood honor—a certain code of the hidalgo who could face hardship beyond human comprehension but would not lift a hand to carry a load, who could kill without warning or cause but yet respect a marriage to an Indian or a Negro slave.

The conquistador tested his arms in the conquest of the Canary Islands, in the first probings of the Indian Ocean after years of forging against the Moors, but he reached his peak as an explorer and plunderer in the Western Hemisphere where he roamed from the central plains of North America to the bottom-most tip of South America. He gave names to the land from the Grand Canyon of the Colorado River to the Straits of Magellan.

He may be condemned for his excesses, for his lack of compassion, for his contempt for and abuse of others, but he must be admired for his faith and courage. He marched and sailed more boldly than any man had ever marched or sailed before. And he will always be remembered because he became less a person than a symbol, a state of mind that acknowledged no defeat no matter how strange or how forbidding the barriers.

THE CONQUISTADOR AND THE THRONE OF SPAIN. The conquistador might betray his companions or assassinate a native emperor, but he lived in the shadow of the Spanish throne and he was aware at all times of the world from which he sprang—a Europe of the sixteenth century dominated by the Spanish kings.

Though Isabella of Castile died the year Columbus returned from his fourth and final voyage, and Spain remained divided—Aragon and Castile—Ferdinand retained control of the Iberian Peninsula. Until his death in 1516 he kept up the war against the Moors, carrying it even to Africa, but with the conquest of Oran and Tripoli he turned his attentions northward. Joining forces with the Pope and the Venetians against France, he added Navarre to Castile the year he died. He was succeeded on the throne by his grandson—Charles I of Spain, Charles V of the Holy Roman Empire—the king to whom the great conquistadores owed their allegiances and loyalties.

Both as king and as emperor Charles kept Europe in turmoil until his retirement in 1556. A thin, bulging-eyed man with a speech defect, good common sense and a limited imagination, he was well-educated for his time, though he knew no Spanish when he began his lengthy reign. A foreigner to his Spanish subjects, the young man from Ghent leaned heavily at first on his advisors as he tried to hold the many parts of his kingdom together. There were Aragon, Castile with its newly acquired Navarre, Granada, the colonies in America, the North African possessions, the kingdoms of Naples, Sicily and Sardinia as well as the Netherlands. The European areas were either straining for local government or coming under the hungry eyes of neighboring kings, and the other areas were expensive to maintain with the deficient treasury that was always to plague Charles. In addition to the conflict he had inherited with France, Lutheranism was splitting Europe apart; and Moslem Turkey, joined with the Barbary States of North Africa, was closing in from the Danube and the Mediterranean.

Charles emerged as his own man only after his historic meeting with Martin Luther at the Diet of Worms in 1521. He moved very quickly in the years that followed—roaming over Europe as no king had before him. He sacked Rome in 1527 and held Pope Clement VII a prisoner. Five years later he led his armies against the Turks and forced them back down the Danube. He personally directed the invasion of France in 1536 and crushed the rebellion of his native Ghent in 1540. Four years later, stopping short of Paris, he accepted the treaty of Crespy.

In the last years of his reign the Wars of the Reformation drained his energies and his budget, and as he reached old age all of the pieces he had held together with force, chicanery and money began to slip away. There was war in Parma and the Piedmont. The French checked his attack through Germany, and the Turks were marching again. Weary and embittered, he abdicated the throne of Spain in favor of his son Philip.

However, despite the problems he faced in Europe, Charles found time to encourage and control the conquistadores. He was meeting with Luther the same week Cortés was preparing the final siege of Mexico City, and he was fighting the Turks and besieging Tunis during the years of Pizarro's conquest of Peru. When he assumed the throne there were only insignificant settlements on the American mainland, yet when he died the conquest was virtually complete and governments had been established.

Charles supported and guided the conquistadores. He settled the differences between them and he legalized their relationships with the natives and the missionary church. He organized the labor force and regulated the trade and shipping. And most particularly he supervised the exploitation of the newly claimed lands.

An energetic and conservative man, Charles V faced the great decisions of the Reformation and the preservation of Europe as he had been born into it, and it is against the background of his personality and the tumult of his reign that the conquistadores must be seen. They sailed from a Spain created by him and his grandparents, and it was to this man that they gave their allegiance with unwavering loyalty. To him they directed their reports of conquest and failure, and it was he who allowed them to share the fruits of their victories.

THE CONQUISTADOR AND THE CHURCH. For the Spaniard the Cross and the Crown were more closely wedded than in any other European country. The years of war against the Moors bred into the Spaniard a conviction, a passion for religion, that welded his country together and convinced him that the church of Spain should be the responsibility of the crown of Spain. Where there were deviations and heresies in the rest of Europe, Spain clamped down the lid on speculation, closed off all discussion that might lead to reformation outside the Roman Catholic Church and cleaned its own house. The reformation under Archbishop Jiménez de Cisneros abolished concubinage, set new standards of morality, education and habit. It established a religious ethic for the clergy without equal in Europe. The crown assumed rights which were retained elsewhere by the Pope, and nowhere in Christendom did he have less authority. The throne alone could approve and appoint the clerical hierarchy. The throne could depose. The throne alone could approve the papal bulls or rescripts that were to govern the religious life of Spain. And the throne controlled the tithes.

From these powers Spain derived certain advantages: religious peace and tranquility when all of the rest of Europe was torn with speculation and conflict. The Counter Reformation at the same time removed Spain from the stream of humanism that was sweeping northward through Europe. There was theology in the Peninsula, but it was mystical and speculative. Though the time of the mystic was "the last bright glow of medieval Catholicism," it was sharply limited. Santa Teresa of the barefoot Carmelites was confined to a convent and her followers were tried by the Inquisition.

Tolerance was abandoned when Isabella, "The Catholic," appointed Tomás de Torquemada head of the Inquisition to clean up religious deviates. The establishment of this institution was a symptom of Spanish religious passion, though the purge that followed was based as much on a misconception of racial purity as it was on religious purity. Intermarried for centuries with Jews and Moslems, the Spaniards tried to cut themselves free from what they believed to be foreign ties. The conversos—Jews (*Marranos*) and Moslems (*Moroscos*) who had accepted the faith—were rooted out on the slightest provocation. And those who had not accepted the faith were expelled.

The Inquisition became a political weapon in Spain more than a religious one. The Suprema which directed its activities was only one of several royal councils, and all of its senior officials were paid by the crown.

However, more misinformation has been spread about the Inquisition than probably any other organization in history. None can deny excess and error, but it must be remembered that it kept prisoners safe from the violence of the mobs, attempted to be just within the pattern of Spanish justice, and avoided the witch-burning that swept through the rest of Europe. The number of persons burned alive was probably smaller in Spain than in other European countries such as England and Sweden.

Much of the terror of the Inquisition lay in its secrecy, as does much of the misinformation regarding it. As the Inquisition and the mystics were each part of the religious fervor that helped to shape Spain, so were the religious orders.

It is estimated that as many as one person in five was professionally affiliated with the church in one capacity or another. And the missionary orders dominated their activities. The Dominicans traveled westward with the conquistadores, bringing with them their affinity for legality—the law of God. They held their places in the many legislative bodies and the scattered governments established by the conquistadores. They fought against and beside them. While they showed no mercy for the transgressor, it was they who forced the humanitarian legislation of the Council of the Indies. It was they who made their fellow Spaniards accept the Indians as God's creatures. The Franciscans were the other order that journeyed westward in the early years, bringing to the continent full power to administer all sacraments, to confirm minor orders, to consecrate churches and provide them with clergy.

The first three Franciscans to arrive in Mexico opened schools where they taught the natives reading, writing and gospel. When the first large body of their fellows arrived in Vera Cruz in 1524, they set the example of humility for their fellow Christians and the natives by walking barefooted from Vera Cruz to Mexico City, and from there they spread out to Christianize and to educate the heathen.

And though the orders did much to make the lives of the natives easier, at no time did they relax their pressure for conversion. When the Araucanian chief—Caupolican—was captured, he was converted and baptized, "causing pity and great excitement among the Castilians who stood around," and after instruction in the True Faith, he was made to sit upon a stake while his co-religionists shot arrows through him. The whipping post on which the erring were chastised was as much a part of the mission as the altar. Spanish religious zeal was actual and passionate. It knew no middle ground, allowed for no compromise and was as much a spur to the conquistador as glory, gold or the king. It was not incongruous for Bernal Díaz del Castillo, one of Cortés' captains and a future historian, to state, "We came here to serve God and to get rich." The desire to convert the native and save his soul was sincere and cannot be underestimated.

THE WORLD THE CONQUISTADORES FOUND. The levels of Indian civilizations varied from the high culture of the Mayans of Yucatan and Guatemala to the most primitive of the aborigines of Tierra del Fuego.

The first Indians contacted on the continent were simple savages living along the coast. Their culture was no greater than that of the American Plains Indians met by Coronado in his northward march.

However, in Central America, Mexico and Peru the conquistadores discovered three civilizations almost as high as many of those of classical Europe and higher than those of Northern Europe at the birth of Christianity. The Mayans who had withdrawn to Central America could write a hieroglyphic as fine as that of Babylon and Egypt, knew astronomy better than the Greeks and proved it in their creation of a three-hundred-and-sixty-five-day calendar that even took into account the leap year and equaled any of Europe's until Pope Gregory's modifications in 1582. While none of the American civilizations ever discovered the arch, large buildings were erected and the stone sculpture of the pyramid temples might even have been cut with the use of iron tools. While the Mayan language remains unread, no Rosetta stone having ever been located, it is believed that its history dates back to 3485 B.C., and definite dating exists in the vicinity of Vera Cruz that places the Mayan civilization as far back as 96 B.C. Yet these people never domesticated animals other than fowl and dogs, and never discovered the wheel. Basically an agricultural civilization, the Mayans were a loose federation of tribes bound together by a highly developed religion with a complex theology.

The Mayans had been thrust out of the Mexican plateau by the more aggressive Aztecs who established what was to eventually become Tenochtitlan—cactus growing on a rock—on Lake Texcoco about 1325—less than two hundred years before the arrival of Cortés and the conquest of the city that was to be called Mexico. A brutal race of warriors, the Aztecs held down their Indian neighbors with cruelty and terror, which was to react against them and aid the Spanish conquest. Lacking the mathematics and the astronomy of the Mayans, the Aztecs took what culture they could from a tribe that has almost been lost in the limbo of history—the Toltecs who seem to serve as a bridge between the high Mayan culture and that of their Aztec successors. Engineers and builders, the Aztecs were able to construct Tenochtitlan on the marshy ground of the great lake. They built canals across their city and causeways to the mainland. They watered the city with an aqueduct which filled the many scattered fountains and reservoirs. Though most of their number lived in reed and mud huts, there were many adobe buildings built around large patios with flower gardens between. And they, like the Mayans and Toltecs, built large pyramid temples. A superstitious people borne down by the weight of a crude religion, the Aztecs were not the equals of their Inca neighbors to the south.

The Incas of Peru had developed a very crude written language, had engineered irrigation, great forts, and cities which are impressive to this day. They developed anesthetics of herbs and could perform surgical operations of great complexity.

The range of civilizations lying so close together confused the conquistadores, who expected to meet the Aztec and Inca level of culture and wealth wherever they went, and it was easy for a Fray Marcos to mistake from a distance the simple adobe pueblo culture of Arizona for the one of Mexico, from which he had just come. The next Tenochtitlan was always just beyond the horizon. If there were rich cultures like the Aztecs' and the Incas', why should there not be more like them in so vast a pair of continents?

The Indian culture was conquered and destroyed so that little more than statues, pottery and legends remain of it. But once it had been found at its highest level, there was no reason for the conquistador to believe it would not be found again. For history, the great crime of the conquistadores was his treatment of what he considered barbarous societies.

THE CONQUISTADOR AND WAR. For the Spaniard, war had become a way of life. He fought the Portuguese, the French, the Moors, and at times his own countrymen. The profession of arms was a glorious service to the Crown and the Cross. There were the enemies of Spain and of God, and a man of honor joined either the army or the Church Militant.

In sixteenth-century Europe there were no soldiers equal to those of Spain—no men better equipped, better trained or better motivated. They were already far from the medieval tradition, being organized professionals who fought in political wars for a king and country, and at least some of them were armed with gunpowder weapons. The local captains recruited their own troops, and the crown levied taxes on the towns and borrowed from the church to pay those troops. While mercenaries continued to be the core of most European armies, the Spanish soldier marched in the vanguard of Spain's wars. With the Iberian Peninsula as a natural fortress, the Spanish monarchs did not hesitate to send their armies abroad. These seasoned campaigners of the wars against the Moors, the French and the Italians were readily available for service in the New World, and, having been raised in the mercenary tradition, they were ready and eager to fight for booty and glory.

The conquistador was foreshadowed by both literature and history. Spain was flooded with romantic novels of the military hero who saved the homeland, rescued noble ladies and won great fortunes. He was the wandering knight who tilted with giants and slaughtered Moors. A century later he was to become Don Quixote, the magnificent innocent; but in the years of the conquistador the warrior was an ideal.

The conquistador was favored by the shifting pattern of war. When Charles VIII of France marched against Naples, he brought about a revolution in the art of war. Europe expected one more battle of precision, procession and movement, a general action won or lost with the death of a single soldier while whole armies surrendered when they were formally outflanked or cut off from their bases. But to everyone's surprise, Charles VIII's pikemen, cavalry and artillery were blended successfully into a modern combat force at Fornovo in 1495. Thirty-three hundred and fifty men were killed, and a way of war was dead in a short quarter hour.

In the years that followed Fornovo, many commanders experimented with new techniques, new ratios of men and horse and gun; and some of these experiments were disastrous failures. But all of the old formalities were meaningless, and a half century elapsed before new ones were developed. And in that half century military tactics were fluid. The light cavalry which was once the strength of every army now fell before the arquebusier. The heavy cavalry was converted from an assault force against a line to the support of infantry already clashing with infantry. The ideal of the warrior hero remained for a time though battle for pleasure gave way to battle for survival, while the tilt and the tournament disappeared.

During this historic fifty years the conquistador spread over the New World, unbound by tradition, prepared to fight in any fashion that would bring him victory. He invented his tactics as he went; and with both his freedom and his ingenuity, he was probably the superior of any fighting man in Europe. It may be merely legend that Cortés offered to capture an African fortress when his emperor quit the battlefield, but no one who knows the Battle of Lake Texcoco can doubt that the aging conquistador could have made his offer good.

THE CONQUISTADOR AND HIS HORSE. The Spaniard—white-faced, bearded and armored—came as a shocking surprise to the Indian, but nothing added to that surprise more than the conquistador's horse. As Coronado's companion, Castañeda, was to write, "After God we owed the victory to our horses." Fifty years after the conquest of Mexico, Cortés' captain, Bernal Díaz del Castillo, was able to recall the horses of the conquest by name, owner and color.

The horse meant as much to the Spaniard as it did to his historic enemy, the Moor. An ancient law even decreed that caballeros should ride on horseback "as honor and tradition demanded." In fact, *caballero* meant only "a rider on a horse" before it came to mean "gentleman," while a *peon* originally meant "a person who walks."

The conquistador's horse was his single most valuable possession, costing as much as six thousand dollars in the New World. And in the early year of the conquest, it was difficult to buy a horse at any price. The voyage from Spain to Mexico took at least two months. If the vessels were becalmed and the water was in short supply, the horses had to be dropped into the sea—in the "horse latitudes." When Cabeza de Vaca sailed as Governor of Paraguay in 1540, he lost sixteen of his forty horses.

Twenty-two years earlier Cortés had had to scour Cuba, Jamaica, Santo Domingo and the other islands before he sailed for Mexico "because horses and Negro slaves are hard to come by." After his tragic retreat on the Night of Sorrows, he still thought of horses ahead of men: "Without His merciful assistance we should have all perished, horses and men." And after the battle he "cured the wounded horses with grease from dead Indians."

The Spaniard rode his horse a la genita in a light, high Moorish saddle, knees up in short shoe stirrups. He guided the short-legged, low-bellied beast—preferably a stallion—with a powerful mameluke bit having a solid curb that put pressure on the neck and not the mouth. The conquistador on horse carried his lance overhand, ready for quick thrusts, and not under his arm as was the tradition in jousting.

The Indians believed the Spanish horses were immortal and when they found the one belonging to Pedro de Moron on the road leading to Mexico City, they cut off its head and sent it from village to village. However, another legend that horses ate human flesh did not die so easily.

THE CONQUISTADOR AND THE PRIZE. One day a young padre objected to Francisco Pizarro's mistreatment of the Indians and urged that the faith of God be made known to them. The old conquistador turned on him with anger, saying, "I have not come for any such reasons. I have come to take away from them their gold." There is no doubting that many of the conquistadores crossed the ocean for no other purpose than to get rich as quickly as possible and sail back to Spain with their booty. Las Casas says the rallying cry in Hispaniola in 1494 was "As God may take me back to Castile." Most of the conquistadores were poor men, the second sons of wealthy families or the descendants of families whose wealth had given out. They had come west believing the Admiral's extravagant claims about the treasures they would find in the land he had discovered. But there was very little treasure found in the early years, and most of the adventurers settled down to plantation life or to gambling away their hours in the towns. A little gold and some pearls were found in the Isthmus, but it was not very much. But the lure of wealth of the Indies remained. And so when the captains of Córdoba and Grijalva returned from Yucatan with tales of a civilization on the continent, the conquistadores were ready to give up their plantations and strike out on the gold trail. Though they fought hard and lived hard, they really found great treasure only twice: in Mexico and Peru. And for most of the men who marched with Cortés, Mexico turned out to be a disappointment. When the great city on Lake Texcoco finally fell, the treasure was gone. Some say it was thrown into the lake; others say it was scattered about the countryside. In all probability much of it was found and smuggled home to avoid paying the king's fifth—the royal share. In any event, the conquest soured in their mouths.

However, the conquistadores were paid off with another prize. From the time of the Admiral's first colony, Spaniards were given the chance to win repartimientos—divisions of lands or towns or homes or mines. In most instances this included the services of the Indians living in the granted area. The repartimiento—or division of spoils—had its foundation in the North African wars, when the king gave away land that had belonged to the Moors.

In time Governor Nicolás de Ovando changed the structure of the grants to encomiendas, which were similar and clearly included the services of the Indians with certain specific restrictions as to their use. The natives were allotted to a conquistador in groups of fifty or a hundred or more for work on farms or in mines and the padres received encomiendas in lieu of pay in many instances. This actually made legal a form of slavery, though the word itself was generally avoided and the crown ordered that only cannibal and rebel Indians could be sold or traded as slaves. The king attempted to justify his position and was even partially sincere when he "commended" the Indians to their Spanish masters, stating that the encomendero—owner of an encomienda—had the right to extract labor or tribute from his Indians, but at the same time making it clear that the Spaniard was obliged to protect the Indians and give them religious instruction. As there was no standing army in the New World, the encomendero was committed to fight for the king, making the encomienda very much like the feudal fief which included a grant of land and the services for life of the peasants who lived on it. Even when the Laws of Burgos came into effect, at least a third of all Indians had to be kept at work in the mines and all Indians were forced to work at least nine months of the year for the Spaniards.

By 1503 it was clear that the Indians were to be forced to "work so that the kingdom of the Spaniards may be enriched and the Indians Christianized." Cortés was not wholly in favor of establishing the encomienda in Mexico, but the pressures to pay off those who had fought with him as well as to create gifts for the absentee grandees in Spain was too great. And a decade after the conquest of Mexico the encomenderos asked that their grants be given in perpetuity to their families. Charles agreed for a time, but eventually changed his mind and limited the grants to only one or two generations. The practice of paying off conquistadores with encomiendas lasted up into the eighteenth century, when the family of Don Diego de Vargas received an encomienda for the reconquest of New Mexico.

The prize of an encomienda, frequently running to thousands of square miles, satisfied many of the conquistadores and was a far greater one than most of them won in gold or silver. But the lure of ready treasure held their attention. In 1530 silver mines were discovered west of Mexico City, and in 1545 the great deposits of Cerro de Potosí were found in Peru. Then on September 8, 1546, a small troop of Spanish conquistadores and four padres camped near the base of a large mountain far north of the towns in New Galicia and discovered the fabulous mines of Zacatecas.

The prizes of the conquistadores varied: the small prize of gold trinkets and plantations on the Islands, the treasures of the Aztecs and Incas, the great encomiendas and finally the silver mines. Toward the end of Charles's long reign the gold and silver he had gambled for began to flow into Spain in quantities so large they rocked the price structures of Europe. Before 1520 most of the wealth was in gold, but after the silver strikes the percentages shifted and vast quantities of silver sent the price of the scarcer metal even higher. During the years of the Admiral's administration—1503-1505—about one million dollars in gold was shipped home. The years of the Mexican conquest brought the figure to ten million and still mostly gold. However, the decade after the silver strikes over sixty million dollars' worth was loaded in galleons for Spain. For the years 1591 to 1595 the exports of silver from the New World rose to over a hundred million dollars. (These rates are comparative: a hundred thousand dollars could put an army in the field, a governor's salary was 3,000 a year, a seaman's 26. A house rented for 31 a year and a gallon of wine sold for 8 cents).

Fifty years later the treasure sources were almost exhausted. And very little of the prize remained in Spanish hands. For the tragedy of Spain was that its kings were forced to spend their money outside the country to buy what was needed to finance armadas and fight wars. There was very little industry at home and even less inclination to create it so long as the wealth flowed in from across the sea. And so the great prize of the conquistadores probably brought about the downfall of the country for which they fought, because Spain, wasting its energies abroad, never kept pace with the rest of Europe.

THE CONQUISTADORES AND THE OTHERS. Three men who were not actually conquistadores became an inseparable part of the conquests. One of these men never crossed the ocean, another came only after the conquest of Mexico, while the third gave up his encomienda to spend a long life attacking the conquistadores.

Juan Rodriguez de Fonseca, the Bishop of Burgos, served from 1493 to 1524 as the chief minister for Spanish colonial affairs. A brilliant and able administrator in a Europe run by clergymen—Wolsey in England, Amboise in France, de Medici in Tuscany, Adrian in Flanders—Fonseca rose through his connections with the royal household and a distant relationship to Isabella herself. As a personal friend of the Grand Inquisitor, Torquemada, he received his first important post as reviewing officer for the Inquisition during the expulsion of the Jews from Spain. In 1493 he helped the Admiral prepare for the second voyage to the New World, and so began a life's work. Most of the expedition's papers were signed for the king by Fonseca, who as time went on became an enemy of the uncompromising Italian sailor. But whatever his relationship to the discoverer, Fonseca satisfied Ferdinand, and in 1507 all Indies affairs were placed in the bishop's hands. Four years later he was appointed Chancellor of the Indies. His titles eventually included Archbishop of Rosano, Lord Bishop of Burgos, Count of Pernia and Prince President of the Supreme Council of the Indies.

The clergyman used his many titles to further his own interests and those of his friends. He worked hard at frustrating Columbus and supported Ojeda and Ovando in their clashes with the Admiral. He cleared the appointment of Pedrarias to Castillo del Oro and blocked an effective hearing for Balboa. He attempted to scuttle Magellan's command before it began and eventually placed his own natural son as a captain on that ill-fated fleet. He strove to support Velásquez over Cortés and was finally called before Pope Adrian VI to answer charges of abuse of office. The Pope relieved Fonseca from his state positions and sent the report of the hearing to Charles, who concurred. Ordered to refrain from meddling in Cortés' affairs, Fonseca withdrew from public life though he refused to resign his absentee bishopric of Burgos, and to the end of his life he remained one of the wealthiest and most influential men in all of Spain. His contribution to the conquistadores is difficult to evaluate. He knew how to administer an empire dominated by paper work, and it was he who saw that the fleets were built and that the supplies needed in the New World were shipped out.

Antonio de Mendoza arrived in New Spain in early 1535. In the fifteen years that he served as the first viceroy, he established a structure of government that was to last for three hundred years. Born only two years before the discovery of the New World, Mendoza, the son of a hero of the Moorish wars, was himself a soldier and a diplomat, having served Charles in Flanders, Hungary and Italy. He arrived in a Mexico torn apart by internal feuds, by the restless conquistadores and the would-be adventurers who swarmed in after the conquest, and by the mistreatment of the Indians. Mendoza found himself in a political jungle made up of those men who were the enemies of Cortés and those who supported the captain-general, and though Mendoza was governor and viceroy, "representing the very person of the king," Cortés retained his title of captain-general and all of his prerogatives of exploration and conquest.

The viceroy was responsible for the government and the courts, for the appointments of the clergy and the conversion of the Indians. A reasonable and understanding man, Mendoza won the approval of the people of Mexico—Spaniards and Indians alike. He regulated the mines and controlled the encomiendas, supported the clergy, established schools, set up a government and organized its protection, explored unknown sections of the province, financed navigation in the Pacific, opened new mines, pushed the pacification of New Galicia and Yucatan, and personally fought in the Mixton War against the wild Indian tribes who threatened the silver operations in Northern Mexico. He blocked the schemes of Cortés, won over Alvarado, met with Cabeza de Vaca to learn of his travels, sent out Coronado's expedition and welcomed back the survivors of De Soto's. The most powerful man on both continents, he used his strength with great care. He wrote his successor that the secret of good government is "to do little and do it slowly."

In addition to establishing a lasting government in the New World, Mendoza also set the tone for it. He lived lavishly, supporting a large household. Eighty loads of hay were needed every day for his stables and twenty-one of wood for his stoves. He lived with pomp and pageantry because he believed this was proper for the king's representative. And he was relieved of this office for what was thought to be a better one—the viceregality of Peru. Shortly after taking over his new post, Mendoza died. And strangely enough for a Spanish administrator, he was mourned.

The third man whose activities were to have a great effect upon the conquistadores was for a brief time one of them. Bartolomé de

Las Casas—called variously Las Casas or Casas—arrived in the New World in 1502 in the fleet that brought Governor Nicolás de Ovando, the Admiral's successor. Already a graduate of the University of Salamanca, Las Casas accepted Holy Orders in 1510 and was the first clergyman ordained in the New World. Ordination did not prevent him from participating in the conquest of Cuba a year later or from accepting a repartimiento for his efforts. Sometime in 1514, the clergyman-conquistador became aware of what was actually happening to the Indians. He gave up his repartimiento and devoted the rest of his life to the Indian cause. When he died in 1566 at the age of ninety-two, he had become recognized among his compatriots as a fanatic saint, the creator of the Black Legend, a colonizer and the Protector of the Indians. He had blocked in part an unjust war in Nicaragua, had fought his fellow clergymen over the human status of the Indians, had lobbied for the New Laws to protect the Indians, had clashed with Fonseca, had served as an advisor to Cardinal Jiménez, the Regent for Charles, had held the bishopric of Chiapa, and for a brief time had even attempted to establish a colony in Venezuela.

Las Casas firmly believed his countrymen were wrong in their treatment of the Indians. He argued that the natives were rational human beings who could be converted peacefully and that their conversion was the only real reason for Spain being in the New World. He expressed himself in numerous books, letters, pamphlets and at hundreds of conferences. He stated his case, and as is typical of men of passionate belief, he overstated it. No one doubts that the conquistadores were guilty of most of the crimes with which he charged them. But Las Casas hurt his cause when he claimed that they had destroyed fifteen to twenty million Indians, which was more than double the population of both continents. His statistics were as wrong as his intentions were good. But even this weakness joined with his strong prejudices did not prevent him from writing one of the finest early histories of the Indies. He knew almost every person of importance during the years of the conquest. He met the Admiral, knew his sons and brothers well. He had access to Fernando Colón's biography of his father as well as a copy of the Admiral's journal. He was a friend of Roldán who revolted against the Colóns in Hispaniola, of Pinzón and Ojeda who sailed on the Columbian voyages. He knew Juan Ponce de León, Magellan, Pedrárias, Bernal Díaz del Castillo, Ferdinand, Charles and Fonseca. He was in Cuba when Grijalva returned from Yucatan and when Cortés sailed. Samuel Eliot Morison,

the maritime historian, has written that Las Casas' is "the only history
of America I should wish to preserve if all others were destroyed."
But for all of his good and hard work in behalf of the Indians, Bartolomé de Las Casas helped his country's enemies more than any
other Spaniard.

THE CONQUISTADOR AND THE JUST WAR. The sins against the Indians were weighed with great care in the conquistador's own time.
And none condemned him more fully than his own contemporaries.
However, he was condemned less for the destruction of cultures which
at core were abominable to the Christian Spaniards, than for his
treatment of the Indians as human beings. A long and complex argument began almost from the moment the first Spaniard met an Indian
on the continent. Learned clergymen prepared a document which
the conquistadores were required to read upon initial contact with
the natives. This one was read aloud to the Indians by padres before
Alonzo de Ojeda attacked at Cartagena. Similar manifestoes were
read to the Indians by other conquistadores.

I, Alonzo de Ojeda, servant of the high and mighty kings of Castile
and León, civilizers of barbarous nations, their messenger and captain, notify and make known to you, in the best way I can, that God
our Lord, one and eternal, created the heavens and the earth, and one
man and one woman, from whom you and we and all the people of the
earth were and are descendants, procreated, and all those who shall
come after us. But the vast number of generations which have proceeded from them, in the course of more than five thousand years that
have elapsed since the creation of the world, made it necessary that
some of the human race should disperse in one direction and some in
another, and that they should divide themselves into many kingdoms
and provinces, as they could not sustain and preserve themselves in
one alone.

All these people were given in charge, by God our Lord, to one person, named St. Peter, who was thus made lord and superior of all the
people of the earth and head of the whole human lineage, whom all
should obey, wherever they might live and whatever might be their
law, sect or belief. He gave him also the whole world for his service
and jurisdiction, and though he desired that he should establish his
chair in Rome, as a place most convenient for governing the world,
yet he permitted that he might establish his chair in any other part of
the world, and judge and govern all the nations, Christians, Moors,

Jews, Gentiles, and whatever other sect or belief might be. This person was denominated Pope, that is to say, admirable, supreme, father and guardian, because he is father and governor of all mankind. This holy father was obeyed and honored as lord, king, and superior of the universe by those who lived in his time, and in like manner has been obeyed and honored by all those who have been elected to the Pontificate, and thus it has continued unto the present day, and will continue until the end of the world.

One of these pontiffs of whom I have spoken, as lord of the world, made a donation of these islands and continents, of the ocean, sea, and all that they contain, to the Catholic kings of Castile, who at that time were Ferdinand and Isabella of glorious memory, and to their successors, our sovereigns, according to the tenor of certain papers drawn up for the purpose (which you may see if you desire). Thus his majesty is king and sovereign of these islands and continents by virtue of the said donation; and as king and sovereign certain islands and almost all to whom this has been notified have received his majesty and have obeyed and served him. And, moreover, like good subjects and with good will and without any resistance or delay, the moment they were informed of the foregoing, they obeyed all the religious men sent among them to preach and teach our Holy Faith; and these of their free and cheerful will, without any condition or reward, became Christians, and continue so to be. And his majesty received them kindly and benignantly, and ordered that they should be treated like his other subjects and vassals: you also are required and obliged to do the same. Therefore, in the best manner I can, I pray and entreat you that you consider well what I have said, and that you take whatever time is reasonable to understand and deliberate upon it, and that you recognize the church for sovereign and superior of the universal world, and the supreme Pontiff, called Pope, in her name, and his majesty in his place, as superior and sovereign king of the islands and Terra Firma, by virtue of the said donation; and that you consent that these religious fathers declare and preach to you the foregoing. And if you shall do so lo, you will do well and will do that to which you are bounden and obliged; and his majesty, and I in his name, will receive you with all due love and charity, and will leave you, your wives and children free from servitude, that you may freely do with these and with yourselves whatever you please and think proper, as have done the inhabitants of the other islands. And besides this, his majesty will give you many privileges and exemptions and grant you many favours. If you do not do this, or wickedly and intentionally delay to do so, I certify to you that by the aid of God I will powerfully invade and make war upon you in all parts and modes that I can, and will subdue you to the yoke and obedience of the church and of his majesty, and I will take your wives and children and make slaves of them, and sell them as such, and dispose of them as his majesty may command; and I will take your effects and will do you all the harm and injury in my power, as vassals who will not obey or receive their sovereign and who resist and oppose him. And I protest that the deaths and disasters which may in this manner be occasioned will be the fault of yourselves and not of his majesty, nor of me, nor of these cavaliers who accompany me. And of what I here tell you and require of you, I call upon the notary here present to give me his signed testimonial.

Those who dominated the royal councils sincerely believed that all actions should be as legal as possible, and as legality was basic to the complex administration of the growing empire, the laws of the royal councils had to be taken seriously, though sometimes the document was read at night in a whisper at some distance from a village about to be attacked. It was not important that the natives could not have understood the document which was read to them in Latin. In most instances, even the conquistadores could not understand it. But it was important that the formality be observed and be recorded.

The just treatment of the natives became a raging controversy in Spain not only because the religious orders saw the inhumanity of the conquests, but also because there was a sense of justice in the entire administration of the empire. The natives were the king's subjects. They belonged to no one else, and if they were human then they had certain rights as subjects of the king and as converted Christians. The Laws of Burgos, passed in December of 1512, made the throne's position clear for the moment. The Spanish conquistador was responsible for bringing the Indians together only by the use of gentleness. Attention was to be paid to their religious instruction. Churches were to be constructed and equipped with ornaments and images. The Indians were to be taught creed, prayer, how to confess, to attend funerals bearing crosses, and all the other basic knowledge which should be part of a Christian life. It was permissible to use the Indians in the mines but they were not to be ill-treated or overworked, and pregnant women were to be released from work. Careful regulations were set down governing the food, beds, clothes, etc., which had to be furnished to the Indians.

The Laws of Burgos became the basis of a series of many laws which were interpreted and added to over the years of Spanish administration. But there is no doubt that they were observed more in the breach than the letter.

The great advocate of justice for the natives was Bartolomé de Las Casas. Convinced that the Laws of Burgos, "the first public recognition of the rights of the Indians," were being ignored, Las Casas began a fifty-year fight for the rights of the Indians. He saw them as a simple people whom God had created without evil or guile, which was in the tradition of the concept of the noble savage—a man who was not contaminated with the sins of civilized society. For Las Casas the Indians were obedient and faithful, patient, peaceful and virtuous, who would be the most blessed people on earth if only they worshiped the one true God.

His contemporary, Oviedo, the historian-conquistador, recorded a different impression: for him the Indians were naturally lazy, vicious, cowardly and in general a lying, shiftless people whose marriages were not a sacrament but a sacrilege. He claimed they lived only to eat, drink, worship heathen gods and commit bestial obscenities.

From these extremes the arguments ran throughout the period of the conquest. Almost every person of position had an opinion. The legality of the question of rights for the Indians came down to a simple and bitter argument: was the Aristotelian theory—some men were by nature slaves—applicable to the Indians?

The Viceroy Antonio de Mendoza, whose firm control brought a semblance of peace to the political scene in Mexico City after the conquest, left a note for his successor recommending that neither those who considered the Indians simple, industrious, humble, without malice or evil, nor those who held the contrary view should be believed. He suggested that the Indians should be treated like any other people and that no specific rules or regulations should be made for them. "There are few persons in these parts who are not motivated in their opinion of the Indians by some interest, whether temporal or spiritual, or by some passion or ambition, good or bad."

The arguments raged through the universities and the council halls. The padres took positions and the conquistadores took positions. The situation became so obviously unjust that in April 1550 the king suspended all conquests in the New World until special groups of theologians and counselors could decide upon a just method for conducting them.

THE CONQUISTADOR AND THE BLACK LEGEND. Time has made it

almost impossible to evaluate the activities of the conquistador without prejudice. He was a Catholic who came from a Europe caught in the passions of the Reformation. The English and Dutch were establishing a national church, and anything supported by or supporting the papacy of Rome was a natural enemy. And Spain not only supported the Pope, but was the strongest bulwark against the Reformation.

Everything that could be done to smear Spain and its empire was grist for the foreign propaganda mills, and Bartolomé de Las Casas, the Bishop of Chiapa and Protector of the Indies, did more than anyone else to feed the presses of the countries envious of Spanish wealth and afraid of Spanish power and the Spanish church. In 1542 he presented to Charles A *Brief Account of the Destruction of the Indies.* Fourteen years later it was published in England as *The Tears of the Indians, Being a True Account of the Cruel Massacres and Slaughter of about Twenty Millions of Innocent People.* During the next hundred years, forty-two editions of this propaganda tract were published in England alone. In some editions drawings of Indians being quartered, fed to the dogs, hunted, boiled, etc., were added. The Spanish court realized the dangers involved in the tract, and at various times its publication was prohibited. But the damage was done. Las Casas may have exaggerated his details but he was not alone in his criticism, and news of the reaction within Spain itself helped create propaganda elsewhere. A secret hearing into the administration of Viceroy Mendoza revealed that at the close of the Mixton War many of the captured Indians were put to death in the presence of Mendoza and that he ordered some of them to be placed in a line and blown to pieces by cannon while others were torn apart by dogs. Some were given over to the Negroes for slaughter and some were hanged. One padre reported that so many natives were destroyed in labor at the mines that for a half league around the mine at Oaxyecac he "could not walk except on dead men or bones; so many birds came to scavenge, they darkened the sky."

There is no question that the Spaniards sinned in their conquest and treatment of the Indians. Nor is there any question that a passionate reformer helped create a picture of that sin beyond its actuality. At the same time it must be remembered that Spain's enemies were prepared to use this knowledge and distort it with hypocrisy because it helped to justify any action they took against the Catholic enemy and against the wealthy Spanish empire.

THE CONQUISTADOR AND COLOR. The Spaniards had for centuries intermarried with moroscos or converted Moors, and when they moved on to the New World they brought with them no color prejudice. They came in small numbers to the new-found land, and from the first voyage of the Admiral intimate relations with the Indians were routine. Within a few generations, there were large numbers of mestizos throughout New Spain, and when the Spaniards supplemented the Indian population with Negro slaves, two new mixtures were added to the color range: the mulatto (white and Negro) and the zambo (Indian and Negro). From these three there would in time be almost unlimited combinations resulting from varied intermarriages. And some Spaniards did marry their Indian women. The church approved such marriages, and the king who wanted married men on the encomiendas not only approved but urged the marriage of Spanish soldiers and the Indian women. In some rare instances Spanish women—in small numbers during the early years—married Indians. The converted Carlos Inca married a Spanish woman born in Pizarro's home town.

Cortés had a child by Doña Marina, his Indian interpreter; and when he tired of her, she married a Spanish officer of Cortés' command. The conqueror of Mexico also lived with two women from the household of Montezuma. De Soto left mestizo children in the Isthmus and an Indian princess with children in Peru. During his travels beyond Florida, he was given two or more Indian women by a chief. Balboa lived with an Indian princess and probably was betrayed because of her. The oldest Pizarro brother founded a famous Peruvian line in his liaison with an Inca princess. Alvarado also left mestizo progeny who became prominent in Latin American history. Juan de Oñate, the settler of New Mexico, was married to a woman directly descended from both Cortés and Montezuma.

In most instances the children of these relationships were raised by the mother; but Cortés sent his son to the Spanish court, and Almagro, the partner of Pizarro, seems to have raised his son himself. The younger Almagro assumed the governorship of Peru upon the assassination of Pizarro, and his being of mixed blood was in no way responsible for his eventual downfall.

The relationship between the conquistadores and Indian women was not always sanctified by marriage, but the Spanish soldiers generally made a practice of converting the women to Roman Catholicism. In later years the children of these liaisons were to face discrimination in gaining certain political offices, but so also were the Creoles—those of all white parentage born in the New World.

The Spaniards had a completely different view of color and prejudice from the North Europeans, and their devotion to their Indian women was in many instances a constant one. Some conquistadores left their companions to live permanently with their Indian wives. One castaway in Yucatan refused to join Cortés because he had an Indian wife, a family and a social status within the tribe which he would not have enjoyed with his own people.

In later years, after the easy relationship between the conquistadores and the Indian and Negro women had produced millions of mixed-blood offspring, the general tendency on the part of these children was to seek recognition for the percentage of white blood which they had. This became a sign of status, but by the time white blood became important, the conquest was established; and with the smallest possible numbers Spain bound its colonial empire to the motherland for centuries.

THE CONQUISTADORES AND THE ADMIRAL. "The vessels were hove to, waiting for daylight; and on Friday they arrived at a small island of the Lucayos, called in the language of the Indians, Guanahani. Presently they saw naked people. The Admiral went ashore in the armed boat. . . ." The date was October 12, 1492. The account is from what has become known as the Journal. It was apparently copied from Fernando Colón's papers by Las Casas, as it is in the handwriting of the Bishop of Chiapa and his notes fill the margin.

This is the first report of the New World, the first record of the natives being called Indians, the first contact with them, and the first landing. The island called Guanahani is generally agreed to be Watling Island in the Caribbean. The arrival of Cristopher Columbus—or as he signed his papers, Cristóbal Colón—was both the beginning of the conquests which were to sweep two continents and a continuation of a pattern of conquest established only a few decades before in the Canary Islands.

The Admiral of the Ocean Seas began a relationship to the Indians that carried over to those who followed him, a relationship for which he must bear some responsibility despite the aura of the hero which has gathered about his name. When he landed on the island of Hispaniola which was to become his headquarters, there is estimated to have been an Indian population of about three hundred thousand. Four years later one third of these were dead. Fifty years later there were fewer than five hundred left alive. Las Casas, who knew the Admiral, had reservations about him. Peter Martyr, the contemporary historian who knew him, "did not particularly admire" him. Most of his contemporaries were impressed with his discoveries, but very few seem to have been impressed with the man himself. In the first place, he claimed too much for his discoveries and embroidered his tales of riches to be found. This could only bring about resentment from both the investors in future expeditions and those who crossed the ocean for easy treasure. For a decade after the discovery the enterprise of the Indies was a losing proposition, costing more than it returned. And the Admiral never wavered in his claims, expecting others to believe as wholeheartedly as he in what he had found. Eventually one of the colonists of Hispaniola was to write: "Neither the Admiral or his brother should come here to these islands." The Colóns had proved a disappointment, but at the same time there were few who could argue then or later his own claim:

I should be judged as a captain who went from Spain to the Indies to conquer a people numerous and warlike, whose manners and religion are very different from ours, who live in sierras and mountains, without fixed settlements, and where by divine will I have placed under the sovereignty of the king and queen our lords, an Other World whereby Spain who was reckoned poor has become the richest of countries.

The Admiral was never a modest man. He was always sensitive, difficult, careless with detail and a poor administrator. He annoyed those who knew him and lost the support of the Throne. But he began the conquest. Balboa and Cortés were already in Hispaniola in 1504 when the Admiral sailed home for the last time.

Authors' Note

THE USE of foreign names has always been a problem for the English writer. Vasco Núñez de Balboa was known to his contemporaries not as Balboa but as Vasco Núñez. Francisco Vásquez de Coronado was known as Francisco Vásquez. Hernando de Soto was Soto. And Columbus was generally known as Colón. The given name of Cortés is frequently found as Hernán, Hernando, Fernán and Fernando. In most instances we have allowed the usage of the period to prevail in the chronicle itself and have followed modern American usage in the commentary.

Indian places and personal names are similarly confusing. In many instances they changed many times over the centuries. Cortés refers to the Aztec capital as Temixtitan. Tenochtitlan—cactus growing on a rock—was in general use at the time and the modern reader will recognize it as Mexico City from Mexitli—a place where the god of war lives.

Translators of the chronicles have been as capricious as the chroniclers in their practice. Some names have been modernized in the texts while others will always remain confused because they were written in haste by tired, semiliterate Spanish soldiers in the field. We have tried to follow a simple practice—clarify only what might seem confusing.

The stories of the conquistadores included in this collection cover the major activities in Central and North America. They were in all instances written by conquistadores themselves or by their friends. Some of the accounts are letters written from the field before or after a battle. Some describe great discoveries, others great disappointments. These are living chronicles, written by men who wrote in anger or in haste or in bitter memory of things they saw, actions of which they were a part. We have tried to keep to the original text, but have not hesitated to take certain liberties: modernizing and simplifying, cutting duplication, adding recognizable place names, dropping details that no longer have any meaning for the modern reader. In short, we have striven to make this a book to be read by anyone interested in one of the most exciting and colorful periods of history. The years of the conquistador were actually brief—Balboa was in Hispaniola by 1502. Coronado and De Soto wandered through what has become the United States in the early 1540's. Most of the men knew each other, were friends or enemies. Some were greater than others, some more understanding, others more brutal, but each cut a bold swath in history. The general preface has been written not to be all inclusive but rather to help set the background and show the breadth of problems that arise in trying to understand these seemingly simple men and their actions. The prefaces and postscripts which have been woven about the original texts attempt to set briefly the time and circumstance. But most of all we have tried to make a book that was entertaining for the modern reader.

I.R.B.
H.M.R.

1

Balboa
Establishes a Colony
at Darien

C A R I B B E A N   S E A

BALBOA
DISCOVERS THE
SOUTHERN SEA
September 1, 1513
January 19, 1514

Acla
Ponca
Careta

Point of Discovery
of Pacific

Torecha

Islas
de las
Perlas

G. de
SAN
MIGUEL

G. de
URABA

San Sebasti

Darien

SOUTH
SEA

W   E

0   10   20   30   40

CUBA

CARIBBEAN SEA

SOUTH
SEA

Rio Abraibe

1

Balboa Establishes a Colony
at Darien

IN THE first flush of discovery by Columbus, expedition after expedition probed the waters of the Caribbean trying to find a way to make the New World pay. One of the first grants of trade was given to Rodrigo de Bastidas, a notary from Seville. Accepting the king's demand for one-fourth of whatever he could find, Bastidas formed a partnership with the master pilot Juan de la Cosa. Cosa had sailed with Columbus and was to make thirteen crossings of the Atlantic before his death. When the partners set sail early in 1501, they had aboard an insignificant young sailor from the small mountain town of Jerez de los Caballeros, in Estremadura, by the name of Vasco Núñez de Balboa. Except for a good family name and his training as a page in a wealthy household, Balboa had nothing more than his personality and his intelligence to offer. He had fought in no campaigns, and he had no money.

The Bastidas expedition moved west from the Islands toward the mainland and discovered Darien in the Gulf of Urabá sometime late in 1501. Several months later, their ships in poor condition, the partners landed in Hispaniola before sailing back to Spain. Balboa remained on the island, and along with a fellow Estremaduran, Hernán Cortés, he enlisted in the campaign against the Indians under Governor Ovando. When the Indians were defeated, Balboa joined the group of planter-loafers who spent their years gambling, wenching, and dreaming of what they would do if given the opportunity.

But for years there was very little opportunity. No one had found out how to make the New World really pay its way, and after the last voyage of Columbus in 1502, there was a lull in activities that was to last for a half-dozen years. Governor Diego de Velásquez colonized Cuba in 1508 and the Council of the Indies back in Spain began to stir again. Alonzo de Ojeda, who had sailed with the Admiral of the

Ocean Seas on his second voyage, was named governor of New Andalusia, which stretched from western Venezuela to the Gulf of Urabá. At the same time an adjoining territory, stretching north from the Isthmus to Honduras, was granted Diego de Nicuesa, a planter from Hispaniola.

Ojeda tried to land several times and lost over seventy men to the Indians' poisoned arrows before he finally built at San Sebastian on the eastern shore of the Gulf of Urabá. Wounded and unable or unwilling to remain, he turned his authority over to an attorney, Martín Fernández de Enciso, and left for home. The attorney left Santo Domingo for his new governorship on September 13, 1510, with one hundred and fifty-two settlers. There was also on board a stowaway who was fleeing boredom and debt—Balboa. The two men clashed almost immediately, and only Balboa's years of experience in the Islands prevented his execution. Unfitted for command, Enciso abused a certain Francisco Pizarro of Ojeda's original group, and so the new colony began with trouble and ended with it. Soon after Enciso's landing at San Sebastian, the Indians killed several colonists, and at Balboa's suggestion the group moved across the gulf to Darien, where a new town was founded. The colonists, completely disgusted with Enciso, elected Balboa and another as joint alcaldes.

To the east Nicuesa attempted to establish his province, but when his town of Nombre de Dios proved a failure, he tried to take over Darien. Balboa and his followers refused to let him even put ashore, and so, rejected and unable to repair his leaky vessel, he put to sea on March 1, 1511, and was never heard of again. Soon afterward Enciso, furious at being ignored in the colony he claimed, also departed, and for the next three years Vasco Núñez de Balboa was in command of the first settlement on the mainland.

Angry with the appointment of Ojeda and Nicuesa, Admiral Don Diego de Colón, son of Christopher Columbus and the Governor and Captain General of Hispaniola, without waiting to hear from the king, confirmed Balboa as the acting captain. Balboa began at once to explore the area and make friends with the Indians.

At the time of its discovery Central America probably had a native population larger than that of North America above the Rio Grande then, and it was Balboa's intention to keep it friendly. He met with and won over what chiefs he could. He defeated and then made friends with others. Though it was eventually to cost him his life, he took an Indian princess as his mistress. He gathered gold in small amounts and captured some slaves. He sent what help he could spare to those Nicuesa had abandoned at Nombre de Dios to the north. From a native he heard of the sea to the southward, but he was too busy to seek it out. In a short time he won over as friends thirty of the small native kingdoms, but even these could not supply the food he needed; and on January 13, 1512, he sent what gold he had to Admiral Colón with a request for food.

A full year was to pass before Balboa realized his boat had sunk. Only two of the men aboard survived and they were to be lost as castaways for eight years before Cortés put ashore in Yucatan. Through the year he waited, Balboa continued his explorations.

Darien was anything but a flourishing colony, and its weaknesses became apparent to the Indians, who began to plot its destruction. One young Indian warned his sister, who had become a mistress of Balboa, and the plot was revealed. Moving quickly, Balboa attacked the Indians' supplies and executed several of their leaders. But by this time the situation in the colony had become desperate. As there were no boats available, the colonists made one and sent it with two men to Hispaniola for help. But as the crown no longer recognized his rights, Diego de Colón had no desire to keep the colony alive. His father had been granted a percentage of everything that resulted from his discovery, and the young Admiral believed that part of everything that came off the mainland should belong to him. The two representatives of Darien pushed on and landed in Spain in May 1513. Meanwhile the colonists became increasingly restless. There were those who had been friends of Enciso and those who had known Ojeda and Nicuesa. And there was hunger. A revolt was planned, but Balboa was able to suppress it. Finally, two boats from Colón in Hispaniola arrived in December 1512, a full year after the Admiral had assured Ferdinand that he was granting every aid to the new colony.

Though these two ships brought supplies, they did not bring Balboa the long-awaited confirmation of his appointment by the king. As the boats departed on January 13, 1513, he sat down and penned a lengthy letter to Ferdinand, detailing the conditions that prevailed in Darien. He attacked his opposition, defended his actions and set forth some of his hopes, at the same time making an appeal for support.

A LETTER OF VASCO NÚÑEZ DE BALBOA TO THE KING.
DARIEN, JANUARY 20, 1513

Most Christian and most puissant Lord,

Some days ago I wrote to your Majesty by a caravel which came to this town, giving your very Royal Highness an account of all that has happened in these parts. I also wrote, by a brigantine which left this town for the island of Española [Hispaniola or Haiti], to let the admiral know that we were in extreme distress; and now we have been supplied by two ships laden with provisions. We had been reduced to such extremities that if succor had been delayed, it would no longer have been necessary. For no remedy could then have delivered us from the consequences of famine In our great need we lost three hundred of the men of Urabá under Alonzo de Ojeda and of Veragua under Diego de Nicuesa.

After much labor, I have united all these parties. I sent to order that the persons who were in the settlement of Diego de Nicuesa should be brought to this town, and I treated them with all the attention that was possible. Your most Royal Highness will be aware that, after Diego de Nicuesa came to this town and then departed for Española, I took as much care of the people that were left in his settlement as if they had been under my own charge. When I found that they were in want, I remembered to send provisions to them.

After a year and a half, I conveyed them to this town, seeing that thus I should further the service of your most Royal Highness. For if I had not helped them they would have been lost, five or six dying of hunger every day, and the survivors being thinned by the Indians. Now all the men who were left behind by Diego de Nicuesa are in this town. From the first day of their arrival here they have been treated as well as if they had been sent by order of your most Royal Highness, for no difference was made with them, any more than if they had come here on the first day. As soon as they arrived, they were given their pieces of land for building and planting in a very good situation, close to those occupied by the men who came with me, for the land was not yet divided and they arrived in time to receive some of the best pieces.

I have to inform your most Royal Highness that both the governors, Diego de Nicuesa as well as Alonzo de Ojeda, performed their duties very badly. They were the cause of their own perdition, because they did not know how to act. They imagined that they could rule the land and do all that was necessary from their beds. But the nature of the land is such that if he who has charge of the government sleeps, he cannot awake when he wishes, for this is a land that obliges the man who governs to be very watchful. The country is difficult to travel through because of the numerous rivers and morasses and mountains. Many men die owing to the great labor they have to endure, and every day we are exposed to death in a thousand other forms.

I have thought of nothing day or night but how to support myself and the handful of men whom God has placed under my charge, and how to maintain them until your Highness sends reinforcements. I have taken care that the Indians of this land are not ill-treated, permitting no man to injure them and giving them many things from Castile whereby they may be drawn into friendship with us. Because of this honorable treatment of the Indians, I have learned great secrets from them, through the knowledge of which large quantities of gold may be obtained, and your Highness will thus be well served. I have often thought of how it will be possible for us to sustain life, seeing that we have been as badly succored from the island of Española as if we had not been Christians. But our Lord, by His infinite mercy, has chosen to supply us with provisions in this land. We have often been in such straits that we expected to die of hunger; yet at the time of our greatest necessity our Lord has pointed out the means of relief.

Your most Royal Highness must know that after we came here, we were forced to travel from one place to another by reason of the great scarcity, and it astonishes me how we could have endured such hardships. The things that have happened have been more by the hand of God than by the hand of men. Up to the present time, I have taken care that none of my people shall go out of here unless I myself go in front of them, whether it be by night or day, marching across rivers, through swamps and water, stripped naked, with our clothes fastened on a shield upon our heads. And when we came to the end of one swamp we had to enter another, and to walk in this way from two to ten days. If the person who is entrusted with the government remains in his house and leaves the work to others, no one else he can send in his place can manage the people as well, or fail to make mistakes which may cause the destruction of himself and all who are with him. I can say this with truth, as one who has seen what happens; for sometimes, when I have been unable to go with the men because I have been detained by some business connected with the sowing of the crops, I have observed that those I sent in my place did not act according to reason.

I, my Lord, have taken care that everything obtained up to the present day shall be properly divided, the gold and the pearls (the shares of your most Royal Highness being put on one side) as well as the clothing and eatables. But until now we have valued the eatables more than the gold, for we have more gold than health, and often I have searched in various directions, desiring more to find a sack of corn than a bag of gold. I assure your most Royal Highness that if I had not personally gone in front of my men, searching for food, there would have been no one left in the town or in the land unless our Lord had miraculously taken pity upon us. The way I have divided the gold procured is to give a proper share to each man engaged in finding it. All receive shares of the food, although some have not gone in search of it.

I wish to give an account of the great secrets and marvelous riches of this land of which God has made your most Royal Highness the Lord, and me the discoverer before any other, for which I give many thanks and much praise for all the days of the world. I hold myself to be the most fortunate man born, seeing that our Lord has been served at my hands rather than at those of another. As so propitious a commencement has been made, I beseech your most Royal Highness that I may be permitted to complete this great enterprise. I am bold to make this supplication because I know that you will thus be well served. But for this purpose your most Royal Highness should order that five hundred or more men be presently sent from the island of Española. With these, and the men already here, although not more than one hundred are fit to bear arms, I will be able to march into the interior of the land, and pass over to the other sea on the south side.

That which I, by much labor and great hardships, have had the fortune to discover, is as follows: In this province of Darien many very rich mines have been found, and there is gold in great quantities. Many rivers have been discovered. Thirty containing gold flow from a mountain about two leagues from this town. This mountain is toward the west, and between the town and the mountain no gold-bearing rivers have been seen, but I believe they exist. Following the course of the great river of San Juan for thirty leagues on the right-hand side, one arrives at a province called Abanumaque. From a son of a cacique [chief], and from other Indian men and women whom I have taken, I have certain intelligence that there are very rich rivers of gold in this province. Thirty leagues up this great river, on the left hand, a very large and beautiful stream flows into it, and two days' journey up this stream there is a cacique called Davaive, a very great lord with a large and populous land. He has such great store of gold in his house that one who does not know this land would hardly believe it. I know this of a certainty. All the gold that goes forth from this gulf comes from the house of the cacique Davaive, as well as all that is owned by the caciques of the surrounding districts. It is reported that they have many pieces of gold curiously worked and very large. Many Indians who have seen them tell me that this cacique

Davaive has bags of gold so heavy that it takes the whole strength of a man to lift one onto his back.

The cacique collects the gold in this manner. Two days' journey from his house there is a very beautiful country inhabited by a very evil Carib race, who eat as many men as they can get. They are a people without a chief, and there is no one whom they obey. They are warlike, and each man is his own master. They are lords of the mines, and these mines, according to the news I have received, are the richest in the world. In that land there is a mountain which appears to be the largest in the world. It rises up on the Urabá side of this gulf, somewhat inland; it may be twenty leagues from the sea. The way to it is in a southerly direction. At first the land is flat, but it gradually rises until it is so high that it is covered with clouds. During two years we have seen its summit only twice because it is continually obscured by clouds. Up to a certain point it is covered with a forest of great trees, and higher up the mountain it has no trees whatever. It rises in the most beautiful and level country in the world, near the territory of this cacique Davaive. The very rich mines are in this land toward the rising of the sun, and it is two days' journey from the rich mines to the abode of Davaive.

There are two methods of collecting the gold without any trouble. One is by waiting until the river rises in the ravines. The freshets then carry the gold down from the mountains in large lumps. When the freshets pass off, the beds remain dry, and the gold is laid bare. The Indians describe the lumps of gold as being the size of oranges or of a fist, and others like flat slabs. The other way of gathering gold is by waiting until the plants on the hills are dry. Then these are set on fire. When they are consumed, the Indians search in the most likely places and collect great quantities of very beautiful grains of gold. The Indians who gather this gold bring it in grains to be melted, and barter it with this cacique Davaive, in exchange for youths and boys to eat, and for women to serve them as wives, whom they do not eat. He gives them also many pigs, fish, cotton cloth, and salt, and such worked pieces of gold as they want. These Indians trade only with Davaive, and with no one else.

Davaive has a great place for melting gold in his house, and he has a hundred men continually working at the gold. I know all this of a certainty, for I have never heard any other account in whatever direction I have gone. I have heard it from many caciques and Indians, from natives of the territory of Davaive, as well as from other parts. I have heard it in many forms, obtaining the information from some by torments, from others for love, and from others in exchange for things of Castile. I also have certain information that, after ascending this river of San Juan for fifty leagues, there are very rich mines on both sides. The river is navigated in the small canoes of the Indians, because there are so many narrow and winding mouths overhung with trees, and these cannot be passed except in canoes three or four *palmos* in breadth. After the river is entered, ships may be built of eight or more *palmos*, which may be rowed with twenty oars. But it has a strong current which even the Indian canoes can hardly stem. When it is blowing fresh the vessels may make sail, assisted by the oars in turning some of the windings.

The people who wander along the upper course of this great river are evil and warlike. It is necessary to be very cunning in dealing with them. I have information of many other things, but I will not declare them now, believing that I shall discover them with the help of God.

Down this coast twenty leagues westward is the province called Careta. It has certain rivers which contain gold, according to the Indians in this town. The Spaniards have not gone there, in order not to rouse the country until we have more men, for we are now few in number. Farther down the coast, forty leagues from this city and twelve leagues inland, there is a cacique called Comogre, and another named Pocorosa, who are at equal distances from the sea. They have many wars with each other. They each have a town inland and another on the seacoast, by which the interior is supplied with fish. The Indians assured me that there were very rich rivers of gold near the houses of these caciques. At the distance of a day's journey from the house of Pocorosa there are the most beautiful mountains in these parts. They are clear of forests, except some groves of trees along the banks of mountain streams.

In these mountains there are caciques who have great quantities of gold in their houses. It is said that they store their gold in *barbacoas* like maize, because it is so abundant that they do not care to keep it in baskets. All the rivers of these mountains are said to contain gold in very large lumps. The Indians go into the water and gather the gold in baskets. They also scrape it up in the beds of streams, when they are dry. That your most Royal Highness may be more completely informed concerning these parts, I send an Indian workman of that district who has collected it many times. Your most Royal Highness must not hold this subject as one for jest, for I am well assured of it by many principal Indians and caciques. I, sire, have myself been very near these mountains, within a day's journey, but I was unable to reach them because of the lack of men; for a man gets as far as he can, not as far as he wishes. Beyond these mountains the country is very flat toward the south, and the Indians say that the other sea is at a distance of three days' journey.

All the caciques and Indians of the country of Comogre tell me that there is such great store of gold in the houses of the caciques of the other sea, that we should be astonished. They declare that there is much gold in very large grains in all the rivers of the other coast, and that the Indians of the other sea come to the residence of this cacique Comogre by a river and bring gold from the mines to be melted, in very large round grains and in great quantity. In exchange for the gold they get cotton cloth and good-looking Indian men and women. They do not eat them like the people toward the great river. They say that the people of the other coast are very good and well mannered.

I am told that the other sea is very good for canoe navigation, for it is always smooth and never rough like the sea on this side. I believe that there are many islands in that sea. They say that there are many large pearls and that the caciques have baskets of them. The river which flows from that territory of the cacique Comogre to the other sea forms itself into three branches, each one of which enters the other sea by itself. They say that the pearls are brought to the cacique Comogre in canoes by the western branch. The canoes with gold from all parts enter by the eastern branch.

It is a most astonishing thing and without equal that our Lord has made you the lord of this land. It should not be forgotten that your most Royal Highness will be served by sending me reinforcements. Then, if our Lord favors me, I will discover things so grand, and places where so much gold and such wealth may be had, that a great part of the world might be conquered with it. I assure your most Royal Highness that I have worked with more diligence for your service than the governors who were lost here, Alonzo de Ojeda and Diego de Nicuesa. I have not remained in my bed while my people were entering and exploring the country. No party has gone into any part of this land unless I was in front as a guide, opening the road with my own hands for those who went with me. If this is not believed, I refer to what I have sent home, the fruits of all those who have labored here.

As one who has more knowledge of the land than anyone else has acquired, I desire that the affairs of these regions which I have originated may flourish and reach such a position as to be of service to your most Royal Highness. Therefore, I must make known what is necessary to be done and to be provided at once, until the land is known and explored.

The chief requirement is that a thousand men should come from the island of Española, for those who might come direct from Castile would not be fit for much until they were accustomed to the country. Your most Royal Highness will please to order that, for the present, this colony be supplied with provisions at the hands of your most Royal Highness, that the land may be explored and its secrets made known. Thus two things will be effected: one, that much money will be gained in the markets; and the other and principal one that, the land being supplied with provisions, great things and vast riches may be discovered.

It is also necessary to provide the means of building small ships for the rivers, and to send pitch, nails, ropes, and sails, with some master shipwrights who understand ship-building. Your most Royal Highness should also send two hundred cross-bows with very strong stays and fittings, and with long ranges. They should not weigh more than two pounds. Money would thus be saved, because each man in this place ought to have one or two cross-bows, as they are very good arms against the Indians, and useful in the chase of birds and other game. Workmen should also be sent to look after the cross-bows, for every day they get out of order owing to the constant damp. Two dozen very good hand-guns, of light metal, are also required; for those made of iron are soon damaged by the constant damp and eaten away with rust. They should not weigh more than twenty-five to thirty pounds, and they should not be long, so that a man can carry one wherever it may be necessary. Good powder is also wanted.

For the present, it is necessary that as large a reinforcement of troops as possible should be sent to the province of Darien, because it is a land full of hostile tribes. There should also be a force at the mines of Tubanama, in the province of Comogre, because it is also a very populous region. At present, most puissant lord, the troops cannot build with lime and stone, nor with mud, but are obliged to make double palisades of very strong wood, with mud between them, surrounded by a good strong ditch. And those who tell your most Royal Highness that forts may be built of stone and lime or of other material, have not seen the quality of the land. What I should urge is that people should come, so that the land may be explored from these two stations of Davaive and Comogre, and the secrets of it made known, as well as those of the sea on the other side toward the south.

In all the matters which I have named, your most Royal Highness would gain money, and it would cost nothing beyond the order to send people here.

Those Indians who eat men, and others at the bottom of the Gulf of Urabá and in the extensive flooded parts, have no workshops nor do they support themselves on anything but fish, which they exchange for maize. These are worthless people, and when canoes of Christians have gone on the great river of San Juan, they have come against them and have killed some of our people. The country where the Indians eat men is bad and useless, and can never at any time be turned to account. These Indians of Caribana have richly deserved death a thousand times over, for they are a very evil race and killed many of our Christians when we lost the ship. I would not make slaves of so bad a people, but would order them destroyed, both old and young, so that no memory may remain of them. I speak now of Caribana and for twenty leagues inland, the people being evil, and the country sterile and worthless. And it will be serviceable to your Highness to give permission to take other natives to Española and the other islands occupied by Christians, to be sold and made profitable, so that other slaves may be bought for their price. It is impossible to keep them here even for a day; for the country being very extensive, they can run away and hide. Thus the settlers in these parts, not having Indians secured, cannot work for the service of your Highness nor extract any gold from the mines.

The settlers would also beseech your Highness to grant them permission to bring Indians from Veragua, from a gulf called San Blas, which is fifty leagues from this town, down the coast. Your Highness will be well served in granting this request, because it is a worthless land, covered with great swamps and forests, and seen from the sea it appears to be inundated. No profit whatever can be made out of these Indians of Veragua and Caribana, except in this way, by bringing them to Christian settlements from which they can be taken to Cuba, Jamaica, and other islands inhabited by Christians, to be exchanged for other Indians, of which there are many in those islands. I must inform your Highness that permission to take the Indians of the islands to the mainland would be very conducive to your service, since, for a distance of two hundred leagues round this town there is no inhabited island, except one in Carthagena, where the people defend themselves well. Thus, by sending the warlike Indians of these parts far from their homes, they will labor well in the islands, and those of the islands here.

As regards the gold that is collected from the Indians, by barter or during war, it will conduce to your service to give permission that henceforth a fifth may be given to your Highness of all that may be obtained. The share being now a fourth, it is looked upon as hard service to discover land and to march in war through great hardships, for in truth they are so great as to be intolerable. The men prefer to seek for gold, rather than to go and die. And if I, or the governor who may succeed me, have to make the Christians go inland on expeditions of discovery, they will never go willingly, and a thing done against the will is never so well done as it should be; while, when it is done willingly, all will be done well and according to our desire. I therefore assure your Highness that if the royal share of gold is a fifth, it will be collected in much larger quantity than when it is a fourth, besides which the country will be discovered according to your Highness' desire.

With respect to the arms and the means of building brigantines, and the shipwrights, these are important points, because without them no good work can be done. If your Highness should order them to be sent, it would be entirely at the cost of the settlers in these parts, without any expense to your Highness. Your Highness should receive all this from me as your loyal servant, and should give it credence because your service will thus be advanced. I do not desire to make towers of wind like the governors whom your Highness sent out. Between them both they have lost eight hundred men. Those whom I have rescued scarcely amount to fifty, and this is the truth. Your Highness will consider all that I have done, and discovered, and endured with these people, without any help but from God and my own industry.

If I have erred in anything in working for the service of your Highness, I beseech that my earnest desire to serve your Highness may be considered. Although, most puissant lord, I have not succeeded in doing all that is necessary in this land, I can certify that I know how to administer better than all those who have come here before. That your Highness may understand this, you must consider how little other governors have discovered until today, and how they have all failed and left these shores full of graves. I do not desire to enlarge upon this, but your Highness should know what each man has been able to do and has done up to this time.

Most puissant lord, I have sent Sebastian del Campo, that you may be better informed of all that has passed here. I entreat your Highness to give him full credence, for he has been informed by me of the whole truth concerning all that can be done in your service, and of that which ought to be done for this land.

Your Highness must know that formerly there were certain disagree-

ments here, because the alcaldes and regidores of this town, filled with
envy and treachery, attempted to seize me. When they failed in that,
they made false charges against me with false witnesses and in secret.
I complain of this because if such acts are not chastised, no governor
you may send here will be free from attacks. For I, being alcalde for
your Highness, have been exposed to a thousand slanders, and if your
representative is not respected, he cannot do what is necessary for your
service. And because the alcaldes and the regidores sent an accusation
against me, which I believe your Highness will see, I appointed two
gentlemen as my judges, that they might draw up a report of my life
and of the great and loyal services which I have done for your Highness in those parts of the Indies where we now are. I send this that you
may see the malice of these people, and because I believe that your
Highness will be pleased with all that I have done for your service. I
beseech that favor may be shown me in proportion to my services. I
also send a report of what passed with respect to those who invented
these calumnies.

Most puissant lord, I desire to ask a favor, for I have done much
in your service. It is that your Highness will command that no bachelor of laws, nor of anything else unless it be of medicine, shall come
to this part of the Indies on pain of heavy punishment which your
Highness shall order to be inflicted, for no bachelor has ever come
here who is not a devil, and who does not lead the life of devils. And
not only are they themselves evil, but they give rise to a thousand law-
suits and quarrels. This order would be greatly to the advantage of
your Highness' service, for the country is new.

Most puissant lord, in a brigantine that we sent from here, on board
of which was Juan de Quizedo and Rodrigo de Colmenares, I forwarded to your Highness 500 pesos of gold from the mines, in very
beautiful grains. As the voyage is somewhat dangerous for small
vessels, I now send to your Highness, by Sebastian del Campo, 370
pesos of gold from the mines. I would have sent more if it had not
been for the impossibility of collecting it during the short time the
vessels were here.

With respect to all I have said, I beseech your Highness to that
which is best for your service. May the life and royal estate of your
Highness prosper by the addition of many more kingdoms and lordships to your sacred rule. May all that is discovered in these parts
increase the power of your Highness, as your most Royal Highness
may desire; for there are greater riches here than in any other part of
the world.

From the town of Santa Maria del Antigua, in the province of

Darien, in the gulf of Urabá, today this Thursday the 20th of January in the year 1513.

The making and creation of your Highness, who kisses your most royal hands and feet, Vasco Núñez de Balboa.

During the months that followed, Balboa received more and more supplies from Hispaniola. Ferdinand, frustrated and angry at the way in which Diego de Colón was blocking activity, had appointed several appeals-judges who could override the Admiral's decisions, and they came to the help of Darien. By early summer several boats had stopped at the small colony. One of them brought about one hundred fifty new colonists, and another brought the long-awaited confirmation to Balboa:

For the present, until such time as we command that a governor and court of law be provided for the province of Darien which is in the tierra firme of the Indies of the Ocean Sea, it is my pleasure and will, considering the competence and ability of you, Vasco Núñez de Balboa, and knowing that it will be to our service, that you be our governor and captain-general of the said island and province and the judicial authority in it.

He was now a captain-general and interim governor by the king's appointment. But about this same time—if not even by the same ship—he learned that the term of office was going to be a short one. The king had reached the end of his patience with the slow progress in the New World, with the many quarreling factions and the constant drain on the treasury. He intended to set up a new government in Darien.

Faced with removal from office, Balboa made the decision which was to make him immortal—discover the South Sea. If he could do this and get the news back to Ferdinand in Spain, there was just the possibility that he would not be replaced. The colony was well fed at the moment, the natives were friendly, and the ships had brought in supplies. The conditions were as good as they were ever going to be.

Organizing his expedition with care, Balboa notified the friendly Indians that he was planning to come through their territory. And on the last day of August 1513, with one ship and nine canoes, he set out with half his colony—about two hundred men—for Careta. Here he left half his men, and pushed on with ninety-two soldiers, two priests, some slaves, servants, women, and war dogs. His own dog

Leoncito who had been with him when he had stowed away on Enciso's ship now drew the pay of a bowman. A two-day march brought the expedition to Ponca in the interior, and for the next five days they made their way through the jungles, swamps and rivers, arriving at the village of Quareca on September 24. Here the Catholic conquistadores were sickened by a morality completely alien to them. Homosexuality was common practice. The chief's own brother was dressed as a woman, as were several others. Balboa did not even consider the lengthy torture prescribed by the Church for such conduct but fed the men alive to his dogs. He pressed on to Torecha.

The moment of discovery was formally recorded by the notary, Andrés de Valdarrabano, and several years later the chronicler Oviedo claimed to have copied the report:

There in Torecha he left part of the troops, and departed with about seventy men; and on the twenty-fifth of the month, the same day that he left, he reached the bohios and seat of the chief named Porque, who had absented himself. Balboa did not bother with him, but passed on, pursuing his journey in search of the Other Sea. And on a Tuesday, the twenty-fifth of September of that year one thousand five hundred and thirteen, at ten o'clock in the morning, Captain Vasco Núñez, going ahead of all those he was conducting up a bare high hill, saw from its summit the South Sea.

And immediately he turned toward the troops, very happy, lifting eyes and hands to Heaven, praising Jesus Christ and His glorious Mother the Virgin, Our Lady; and then he knelt down on both knees and gave much thanks to God for the grace He had shown him in allowing him to discover that sea, and in doing so to accomplish so great a service to God and to the Catholic and Most Serene Kings of Castile . . .

And he commanded that all those who accompanied him should kneel down likewise and give the same thanks to God, and should pray very devoutly that He permit them to discover and see the great secrets and riches which lay in that sea and coast, to the greater exaltation and growth of the Christian faith and for the conversion of the Indians native of those austral regions, and for the great prosperity and glory of the royal throne of Castile and of its princes present and to come.

Everyone did so very willingly and joyously, and then the captain caused a fine tree to be felled, of which was made a tall cross which was planted and fixed on that same place and high hill from where that austral sea was first seen. And because the first that was seen was a gulf or bay entering into the land, Vasco Núñez commanded that it be called the Gulf of San Miguel, because it was the feast of the archangel four days later. And he also commanded that the names of all the men who were there with him should be written down so that the memory should remain of him and of them, because they were the first Christians who saw that sea; all of whom sang the hymn of the glorious holy doctors of the Church, Ambrose and Augustine, as a devout priest who was there, named Andrés de Vera, sang it with them, saying: "Te Deum laudamus: Te Dominum confitemur."

The report prepared by the notary was signed by the sixty-seven caballeros and hidalgos present. Among them was the soldier of Ojeda's original colony who had clashed with Enciso—Francisco Pizarro.

The exact date of the discovery comes into doubt as the notary placed the twenty-fifth on Tuesday instead of Sunday, and it is doubtful if the padres accompanying the expedition would have confused the Sunday of a week, whereas the notary might easily have confused the day of the month.

Coming down from the height, Balboa stopped at a small, empty village near the sea. At ten in the morning two days after his discovery, he marched to the shore. He wore his full uniform, armor and helmet, and one of his men carried the flag. Marching back and forth along the beach of the South Sea, he made his claim.

Long live the most high and mighty Sovereigns, Don Fernando and Doña Juana, Kings of Castile and of León and of Aragon, et cetera, in whose names and for the royal Crown of Castile I take and assume royal possession corporal and present of these austral seas and lands and coasts and islands with everything annexed to them or to which title might or could exist, ancient or modern, in times past, present or to come, without gainsay whatsoever.

And should any other prince or captain, Christian or infidel, of whatever law or sect or condition he may be, pretend to any right to these lands and seas, I am ready and prepared to deny him and to defend them in the names of the Kings of Castile present and future, whose is this empire and the dominion of these Indies, islands, and mainland, northern and southern, with their seas, in the arctic pole as in the antarctic, on both sides of the equinoctial line, within and without the Tropics of Cancer and Capricorn—so that each thing and part of it belong and appertain most completely to their Highnesses and to their successors, as I declare more at length by writ, setting forth all that may be said or can be said and alleged in behalf of their royal patrimony, now and for all time so long as the world shall last until the final universal judgment of all mortals.

When he was done, the men edged forward and tried the water with their hands and put it in their mouths to see if it was fresh or salty like the North Sea. And when they realized that it was salty, they accepted it for an ocean and thanked the Lord. And Balboa took a dagger from his belt and cut a cross on a nearby tree and threw sea water on it. Then he made crosses on two other trees, completing the Holy Trinity, and the men who were with him began making crosses on other trees. And when they were done, they believed they had completed the formalities that would secure possession of the entire South Sea. Then the group signed their names a second time to the notary's account, attesting to the accuracy of Balboa's claim. Only three years had passed since the captain had stowed away in a flour barrel aboard Enciso's ship.

The expedition spent over a month on the shores of the South Sea. On November 3 they started home, crossing through a small native kingdom governed by a woman whom they failed to meet. Balboa reached Darien on January 19, 1514, hoping to rush the news of his discovery to Spain and, in the glory of it, retain his captaincy and governorship. But on his return, he learned that a new governor had already been appointed and that the official documents made no reference to the acting captain. Balboa carefully penned his report, sent it on to Ferdinand and waited to see what would happen. The worst did.

The man selected to replace the thirty-seven-year-old adventurer was Pedrarias Dávila. The two men were to become father and son, and mortal enemies. Pedrarias was almost seventy when he was selected for his new office. He was a hero of the Algerian wars; a friend and protege of Fonseca—the powerful Bishop of Burgos who controlled the Council of the Indies—and of the husband of Doña Isabella, who was as strong-minded and as influential as her husband was unscrupulous and petty. The appointment of Padrarias as well as that of a new bishop for Darien showed the hopes that Ferdinand had for the small colony of huts built on the Gulf of Urabá.

The bishopric cost the king seven hundred gold pesos and was the subject of the first bull signed by the newly elected Pope Leo X. In

Spain everything that could be done to support the new colony was being readied. Almost two thousand recruits were enlisted. A small armada was prepared and provisioned. And on February 26, 1514, the fleet set sail with full pomp and ceremony. It returned the same day driven back by storms. Soon afterward Pedrarias tried a second time, and after an unpleasant voyage the armada landed at Darien with as much ceremony as it had departed from Spain.

Within a week the residencia of Balboa began. He was held by the courts until a full investigation of his activities had been completed. His enemies had all the time they wanted to satisfy their hatred of the man who had governed them for three years. In addition, Enciso returned to add his complaints to the list.

While Balboa was involved in satisfying the court which had no desire to be satisfied, Pedrarias assumed control of his province. He had almost three thousand people to feed, colonists who had been granted a total of almost four thousand square miles by their generous sovereign, and a camp split between Balboa's friends and enemies.

Pedrarias began sending small expeditions to scour the countryside for gold, and at the same time he began planning longer and more ambitious ones. All of the innocents who had sailed so recently from Spain had great hopes for the future. But they did not last long.

The results of the gold-seekers were disappointing, and, much worse, an epidemic struck the town. The jungle weather, the poor food, the unsanitary conditions fed one upon the other and eight hundred died quickly. Then starvation set in, though this was more difficult to explain to the colonists. There was ample food, but Pedrarias and his officials saw no need to distribute the supplies and made no effort to bring in additional provisions, and so through greed and neglect men starved in the muddy streets of Darien.

Nothing that happened swayed the new governor from his intention to get rich as rapidly as possible. His captains ravaged the Isthmus and set up a reign of terror among the Indians which was equaled only by that of Juan Ponce de León in Puerto Rico. The Indians became fair game for killing, torture, rape and sport. The slaughter was widespread and there was no one in the new government interested in preventing it. Gold was found in sufficient amounts to keep the colonists eager and hunting.

In December of 1514 Balboa was still attending the hearings against him. His knowledge of the country, the Indians, his own people, went unsought. He had survived the epidemic and the starvation, but he had not yet been released to go his own way. Then that same month a letter written in August arrived in Darien.

LETTER FROM KING FERDINAND TO BALBOA

Because my special emissary has not yet arrived and I am awaiting his coming to take measures in everything to do with those regions and in what concerns you, this will be only to tell you how greatly I was rejoiced to read your letters and to learn of the things you discovered in those regions of Tierra Nueva de la Mar del Sur and the Gulf of San Miguel, for which I give Our Lord much thanks, in the hope that it will all be to His service. I am grateful to you, and I deeply appreciate your labor and achievement in this as that of a most true and loyal servitor. And I also hold in service all those who went with you on that journey, and the hardships and hunger and suffering which you and they endured. And since it has been so great a service to God and to us, and to the welfare and resources of these realms, you must expect that you and they will be well rewarded and remunerated, and that I will always keep in mind your services and theirs, to the end that you may receive favors. As regards yourself, I will so dispose that you be honored and your services recompensed, for in truth I well comprehend that in everything that you have undertaken you have done very well.

I am pleased with the way you behaved to the chiefs on that march, with kindness and forbearance, leaving them well disposed, because that good treatment and reasonableness and leaving of them at peace will cause others to do what is expedient in our service, there and everywhere else.

When your letters came, Pedrarias had already left. I am writing to him to look to your affairs with care and to favor you as a person whom I greatly desire to gratify and who has greatly served me, and I am sure that he will do so.

Ferdinand made it clear that he respected the opinions of the replaced captain. But Pedrarias ignored the king's letter as well as Balboa's plea that he stop plundering the Indian villages. The officers of Pedrarias seemed determined to wipe out the native population if this would bring more gold. When the senior officer of the expeditions had more treasure than he wanted to account for, he stole a boat and sailed directly for Spain, where he remained in hiding for two years.

In March 1515, a ship arrived with orders from Spain, and though Pedrarias tried to keep the contents a secret, the bishop forced their release.

The new directives rocked the colony. Pedrarias' enemy Balboa was made the governor of a newly created province with full powers. He was his own chief justice and he could appoint his own officials. He could also remove any who had been appointed within the borders of his province by someone else. And in addition he was named Adelantado of the Coast of the South Sea which he discovered. This was a title newly created, and Balboa's for life with all the honors and liberties which went with it. It seemed for the moment that everything Balboa had sought was suddenly his. However, when he looked at the directives carefully, he found that the situation had not actually altered. He would have to request his supplies and men from Pedrarias, and he would have to report directly to the older man. The letter which Pedrarias received confirmed both Balboa's appointment and the power of his enemy.

The King to the Governor:

I command and charge you that in what concerns the said office as in every other thing in which the said Vasco Núñez may apply to you, you treat him and favor him and look after him as someone who has also served us, and in such manner that he recognizes in you the will I have to favor him . . . and you must give him full liberty in the things of his administration so that he does not lose time coming to consult things with you, notwithstanding that I have ordered that his appointment be subordinate to your gobernacion, for I very much prefer that he should undertake this than that it be done by anyone else . . . and it will be most desirable that the good treatment you give Vasco Núñez be seen, for thus people will have a more apt will to serve us. . . .

It appeared that nothing could make the old man help Balboa. In fact, he forbade the newly appointed Governor of the South Sea Coast to leave Darien, and he rushed his own expeditions to the Pacific so that he could strip the coast and in particular the Pearl Islands which Balboa had discovered. In pained anger, Balboa wrote several times to the king protesting what was happening. But the power of Pedrarias and his sponsor Fonseca was almost unlimited.

The correspondence of the two men with the court in distant Spain spilled over with their mutual hatred.

Balboa wrote:

With regard to the Governor, although he is a distinguished personage, your Highness knows that he is very old to serve in these parts, and he suffers greatly from a serious illness so that he has never been well for a single day since he came here. He is an excessively hasty man; he is a man who does not much care even if half the troops are lost on the expeditions. He has never punished the destruction and killings done in the entradas both to chiefs and Indians. He has refrained from punishing thefts of gold and pearls which the captains have very obviously stolen in the entradas; there was one captain who gave six hundred pesos of the stolen loot he brought, and nothing more was said about it. It is not known why this captain and others have been allowed to go to Castile; their thefts were publicly discussed. We have seen many times that if any of the men who accompanied the captains in the entradas complained of them, they intimidated him in such fashion that no one else dared to complain. Pedrarias is a person who is delighted to see discord between people, and if there is none he creates it, speaking ill of one to the other; this vice he has to a very great extent. He is a man who, absorbed in his profit-getting and greed, does not remember that he is Governor or occupy himself with anything else; because it matters nothing to him whether the whole world be lost or won, just as if he were not Governor.

And Pedrarias sent on his opinion of the adelantado:

What must be said about Vasco Núñez is his character, and how it is public and notorious that he does not know how to speak the truth, nor to resent or take offense at being taxed with anything wrong that he has done, of whatever nature it may be; that he has no love or good will for any worthy person, but likes to converse and be intimate with people of low degree. That he is most excessively avaricious; covets greatly any good thing possessed by another; is very cruel and disagreeable; never forgives; never submits to any advice; has no self-control nor can use any to resist any vicious appetite; is very mercenary; has neither obedience nor reverence for the Church and her ministers; is of most evil conscience; is always set on tricking the person with whom he converses; when one asks counsel of him he gives it contrariwise. That he is very determined to procure, by fair means or foul, to be superior to what he was already trying to be, by confederations and combines and by any other means he finds handy even if it be contrary to all loyalty and service owed to God and their Highnesses.

The letters came to nothing and Balboa resorted to trickery. He waited until Pedrarias himself decided to visit and claim the province of the South Sea coast, and then he sent a friend secretly to Hispaniola to recruit volunteers so that the colony across the mountains could be established and the explorations which the king had ordered could begin.

Two full years passed between the time Balboa received his appointment and the time his sixty volunteers arrived from Hispaniola. But the volunteers only served to create greater problems. Pedrarias became infuriated at the thought that Balboa might establish himself as a governor, and he had the younger man arrested and caged like an animal inside the governor's house for two months.

Then suddenly and to the surprise of everyone, Pedrarias released Balboa, adopted him as a son, married him by proxy to a daughter in Spain, and agreed to help in the establishment of the province across the mountains. Few in Darien knew, at the moment Pedrarias freed Balboa, that Ferdinand was dead and his grandson and heir, Charles, was withholding support from Fonseca. The canny old governor of Castilla del Oro was taking no chance that Balboa might suddenly become important in Spain.

But Pedrarias was not given to excess generosity. He would allow Balboa to cross over into his own province only after the conquistador had established a settlement at Acla at the entrance of the mountain pass that led across the Isthmus. Balboa accepted the conditions, and though the colony was now down to fewer than six hundred persons, and most of them scattered, he took what men he could find and by March 1517 he had built the settlement.

At long last Balboa was allowed to leave for his own province and return to the scene of his discovery. He cut the timbers for two boats which he would use to explore the Pacific, believing that the timbers of the Acla area would not be so easily destroyed by seaworms. Then he hauled his timbers over the mountains, carrying a hundred-pound plank on his own back. But when he went to assemble the boats, he discovered the lumber was worthless.

Frustrated and weary, Balboa and his men set out to cut new

timbers. They completed their first vessels and dragged them to the sea only to watch them settle to the bottom. Still unwilling to quit the venture, they dragged the ships ashore, caulked them as best they could and sailed for the Pearl Islands. But here they found that Pedrarias' captains had already decimated the local population and destroyed the oyster beds. Though the results were disappointing, Balboa was a governor in his own province. And this amount of success was enough to anger Pedrarias.

To make matters worse for Balboa, two pieces of information were received at Darien. One was a letter from the court directing Pedrarias to "permit Vasco Núñez to do what he wishes." The other piece of news arrived on September 15, 1517. A new governor was going to be appointed for Darien.

No news could have frightened the old tyrant more, for a new governor meant a residencia—a lengthy investigation into the government of Pedrarias. There was nothing personal in this procedure. It was the way in which the Spanish empire policed itself. But Pedrarias had many reasons to fear investigation and even more to fear Balboa's presence at the hearings.

News of the possible change reached Balboa on the South Sea coast in November. And he was concerned himself, but for strangely different reasons. The removal of Pedrarias, who was now helping him, however reluctantly, might slow down his own explorations. Balboa decided to find out what was happening in Darien.

What followed is told by Pascual de Andagoya, who begins his report with his departure from Spain in the fleet that brought Pedrarias to Darien. Andagoya accompanied Balboa in the conquistador's second crossing of the Isthmus, and he was probably present at his death. Andagoya himself went on to Panama in later years, marrying a woman of the Pedrarias household and rising in time to Inspector General of the Indians on the Isthmus. In his explorations of a province called Biru he was the first European to hear of the Inca empire to the south. It was a confusion of the name *Biru* that eventually resulted in *Peru* so many miles away. What happened to Andagoya in South America is another tale. In his record of the years of conflict between Pedrarias and Balboa, he reports events in which he himself had a part.

In the year 1515 Pedrarias de Ávila, who had been appointed governor of the mainland, Castilla del Oro, by the Catholic king of glorious memory, embarked at Seville with nineteen ships and fifteen hundred men—the most distinguished company that had yet set out from Spain. The first land of the Indies at which he arrived was the island of Dominica. This island has a large and beautiful harbor, and is hilly and wooded. Here he disembarked with his troops to find out whether there were any inhabitants. Some of the Spaniards, entering the woods, met with Indians armed with poisoned arrows, watching for an opportunity to kill a stray Spaniard. These Indians are a war-like people. They eat human flesh, and both men and women go about stark naked. This island has not been occupied because the conquest would be very dangerous and of little value.

Continuing his way to the mainland, Pedrarias arrived at the province of Santa Martha, where he landed all his men. A company of his troops came to a village deserted by its inhabitants, where they captured some spoil and found some gold in a tomb. The people of this island are almost the same as those of Dominica. They are armed with poisoned arrows. Here they found certain cloths and the seats on which the devil sat. He was figured on them in the form in which he appears to the people. Although they did not worship him, as being a thing which appeared to and conversed with them, they noted his form and represented it on their cloths.

From there Pedrarias sailed for Tierra Firme, without stopping any-where except at Isla Fuerte, which is in front of Carthagena. The Indians get their salt from this island, and a great number of bags of salt were found. Continuing his voyage, he arrived at a province called Darien, which is at the end of the gulf of the same name. Here he found some Spaniards, who had Vasco Núñez de Balboa for their captain and alcalde. Their settlement was on the banks of a river, a league and a half from the sea.

A year before these people arrived at that province, the captains Diego de Nicuesa and Alonzo de Ojeda departed from San Domingo, each one with his fleet. Ojeda went to the coasts of Paria and Santa Martha, where most of his people perished in the wars with the Indians or from disease. The survivors took Francisco Pizarro, who was after-wards governor of Peru, as their captain and leader. They followed the coast until they reached Darien, where they established themselves, and sent a ship to San Domingo with the news of what had happened. The judges who were there appointed the said Vasco Núñez as alcalde.

Diego de Nicuesa went with his fleet to the coast of Veragua. Leav-ing the remainder of his people on a hill called the hill of Nicuesa, where Nombre de Dios stands, he took a brigantine with some of his men. He knew not where to go, the whole coast being marshy, covered with forest, unhealthy, and thinly peopled. He sailed along the coast in search of the people left by Ojeda, and to discover some country where he might settle, for the coast of Veragua as far as Darien was under his jurisdiction. Ojeda had received the other coast of Santa Martha and Carthagena. Having arrived at Darien, he found Vasco Núñez and his followers. They received him as a stranger, and would neither give him provisions nor receive him as their governor. They made him embark in a boat with some sailors, and it is even said that this boat was caulked with a blunt tool only. I heard this from the caulker himself who did the work. Thus Nicuesa was lost, and it was never known what became of him. When the people he had left at Nombre de Dios found that their captain did not return, they followed him and, arriving at Darien, submitted to the authority of the others.

The Admiral Colón discovered these coasts, both the one and the other.

Pedrarias arrived at Darien at the end of July 1514. He was received by the people who were there, and landed all his troops. The settlement was small, and there were few resources in the land. The provisions on board the ships were disembarked and divided among all the people. The flour and other stores were injured by the sea, and this, added to the evil nature of the land, brought on so much sickness among the people that they could not be cured. In one month seven hundred men died of sickness and hunger. Our arrival weighed so much on those who were already settled at Darien that they would do no act of charity for anyone.

As in united enterprises, until experience has shown the way, the correct method of acting is very seldom adopted. Thus Pedrarias was appointed jointly with the bishop and officers (without whom he could do nothing). These, seeing how the people were dying, began to send out captains in various directions, not to make settlements but to bring as many Indians as possible to Darien. They seldom succeeded, but lost many of their people in fights with the Indians. As there were so many voices in every measure, each one given from motives of interest or wilfulness, neither was good order preserved nor was any evildoer punished.

It was only a short time since Vasco Núñez had reached a point near the South Sea, from which he had seen it. The captains and troops who went forth in that direction, where the country is healthier and more thickly peopled, brought back great troops of captive natives in chains, and all the gold they could lay their hands on. This state of things continued for nearly three years. The captains divided the captive Indians among the soldiers, and brought the gold to Darien. They gave each man his share. To the bishop, the officers who had a vote in the government, and the governor, they gave a share of the Indians. As they were appointed captains by the favor of those who governed, from among their relations and friends, although they had committed many evil deeds, none were punished. In this manner the land suffered for a distance of more than a hundred leagues from Darien. All the people who were brought there, and there was a great multitude, were immediately sent to the gold mines, for they were rich in that land. As they came from a great distance and were worn out and broken down by the great burdens they had to carry, and as the climate was different from their own, and unhealthy, they all died. In these transactions the captains never attempted to make treaties of peace, or to form settlements, but merely to bring Indians and gold to Darien and waste them there.

About thirty leagues from Darien there was a province called Careta, and another, at a distance of five leagues from it, called Acla. In these two provinces there were two lords who were brothers. One of them wished to possess all and there were great wars. A battle was fought in a place called Acla, where Pedrarias afterward established a town of Christians. Before the battle this place had another name, for Acla in the language of that land means "the bones of men," and the province retained that name because of the quantity of bones strewn on the battlefield. After this war there were so few Indians that they made no resistance when we arrived.

These people were more civilized than those of the coast of Santa Martha. The women were very well dressed, in embroidered mantles which extended from the waist downwards, and slept on beds of the same material. The dresses of the women reached down so as to cover the feet, but the arms and bosom were uncovered. The men went about with their private parts covered with a bright colored sea shell, very well carved, which was secured around the loins by cords. In this way they were able to run and walk with great freedom. These shells were used as articles of barter with the inner lands, for they were not found anywhere except on the seacoast. The land is covered with forest like that of Darien, though it is more healthy and there are gold mines in many parts of it.

At this time a captain named Gaspar de Morales set out to discover the South Sea. He went out on it as far as the islands of Pearls, where the lord was friendly and gave him rich pearls. He was the first man who visited them. The first province to the west of Acla is Comogre, where the country begins to be flat and open. From this point forward, the country was populous, though the chiefs were of small account, being only a league or two apart from each other. In this country there is a province called Peruqueta, extending from one sea to the other, and including the Pearl Islands and the gulf of San Miguel. And another province, which was called the land of confusion because there was no chief in it, is called Cueva. The people are all one, speaking one language, and are dressed like those of Acla. From this province of Peruqueta to Adechame, a distance of forty leagues still in a westerly direction, the country is called Coiba, and the language is the same as that of Cueva, only more polished, and the people have more self-assertion. They differ also in the men not wearing shells like those of Cueva, for they go quite naked without any covering. The women are adorned like those of Acla and Cueva. From these provinces were taken most of the Indians who were brought to Darien. They were the nearest and most populous, and no sooner had one captain returned from them than another set out.

One of the captains of Pedrarias, a certain Meneses, established a settlement called Santa Cruz, in the territory of a chief named Pocorosa, in the province of Cueva, on the north sea. From this settlement he advanced into Cueva with part of his forces and was defeated by the Indians, several of his people being killed. Then, seeing that the Spaniards in Santa Cruz were defeated and reduced in numbers, the Indians attacked them. They killed them all so that no one remained alive except a woman, whom the chief took for himself and lived with as his wife for several years. His other wives, being jealous that the chief liked her better than them, killed her and gave their lord to understand that an alligator had eaten her when she went to bathe in the river. Thus this settlement was destroyed.

Wishing to know whether these people had any notion of God, I learned that they knew of the flood of Noah; they said that he escaped in a canoe with his wife and sons, and that the world had afterward been peopled by them. They believed that there was a God in heaven, whom they called Chipiripa, and that he caused the rain and sent down other things which fall from heaven. There is no report concerning the origin of these people, nor can they give any, except that they are natives of the country. A principal woman of this land said there was a belief among the chiefs (for the common people do not talk of these things) that there is a beautiful woman with a child in heaven, but the story goes no further.

Vasco Núñez was in Darien after he had undergone his residencia. He sent one Francisco Garavita to the island of Cuba, without the knowledge of Pedrarias. Garavita returned with a ship and some men to the port of Darien, which is a league and a half from the town. Without disembarking his men, he made known to Vasco Núñez that he had arrived. This came to the knowledge of Pedrarias. He discovered that the vessel came to take Vasco Núñez to the South Sea, where he intended to form a settlement. Thereupon Pedrarias seized Vasco Núñez and made a cage in his own house into which he put him. Then he made an agreement with him and gave him his daughter in marriage, who was then in Spain. Having thus received Vasco Núñez as his son-in-law, Pedrarias sent him to the province of Acla to form a settlement, that which is now called Acla. From there Vasco Núñez sent people to the Rio de la Balsa and made two ships, that he might embark on the South Sea and discover what there might be in it.

Vasco Núñez came to that river, near a populous district which had no chief, for the heads of families were the chiefs among that people and all lived in friendship with each other. This province borders on that of Cueva, and the people are the same. It is wooded and flat, and fertile in yielding crops for bread. In this river we made two ships. We brought many Indians to Acla, to carry the materials for the ships, and the food for the carpenters and other workmen. We conveyed these ships down to the sea with great labor, for we met with many torrents forming hollows which we had to cross. When we got down to the gulf of San Miguel, there was a high tide. The carpenters did not know the wood, and it proved to be such that all the planks were eaten through and honeycombed. Thus there was much trouble before we could pass in the ships to the islands of Pearls, where the ships came to pieces. We made others of good timber, which were larger and better.

Vasco Núñez was to be absent on this expedition for a year and a half, at the end of which time he was to send an account to the governor of what he had done.

At this time the King heard of the differences in the government arising from the officers having votes, and he ordered that Pedrarias should govern alone. Since Vasco Núñez had never paid much respect to the officials, nor sent them any of the Indians he had captured, as the other captains did, they bore him no good will, and they told the governor he had rebelled. They persuaded the governor to go to Acla to get news of Vasco Núñez and send for him, and the officials accompanied the governor. Vasco Núñez, having built the ships, had come to the gulf of San Miguel and landed in a populous district called Pequeo. There he remained for two months, seizing Indians and sending them to Acla for more cordage or pitch, which were required for the ships. Here we received news that Lope de Sosa had been appointed in Castile to come out to this land as governor. Vasco Núñez assembled certain of his friends who were honorable men, and arranged that one Valdarrabano should go with a small force to the neighborhood of Acla, where he should secretly send a man at night to the house of Vasco Núñez and find out about the new governor. If it was true, all the people were to return so that the new governor might not break up the expedition. We were then to have gone to settle at Chepabar, which is six leagues nearer Acla than Panama. But the man was seized for having come in at night like a spy, and because the governor had ordered that any one who arrived was to be sent to Darien. Soon afterward the governor, with the officials, arrived at Acla; and when Valdarrabano came in, he sent his letters to the governor. The officials began to accuse Vasco Núñez and advised that he should be sent for and made prisoner. The governor wrote him a letter ordering him to come and disprove the things of which he was accused. Vasco Núñez presently arrived and was put in a house at Acla as his prison, with guards over him. Pedrarias, considering him as his son-in-law, would not act in the matter but entrusted the case to the licentiate Espinosa, who was alcalde. This official drew up the process and sentenced Vasco Núñez. Valdarrabano, Botello—who was the man that had been sent into Acla at night—and Arguello—who was the friend of Vasco Núñez and had sent him certain letters—to have their heads cut off.

This sentence was executed, and Pedrarias set out for the islands of the Pearls with all the troops that were at Acla.

Sometime in the third week of January 1519, Vasco Núñez de Balboa was executed. "And a pole was raised on which the head of the adelantado was exposed for days." Only later was it learned that the member of his party who was supposed to have gone into town to find out what was taking place had betrayed him, and betrayed him because he wanted the young Indian princess who had been given to Balboa by her father shortly after the conquistador's arrival in Darien.

With Balboa dead, Pedrarias now claimed for himself the discovery of the South Sea. And though the court named two successors to replace him, each died on arrival in the New World, and Pedrarias remained in command. He abandoned Darien shortly after the execution of Balboa and established Panama City on the western side of the Isthmus, making good his claim of the territory. He died in office at about ninety years of age.

The crown recognized his services, gave his widow 488 square miles of territory as a benefit and appointed the son-in-law who married Balboa's proxy-wife governor of Nicaragua. Pedrarias' other daughter was married off to Hernando De Soto when he returned from Peru with a hundred thousand gold pesos.

As for Balboa, the records were expunged. His name was dropped from the history of the colony he had established. Most of his letters were lost or removed from the files. The town he had governed was returned to the jungle. His years of trying to win the Indians came to nothing as his successors almost obliterated the native population. But such men as Pizarro, Belalcázar, Bernal Díaz and De Soto were to go out from Darien as conquistadores with his example of efficient, well-planned expeditions before them.

2

Córdoba

Discovers Yucatan;

Grijalva

Explores the Mexican Coast

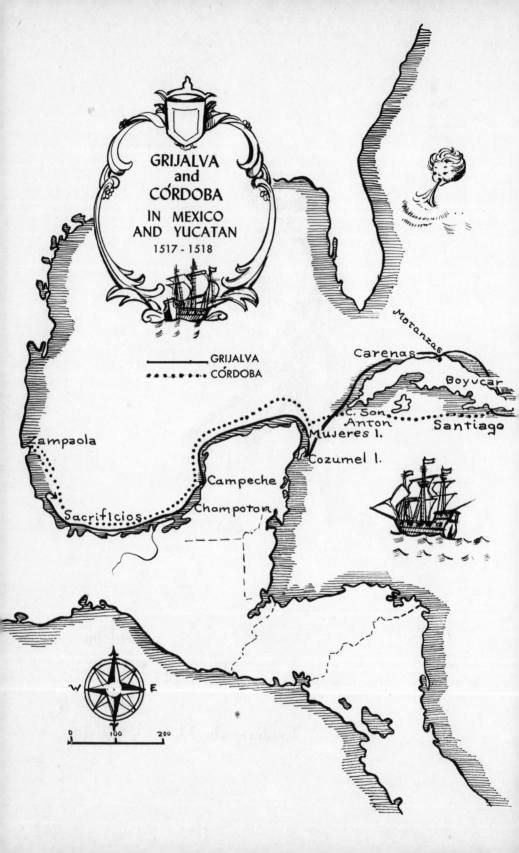

GRIJALVA
and
CÓRDOBA

IN MEXICO
AND YUCATAN

1517 - 1518

——————— GRIJALVA
• • • • • • CÓRDOBA

Matanzas

Carenas

Boyucar

C. Son
Anton

Santiago

Mujeres I.

Cozumel I.

Zampaola

Campeche

Sacrificios

Champoton

W   E

0   100   200

2

Córdoba Discovers Yucatan, and Grijalva Explores the Mexican Coast

THE SPANISH settled in on the islands of the Caribbean, they established towns which remain to this day, and they built their large plantations. Some few joined Pedrarias on the Isthmus where they repeated the process—building towns and plantations. They prospered but not so fast or so greatly as they wanted, partly because the Caribbean Indians did not lend themselves well to routine planting chores. They became ill and died, or they rebelled and were killed.

And so for two reasons the Spaniards sailed again: the search for slaves to keep the plantations operating, and the search for the greater wealth of gold and empires.

In 1516 two slavers left Santiago, Cuba, with a license from Governor Diego de Velásquez. And though one of the vessels was left on the mainland with twenty-five Spaniards, the captains returned to Cuba with a cargo of Indian slaves. However, as soon as the vessel arrived, the Indians freed themselves, stole the boat and sailed it home. They attacked the Spaniards who had remained behind, and when Velásquez sent a rescue ship for the twenty-five Spaniards, all he found was a cross cut on a tree with the inscription, "We are going to Darien." But the rescue vessel did not waste its efforts. It returned to Cuba with a cargo of four hundred Indian slaves, worth about twenty thousand gold pesos.

Governor Velásquez was satisfied with the results of his slavers, and on February 8, 1517, he sent out another expedition. This one was more fully equipped. There were three vessels, one belonging to Velásquez and the other two belonging to Francisco Hernández de Córdoba, a wealthy planter, and two of his friends. Córdoba, "a gentleman and a person of quality," owned an Indian village as well

73

as a large plantation. And he needed slaves as much as any other man on the Island. He was accompanied by the pilot, Anton de Alaminos, who had sailed with the Great Admiral in 1502 as a ship's boy, and with Juan Ponce de León to Florida in 1513. Bernal Díaz del Castillo accompanied this voyage. A half century later he wrote about it in his *True History of the Conquest of New Spain*.

When he penned his account, the aged conquistador had outlived most of his companions—only four others were left alive of those who had marched with Cortés, and Bernal Díaz mentions none of those who had sailed with Córdoba. As he said, "We are very old and bowed down by infirmities and very poor," but his memory remained clear, though he did confuse the year that Juan Ponce de León reached Florida. Yet this is a small detail to a man who wrote to assure his companions and himself their due share of the credit for the Córdoba expedition and the conquest of Mexico that followed it.

THE EXPEDITION OF HERNÁNDEZ DE CÓRDOBA TO YUCATAN

THE ACCOUNT OF BERNAL DÍAZ CASTILLO

On February 8, 1517, we sailed from Havana and twelve days later doubled the Punta de San Antonio. We sailed toward the west, knowing nothing of shoals, currents or the winds at that latitude. A storm struck us which lasted two days and nights, and we were almost lost. The weather having improved, we continued our voyage, and twenty-one days after leaving port we sighted land, which made us happy. This land had never been discovered nor was there any knowledge of it till then.

From the ships we saw a large town about two leagues from the coast. Since it was larger than any we had ever seen in Cuba or Española, we named it "Great Cairo." We sailed as near as we could to the coast to see if there was enough depth in which to anchor. One morning, March 4, we saw approaching ten very large canoes, which they call *piraguas*, full of natives, as many as forty to a canoe. When they arrived near our ships, we made signs of peace and tried to talk to them with our hands, as we then had no interpreter who understood the languages of Yucatan and Mexico. They came aboard without fear, and more than thirty entered the 'lagship. We gave each of them a string of green beads. The principal one, a cacique, said by signs that he would come the next day and bring more canoes in which we could go ashore.

These Indians were dressed in cotton shirts like jackets, and their private parts were covered with some narrow cloths they called *masteles*. The men are more intelligent than the Cuban Indians because those in Cuba went about with their privates showing; the women here wore some cotton cloths, called *naguas*, down to their thighs.

The next morning the same cacique came back with a dozen large canoes and, with a cheerful face and signs of peace, told us to come to his town where he would give us food and whatever was necessary. He kept saying in his language, *"Cones catoche,"* which is to say, "Come here to my house." For this reason, we named that country "Punta de Catoche," and so it is on the charts.

Seeing the great cajolery of the cacique, we agreed to go ashore, but taking the greatest supply of arms we could. We followed the cacique until we came to some bramble thickets, where we were attacked by several squadrons of Indians whom the cacique had placed in ambush there. They wore cotton armor which reached to the knees, carried lances, shields, bows and arrows, and slings and stones. After wounding fifteen of our men with arrows, they came to hand-to-hand fighting and did us great damage. They soon fled when they found out how well our swords cut and about the crossbows and muskets. Fifteen of them were killed.

A little beyond where this fight took place was a small plaza and three stone houses of worship, where they had many clay idols, some like faces of devils, some of women, and others of evil figures which appeared to be of Indians practicing sodomy with other Indians. Within the houses were some little wooden chests. In these were other idols and some small medallions of half-gold, mostly copper, some pendants and diadems, and other small figures of little fish and ducks of the country, all of low-grade gold. After we had seen everything, including the gold and the houses of stone, we were very content to have discovered such a land, as at that time Peru was not yet discovered. While we were fighting with the Indians, the cleric González took charge of the chests, the idols and gold and carried them to the ship.

In these fights two Indians were captured who were afterward baptized as Julian and Melchior. Both were cross-eyed. The fight over, we returned to our ships and continued along the coast.

Believing this to be an island, as the pilot Anton de Alaminos declared, we sailed along with great care, navigating by day and lying to at night. After fifteen days of this we saw what appeared to be a large town near a large ensenada and bay. Since it was the Sunday of Lazarus, we called the town by his name. So it is in the charts, but the natives call it Campeche.

We thought here to find water, of which we were in great need. The casks we brought were not tight because our fleet was composed of poor men without enough gold to buy good ones. Mindful of what had happened to us at Punta de Catoche, we went ashore well armed, disembarking near the town where there was a good well. Here the people of the town drank, since in these lands there are no rivers. When our casks were filled and we were ready to return, there came from the town some fifty Indians, apparently caciques, and asked us by signs what we were looking for. We gave them to understand for water and then to go at once to our ships. They pointed, questioning with their hands whether we came from where the sun rises, and said "Castilan, Castilan." We did not reflect on this talk of "Castilan." After this they told us by signs to go with them to their town.

We agreed to go, and they took us to some very large buildings, well built of masonry, which were the temples of their idols. On the walls were figures of many bodies of serpents and large snakes and other evil-looking figures. One place there, like an altar, was full of drops of blood. In another they had something like the sign of the cross, all painted, at which we wondered as something never seen or heard of before. It seems that at that season they had sacrificed some Indians to these idols to give them victory over us.

Some Indians brought rotten mantles full of dry reeds and placed them on a level place; behind them came two squadrons of Indian archers, well armed and in good order. Then came ten Indians wearing long white cotton mantles down to their feet. They had great long hair all matted with blood. These Indians were the priests of the idols, and in New Spain are commonly called papas. They brought perfumes and with clay braziers full of red-hot coals they began to perfume us. By signs they told us to leave their country before they lighted and finished burning the wood they had piled up. If not, they would kill us.

Seeing their numbers and their arrogance and our wounds not yet being healed from Catoche, we became frightened and agreed to go, embarking with our casks of water.

We sailed for six days with good weather, when a norther came up which lasted four days and nights and nearly wrecked us. God chose to aid us and we were able to survive the storm and continue along the coast. We were again in need of water because of our poor casks. We thought that wherever we went ashore we could take it from watering places or wells we should dig. Continuing our voyage, we saw a town and, about a league before reaching it, what looked like a river or arroyo. As the tide falls very much along that coast, we anchored more than a league from shore. A little after midday we landed in that ensenada with all our water vessels, arms, crossbows and muskets. From the town to where we disembarked was about one league. Nearby were some wells, cornfields, and small stone houses. The town is named Champoton.

While taking on water many squadrons of Indians came from the town, fully armed and their faces painted white and black and with ochre. Some of us wished to embark at once, but it was the opinion of most that we would be attacked while doing so. Others were of the opinion that we should attack them that night according to the proverb: "Who attacks, conquers." It also seemed to us that there were about two hundred Indians to one of us.

While in these consultations, it dawned, and now in bright day we saw more Indian warriors coming along the coast with banners flying and with plumes and drums. They joined the first who had come the night before and soon made up their squadrons and approached us from all sides. They sent us such a stream of arrows, darts and stones thrown from slings that they wounded more than eighty of our soldiers. They closed in on us and brought us to a bad pass, even though we gave them a very good fight with sword and knife thrusts. The crossbows and muskets never stopped playing. Meanwhile the Indians shouted in their language, "*Al calachuni, calachuni,*" which means, "Attack the captain and kill him." They gave him ten arrow wounds and three to me. They gave great lance thrusts to all our soldiers and carried two away, Alonso Boto and an old Portuguese.

Seeing that our good fighting was of no avail, that over fifty soldiers had been killed and all of us were wounded, we agreed with stout hearts to break through the middle of their battalions and take refuge in the boats. Forming a squadron, we broke through them. When we reached the boats, we were so many that they could not sustain us. Holding the sides as best we could, we reached the ship of least draught, which came with great haste to help us. On boarding her many of the soldiers were wounded, especially those who were holding onto the sterns of the boats. It pleased God that with much difficulty we should escape with our lives from these people.

On the charts the pilots and sailors call this Costa de Mala Pelea —Coast of the Bad Fight. Some soldiers cursed the pilot, Anton de Alaminos, and his voyage and discovery of an island, because he always insisted that it was not mainland.

There was not a man among us who did not have two, three or four wounds. Only one soldier remained without wounds. We agreed, therefore, to return to Cuba. As most of the sailors were wounded, we had no one to manage the sails. We left the ship of the least draught at sea, setting her on fire after taking out the sails, anchors and cables, and we divided the sailors between the two other ships.

We had another great trouble, however, which was the lack of water, as we could not take away the casks and barrels we had filled in Champoton. Such great thirst did we endure that our tongues and mouths were like cracks in the dry ground. How difficult it is to discover new lands! One cannot imagine what we passed through except those who have gone through the same excessive hardships.

The pilot Alaminos took counsel with the other two pilots, advising that we should cross over to Florida because he found from his chart and the latitude that he was only some seventy leagues from there. Once in Florida, he said, there was a better route and more certain navigation to Havana than the route by which we had come. It was as he said, because, as I had understood it, he had come with Ponce de León to discover Florida about fourteen or fifteen years before, and in that same country Juan Ponce had ben defeated and killed. After four days of sailing, we saw the land of Florida.

On reaching shore near an estuary opening from the sea, the pilot Alaminos recognized the coast. He said that he had been in that place when he had come with Juan Ponce de León, and that the Indians of that country had made war on them and had killed many soldiers, and that we should be prepared with unusual care. We at once put out two soldiers as scouts, and at low tide we dug some very deep wells on a wide beach. It pleased God that we should strike good water. We were overjoyed, and what with filling ourselves with it and washing clothes we were there for the space of an hour. When we wished to embark with our water, one of the two sentinels came running, shouting, "To arms, to arms, many warlike Indians are coming by land and others in canoes by the estuary!"

The shouting soldier and the Indians arrived at almost the same time. They were large men, dressed in deerskins and armed with very large bows and good arrows, and lances and something like swords. They came straight toward us, shooting arrows, and soon wounded six of us. But we attacked them so swiftly with knife thrusts and sword wounds and with the muskets and crossbows that they left us and went to the estuary to aid their companions, who were in canoes and fighting hand to hand with some sailors. These Indians had already captured a boat and were taking it up the estuary with their canoes, and had wounded four sailors and the pilot Alaminos in the throat.

We attacked them in water above our waists and made them turn loose the boat. Stretched along the shore and in the water were twenty-two of them. After this fight was over, we asked the soldier who had warned us what had happened to his companion, one named Berrio. He said he saw him go away with his hatchet to cut down a palmetto and that he had gone toward the estuary by which the Indians had come. He must have been killed as he gave the alarm. This soldier was the only one who was not wounded in the affair at Champoton and his luck was to come here to die.

We embarked in the boat and carried our sweet water with us. The soldiers were as joyful with this as if we had given them their lives. One soldier jumped from the ship into the boat and, taking a bottle to his breast, drank so much water that he swelled up and died within two days.

Having embarked with our water and taken on the boats, we made sail for Havana and passed that day and night near some shoals called the Bajos de los Martires. The deepest water was only four fathoms, and the flagship touched ground between some small islands and made much water, so that we feared we would founder. But sick and wounded as we were, we worked at the pumps and managed the sails until our Lord carried us to the town of Havana, where a Portuguese diver took out the water from the flagship. When we saw ourselves on land, we gave many thanks to God.

We wrote posthaste to Diego Velásquez, the governor, giving him to understand that we had discovered land with great settlements and houses of stone and mortar, the natives of which were dressed in cotton clothes, had their private parts covered, possessed gold and maize crops, and other things which I do not remember. Our captain, Francisco Hernández, went by land to a town named Santo Espiritu of which he was a citizen and where he had his Indians. He died in ten days from his wounds. Our ship went to the Puerto de Santiago where the governor was. We put ashore the two Indians, Melchorejo and Julianillo, whom we had captured at Punta de Catoche, and took out the chests of diadems, ducklings, little fish and other things of gold and also many idols. They extolled all these so highly that their fame spread through all the islands such as Santo Domingo and Jamaica and even in Castile, and it was said that no better lands had ever been discovered in the world.

As the idols were of clay and there were so many kinds of figures, they said that they were those of the Gentiles. Others said they were the work of the Jews whom Titus and Vespasian had banished from Jerusalem and sent out over the sea in certain ships which had come to this country. As at that time Peru had not been discovered, and was not for twenty years more, they were considered something great.

Another thing Diego Velásquez asked those Indians was whether there were any gold mines in their country, and by signs they gave him to understand that there were. They were shown gold dust and they said that there was much in their country. But they did not tell the truth, because it is clear that neither at the Punta de Catoche nor in all Yucatan are there any mines of gold or silver. They also showed them the heaps of earth where they put the plants from whose roots they make the cazabi bread, called in Cuba *yuca*. The Indians said they had them in their country and that they were called *tlati* for the ground in which they were planted. Thus, yuca with tlati is to say Yucatan. To explain this the Spaniards with Velásquez who were talking with those Indians said that their country was named Yucatan and so it kept this name, although in their language it is not so called.

Leaving aside this talk, I say that all the soldiers who went on this voyage of discovery spent the poor little property we had and returned to Cuba wounded and in debt. By our count we found that fifty-seven had died, including the captain, and this was the profit we derived from that expedition of discovery. Diego Velásquez wrote to the judges who governed the Council of the Indies that he had discovered it and in so doing had spent a great sum of gold pesos. Juan Rodríguez de Fonseca, Bishop of Burgos, and Archbishop of Rosana, as he was called, was president of the Council, and he published it so and wrote it to his Majesty in Flanders, giving much praise in his letter to Diego Velásquez. He made no mention of us who discovered it.

Córdoba reached Florida from Yucatan, which has since become a part of Mexico, about April 17 and he returned to Cuba about May 1. Bernal Díaz says he died ten days later of his wounds. Las Casas says he survived another six months. Córdoba was not important to Velásquez.

The pilot Anton de Alaminos reported that they had found an island with much gold and an Indian village of considerable size which they named Great Cairo. The people were infidels or non-Christians, and the largest infidel town the Spaniards knew was Cairo, so the transfer was logical.

The conquistadores spread names through the whole world in this fashion. The Romans had called North Africa Mauretania; the people there became the Moors. They were infidels like those whom the Spaniards met in the Philippines a half-world away and so the name Moros was given to the natives of the Philippines.

Although Córdoba had lost fifty men and had been wounded ten times, Velásquez began to plan the next expedition with great speed. He selected the same pilot and put out the expedition under the command of his own nephew, Juan de Grijalva.

The best account of Grijalva's expedition appears in *History of the Indies*, by Bartolomé de Las Casas, "the Protector of the Indians," and one of the most biased historians who ever wrote of his own times. However, despite his own comments about the activities he found in the New World, Las Casas or Casas knew the men who were making the history of the time and heard them tell their own stories. While he was furious about the treatment of the Indians and critical of the activities of many of the conquistadores, he kept his facts straight in most instances. He even seemed to like Juan de Grijalva.

THE DISCOVERY OF NEW SPAIN IN 1518 BY
JUAN DE GRIJALVA

THE ACCOUNT OF BARTOLOMÉ DE LAS CASAS

Velásquez had three ships and a brigantine fitted out with everything necessary for the voyage and with many trade goods to exchange for gold. He found volunteers well disposed to go back, as well as many who had not gone before, up to two hundred men. He sent as pilot of the fleet the same Anton de Alaminos, who had discovered the country with Francisco Hernández. As captains of the three ships went a Francisco de Avila, nephew of Gil González de Avila; Pedro de Alvarado—who was to become one of the great conquistadores; and a Francisco de Montejo, who in the end was the man who discovered the land and kingdom of Yucatan.

Diego Velásquez ordered the captain general, Juan de Grijalva, under no circumstances to settle in any part of the country discovered by Francisco Hernández, or in any other he might discover. He was simply to trade and leave the people among whom he went in peace and with love for the Christians.

The four ships sailed from the Puerto de Santiago in the beginning of the year 1518 [January 25] and went to the Puerto de Matanzas on the north coast. Here they took aboard cazabi, pigs, and other supplies from the haciendas of some of the Spanish residents. Departing from that port and from Carenas, which they also entered to take supplies, on May 3 they struck land in the Isla de Cozumel, which is close to Yucatan.

Some Indians came out to the ships in their canoes and brought gourds of honey, which they presented to the captain, who gave them some Castilian things. Grijalva had an Indian interpreter, one of those whom Francisco Hernández had brought with him to Cuba from that country. Since no town was to be seen, they raised sail and went coasting along the island. They saw many stone houses and masonry buildings, high and conspicuous, which were the temples of their gods. There was a large temple, well built, close to the sea, which looked like a large fortress. They anchored in front of it, but could not go ashore as it was already late.

Early in the morning a canoe full of Indians came to the ships. Captain Juan de Grijalva told them through his interpreter that he wished to go ashore and see the town and talk with its lord, if it would not displease him. They answered that he would not be displeased. Those who could got into four boats and went to shore. On reaching the temple, they looked at the buildings, which were admirable. Here Grijalva had Mass said before the Indians by a padre he had with him. It was very indiscreet and improper to celebrate the true sacrifice in a place where so many sacrileges were committed without first looking over the place, blessing it and sanctifying it. Neither was it decent to celebrate it before infidel Indians who did not adore nor give honor to the Creator of all things, Who was there consecrated.

An old Indian came before them. He seemed a man of authority and must have been a priest of the idols. He put down a clay brazier, well made, full of live coals, and placed in it some aromatic thing with which he incensed and perfumed certain idols or statues of men. Then the Indians brought the captain a present of some large turkeys and some gourds of bee honey.

The captain gave them some beads, bells, combs, looking glasses and other trifles. He asked them through the interpreter if they had gold, saying that they would buy or trade it for such things. This was, as always, the beginning of the Evangel which the Spaniards were accustomed to preach and was the theme of their sermons. See what article of faith the Christians first showed them: that there was in heaven a Lord and Creator of all things, who was called God, but if they had gold there was never another, so that the Indians should understand that that was the end and final desire and the cause of their coming to those countries, of their voyage and their hardships. The Indians brought some pieces of low-grade gold such as they put in their ears and noses for adornment.

While there the captain issued a proclamation that no one should barter for gold or for anything else but should bring to him any Indian wishing to trade. He asked for the lord of the town, but they answered that he was not there, having gone to a certain country or town on business. It may well be believed that he was present because it is the custom of the caciques and the lords of the Indians when any new people arrive, especially Spaniards, to order their people not to say they are present. They go about among their vassals and people disguised like one of them, seeing and hearing what is going on.

When Grijalva saw that there was no gold in abundance, he decided to embark and go on, coasting along the island and running along the land of Yucatan, which could be seen and which they also thought to be an island much larger than Cozumel. The wind turned contrary and they could not go on, so they decided to turn back to the place which they had left. When the Indians saw them coming back, they feared that perhaps the Spaniards had repented of not having sacked the town and were returning now to do so, and they all left the town, taking with them all they could of their little jewels. Our people found the town entirely vacant. There was some corn and fruit, which did not taste badly to them. Taking what they wished of this, they again made sail and started to coast along the shore of

Yucatan. They arrived there on May 13. They then went in search of the cacique Lazaro, lord of the town of Campeche whom Hernández had named Lazaro, and from whom he and his men had received fine hospitality and agreeable treatment. On the way they saw great and beautiful buildings of masonry, all whitened, and high towers. These were the temples of their gods.

They arrived at this town, which I believe was Champoton and not Lazaro, and anchored as near to it as they could. An infinite number of Indians came to the beach when they saw the ships. All that night they kept watch, making a great noise with their trumpets and drums and many other instruments. Grijalva decided to land with his men and go to the town under pretense of taking water, or truly so if he needed it. This also had been the theme of Francisco Hernández.

They disembarked before dawn in order to land more safely and with less disturbance to the natives who were peacefully on shore in their land and in their houses which the Spaniards should have greatly respected. It is manifest that the Indians should have been disturbed and have had a strong suspicion that this new people came to do them harm, especially after the damage which Francisco Hernández had inflicted on them if this town was Champoton.

If it was Lazaro, it was sufficient for them to take note of the fact that their neighbors had received those evil works, to make them change their minds and become suspicious, more especially because the Spaniards were landing in their country and town without their license and at night. The Spaniards went ashore and placed some cannon near the village. The Indians who were guarding the town went after them with their arms, bows and arrows, lances and shields, declaring by their gestures and signs that they should leave the country, and making movements like threats that they were going to attack them.

Captain Grijalva then began to make protestations and justify his deeds before the Spaniards, calling them to witness that neither he nor they had come to do any harm to these people but to take water of which they were in need and to pay for it, and other words which went with the wind and were of no effect to excuse the harm and the evil which afterward happened. See whom he used for witnesses of his protestations, and what they availed. The Indians, who were quietly in their houses, could not understand them. They saw only a strange and warlike people and what damage had been done the year before and that they were not coming in, as the saying is, by the door, as they had not asked for a license to enter the country. Besides, they were coming in by night, a means of entry which manifestly was bound to engender in the minds of those Indians a just and reasonable fear and suspicion.

Grijalva made the Indian whom he had brought with him from the Isla de Cozumel tell them that he did not wish to do them any harm but to take water and leave the country. The Indians showed them a well a stone's throw from the town, telling them to take it there and then to go away at once. The sailors and ship's boys went with their casks and filled these and their other vessels. The Indians, thinking that they were very slow about it or judging that they had turned stubborn, told them to hurry up, coming toward them as if they were going to shoot arrows at them. While the Indians were very insistent on this and the Spaniards did not leave, two Indians came out of their squadron and went toward the Spaniards. One of them carried something like a lit match and placed it on top of a stone. He spoke in his own language as if setting a limit within which if the Spaniards did not go away they would make war on them. The limit was until the fire should be put out or burn out. When this happened, as the Spaniards did not go away, the Indians attacked them with a great shout.

The Spaniards, who were not asleep, first discharged their cannon and then with their accustomed impetus, especially against native people, they killed as many as possible with muskets and crossbows, and then with their swords, cutting in half the naked bodies. The Indians assembled inside a barricade of stone and wood, and the Spaniards did not have enough room to do them so much harm. Captain Grijalva himself, who by nature was not cruel but mild and of a good disposition, also prohibited the Spaniards from pursuing them.

In this assault the Indians killed a Spaniard with an arrow and wounded many, among them Juan de Grijalva himself. Afterward some Indians came to ask a truce or peace. Grijalva sent two or three Spaniards to the palisades, where they were given a wooden mask covered with thin gold leaf, which the cacique sent to the captain as a sign of peace. Many disarmed Indians came to see the Spaniards, but did not dare come close to them. The Spaniards collected their water and cannon and embarked in the boats, leaving their love penetrating to the entrails of these people.

They left Champoton, sailing south in search of some port to careen one of the vessels which was making much water. They found one ten leagues from Champoton, which they named Puerto Deseado, where they careened the ship. A canoe with four Indians came to pursue their business of fishing or as small traders, and Grijalva ordered them seized under color of learning our language to serve as interpreters. This was highly iniquitous. He thought nothing of making slaves of them without their meriting it and depriving them of their wives and sons, and leaving the sons and fathers in anguish and sadness.

From Puerto Deseado the great country of New Spain appeared toward the right hand as if toward the north. The pilot, Alaminos, believed it was another island, thinking also that Yucatan was an island. On asking the Indians what land it was, they answered "Colua," the last syllable sharp. This is the one which we afterward called Nueva España. Whether an island or a distinct land, the captain felt impelled to go to it and take possession of it, as if the thousands of possessions already taken for the kings of Spain in all this hemisphere were not sufficient.

From Puerto Deseado they followed the coast which runs west and reached a large river which they named San Pedro y San Pablo, about twenty-five leagues from Puerto Deseado. Five leagues farther on they came to another larger one, whose force carried fresh water two and three leagues into the sea. This river Grijalva baptized with his own name. This or the town or the country itself is called by the natives Tabasco. It is a most happy land and most abundant in cacao, which are the seeds they use for a smooth drink and for money in all New Spain. They went up this river nearly a league where the principal town was. Here they let drop their anchors.

The Indians were astonished to see such great vessels and men bearded and dressed and altogether of a new kind and different skill. Six thousand men sallied forth to prevent the landing in their country and town. As it was late, both parties passed all night in keeping watch. When it became light, over one hundred canoes filled with armed men placed themselves near the ships. One canoe advanced and a man of authority stood up in it and asked what they wanted or were looking for in countries or lordships which did not belong to them.

Through the interpreters Grijalva answered that he and the Christians did not come to do them any harm but to search for gold and that they brought things to pay for it. With this answer the captain of the canoe returned and gave the news to his king and lord, saying that the Christians looked to him like good people. He returned and told Captain Grijalva that this lord and all his subjects were pleased to be friendly with him and the Christians, and would give them the gold which they had and receive what they brought from their country.

He brought a large and very beautiful gilded wooden mask and some pleasing things made of different colored feathers, and said that his lord would come the next day to see the Christians. Grijalva gave him some strings of green glass beads, some scissors, knives, and a hat of red frieze. The scissors and knives were what did the business because with these the mediator of peace and friendship thought he was very fortunate. The cacique and lord of the country decided to visit the Christians and entered a canoe with unarmed rowers and boarded the ship of Captain Grijalva as assured as if he were his own brother.

Grijalva was a gentleman about twenty-eight years old. He wore a loose coat of crimson goods with the rest which corresponded to it— rich things. The cacique was received by Grijalva with much respect, and they embraced and seated themselves. They understood very little of what each other said, conversing more by signs and words which the Indian who had been captured at Puerto Deseado spoke to the Indian brought from Cuba. It all amounted to the cacique saying that he was pleased at the captain's coming and desired to be his friend. Then from a chest or coffer he began taking out pieces of gold and some of wood covered with gold leaf, just as if they had been made for Grijalva to his measure. The cacique, with his own hands, began to arm him from head to foot, taking off any which did not fit and putting on others which went better with the rest. In this way he armed him all with pieces of fine gold just as if he was doing it with a complete equipment of steel made in Milan. Besides this armor he gave him many other jewels of gold and feather work. The beauty of Grijalva then was something worth seeing. But it is more meritorious and praiseworthy to consider the liberality and humanity of that infidel cacique.

Grijalva thanked him and recompensed him by having a very rich shirt taken out and put on him. Then he took off his crimson jacket and put that on him, along with a cap of very good velvet and some new leather shoes. Finally he dressed him and adorned him as best he could and gave many other trade goods of Castile to all those who had come with him. A crimson coat was worth among the Spaniards of that place sixty or seventy ducats or gold pesos at the least. But what the cacique gave Grijalva would amount to more than 2000 or 3000 castellanos or pieces of gold.

It is said that this cacique saw in the ship one of the Indians

Grijalva had captured. He said he would give for him in exchange as much gold as the Indian weighed. Grijalva did not agree, thinking perhaps that he could get more. I do not believe this. For one reason, the greed for gold in him and in those of his company did not boil so little that he would leave the six or seven *arrobas* of gold he would weigh, for an Indian they captured fishing in a canoe, and who probably was not of more quality and property than others. The other reason is that it does not seem that Grijalva complied with the civility showed him by the cacique in not granting him what he asked, if in truth he offered such an exchange. Finally, however, whatever may have been the case, the cacique was contented with the Spaniards and they with him, to such an extent that from now on the anxiety to settle and remain in that country began, and murmuring at Grijalva because he would not agree.

They departed from the Rio de Tabasco, called from then on Rio de Grijalva, and went coasting along as near the land as possible. They found the coast full of settlements and of people who came out to look at the ships, as they had never seen others. They took some Indians by force, something which could not but cause scandal and fail to offend the Lord, taking them against their will. They at once asked them by signs if there was any gold in that country, and they said there was much. They turned some of them loose, telling them to bring gold for which they would pay with the trifles of Castile. Now the coast turned from the west to the north. Continuing with their course they anchored with their four ships close to an islet. There were buildings of masonry on it, especially a very high one which must have been their temple, where there was an idol and many heads of men and dead bodies. From this they found out that the natives must offer men to their idols, and for this reason they named it Isla de Sacrificios.

The next day many Indians with banners appeared on the coast and made signs to the Spaniards to come ashore. The captain sent Francisco de Montejo with some men to find out what they wished and whether they were for peace or for war. When he reached the beach, the Indians came to him very joyfully, showing signs of peace. They presented him with many beautiful cotton mantles.

Montejo showed them some things made of gold and asked them by signs if they had any. They answered "Yes" and said they would come back the next day with some. They did come back as they said and made signs and gestures calling the Spaniards to come ashore.

Grijalva went with some of his men and found shelters made of boughs of trees, very fresh, and leaves on the ground where the Spaniards sat on account of the sun. On the same ground was the table, a very beautiful mantle, on which were clay vases well made like deep crocks, and full of birds cut up in small pieces with a fragrant broth like a stew. They had put down an abundance of bread made of maize mixed with a mass of black beans—frijoles—and divers fruits. They offered the Spaniards some colored cotton mantles, all with great pleasure and joy, as if they were among their own brothers. Among other gifts, such as they make to their guests, they gave to each Spaniard a lit reed full of aromatic things very fragrant, through which you draw in the smoke with the breath and it comes out through the nostrils. They were given in exchange some strings of colored beads, two hats, some combs, and other small things.

The next day there came a squadron of Indians among whom were two, an old man and a young one, who were principals and seemed to be lords, father and son. Before reaching the captain they put their hands on the ground and kissed them, which must be a ceremony signifying peace and friendship and kind reception. This done, they embraced the captain as if he were a relative they had not seen for many days. They spoke many words in their language, and the captain in his, without their understanding each other, but it all added up to the Indians showing much love and joy with his coming. No less was the pleasure of Grijalva and his men in finding such good and kind people, for the hope of getting rich here increased again. The old lord ordered the Indians to bring boughs and green leaves at once to make bowers where the Spaniards might place themselves. In ordering the Indians the old man and the young one displayed authority and command like lords.

The old man made signs to the captain and the other Spaniards to sit down. First he gave them each reeds of the odors already described. Many Indians came and went, all unarmed, in the simplest manner, and it seemed as if they were inviting each other to come and see the Spaniards. They all showed great joy and talked to them as if they were very close relatives or very friendly neighbors. What was most important and the desire of the Spaniards was that they began, by order of the old lord, to bring many different coral jewels, very beautiful and of marvelous workmanship; a collar of twelve pieces of gold with many pendants; some strings of round clay beads, gilded so that they looked like all gold; other smaller ones very well gilded; other earrings; two masks of mosaic work of turquoise with some points of gold; a very rich fan of different color feathers, as well as some little things of gold leaf.

The day passed in this with great rejoicing of all, the cacique embracing the captain, begging him by signs to come back the next day to the same place, saying he would then have much more gold brought. At daybreak on the following day many people appeared on the beach with some white banners which must have been signs of peace and friendship.

Captain Grijalva went ashore with a goodly number of Spaniards, and when the cacique saw him, he went to him, put his hands on the ground and kissed them, and then embraced the captain with a joyful face. The captain ordered an altar to be set up and our chaplain to say mass.

When the cacique saw that this was a religious symbol and the ceremonies of divine worship, he had some braziers brought with live coals and put them in front of the altar and threw in them some incense and aromatics. These people of New Spain were the most religious that have ever been seen among the natives who had no knowledge of the true God. He was astounded, and the Indians with him had their eyes fixed on the ceremonies of the mass, as among the Indians the greatest attention is paid to the actions and works they see us perform.

When the mass was over the lord ordered food to be provided, which was done. The meal over, the cacique ordered jewels and gold to be fetched. There were many and divers things, all richly wrought. Among the jewels traded here it is said there was an emerald worth 2000 ducats. All the gold given was worth more than 1000 ducats, without counting the value of the manufacture of some of the pieces which might be worth more than the gold they contained.

What the captain gave him in recompense would not relieve the cacique from poverty—a sash, a hood of colored frieze, in which was a medal—not gold but counterfeit; a shirt with loops and some embroidery of thread, not silk; a cloth for the hair; a leather belt with a pouch; a knife; and some scissors; some women's shoes and drawers; two mirrors; two combs and some strings of glass beads of different colors, all of which might be worth in Castile three or four ducats.

That cacique and his people, esteeming themselves very rich with what Grijalva had given them and possibly thinking they had cheated the Spaniards more than half of the right price, came back the next day with richer jewels with which again to cheat, receiving in return more of the trifles of Castile. And so it was for several days. Thus, we were accustomed to trade with the Indians.

From all this trade the Spaniards saw that there was a considerable quantity of gold in the country and that the people were peaceable, frank and liberal. Consequently there was a great opportunity to fill their pockets and become rich lords at very little cost. They now began to renew the clamor to their captain Grijalva. With great importunity and murmuring, they said that since God had shown them a country so rich and a people so well disposed where they could be very happy, he should consider it well to make a settlement there. He should let Diego Velásquez know their good luck by sending him one of the four ships with all the gold and jewels that they had traded so that he might send them more men, goods, arms, and other things necessary for the settlement. They all declared that Diego Velásquez would consider it a good deed, notwithstanding that in his instruction he had prohibited them from making a settlement and that they should only discover and trade.

Juan de Grijalva's nature was such that he would not have made a bad friar, considering his obedience and even humility and other good qualities. For this reason, even if all the world had joined against him he would not have broken his instructions willingly on a single point or letter of what was ordered even if he knew that they would make pieces out of him. I knew him and often talked with him, and I always understood him to be a person inclined to virtue, obedience, and good customs, and very obedient to his superior's orders. Thus, in spite of the begging, demands, and importunate reasons they all made on him, they were not able to get him to make a settlement. He alleged that he was prohibited by the one who had sent him, and that he had no more authority or power than to discover and trade and that in compliance with these instructions he would discharge his duty.

In view of his determination everybody began to swear at him and hold him in contempt. It was a marvel that they did not lose their shame and all go ashore and make a settlement, leaving him or sending him in the ship to Diego Velásquez. As one of the ships was making much water and was in need of careening, Grijalva agreed to send it to the Isla de Cuba with the sick and the good news of the rich country and kind people as well as the gold and the jewels which he had obtained in trade. With this embassy he sent Pedro de Alvarado, who finally reached Cuba and gave an account of the riches they had found. All those on board the ship complained about Grijalva because, despite the wishes of all, he did not wish to settle in such a happy and rich country.

Diego Velásquez was moved to anger against Grijalva because he had not done it, although he had ordered him and given instructions to him in no manner to make a settlement. Diego Velásquez, however, was of such a character, terrible for those who served him and aided him, and he easily became enraged against those about whom people spoke badly, as he was more credulous than he should have been. Finally, angry with Grijalva because he had not made a settlement contrary to his orders, he determined to send another fleet before Grijalva should arrive, and send another captain. In the end he fell on one who did not obey him as faithfully as did Grijalva, so that he finally lost his property and honor and from that time on had a bitter and sad life, and at last was ruined. God knows, therefore, where his soul went. There are many reasons for which God should punish him for having made himself rich with the blood of the people of Cuba and the killings in Española. Leaving these aside, it seems that our Lord wished to afflict him for not thanking Grijalva for the obedience which he observed in complying strictly with his order not to make a settlement, where Grijalva himself would have been much better off. So God allowed him to send a man [Cortés] who even before he left denied him.

After Pedro de Alvarado left for Cuba, Grijalva with three ships sailed up the coast exploring it for many leagues. He came near the province of Panuco and seeing that it was all one country and believed to be mainland, they agreed to turn back by the route over which they had come and direct their voyage for Cuba to give and account to Diego Velásquez of the success of their discovery and journey. After more trading and more murmuring against Grijalva because he would not make a settlement, they began the return, stopping again at Champoton for water.

Here it is said they found an ambush of armed men with bows and arrows which they discharged against the Spaniards. The citizens and relatives of those at Champoton, seeing that Francisco Hernández and his company worked such great ravages and killed so many, would be grieved, as is natural, and consequently think all Spaniards were unjust and cruel. They decided, then, not to receive them but to kill them all. Finally the Spaniards took all the water they wished in spite of the Indians, because people without arms or defense would always have to be the under dog.

From there Grijalva and his ships took their course for the Isla de Cuba and after many great hardships by wind and sea and contrary currents they came to the port of Matanzas, near Havana. Here Grijalva found a letter from Diego Velásquez telling him to make all possible speed to reach Santiago, where he was. He should make known to all the men who came with him that those who wished, should remain in Havana in order to return and settle the new country. The rest could go back to their homes because Velásquez was preparing to send men for the settlement.

On November 13, 1518, Diego de Velásquez was appointed Adelantado of Yucatan on the proviso that he conquer and settle at his own expense. What followed is the story of Hernán Cortés.

The future conquistador of Mexico seems to have been a friend of Grijalva's, for he stopped at the discredited captain's home on the south coast of Cuba before departing for Yucatan and Mexico.

In 1523, Grijalva sailed with the conquistador Garay from Jamaica, but as was Grijalva's luck, that expedition fell apart at Vera Cruz and most of its members joined Cortés. Captain Grijalva himself was killed in an Indian uprising in Nicaragua four years later.

3

Cortés
Conquers
Mexico

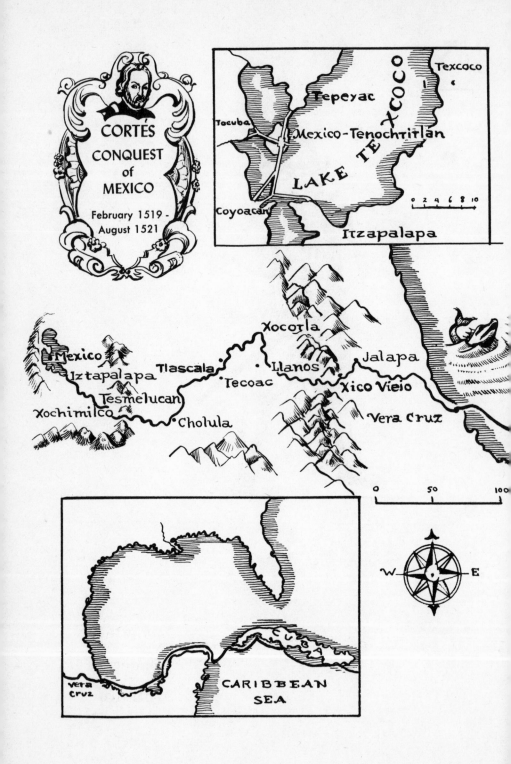

CORTÉS
CONQUEST
of
MEXICO

February 1519 -
August 1521

Texcoco

Tepeyac

Tocuba

Mexico-Tenochtitlan

LAKE TEXCOCO

Coyoacan

0 2 4 6 8 10

Itzapalapa

Xocotla

Mexico

Iztapalapa

Tlascala

Llanos

Jalapa

Tecoac

Xico Vieio

Tesmelucan

Vera Cruz

Xochimilco

Cholula

0   50   100

Vera
Cruz

CUBA

CARIBBEAN
SEA

W — E

3

Cortés Conquers Mexico

HERNÁN CORTÉS, who among all the conquistadores was to prove himself the greatest commander in the field, was born in the small town of Medellin in Estremadura in 1485. This was the year Harry Richmond crowned himself Henry VII of England and founded the Tudor line, and it was seven years before Columbus' first voyage.

The parents of Hernán Cortés were respectably poor. His father, Martín, was a captain in the king's light cavalry and his mother was a housewife. Though attempts were made in later years to find more notable family connections for the conquistador, they came to nothing.

At the age of fourteen Cortés journeyed to Salamanca, where he entered the university to study law. Two years later he returned home without having completed his courses but with more education than most of his contemporaries.

In 1502 he decided to leave Spain and try his fortunes elsewhere. There were two opportunities for a youth of enterprise: Italy with the Great Captain Gonzalo de Córdoba, or the Indies. Cortés decided to try for a future in the Islands—only ten years discovered and still largely unknown. Besides, his father's friend, Don Nicolás de Ovando, was the newly appointed governor of Hispaniola. However, the youthful adventurer failed to sail with Ovando's fleet because he was injured in a fight over a woman, and two years elapsed before his parents gave him the money for his journey and he was finally able to arrange his passage.

The New World which Cortés entered was one of total confusion. Adventurers had been crossing the Atlantic as quickly as boats could be readied. They conceived the towns they built as little more than bases for conquest—a collection of huts in which to gamble, drink and dream. What form conquest would take none of them really knew.

The nineteen-year-old Cortés had not come so far just to settle down as a planter, and he joined the war in Haiti and fought ably enough to receive a repartimiento. As there was nothing else to do, he spent the next five or six years building up his plantation and getting into trouble with women.

His father's friend Ovando was replaced as governor by Admiral Don Diego de Colón, son of the discoverer, and in 1511 Cortés sailed under the command of Diego de Velásquez in the conquest of Cuba. He was reported as being a popular soldier, and though this campaign was small and almost insignificant, it was here Cortés received his only training in military tactics. He established himself in Cuba on the encomienda with which he was paid for his services and promptly got into trouble again.

This time he alienated Velásquez, who had been named governor of the island. Whether Cortés became involved with a woman or whether he was part of a conspiracy to remove Velásquez from office is muddied by history. But he spent a brief time in jail before he was released, married, and reconciled to Velásquez. This governor was to become increasingly important in the life of Cortés.

A poor noble, one of many who had come to improve his fortunes, Velásquez was a veteran of fourteen years' service in the European wars. An active, hard-working man, he founded many towns, Havana and Santiago among them. But he was an absolute commander among men as restless and eager as himself. In 1517 he supported the voyage of Juan de Grijalva which skirted the coast of North America. Among the captains of the four ships were Pedro de Alvarado and Montejo. Bernal Díaz sailed with them. On the shore of the continent the Spaniards heard of Montezuma and Mexico for the first time, and Grijalva sent Alvarado back to Santiago with the report of Montezuma's distant country and samples of treasure.

Velásquez, who had no authority for further conquest, asked permission to prepare an expedition to rescue certain Christians who were known to be prisoners in Yucatan. The small armada of eleven ships was prepared in haste; and after reviewing names with great care, the governor selected Hernán Cortés to be the captain.

Cortés, the governor and his council met and prepared the rules for the voyage. Every effort would be made to spread the faith; there was to be no blasphemy, no consorting with native women and no gambling. When the governor started to pinch pesos in financing the small flotilla, Cortés spent his own money as well as all he could borrow. And by the time all expenses had been paid, he had contributed perhaps as much as two-thirds of the total. It may have been the large piece of the expedition which Cortés had bought, just jealousy, or an old commander fearing the popularity of a young one, but Velásquez became wary of his captain and prepared to replace him.

With the assurance and haste that were to separate him from other men, Cortés provisioned his ships and sailed the very night he received word of the governor's plan. The fleet coasted Cuba, stopping at several ports for more provisions and volunteers, and though the governor ordered Cortés' arrest, no one attempted to stop him.

Cortés sailed from Cuba on February 10, 1519, and gave command of the first vessel to Pedro de Alvarado, on whom he was to lean heavily in the years that followed. They landed on the coast and spent the next several months winning over some of the local Indians, subjugating others, and founding the Villa Rica de la Vera Cruz—the Rich Town of the True Cross.

From mid-April to August, Cortés played politics as shrewdly as he had ever played them in his life. The expedition he commanded had authority to trade and convert natives, and it was directly responsible to Governor Velásquez, absent in Cuba but well represented among Cortés' officers. However, with the foundation of a new town, a government was organized, and at its request Cortés resigned command as Velásquez' man and consented to become captain-general of an expedition prepared to conquer an empire.

Knowing how irregularly he was acting, Cortés prepared his case for the king. From this moment to the end of his career, he tried to temper his actions with legality and tied his ambitions to the crown's best interest. He was daring in what he did, but he was never rash. He knew that whatever came of his plans, Charles of Spain alone would be his judge, and it was Charles he would have to satisfy.

There was opposition to his plot to cut himself free of Velásquez, and though Cortés worked hard to win over his enemies, dissension remained. Cortés was a firm commander. With so many noble temperaments he had to be. He was prepared to hang a man who robbed an Indian. He cut off the feet of one who tried to desert, and when he broke up a plot against his life he hanged the assassin near his door.

By trickery, force and diplomacy Cortés prepared for the coming conquest. He won over the Indians of the coastal area completely.

It was during these four months on the coast that he learned to deal with Indians in their own tongue. He found a shipwrecked sailor named Gerónimo de Aguilar who had lived for eight years with the Mayans. And he found a woman slave who knew both the language of the Mayans of the coast and the Aztecs of Mexico. Cortés could speak Castilian to Aguilar, who could translate into Mayan for the woman, who could in turn translate the Mayan into Aztec. In time the woman also learned Castilian, and Aguilar was no longer necessary. The men of the expedition called her Marina and gave her the title of Doña. The Indians, unable to pronounce the r, corrupted it to an l and added tzin to the name—creating Malintzin. Her position became such among her people that Cortés himself was named after her—Malinche. In the first distribution of women, Cortés gave her to Puertocarrero, one of his captains. Later when Puertocarrero left for Spain, Cortés took the woman for himself. She bore him at least one son and possibly a daughter. When he no longer had any use for her, he married her off to one of his officers.

For a time during the conquest, Cortés lived with Doña Ana, a daughter of Montezuma, but on her death he lived with other daughters of the emperor. Two of them bore him sons, and one, a daughter. In the years that followed he had another natural daughter by a certain Leonor Pizarro, and at the height of his career after the death of his first wife, he married into a fine Spanish family. He recognized all his children and raised them as his own. Two of his sons he named for his father, and Doña Marina's boy was not only educated at the court of Spain but was eventually created a Knight Commander in the Order of the Apostle Santiago.

With his supplies in hand, Vera Cruz as a base, a friendly Indian force at his back, a means of communicating with the Indians at his side, Cortés sent one of the vessels back to Spain with a report of the actions of the town council of Vera Cruz. He explained his intentions to his king: "I shall make Montezuma a prisoner or dead or a subject of the royal crown." Cortés directed the ship's master to sail directly to Spain and avoid Cuba. The failure to obey this order eventually created great problems. However, after the ship had departed, Cortés made one of the boldest decisions of his life:

There were those who wanted to leave when they saw how large and populous the country was, and how few we were. And so I felt that if I left the ships there, they would leave with them. And if all those who felt this way deserted, I would be left almost alone, and the great service which I had rendered to God and your Highness in this country would be undone. So I decided to beach the ships on the pretext that they were no longer seaworthy. In this way everybody lost hope of ever leaving the country, and I set out on my march securely, without fear that when I turned my back, the people I had left in the town would fail me.

When everything was as ready as he could possibly make it, Cortés turned his back to the sea on August 15 and began his long march. Though history quibbles over the exact number, he had about four hundred men and thirteen horses with him.

By this time, he had already received messengers bearing gifts and warnings from Montezuma, but Cortés had fought Indians before. He knew how poor their weapons were. He knew how their mass tactics set them up for his guns and horses. He knew also that he had reached that moment in his career when he could no longer turn back, and that all the dreams which had filled Spanish heads since Columbus had first reported the discovery were now becoming a reality. The fine gifts which Montezuma sent to keep the Spanish away were like a golden lure. There was one strength, however, Cortés possessed which he himself did not know about and which, as much as anything else, was to have a final bearing in his conquest.

The Aztecs whom he marched against were a warrior people, but they were also superstitious. In the dim past they had driven the Toltecs and their gods out of Mexico, and more than anything else they feared the return of one of those gods.

The legend was simple. Once long ago there was a man named Quetzalcoatl who had come among the Toltecs, a stranger and a chief of a strange group of men who had white skin and blond hair. He taught the Toltecs how to plant and work metal and build. He developed their calendar, and he was kind to them until the Aztecs drove him away. But he said he would return to lead his people out of bondage. And everything which he had forecast would come true by the Aztec calendar in Ce Acatl—the Thirteen-Age—which was the year Cortés began his march into Mexico.

Montezuma was to refer to this prediction when the two men met. This was the secret, unknown factor that helped Cortés. But he had still other assets he had not counted upon—the bitter hatred the subject tribes bore the Aztecs and the incredible boldness of his own men.

In keeping with his firm desire to maintain a legal form for his actions as well as to let his king know what he was doing and why, Cortés wrote Charles five letters during his years of conquest. In their simplicity they are the writings of a soldier in the field. As documents in history there are few to equal them for what they have to tell. Some scholars have compared them favorably to the writings of Caesar from Gaul. In many ways they are similar: minute reports of military actions which reveal their writers.

Cortés tells Charles everything he wanted him to know. He explains his military tactics. He describes his companions and their actions. He gives a detailed description of the Mexico he found. And he keeps Charles dangling and eager about the possibilities of vast wealth. But he no more than mentions Doña Marina and his officers. He neglects to explain why the Aztecs rose against Alvarado while the captain was away. He rarely credits group decision when it suits his need. He makes little or nothing of the attempt upon his life before the reconquest and the fact that he hanged the would-be assassin. But what Cortés does tell is one of the truly great stories of history—a tale of adventure, of brilliant tactics, of exotic peoples, of vast treasure and new lands being opened up to European eyes. He tells even more: the tragedy of two cultures clashing in total conflict—without tolerance or quarter.

The tragic relationship between Montezuma and the Spanish is never simple, though it is often compassionate and always exciting. Cortés wrote to impress his king and to report what he had done. But he wrote so well that he reveals himself completely.

The letters themselves have a colorful history. The first of the five has never been found. It was dated July 10, 1519, and Cortés handed it to Alonzo Puertocarrero, the first master of Doña Marina, when the last ship sailed before the destruction of the fleet. The letter may have been suppressed because Cortés severed relations with Velásquez, who had powerful friends. However, the loss may not be great because a different letter left Mexico on the same voyage, a letter describing the same period of time. This letter was signed by the magistrates of Vera Cruz. It explains why they asked Cortés to abandon Velásquez and lead them against Montezuma. This letter of the magistrates was lost for centuries until it finally turned up in the imperial archives in Vienna, where King Charles had been staying when he received it.

The second letter of Cortés was dated from Segura de la Frontera, October 30, 1520, and was the first account ever written of Mexico. On May 15, 1522, Cortés wrote the third letter about the reconquest of Mexico. In two later letters to King Charles he describes the years that immediately followed the conquest. There is one other important first-hand account of the conquest. One of the captains of Cortés, Bernal Díaz del Castillo, wrote *The True History of the Conquest of Mexico* twenty years after the event. A magnificent work which supplements the captain-general's, *The True History* was written by an old warrior to set the record straight after it had been corrupted by Francisco López de Gómara's *History of the Conquest of New Spain*, published in 1552. The Díaz refutation was so strong that the Spanish court suppressed and withdrew Gómara's book from circulation, even though Gómara had known the captain-general in Spain during his last years and had dedicated his work to Cortés' second son.

LETTER FROM HERNÁN CORTÉS TO KING CHARLES FROM THE TOWN OF
SEGURA DE LA FRONTERA ON OCTOBER 30, 1520

We mounted the pass between the two mountains and, descending it, beheld one of the provinces of the country of Montezuma, called Chalco. About two leagues before we reached the town, I found a very good dwelling place, so large that all my company were very comfortably lodged in it, although I had with me four thousand Indians.

Among the chiefs who came to me here was a brother of Montezuma. He brought me about three thousand dollars in gold and told me, in Montezuma's name, to go back and not insist on coming to his city, for food was scarce and the roads were bad; and, as it was all on the water, I could enter it only in canoes. They said I had only to ask what I wanted, and their sovereign Montezuma would order it to be given to me, and would even agree to give me an annual tribute, which could be taken to the coast or wherever I wished.

I received them very well and gave them some Spanish articles, which seemed to please them very much, especially the one who was said to be a brother of Montezuma. I replied to his embassy that if it were in my hands to return, I would do so to please Montezuma, but that I had come to this country by order of Your Majesty, and that you

had ordered me to give an account of Montezuma and his great city,
for Your Majesty had known about both for a long time. I said also
that they should tell him I hoped he would approve my visit to see
him; only good would come of it for him and his country. If, after I
had seen him, he did not wish to have me there, then I would return;
for he and I could better decide between us how he could serve Your
Highness, rather than through third persons. They left with this
answer.

At daybreak I set out for Amaqueruca, two leagues from here in
the province of Chalco, where we were lodged in good houses belonging to the chief of the town. Many persons who seemed to be of high
rank came to speak to me, telling me that Montezuma had sent them
to wait for me here and see that I was provided with everything necessary. The lord of this place gave me some forty female slaves, and
three thousand *castellanos*. During the two days I was there, they
provided us amply with food.

Accompanied by those chiefs, I left the following day, and slept
four leagues farther on in a small town, almost half of which was
on the water of a great lake. On the land side there is a chain of very
rugged and stony mountains. Here the Indians would have been very
willing to try their strength against us, except that they wanted to do
so with safety by surprising us at night. I anticipated their intention
and kept a good guard that night. When their scouts came, some by
canoes and others from the mountains, some fifteen or twenty were
taken by our men and killed. Only a few returned to give the information they had come for; and finding us always so well prepared, they
decided to change their tactics and treat us well.

The next morning just as I was ready to leave the town, some ten
or twelve chiefs arrived, among them a great lord, a youth of about
twenty-five years, to whom all showed so much attention that after he
had descended from a litter in which he had come, all the others began
clearing the road of the stones and straw before him. He told me that
Montezuma begged me to pardon him for not coming in person to receive me, as he was indisposed, but that inasmuch as I was still determined to go to him, we would meet in his city. Then I should learn
his disposition towards Your Highness' service. He still asked me if it
were possible not to go there, as I would endure much trouble and
privation, and said that he was ashamed not to be able to provide for
me there as he desired. With this, they fell on their knees, protesting
so much that it only remained for them to say that they would defend

the road by force if I still insisted on proceeding. I calmed them, saying that my going there would do them no harm but would bring them many advantages. So after I gave them some presents they left.

I then continued along the road by the shore of that great lake. Soon I saw, two musket-shots distant from the shore, a small city which might have had one or two thousand inhabitants, and which was all afloat on the water, having many towers but, as it seemed, no entrance. About a league from there we reached a great causeway as broad as a horseman's lance, extending within the lake about two-thirds of a league. This led to the city, which, though small, was the most beautiful we had yet seen, not only because of the well-decorated houses and towers but also the excellent construction of its foundations in the water.

In this city we were very well received. The lords and chiefs came to speak with me and prayed me to remain and sleep there. However, Montezuma's messengers who were with me told me not to stop but to go on to another city called Iztapalapan, about three leagues distant, belonging to a brother of Montezuma; and I did. The exit from the city where we dined is by another causeway, a long league in length, which extends to the mainland.

When we arrived in Iztapalapan, the chief of it came out to receive me, as well as one from another great city nearby called Calnaalcan. They were accompanied by many other chiefs, and they gave me three or four thousand *castellanos*, some female slaves and some wearing apparel, receiving me very well.

The next day I left, and after going half a league I reached another causeway leading out a distance of two leagues into the middle of this great lake where stands the great city of Temixtitan. This causeway is two lances broad and so well built that eight horsemen can ride abreast. Within these two leagues there are three smaller cities, which have a great trade in salt, which they make from the water of the lake and from the crust of the land bathed by the lake.

I followed the causeway for about half a league before I came to the city proper of Temixtitan. At the junction of another causeway from the mainland I found another strong fortification with two towers, surrounded by walls twelve feet high with castellated tops. This commands the two roads and has only two gates; they enter by one, and leave by the other. About one thousand of the principal citizens all richly dressed came out to meet me. Each one, in approaching me and before speaking, would use a ceremony which is very common among them, namely, putting his hand on the ground and afterward kissing it, so that I was kept waiting almost an hour until each had performed his ceremony.

There is a wooden bridge ten paces broad in the very outskirts of the city, across an opening in the causeway, where the water may flow in and out as it rises and falls. They can also use this bridge for defense, removing and replacing long broad wooden beams whenever they wish. There are many of these bridges in the city, as Your Highness will see in the account which I shall make of his affairs.

Having passed this bridge, we were received by Montezuma, with about two hundred chiefs, all barefooted and dressed in a kind of very rich livery. They approached in two processions near the walls of the street, which is very broad and straight, and very beautiful, and very uniform from one end to the other, being about two thirds of a league long, and having on both sides very large houses, both dwelling places and mosques.

Montezuma came in the middle of the street with two lords, one on each side. One was the same great lord who had come in the litter to speak with me, and the other was the brother of Montezuma and lord of Iztapalapan, from which I had come that day. All were dressed in the same manner except that Montezuma was shod and the other lords were barefooted. Each supported him below his arms. As we approached each other I descended from my horse and was about to embrace him, but the two lords in attendance prevented me from touching him. They, and he also, made the ceremony of kissing the ground. When this was done, he ordered his brother to take me by the arm, and the other attendant walked a little ahead of us. After he had spoken to me all the other lords in the two processions saluted me, one after the other, and then returned to their places.

When I approached to speak to Montezuma, I took off a collar of pearls and glass diamonds that I wore and put it on his neck. After we had gone through some of the streets, one of his servants came with two collars wrapped in a cloth. They were made of colored shells which they greatly esteem. From each of the collars hung eight golden shrimps a span long, and executed with great perfection. When he received them he turned toward me and put them on my neck. We proceeded through the streets until we came to a large and handsome house, which he had prepared for us. There he took me by the hand and led me into a spacious room, where he made me sit on a very rich platform and told me to wait there. Then he went away.

After a little while, when all the people of my company were distributed to their quarters, he returned with many valuable pieces of gold and silver, and five or six thousand pieces of rich cotton stuffs, woven and embroidered in different ways. After he had given them to me he sat down on another platform, which they immediately prepared near the one where I was seated, and said:

"We have known for a long time, from the chronicles of our forefathers, that neither I nor those who inhabit this country are descendants of its aborigines, but from strangers who came from distant parts. We also hold that our race was brought to these parts by a lord whose vassals they all were, and who returned to his native country. After a long time he came back, but it was so long that those who remained here were married with the native women of the country, and had many descendants, and had built towns where they were living. When, therefore, he wished to take them away with him, they would not go, nor still less receive him as their ruler. So he departed. And we have always held that his descendants would come to subjugate this country and us, as his vassals. According to the direction from which you say you come, which is where the sun rises, and from what you tell us of your great lord or king who has sent you here, we believe and hold for certain that he is our rightful sovereign, especially as you tell us that since many days he has had news of us. Hence you may be sure that we shall obey you and hold you as the representative of this great lord of whom you speak, and that in this there will be no lack or deception; and throughout the whole country you may command at your will (I speak of what I possess in my dominions), because you will be obeyed and recognized, and all we possess is at your disposal.

"Since you are in your rightful place and in your own homes, rejoice and rest, free from all the trouble of the journey and the wars which you have had, for I am well aware of all that has happened to you between Puntunchan and here, and I know very well that some of the people you have met have told you many evil things about me. Do not believe more than you see with your own eyes, especially from those who are my enemies and were my vassals, yet when you came, deserted to help you. I know they have told you also that I have houses with walls of gold and that the furniture of my halls and other things of my service are of gold, and that I am, or make myself, a god, and many other things. The houses you have seen are of lime and stone and earth."

And then he held up his robes, and showing his body, he said to me: "Look at me, and see that I am flesh and bones, the same as you and everybody, and that I am mortal and tangible." And touching his arms and body with his hands, "Look how they have lied to you! It is true that I have some things of gold which have been left to me by my forefathers. All that I possess you may have whenever you wish.

"I shall now go to other houses where I live; but you will be provided here with everything necessary for you and your people, and you shall suffer no annoyance, for you are in your own house and country."

I agreed with what he had said and especially confirmed his belief that it was Your Majesty whom they were expecting. After this he took his leave. We were well provided with chickens and bread and fruits and other necessities. I passed six days there and was visited by many of the lords.

I have already mentioned at the beginning, Most Catholic Lord, that when I started from Vera Cruz in search of this lord, Montezuma, I left there a hundred and fifty men to build a fort which I had begun. I also stated that I had left many villages and forts in the neighborhood of that town under the royal dominion of Your Highness, and the natives as very loyal vassals of Your Majesty.

While I was in Montezuma's city I received letters from the captain whom I had left in my place at Vera Cruz, informing me that Qualpoca, lord of Almeria, had sent messengers to him saying that if he had not yet appeared to give his obedience to Your Highness, it was because he had to cross an enemy's country. However, he asked that four Spaniards be sent to accompany him, and then he would come immediately. The captain, believing that the words of Qualpoca were true, since many others had done the same, had dispatched him the four Spaniards. But after the chief got them in his power, he tried to kill them in such a way as would make it appear that he had not done it. He killed two of them, but the other two escaped to the forests. The captain had then attacked Almeria with fifty Spaniards, two horsemen, two field pieces, and about eight thousand friendly Indians. He slaughtered many of the inhabitants, drove out the rest, and burned and destroyed the city, because the Indians with him were their enemies. Qualpoca, however, together with the other chiefs, escaped.

The captain learned from his prisoners that on orders from Montezuma Qualpoca had killed the Spaniards we had sent. It had been directed that as soon as I left the town of Vera Cruz, Qualpoca should attack those vassals who had rebelled against Montezuma and offered themselves to the service of Your Highness; and that Qualpoca was to use every means to kill the Spaniards I had left there who might aid the rebels.

Six days after I had arrived in Temixtitan I decided from what I had seen of the country that it would be conducive to Your Royal Highness's service and to our security, that Montezuma should be in my power, and not at his entire liberty, so that he might not relax his intention and disposition to serve Your Highness. I thought this especially because we Spaniards are somewhat touchy and importunate, and if we should happen to anger him he could do us such injury with his great power that there would remain no recollection of us; and also because, having him in my power, all the other countries who were subject to him would come to the knowledge and service of Your Majesty, as afterward happened.

I determined to seize him and confine him in my quarters, which are very strong. Thinking over the ways in which I could do this without provoking any scandal or commotion upon his arrest, I remembered what my captain at Vera Cruz had written about what had happened in Almeria, and that all that had happened there was by Montezuma's command. I stationed sufficient guards in the cross streets and went to the palace of Montezuma as I had at other times. After talking with him lightly on pleasant subjects, he gave me some valuables in gold, and one of his daughters, and he gave daughters of other lords to some of my companions. I told him then that I had learned what had happened in Almeria and about the Spaniards who were killed there, and that Qualpoca gave as his excuse that all he had done had been by Montezuma's orders, and that as his vassal he could not have done otherwise. I said that I did not believe Qualpoca's excuse and that Montezuma ought to send for him and the other chiefs so that the truth might be known and they be punished. Otherwise the reports of those wicked men might provoke Your Highness to anger, so that instead of the favors Your Highness would now grant him, evil would result.

Montezuma immediately sent for some of his people, to whom he gave a small stone figure, like a seal, which he wore tied to his arm. He ordered them to go to Almeria and bring Qualpoca; to find out what others had taken part in the murder of the Spaniards and to bring them also; and if they resisted to bring them as prisoners;

and if they should resist imprisonment to call upon certain tribes in the neighborhood, which he then named, to seize them by force of arms; but on no account to return without them.

These men immediately left, and after they had gone I told Montezuma I was very grateful to him for the diligence he had used in the imprisonment of those men, for I must render an account of those murdered Spaniards to Your Majesty. To enable me to give this, it now remained only that he should stop in my quarters until the truth was established that he was blameless. I earnestly prayed him not to feel pained at this. He would not be kept a prisoner but would have entire liberty; I would place no impediment to his service and authority in his dominions. There was much argument and conversation about this, but finally he agreed to come with me and immediately gave orders to prepare the apartment he wished to occupy.

Then many lords came and brought the litter. Weeping, they placed him on it in profound silence. We went to my quarters without causing any commotion in the city. Some disturbance had begun, but when Montezuma heard of it he ordered it stopped. All was completely quiet as though nothing had happened. This continued all the time I kept Montezuma prisoner, for he lived at his entire pleasure and with all his service, just as in his own palace. I and my company did everything we could to please him.

Some fifteen or twenty days later, those who had been sent to Almeria returned, bringing Qualpoca and one of his sons, with fifteen others they said had taken part in the murder of the Spaniards. Qualpoca was carried in a litter very much in the style of a lord, as he in reality was. They were all delivered to me and I kept them in prison. After they confessed that they had killed the Spaniards, I had them questioned as to whether they were vassals of Montezuma. Qualpoca answered, asking if there existed any other lord of whom he might be vassal, as much as to say that there was no other. I then asked them if what they had done was by Montezuma's orders. They answered "No," although later, when the sentence that they should be burned was carried out, all with one voice said it was true that Montezuma had ordered them to do it and that they had obeyed his command. They were burned publicly in one of the squares without causing any disturbance. As soon as they confessed that Montezuma had commanded them to kill the Spaniards, I ordered him to be put in chains, which frightened him considerably.

I talked to him that same day and then I had the irons removed. He remained very satisfied, and thereafter I tried to please him and keep him happy. I always made a point of saying publicly to all the natives that Your Majesty wanted Montezuma to continue in authority, recognizing the suzerainty of Your Highness, and that Your Highness would be well pleased by their obeying him, and regarding him as their lord, as they had before I came to the country.

I treated him so well that when I offered him his liberty, as I did frequently, he told me each time that he was content to remain in my quarters because nothing that he wished was wanting, whereas if he went back to his own palace the lords of the country, his vassals, might press him for things contrary to his own wish and to Your Highness's service. Should anyone attempt to make suggestions to him now, he could excuse himself by answering that he was not free, and thus evade them.

When I was satisfied that he was wholly devoted to the service of Your Royal Highness, I prayed him to show me the gold mines. He gladly agreed and immediately sent some of his servants to the four provinces from which he said he got the gold, and asked me to send Spaniards with them to see how it was taken out.

According to what these Spaniards told me, there is every facility for making plantations and procuring gold. Therefore I begged Montezuma to establish a plantation for Your Majesty in the province of Malinaltepeque, which seemed the best suited. He put such effort into it that within two months sixty bushels of maize and ten of beans had been sown, as well as two thousand plants of cacao, which bears a fruit somewhat like almonds. This fruit they sell ground, and prize it so highly that it is used instead of money all over the country. Montezuma built four good houses, in one of which, besides the living apartment, they made a water tank, and put five hundred ducks in it. They value ducks because their feathers, plucked every year, are used in making clothes. They also placed fifteen hundred chickens on the plantation, not to speak of other farm stock which the Spaniards judged to be worth twenty thousand dollars of gold.

I also asked Montezuma to tell me if on the sea-coast there was any river or bay where ships could enter safely. He said he did not know, but that he would have the coast drawn for me, with its bays and rivers. I might then send Spaniards to see them and he would give me guides. I immediately named ten men, among them some pilots and persons acquainted with the sea. They explored the whole coast from the port of San Juan where I first disembarked. They covered about sixty-odd leagues but found no river or bay where ships could enter. Finally they reached Cuacalco, where the chief received them very well and gave them canoes to explore the river. From their observations they judged its depth to be about the same—two and a half to five or six fathoms—for thirty leagues up from its mouth. There are many large towns along the banks with an innumerable population. All the province is level and rich and abundant in produce. The people of this province are not vassals of Montezuma but rather his enemies. The lord of the province sent word, when the Spaniards arrived, that the Culuans must not enter his country because they were his enemies, but that he offered himself to Your Royal Highness with all his country, and he prayed me to consider him a friend.

I immediately dispatched a captain with one hundred and fifty men to lay out and build a town and construct a port; for the chief of that province had offered to do this as well as everything else that might be necessary or commanded by me.

In the past chapters, Most Powerful Lord, I have said that at the time of my coming to Temixtitan a great lord had come on behalf of Montezuma to meet me on the road. As I learned afterward, they were near relatives, and this lord's dominions, called Haculuacan, adjoined those of Montezuma. The capital is a very great city on this salt lake, six leagues by canoe and ten leagues by land from Temixtitan. The city is called Texcoco. It may have about thirty thousand families and there are very wonderful houses, mosques, and very large well-built oratories; it also has extensive market places. Besides this city he possesses two others, one called Acolman, at three leagues from Texcoco, and the other called Otumpa, six leagues distant.

To prove his loyalty to the service of Your Majesty, Montezuma, at my request, sent to seize and imprison this rebellious lord.

A few days later Montezuma held a meeting of all the lords of the city and the neighboring countries. He asked me to join them. When I arrived, he said, "My brothers and friends, you know that, for a long time, you, and your fathers and grandfathers, have been and are subjects and vassals of my forefathers and myself, and that you have always been well treated by them and by me, and that you have likewise done what good subjects are obliged to do toward their rightful sovereign. I also believe that you have kept in mind, from your forefathers, that we are not natives of this country, and that they came to it from another, very far off; that they were brought here by a sovereign, whose vassals they all were, who left them in it, but who returned after a long time; that he found our forefathers already settled and established in this country, and married to the women, and having a great increase of sons, so that they did not choose to return with him, nor much less to receive him as their sovereign; and that he departed, saying that he would return, or send such a force that they would be compelled to submit. You also know that we have always expected him, and, according to what the Captain has told us of that King and Lord who has sent him here, and according to the direction from which he says he comes, I hold it to be certain, and you must also hold it thus, that his sovereign is the one we have been expecting, and knows of us.

"Since our predecessors did not act justly toward their sovereign lord, let us do so, and let us give thanks to our gods, because that which they looked for has come to pass in our times. I heartily pray you, inasmuch as all this is well known to you, that, as you have obeyed me as your sovereign, henceforward you will regard and obey this great king, because he is your rightful sovereign, and, in his place, you must hold this, his Captain. All the tributes and services which until now you have paid to me, you do give to him, because I also shall pay tribute and serve in all that he may command me. In so doing, you will do your duty as you are obliged, and you will, moreover, in doing this, give me much pleasure."

He told them all this, weeping the greatest tears, and with the greatest sighs a man can give vent to. And all those lords who had heard him were likewise weeping so much that for a considerable time they were unable to answer. I assure Your Sacred Majesty there was not one Spaniard who heard this discourse who did not feel great compassion.

After they had somewhat restrained their tears, they answered that they regarded him as their sovereign, and they promised to do all that he ordered and do it gladly; that henceforth, for all time, they gave themselves as vassals of Your Highness, and would comply with all that should be commanded them in the royal name of Your Majesty; and that they would concur with their tributes and services, which heretofore they had given to Montezuma. All this passed before a notary, who at my request recorded it in due form in the presence of many Spaniards for witnesses.

This decision and offer of these lords having been completed, I spoke to Montezuma one day, and told him that Your Highness was in need of gold for certain works ordered to be made. I besought him to send some of his people, and I would also send some Spaniards to those lords who had submitted themselves, to pray them to assist Your Majesty with some part of what they had. Besides helping meet Your Majesty's need, this would testify that they had begun to render service, and Your Highness would the more esteem their good will. I told Montezuma that he also should give gold from his own treasures for Your Majesty. He asked me to choose the Spaniards I wished to send, and he distributed them through many provinces and cities, some of them eighty and one hundred leagues from Temixtitan. He sent some of his people with them, ordering them to tell the lords that I had commanded each one of them to contribute a certain measure of gold. This was done, and all those lords to whom he sent gave readily, not only in valuables but also in bars and sheets of gold, besides all the jewels of gold and silver, and the featherwork, and the stones, and the many other things of value which I assigned and allotted to Your Sacred Majesty, amounting to the sum of one hundred thousand ducats and more. These, besides their value, are so marvelous that for the sake of their novelty and strangeness they have no price, nor is it probable that all the princes ever heard of in the world possess such treasures.

Before beginning to describe this great city, and the others which I mentioned, it appears to me that to understand them better I should describe Mexico, which is where this great city, and some others of which I have spoken, and the principal seat of Montezuma's dominion are. This province is circular and completely surrounded by high and rugged mountains. Its plain is perhaps seventy leagues in circumference, in which there are two lakes occupying almost all of it, for a canoe travels fifty leagues within their borders, and one of these lakes is of fresh water, and the other larger one is salt. The lakes are divided from each other by a small chain of very high hills in the middle of one end of this plain, except for a strait between these hills and the high mountains; the strait is about a bow shot across. Communication between one lake and the other, and between the cities and the other towns round about, is by means of canoes, with no need of going by land.

This great city of Temixtitan is built on the salt lake, and from the mainland to the city is a distance of two leagues from any side you enter. It has four approaches by means of artificial causeways, two cavalry lances in width. The city is as large as Seville or Córdoba. Its streets are very broad and straight. Some of these, and all the others, are one-half land and the other half water on which they go about in canoes. All the streets have openings at regular intervals to let the water flow from one to the other, and at all of these openings, some of which are very broad, there are bridges, very large, strong and well constructed. Ten horsemen can ride abreast over many. I perceived that if the inhabitants wished to practice any treachery against us, they had plenty of opportunity because they might, by raising the bridges at the exits and entrances, starve us without our being able to reach land. Consequently as soon as I entered the city, I made great haste to build four brigantines capable of taking three hundred men and the horses to land.

The city has many squares where markets are held and trading is carried on. There is one square, twice as large as that of Salamanca, all surrounded by arcades. Daily more than sixty thousand souls buy and sell there, and there are found all the kinds of merchandise produced in these countries, including food products, jewels of gold and silver, lead, brass, copper, zinc, stone, bones, shells and feathers. Stones are sold, hewn and unhewn, adobe bricks, wood both in the rough and manufactured in various ways. There is a street for game where they sell every sort of bird, such as chickens, partridges, quails, wild ducks, fly-catchers, widgeons, turtle doves, pigeons, reed-birds, parrots, owls, eaglets, owlets, falcons, sparrow hawks and kestrels, and they sell the skins of some of these birds of prey with their feathers, heads, beaks and claws. They sell rabbits, hares and small dogs which they castrate and raise for the purpose of eating.

Each kind of merchandise is sold in its respective street, and they do not mix their kinds of merchandise of any species; thus they preserve perfect order. Everything is sold by a kind of measure and, until now, we have not seen anything sold by weight.

There is in this square a very large building, like a Court of Justice, where there are always ten or twelve persons sitting as judges and delivering their decisions upon all cases which arise in the markets. There are other persons in the same square who go about continually among the people, observing what is sold and the measures used in selling, and they have been seen to break some which were false.

This great city contains many mosques, or houses for idols, very beautiful edifices situated in the different precincts of it; in the principal ones of which are the religious orders of their sect for whom, besides the houses in which they keep their idols, there are very good habitations provided.

Among these mosques, there is one principal one. No human tongue can describe its greatness and details, because it is so large that within its high-walled circuit a village of five hundred houses could easily be built. Within and all around it are very handsome buildings in which there are large rooms and galleries, where the religious who live there are lodged. There are as many as forty very high and well-built towers, the largest having fifty steps to reach the top. The principal one is higher than the tower of the chief church in Seville. Within these are the images and figures of the idols, although, as I have said, there are many outside.

The principal idols, in which they have the most faith and belief, I overturned from their seats and rolled down the stairs, and I had the chapels where they kept them, cleansed, for they were full of blood from the sacrifices. And I then set up images of Our Lady and other Saints in them. This grieved Montezuma and the natives not a little. At first they told me not to do it, for if it became known throughout the town, the people would rise against me, as they believed that these idols gave them all their temporal goods. And if they were ill-treated, they would be angered and give nothing, even take away all the fruits of the soil and cause the people to die of want.

I made them understand by the interpreters how deceived they were in putting their hope in idols made of unclean things by their own hands. I told them they should know there was but one God, the Universal Lord of all, Who had created the heavens, and earth and all things else, and them and us, Who was without beginning and immortal; that they should adore and believe in Him, and not in any creature or thing. I told them all I knew of these matters so as to win them from their idolatries and bring them to a knowledge of God, Our Lord.

All of them, especially Montezuma, answered they had already told me they were not natives of this country, and that it was a long time since their forefathers had come to it. Therefore they might err in some points of their belief, as it was so long since they left their native land, whereas I, who had recently arrived, should know better than they what they should believe and hold. If I would tell them and explain to them, they would do what I told them.

Montezuma and many chiefs of the city remained with me until the idols were taken away and the chapels cleansed and the images put up, and they all wore happy faces. I forbade them to sacrifice human beings to the idols, as they were accustomed to do, for besides its being very hateful to God, Your Majesty had also prohibited it by your laws and commanded that those who killed should be put to death. Henceforth they abolished it, and in all the time I remained in the city, never again were they seen to sacrifice any human creature.

There are many large and handsome houses in this city, for all the lords of the country, vassals of Montezuma, inhabit their houses in the city a certain part of the year. Moreover there are many rich citizens who likewise have very good houses. Besides having very good and large dwelling places, all these people have very beautiful flower gardens of divers kinds in the upper as well as in the lower dwellings.

Along one of the causeways leading to the city there are two conduits of masonry, each two paces broad and five feet deep, through one of which a volume of good fresh water, the bulk of a man's body, flows into the heart of the city. All supply themselves from this and drink it. The other, which is empty, brings the water when they wish to clean the first conduit, for while one is being cleaned, the water flows through the other.

So far, the extent of Montezuma's kingdom is not known, but everywhere within two hundred leagues on this and the other side of this capital, wherever he sent, his messengers were not disregarded, although there were some provinces in the midst of these countries with which he was at war.

All the other lords of this country and province, especially those of the neighborhood, resided, as I have already said, a greater part of the year in the capital. And all, or at least most of them, had their first-born sons in the service of Montezuma. There were fortified places in the dominions of these lords, and Montezuma sent his own people among them as governors and collectors of the taxes and rents he received from each province. These men kept an account of what each province was obliged to give, by means of characters and figures written on the paper they make, showing the amount each province was taxed according to the quality of its land. In this manner, produce from all the said provinces came into his possession.

He was so feared by the present as well as by the absent, that there was never a prince in the world more so. He had many pleasure houses within and without the city, each as well constructed to serve for its particular kind of pastime as could be described or desired for so great a lord. Within the city, he had residences such and so marvelous that it seems to me almost impossible to speak of their excellence and grandeur. So I limit myself to saying that there is nothing comparable with them in Spain.

He had a house, a little inferior to this one, where there was a beautiful garden with arbors overhanging it, of which the marbles and tiles were of jasper beautifully worked. In this house there were apartments for two great princes and all their servants. It had ten pools of water, in which were kept all the many and divers breeds of waterfowl found in these parts, all domesticated. For the seabirds, too, there were pools of salt water, and for those of the rivers and lakes there was fresh water, which for the sake of cleanliness they renewed by means of pipes. To each kind of bird they gave the food which suited its habits in its free state; so that to those which ate fish they gave it, and likewise worms, maize and smaller seeds were supplied as required by the different birds. I assure Your Highness that all those birds which ate only fish received each day two hundred and fifty pounds, caught in the salt lakes. Three hundred men had the charge of these birds, for their sole employment. There were others who were occupied only in curing the birds which were ailing. Over each pool for these birds, there were beautifully decorated galleries and corridors where Montezuma came to amuse himself by watching them. There was an apartment in this house in which were men, women and children, white of face, body, hair and eyelashes from the day of their birth. There was another very beautiful house with a large court paved with flags in the pattern of a chess board.

There were also houses about nine feet in height and about six paces square. One half of each was covered with a roofing of square tiles, and the other half, which was open, had a stout lattice of wood. Each of these houses contained a bird of prey, representing all the sorts known in Spain from the kestrel to the eagle, besides many other kinds which had never been seen there; and there were great numbers of each of these kinds. Across the tops of these houses there was a perch, and another one out beyond the lattice, so that the birds might use the one at night and when it was raining, and the other to sun themselves and take the air. All these birds were fed daily on chickens, with no other food. There were certain large rooms in this palace fitted with great cages, very well constructed and joined with heavy timbers, in all or most of which were kept lions, tigers, foxes and every kind of cat in considerable numbers. These were also fed on chickens. Three hundred other men had charge of these animals and birds.

There was another house where many monstrous men and women lived, among whom were dwarfs, hunchbacks, and deformed; and each monster had a room apart, with persons to take charge of them. I do not mention the other things Montezuma had in this city, because they were so many, and so various.

While all was quiet in this city, and many Spaniards were distributed about the country pacifying the people, I hoped that ships might arrive with the answer to the account I had sent Your Majesty, so that I might forward what I now send, together with all the gold and jewels I had collected for Your Highness. Finally some natives came to tell me that eighteen ships had arrived on the coast below the port of San Juan, and they did not know whose they were.

Following the Indians, there came also a native of the island of Fernandina, who brought me a letter from a Spaniard whom I had stationed on the coast. In this letter he said that "on such a day, a single ship had arrived off the harbor of San Juan." He had examined all the coast as far as the eye could reach, but had discovered no other, and therefore believed it to be the ship I had sent to Your Majesty, since it was time for this to return.

I dispatched two Spaniards by different roads so that they might miss no messenger coming from the ship. I directed them to learn how many ships had arrived, from where they came, and what they brought, and to return as quickly as possible to tell me. I likewise sent another Spaniard to Vera Cruz to announce what I had already learned about these ships, so that they might get additional information for me. Another went to the Captain whom I had sent to form a settlement at the port of Quacucalco. I wrote him to stop wherever that messenger met him, and not proceed any further until I should write to him again. However, he already knew of the arrival of the ships when he received my letter.

For the next fifteen days I had no further news or answers from the messengers, and I was considerably alarmed. Then other Indians, also vassals of Montezuma, arrived. From them I learned that the ships had already anchored at San Juan, and the people had disembarked. They had brought about eighty horses, eight hundred men, and ten or twelve pieces of artillery. All of this report was pictured on paper of the country, to be shown to Montezuma.

The messengers also told me that the Spaniard I had stationed on the coast, and the other messengers I had sent, were held by these people, and had asked the Indians to tell me that the captain of these people would not allow them to return. When I heard this news, I decided to send a padre, bearing a letter from me, and another letter from the alcalde and the municipal officers of Vera Cruz who were with me, addressed to the captain and people who had arrived at that port of San Juan.

Within five or six days after the padre had gone with the dispatch, twenty Spaniards, whom I had left in Vera Cruz, arrived with a cleric and two other laymen whom they had captured there. From them I learned that the armada and people in the port belonged to Diego Velásquez, and had come by his orders, under a certain Pánfilo de Narváez, a householder of the island of Fernandina, as their captain; that Narváez came with a commission as captain-general and lieuten-ant-governor of all these parts, by appointment of Diego Velásquez, with faculties from Your Majesty for all this.

It appeared that Narváez knew of everything I had done in the country in the service of Your Highness; about the cities and towns I had pacified and about the great city of Temixtitan; about the gold and jewels we had obtained here, and all else that had happened to me. Narváez had sent these men to Vera Cruz to try to win over the inhabitants to rebel against me.

Almost simultaneously there arrived one of the Spaniards who had gone to Quacucalco, bringing letters from his captain, one Velásquez de León, who also informed me that the expedition was under Pánfilo de Narváez, who came in the name of Diego Velásquez. This León forwarded to me a letter which Narváez had sent him by an Indian, for he was a relative of Diego Velásquez and brother-in-law of Nar-váez. The letter told how Narváez had learned from my messengers that León was there with our people. It ordered him to come back immediately with them, because he would thereby fulfill his obliga-tions toward his relative. whom he believed I held by force, and other similar things.

The captain, being devoted to Your Majesty's service, immediately left to join me with all his forces. Afterward I learned from that cleric and the two who accompanied him about the intentions of Diego Velásquez and Narváez; how they had dispatched that armada and force against me, because I had sent the description of this country and the presents to Your Majesty instead of to Diego Velásquez. I learned how they came with intent to kill me and many of my company whom they had already condemned. I learned also that when the licentiate Figueroa, the judge residing in the island of Hispaniola, and Your Majesty's judges and officials there learned that Diego Velásquez was preparing this armada, they had perceived the harm that would come to Your Majesty by their coming, and had sent one of the judges, the licentiate Lucas Vásquez de Ayllon, to order Diego Velásquez not to dispatch the armada. But Velásquez still sent the armada, and the licentiate Ayllon had come with them hoping to prevent the harm which would follow from their arrival, for it was obvious to him and to everybody that the armada came with evil intentions.

I sent this cleric back to Narváez with a letter in which I told him I had learned he was captain of the armada, and that I was glad it was he, as I had thought otherwise, seeing my messengers had not returned. I said, however, that I marveled he did not write me or send me some messenger announcing his arrival, for he knew that I would be rejoiced at it, not only because of our old friendship but also because he had come to serve Your Highness, which was what I most desired. Instead of which, I said, he had sent corrupters and letters of seduction to those under me in Your Majesty's service, inciting them to rebel against me and join him, as if we were infidels the one and Christians the other, vassals of Your Highness the one and traitors the other. I asked him as a favor that henceforward he would not use these means with me, but first let me know the cause of his coming. I said I had been told that he called himself captain-general and lieutenant-governor for Diego Velásquez, and had named alcaldes and municipal officers and had executed justice, all of which was against the good service of Your Majesty and against all your laws. If he had such authorizations from Your Highness, I asked as a favor that he present them to me and to the municipal authorities of Vera Cruz, as they would be obeyed. I told him further that I was in Temixtitan where I held the monarch prisoner and had a great sum of gold and valuables belonging not only to Your Highness but also to my company and myself, which I did not dare to leave since I feared that if I left the city the people might rebel, and such a quantity of gold and jewels and such a city would be lost, which meant the loss of the whole country. I likewise gave a letter to this cleric for the licentiate Ayllon, who, as I afterwards learned, had been sent away as a prisoner by Narváez before the cleric arrived.

On the day the cleric left, I received a messenger from the citizens of Vera Cruz, who informed me that all the natives had risen in favor of Narváez, who had told them I was a traitor and that he had come to take me and all my company prisoners and make us leave the country. As Narváez's people were many, and mine few, and he had brought many horses and much artillery, and I had little, they wished to be on the winning side. The messengers informed me also that they had learned that Narváez would occupy Cempoal, and they believed that, aided by the Cempoalitans, he would attack nearby Vera Cruz. They let me know they were leaving the town rather than fight, and to avoid scandal they would go up the mountain to the house of a chief, vassal of Your Highness and our friend, where they would remain until I sent them directions what to do.

When I saw the great mischief that was spreading, I decided to go to Narváez myself, because the Indians would not dare to rebel on seeing me, and also because I thought I could make some sort of arrangement with Narváez so that the evil could be stopped at the outset. I started the same day, leaving the fort well provided with maize and water, and a garrison of five hundred men, with some cannon. Taking the others (some seventy men), I pursued my road, accompanied by some of Montezuma's principal people.

Before I left, I made some explanation to Montezuma, telling him to look to the fact that he was a vassal of Your Highness, and that now he would receive the favors from Your Majesty for his services to you. I entrusted to him those Spaniards who would take care of all the gold and valuables he had given me for Your Highness. I told him also that I was longing to see the people who had arrived and to learn who they were, for I believed they were bad people and not vassals of Your Highness. He promised to provide those left behind with everything necessary and to take great care of all I left there. He prayed me also to let him know if these were bad people, and he would immediately raise many warriors to attack them and drive them out of the country. I thanked him for all this, and assured him that Your Majesty would order many favors to be shown him. I gave jewels and stuffs to him, to his son, and to other lords who were with him at the time.

On the way to the coast, I met Juan Velásquez returning with all his people. He is the captain I had sent to Quacucalco. I sent those who were indisposed to the city and went on with him and the others. Fifteen leagues beyond Churultecal, I encountered that Fray Olmedo, whom I had sent to the port to learn what sort of people had come in the armada. He gave me a letter from Narváez, telling me that he brought powers to hold this country for Diego Velásquez, and that I should immediately come to him and submit to them, and that he had established a town with alcaldes and municipal officers.

Fray Olmedo told me also of a native lord, a vassal of Montezuma, who was governor of all his country along the coast. This lord had spoken to Narváez on behalf of Montezuma, giving him gold. Narváez had given him some trifles and had sent messengers to Montezuma, saying that he would deliver him and that he wished no gold; but that once he had me and those with me prisoners, he intended to depart and leave the country and the natives in their full liberty. Finally I learned that his intention was to possess himself of the country by his own authority, without asking recognition from anyone; and that if I and my company refused to accept him as captain or justice in the name of Diego Velásquez, he would come against us and capture us by force, and that for this purpose he had confederated with the natives, especially with Montezuma, by means of his messengers.

When I saw the harm against Your Majesty that would result from such a plan I did not hesitate to go on, hoping to dissuade him from his evil intention.

Fifteen leagues before arriving at Cempoal, where Narváez camped, I was met by the cleric sent by the citizens of Vera Cruz, by whom I had written to Narváez and the licentiate Ayllon. He was accompanied by another cleric, and a certain Andres de Duero, who had come with Narváez. They told me Narváez' answer to my letter: that I might still obey and recognize Narváez as my captain, and that I must yield the country to him. Otherwise I should be punished, as Narváez had brought great forces and most of the natives were in his favor. If I would deliver the country to him, he would give me all the ships and provisions I desired and would allow me to go away with all those who wished to leave with me, taking everything I desired without any hindrance from him. One of the clerics told me that Diego Velásquez had authorized this offer and had given his instructions to Narváez and the two clerics jointly, so that they could make all the concessions I wished.

I answered that I did not perceive any warrants of Your Highness directing me to deliver the country to them, and that if Narváez had brought any he should present them before me and the Municipal Council of Vera Cruz, according to Spanish law and custom. Only then would I be ready to obey and comply with them. Until then, I would not do as he said for any interest or concession, for I and those with me would rather die in defense of the country which we had won for Your Majesty than forfeit our loyalty to our king. They advanced many other propositions to win me over, but I could accept none without having seen the warrants of Your Highness authorizing me to do so; and these they could not produce.

In conclusion, these clerics, Andres de Duero and myself agreed that Narváez and I, with as many others, should meet with perfect surety on both sides, at which time he would satisfy me of the warrants, if he had brought any, and I would give my answer. I, on my part, sent him a safe conduct, and he sent me another which it seemed to me he had no thought of observing. For he had planned that during the visit some way should be found to surprise and to kill me. Two of the ten who were to come with him had been designated to do this, while the rest were to fight with my attendants. And so it would have been, if God had not succored me by a warning which one of those concerned in the treachery had sent me together with their safe conduct.

Knowing all this, I wrote a letter to Narváez, and another to the three commissioners, telling them I had discovered their treacherous intention and would not go as had been agreed. I immediately sent them requisitions and mandates, by which I required Narváez to make known to me any warrants he brought from Your Highness, and said that until he had done so he should not, under certain penalties I imposed, call himself captain or justice or meddle with any duties pertaining to these offices. By the same mandate, I commanded all the persons who were with him not to regard or obey him as captain or justice, and summoned them to appear before me within a certain time. Narváez' answer was to imprison the notary who delivered the mandate, and the persons accompanying him.

Seeing that I could in no way prevent this great evil, and that the natives were revolting, I gave orders to Gonzalo de Sandoval, alguacil mayor, to seize the persons of Narváez and those who called themselves alcaldes and municipal officers. I gave him eighty men to make the arrest, while I, with the remaining hundred and seventy, followed on foot without artillery or horses, to aid him if Narváez and his companions should resist. On the same day, we arrived near the city of Cempoal where Narváez and his people were quartered.

I planned to go by night, unperceived if possible, directly to the quarters of Narváez, which I and my men knew very well, and seize him there. Once he was a prisoner, no trouble would arise, for the others wished to submit to justice, especially as most of them had been forced to come by Diego Velásquez, fearing that unless they did he might take away their slaves in the island of Fernandina.

On the feast of Pentecost, a little after midnight, I attacked the quarters. I had encountered the sentinels Narváez had placed, and my vanguard captured one of them, from whom I informed myself of their position. The other escaped, however, and when I approached, Narváez and all his men were already armed and had saddled their horses. They were well prepared, with two hundred men guarding each quarter. We moved so quietly that when they heard us and seized arms I was already inside the courtyard of his quarters, where all the people were gathered. They had taken possession of three or four strong towers. In the one where Narváez was lodged, nineteen guns had been placed on the stairs. We reached the top of that tower so quickly that they did not have time to put fire to more than one of the pieces, which by God's will did not go off. Although asked many times to yield themselves to Your Highness, the men with Narváez surrendered only when we set fire to the tower. And so, with the loss of only two men, all those we wished to take were made prisoners within an hour.

The bad intentions and wicked disposition of Diego Velásquez and Narváez having come to light, all rejoiced greatly that God should have ordained and provided such an ending. For I assure Your Majesty that if God had not mysteriously intervened, and had Narváez been victorious, it would have been the greatest injury which Spaniards had done to one another for a long time past.

Narváez would have succeeded in his purpose, as Diego Velásquez commanded him, which was to hang me and many others of my company so that no one should recount what had happened. And the Indians had perceived that if Narváez were to capture me, it could not be without loss to himself and his people, nor without many of us perishing. Meanwhile they could kill those whom I had left in Temixtitan, which indeed they attempted to do. Afterward they intended to join forces and attack those who remained here, and free their country so that not even a memory of the Spaniards should survive. Your Highness may be assured that if they had achieved all this, this country, which has now been conquered and pacified, would not have been recovered within twenty years.

So many peoule could not be maintained together in Cempoal, because of its being nearly destroyed and because it had been plundered by Narváez and abandoned by its inhabitants. Therefore, two days after Narváez had been taken prisoner I sent two captains, with two hundred men each, one to the port of Quacucalco, which, as I have told Your Majesty, I had founded, and the other to that river which the people from Francisco Garay's ships said they had seen. I likewise sent two hundred men to Vera Cruz, where I ordered Narváez' ships to depart. I remained with the rest of the people in Cempoal to provide whatever Your Majesty's service required. I also sent a messenger to Temixtitan, by whom I made known to the Spaniards I had left there what had happened to me.

These messengers returned within twelve days, bringing me letters from the alcalde there, telling me that the Indians had assaulted the fort in the capital on all sides and set fire to it in many places; that they had sunk mines, and that our people had been in much trouble and danger; and that if Montezuma did not order the war to cease they would yet perish, for they were closely surrounded. Though there was now no fighting, no one could go two paces outside the fort.

As the Indians had captured a great part of the provisions I had left, and had burned my four brigantines, my men were in extreme need, and begged me for the love of God to come to their aid in all haste. I saw that if I did not rescue them, besides the Indians killing them and taking all the gold and silver and other valuables, the noblest and greatest city recently discovered in the world would be lost, and with it all else that had been gained, for it was the capital to which all gave obedience. I immediately sent messengers to the captains whom I had sent off with expeditions, telling them to return immediately from wherever they were found, and to come by the shortest route to the province of Tlascaltecal, where I would unite with them. When we joined forces and made a review, there were seventy horsemen, and five hundred foot soldiers.

I started in all haste with these troops for the capital. The whole length of the road no one from Montezuma appeared to receive me. All the country had risen, and was almost deserted, which made me suspect that the Spaniards whom I had left in the city were dead, and the natives had gathered to await me at some pass, where they would take me at a disadvantage. Fearful, I advanced with the utmost precaution until I reached the city of Texcoco on the shore of that great lake. I inquired of some of the natives there about the Spaniards who had remained in the great city, and was told that they were alive. A

canoe arrived with one of the Spaniards who had remained in the
city. I learned from him that they were all alive except five or six the
Indians had killed, and that the others were still besieged. They were
not allowed out of the fort, nor did the Indians provide them with
anything except on payment and at a heavy price. Afterward, however, when they heard of my coming, they had behaved somewhat
better toward them. Montezuma said he was waiting only for my
arrival to give them again the freedom of the city. With the same
Spaniard Montezuma also dispatched a messenger to me with word
that he believed I already knew what had happened. He thought I
might be angry on account of it, and inclined to vengeance, and
begged me to put aside my anger because he was as much grieved as
I and nothing had been done by his wish or consent. He sent me
news of many other things, to appease the anger he supposed I felt.
He asked me to come to the city and said that whatever I ordered
would be complied with no less than before.

I sent word to Montezuma to say that I was not angry with him in
any way, as his good will was well known to me, and that I would do
as he desired. I left for the city and entered about noon the next day.
I saw few people about. Some of the gates at the cross streets and
entrances to the streets had been removed. I did not like this, though
I thought it had been done from fear, and that my arrival would reas-
sure them. I marched directly to the fort and the principal mosque adjoining where all my people were quartered. They received us with as
much joy as if we had given them their lives anew, and we rejoiced
all that day and night, believing that peace had been restored.

The next day after Mass I sent a messenger to Vera Cruz to give
them the good news that the Christians were alive and that I was safe
in the city. The messenger returned within half an hour with his head
all bruised and broken, calling out that the Indians in the city were
in battle array and had raised all the bridges.

Immediately such a great multitude fell upon us from all sides that
neither the roofs nor the houses could be seen for the crowd. They
came on with the most frightful yells. With their slings, they threw
so many stones into the fortress it seemed as if they rained from the
heavens, while arrows and missiles were so thick we could hardly
move about.

I sallied forth against them on two or three sides, where they fought
us very valiantly. In one place where a captain had gone out with
two hundred men, they killed four and wounded him and many

others before they could retreat. On the other side, where I was engaged, they wounded me and many other Spaniards. We killed few of them, for they retreated to the other side of the bridges, and from the roofs and terraces did us much injury with stones.

Some terraces were captured and set on fire; but they were so many and so strong and so filled with people well supplied with stones and other weapons that we were not strong enough to take them all or to defend ourselves against their attack at their pleasure. They attacked the fort so violently, and set fire to it in so many places, that on one side a great part was destroyed without our being able to prevent it. We were only able to put out the fire by breaking down a part of the walls. Had it not been for the strong guard of musketeers and archers with some field pieces I placed there, they would have scaled that part without our being able to resist them.

We fought all that day until the night was well advanced, and even throughout the night they kept up their cries and yells. During the night I had those breaches caused by the fire repaired, and I distributed the watch and the guards because on the next day we would have to fight stoutly; and I cared for more than eighty wounded.

At dawn the following day, the enemy opened battle more stoutly than the day before. There were so many of them that the artillery had no need to aim but just to shoot into the masses of Indians. Although the artillery did much damage, for thirteen arquebuses were playing besides muskets and archery, it seemed as if they did not feel it. When one discharge would sweep away ten or twelve men, more would immediately fill their places as if no harm at all had been done. Leaving such guard as could be spared in the fort, I again made a sortie, and captured some bridges and burned some houses, killing many of the defenders. But they were so numerous that although we did them a good deal of damage, we made very little impression on them. We had to fight all day long, while they fought by hours, because they relieved one another and even so they had more than enough men. That day they also wounded some fifty or sixty Spaniards, although none of them died; and I fought until nightfall, retiring only from sheer fatigue into the fort.

We spent that whole night and the next day in making three engines of wood, each accommodating twenty men, so that the stones they threw from the roofs could not hurt us, the engines being covered with planks. Inside there were archers and musketeers, and others armed with pikes, pickaxes and bars of iron for making breaches in the houses and knocking down the barricades which the Indians had made in the streets. While these machines were being made, fighting continued. Whenever we went out of the fort, they tried to enter, and were repulsed only with great difficulty.

Montezuma, who, with one of his sons and the many other chiefs whom we had captured at the beginning, was still a prisoner, asked to be carried to the roof of the fort where he could speak to the captains and the people and ask them to stop.

I had him taken there. When he reached the parapet on the top of the fort, intending to speak to the people who were fighting there, one of his own subjects struck him on the head with a stone with such force that he died within three days. I then had him taken out, dead as he was, by two of the Indian prisoners, who bore him away to his people. I do not know what they did with him, except that the war did not cease but went on more stoutly and more fiercely every day.

Having completed the engines, we sallied out the next day carrying them before us, followed by four pieces of artillery, many archers and shield bearers, and more than three thousand natives of Tlascaltecal who had come with me and helped the Spaniards. When we reached one of the bridges, we placed the engines and scaling ladders against the walls of the terraces in order to scale them.

But the defenders were so numerous and threw so many and such large stones at us from above, that they damaged the engines, killing some of the Spaniards and wounding many without our being able to advance one pace. We fought from morning till noon, when we returned to the fort with infinite sorrow.

The courage of the Indians was increased so much by this that they attacked us almost at the very doors, and occupied the great temple. About five hundred who appeared to be notable persons ascended the highest and principal tower, carrying up a large supply of bread and water and other stores. Most of them had long lances with broad points, all longer and broader than ours, and not less sharpened. From their vantage point they did great injury to our people in the fort. Two or three times the Spaniards attacked the tower and attempted to mount it, but it was very high and the ascent very steep. Those above were well supplied with stones and other arms, and favored by the fact that we could not capture the neighboring terraces. And so every time the Spaniards attempted to ascend, they were beaten back, and many were wounded. Others of the enemy who saw this from other parts took fresh courage and attacked the fort fiercely.

Observing that if they succeeded in holding that tower, besides doing us so much injury from it, they also gained fresh courage to attack us, I sallied out from the fort, although my left hand had been maimed by a wound on the first day. I advanced to the tower with some Spaniards and easily succeeded in surrounding the base, although the Indians guarding it were not idle. I began to ascend the tower, but they defended the ascent very stubbornly, throwing down three or four of my followers. With the help of God and His Glorious Mother (for whose house that tower had been set aside, her image being placed in it), we reached the top and forced them to jump down on some terraces about a pace broad which extended around it. This tower had three or four such terraces about sixteen feet one above the other. Some of the enemy fell all the way down and were immediately killed by the Spaniards who surrounded the base of the tower. Those who remained on the terrace fought so valiantly that we were more than three hours in completely dispatching them. Not one escaped.

Your Sacred Majesty may believe that we captured this tower only because God had clipped their wings; twenty of them were sufficient to resist the ascent of a thousand men even though they fought valiantly till death. I set the tower on fire, as well as others in the mosque, from which they had already carried off the images we had placed in them.

Some of their pride was taken out of them by our capturing this vantage point, so that they fell back a little on all sides. Afterward, when I returned to the roof, I spoke to their captains and told them to look about and see that they could not hold out anywhere, and that every day we did them great harm and killed many, and that we were forced to burn and destroy their city, for I would not stop till there was nothing left of it or them. They said they were aware they had sustained much damage from us, and that many of them had perished; but they were all fully determined to die or be rid of us, and I might see how all these streets and squares and terraces were filled with people, so numerous that if twenty-five thousand of them perished for every one of ours, they would finish with us first, for we were few and they were many. They said that all the high roads leading into the city had been destroyed (as, in fact, they had destroyed all save one), and we had no way of escape save by water. They knew very well that we had few provisions and little fresh water and could not hold out much longer, for we would die of hunger even if they did not kill us. They were right of course, for, had we no other enemy save starvation and thirst, these would suffice to kill us in a short time. We exchanged many other arguments, but they came to nothing.

When night set in, I sallied forth with some of my men and took them by surprise, capturing a street from them and burning more than three hundred houses. I quickly returned by another street, in which I also burned many houses. In particular I destroyed some terraces which overlooked the fort. During the same night I ordered the engines to be repaired.

In order to follow up the victory God had given us, I went out at daybreak into the same street where we had been routed the day before. There I found not less resistance than on the former occasion. Our lives and honor were at stake. This street led to the only sound causeway extending to the mainland, but before reaching it we had to pass by eight very large and deep bridges, and there were many quite high terraces and towers. We set our determination and spirit in it so that, God helping us, we gained four of the bridges that day and burned all the terraces and houses and towers to the last of the bridges. They had, however, during the night before, made a number of very strong barricades of adobe and clay at all the bridges, so that our crossbows could do them no harm. We filled in the bridges with the adobe and earth from the enclosures, and with stones and wood from the houses we had burned. That night I took precautions to guard those bridges so that the Indians might not retake them.

The next morning I again sallied forth, and again God gave us good fortune and victory. We captured all the bridges. At the same time some of the horsemen followed victoriously in pursuit of the fugitives as far as the mainland. While I was engaged in repairing the bridges, I was called in great haste and told that the Indians who attacked the fort were suing for peace, and that a number of their chiefs and captains were awaiting me. Leaving my people and some field pieces there, I went with two or three horsemen to see what the chiefs wanted. They said that if I would assure them they would not be punished for what had occurred, they would raise the siege, re-establish the bridges, restore the causeways and serve Your Majesty as they had before. They besought me to have brought there one of their people, a native priest whom I had made a prisoner and who was a sort of superior of their religion. He came and spoke with them, and made an agreement between them and me. As they had promised, they immediately sent messengers to the captains and people in outside camps, telling them that the attack on the fort should cease, as well as all other hostilities. And so we took our leave and I entered the fort to eat.

When I was about to begin, someone came hastily to say that the Indians had regained the bridges we had captured that day, and had killed some Spaniards. God only knows how much disturbance this caused me, for I was thinking that we had assured a passage for our retreat.

I mounted my horse with all possible haste and rode through the length of the street with some other horsemen following me. Without halting anywhere, I again dashed through the Indians and recaptured the bridges, pursuing the enemy to the mainland. As the foot soldiers were very tired, wounded and dismayed, none of them followed me, and this left me in a very dangerous situation after I had passed the bridges. When I tried to return, I found them retaken, and more deeply dug out than when we had filled them up. From one side to the other all the causeway was full of people, not only on land, but also in canoes on the water. They goaded us and stoned us in such a manner that if God had not interposed to save us, it would have been impossible to escape. Indeed it was already announced in the city that I was dead.

When I reached the last bridge nearest the city I found all the horsemen who had gone with me fallen into it, and one horse loose, so that I could not pass but had to return alone in face of my enemies. I forced something of a passage, so that the horses could get by. Finding the bridge free, I crossed through with difficulty, for I had to jump the horse from one side to the other—almost six feet. But as I and he were armored, the Indians did not hurt us beyond slight body wounds. And so victory was theirs that night, for they held the four bridges.

Leaving a guard over the other four, I went to the fort and had a wooden bridge constructed which forty men could carry. We were daily receiving great damage from the Indians, and feared also that they might destroy that causeway as they had the others, when we would all inevitably perish. All of my company, or nearly all, were wounded so badly that they could no longer fight, and they pleaded with me to leave. I decided to withdraw that same night. I collected in a room all the gold and jewels belonging to Your Majesty that could be carried, and gave it to the officials of Your Highness, whom I designated in your royal name, beseeching and requiring the alcaldes and municipal authorities, and all the people who were there, to help me take it away.

Having abandoned the fort and considerable treasure belonging not only to Your Highness but also to the Spaniards and myself, I set forth as secretly as possible, taking with me a son and two daughters of Montezuma, Cacamazin, the lord of Aculuacan, and another of his brothers, whom I had put in his place, and some other chiefs whom I held as prisoners.

When we reached the bridges which the Indians had removed, we laid down the bridge which I carried with little trouble at the first crossing, for there was none to offer resistance save some watchmen. These shouted so loudly that before we came to the second crossing, an infinite multitude of the enemy had risen against us, battling on every side both on water and land. I crossed rapidly with five horsemen and five hundred foot soldiers, with whom I passed all the other broken bridges, swimming until I reached the mainland. Leaving those people there, I returned to the others and found that they were fighting stoutly; but the injury our people received was beyond calculation. Not only the Spaniards but also the Tlascalans who were with us, were nearly all killed. Though they killed many natives, many of the Spaniards were killed, with their horses; and all the gold and jewels and many other things which we carried, and all the artillery, were lost.

When the survivors were collected, I pushed them on ahead, while I took the rear guard with three or four horsemen and about twenty foot soldiers who remained with me. We fought the Indians until we arrived at a city called Tacuba at the end of the causeway. God only knows how much trouble and danger I endured. Every time I turned to face the enemy, I came back full of arrows and darts and stones, for with water on both sides, they could assail us with impunity. When we attacked those on land, they would escape unhurt into the water. With great difficulty and fatigue, I conducted my remaining people to Tacuba without being killed myself.

When I reached the city, I found all the people in a panic in the square. They did not know where to go, and I tried to hurry them out of the country before more of the inhabitants should gather and capture the roofs, from which they could do us great injury. The vanguard said they did not know the way, so I sent them to the rear and took the lead myself until we had got clear of the city, where I awaited them at some farms. When the rear guard came up, I learned that they had sustained some injury, and that some of the Spaniards and Indians had been killed, and that much of the remaining gold had been lost and left on the road, where the Indians gathered it up. I held the Indians in check there until all the people had passed on.

No horse of the twenty-four left could still run, nor any horseman raise his arms, nor a sound foot soldier move. When we reached some buildings on a hill we fortified ourselves in them, and the enemy surrounded us and besieged us until night. We did not have an hour's rest. We counted over one hundred and fifty Spaniards killed in this fight, forty-five mares and horses, and more than two thousand of the Indians who had aided us. The son and daughters of Montezuma and all the chiefs whom we carried prisoners were also killed.

At midnight, believing we were not observed, we left. We did not know any road, nor where we were going, except that an Indian of Tlascaltecal told us he would guide us to his country if they did not stop us on the way. There were some watchmen near who heard us and alarmed many towns round about, from which numbers of people gathered and pursued us until daybreak.

When I saw that our enemies were gathering from all sides, I got our people who were still fit for service into order, making squadrons, and placing them in the vanguard, rear guard, and on the flanks, with the wounded in the center. I likewise distributed the horsemen. And so we continued all that day, fighting on all sides. During the whole night and day, we did not advance more than three leagues. When night came on, Our Lord was pleased to show us a tower and good lodging place on a hill, where we again fortified ourselves. They left us in peace during that night, although at dawn we had some disturbance from a false alarm caused by our own fears of the multitude which kept coming in pursuit of us.

The next morning I departed, followed on all sides by the enemy, yelling and raising the whole country, which is thickly populated. We marched along some lakes till we reached a populous town, where we thought we would have to fight with the townspeople. But when we arrived there, they fled.

I rested there that day and the next because my people, both the wounded and the sound, were very weary and exhausted with hunger and thirst, and the horses likewise were very tired. We found some maize there which we ate and carried away with us on the road, boiled and roasted. We left the next day, always pursued by our adversaries. When it was already late, we reached a plain where there were some small houses in which we lodged that night, suffering for lack of food.

Early next morning we began our march, our enemies still following our rear guard. Constantly skirmishing with them, we arrived at a large town two leagues distant, where there were some Indians stationed on the top of a small hill. With five horsemen and twelve foot soldiers, I started round the hill behind which was a great city of many people with whom we engaged fiercely. On account of the rocky country and the great number of people, we had to retire to the town where our people were. I came out of this very badly wounded in the head by two sling stones. After binding up the wounds, I made the Spaniards leave the town because it did not seem to me a safe camp for us. We marched on with great numbers of Indians pursuing us, fighting so stoutly that they wounded four or five Spaniards and as many horses. They killed one horse, and God only knows how great was its value to us, and what pain we suffered at its death, because, after God, our only security was the horses. But we consoled ourselves with its meat, and ate it without leaving even the skin, so great was our want.

Seeing that the enemy increased every day and grew stronger, and that we were becoming weaker, that night I ordered the wounded and the sick, whom we carried behind us on our horses, to provide themselves with crutches so that the horses and the able Spaniards would be free to fight. From what happened to us the next day, it seemed that the Holy Ghost had inspired me with this thought. After we had left the camp in the morning and marched about a league and a half, so great a multitude of Indians came out to encounter me that all about us we could not see the ground, so completely was it covered by them. They attacked us on all sides so violently that we could not distinguish each other for being so pressed and entangled with them. Certainly we believed that to be our last day. But Our Lord was pleased to show His great power and mercy to us, for with all our weakness we broke their great pride and haughtiness. They were so many that they hindered one another and were unable either to fight or to fly, and many of their important persons perished.

We spent a great part of the day in this struggle, until it pleased God that one of them who must have been an important chief fell. With his death all the battle ceased. After this we continued on our way more easily, although some of them still harassed us, until we reached a small house in the plain, where we lodged that night, and on the open ground. From there we first saw the mountains of Tlascaltecal. Joy filled our hearts, because we recognized the country and knew our way, even though we were not certain we would find the natives faithful and friendly. We feared that, seeing us so reduced, they might wish to put an end to our lives, and so recover the liberty they had formerly enjoyed.

The next morning at daybreak we began to march by a very level road which led directly to Tlascaltecal. On this day, which was Sunday, July 8, we left all the country of Culua and entered the province of Tlascaltecal at a village called Gualipan. There the natives received us very well and somewhat relieved our great hunger and wearinesss, although for much of the provision they asked payment and would accept only gold. This we were obliged in our great necessity to give.

We remained three days in this town. All the chiefs of the province and some of those of Quasucingo came to speak to me, showing great sympathy for what had happened to us. They tried to console me by reminding me they had often told me the Culuans were traitors against whom I should be on my guard, but that I would not believe it. Inasmuch as I had escaped alive, they said I ought to rejoice, for they would aid me until death to obtain satisfaction for the injury the Culuans had done me. They added that they felt obliged to do this as vassals of Your Highness, besides which they also suffered because of the many sons and brothers who had perished in my company, and on account of other past injuries. They said they would be my true and steadfast friends until death.

As I now came wounded and almost all of my company exhausted, the chiefs wanted us to go into the city, four leagues from this town, where we might rest and they would care for us and restore us. I was very grateful to them and accepted their invitation and gave them a few things from the valuables which had escaped. At this they were well contented and I went with them to the city, where I was well received. The chief brought me a bedstead of finely finished wood, with some bedclothing for me to sleep in, for we brought none; and he helped everybody with all that he had and could.

When I quit this city for Temixtitan, I had left there some sick persons and some of my servants with silver and wearing apparel belonging to me, and some other household things and provisions, in order to march forward unencumbered, lest anything should happen to us and all the documents and agreements which I had made with the natives of these parts should be lost. All the clothing of the Spaniards who came with me had been left, for in our retreat they only took

away what they wore, and their bedding. I learned that another servant of mine had come from Vera Cruz, bringing provisions and other
things for me. He had been accompanied by horsemen and forty-five
foot soldiers, and had brought with him the others I had left there.
He carried all the silver and clothing, my own as well as that of my
companions, with seven thousand dollars of melted gold which I had
left there, without counting other valuables, and another fourteen
thousand dollars of gold in pieces, which had been given in the province of Tuchitepeque to that captain whom I had sent to build the
town of Quacucalco. He carried also many other things which were
worth more than thirty thousand dollars of gold. This I learned, and
also that the Indians of Culua had killed them all on the road and
taken their treasure. I likewise learned that they had killed on the
roads many other Spaniards who were coming to the city of Temixtitan believing that I was there at peace and that the roads were
secure.

I assure Your Majesty that all of us were plunged into such sadness
by this news that it could hardly have been worse, because the loss
of these Spaniards and the treasure recalled the deaths and losses of
the Spaniards who had been killed in the city, at the bridges, and on
the road. It especially made me suspect that the people of Vera Cruz
might have been attacked, and that those whom we considered our
friends might have rebelled upon hearing of our defeat.

To learn the truth, I immediately dispatched messengers accompanied by Indians to guide them. I ordered them to avoid the high road
until they arrived at Vera Cruz, and to let me know at once what had
happened there. It pleased Our Lord that they should find the Spaniards very well, and the natives perfectly faithful. It was a great relief
to learn this after our losses and griefs, though it was bad news for
them to hear of our disaster and rout.

I remained twenty days in this province of Tlascaltecal, healing my
wounds which, with the poor care on the road, had become much
worse, especially the wound on my head; and I also had all the
wounded of my company cared for. Some of the men died. Some
remained maimed in their arms, others in their legs, for their wounds
were very bad and there was very little means for curing them. I
myself lost two fingers of my left hand.

Seeing that many of our people were dead and the survivors
wounded and disheartened, and fearing other dangers and troubles
still ahead, my men pleaded with me to withdraw to Vera Cruz. There

we could fortify ourselves before those natives whom we still considered our friends, seeing our rout and diminished numbers, could join with our enemies and, taking the passes over which we had to cross, attack us on the one side and our people at Vera Cruz on the other. Being there together, and having ships, we would be stronger and better able to defend ourselves in case they should attack before we summoned aid from the Islands.

I remembered, however, that Fortune is always on the side of the daring, and that we were Christians, confiding in the very great mercy of God, Who would never permit us to perish. I considered that to show so little courage before the natives, especially our friends, might cause them to abandon us the sooner, and turn them against us; that this great and noble country, at peace and on the point of being secured under Your Majesty, would be lost. The war must be continued to bring about the pacification of this country as it was before, and I determined on no account to go to the seaport. Rather, disregarding all difficulty and danger which might offer, I said that I would not abandon this country; for besides its being disgraceful to me and very dangerous to all, we would act treasonably toward Your Majesty. I was determined to return against the enemy from all possible points, and to take the offensive against them in every way I could.

After stopping twenty days in this province, although I was not yet well of my wounds, and those of my company were still somewhat weak, I left for the province of Tepeaca, which belonged to the confederation of Culua, our enemy. I had been informed that the inhabitants there had killed ten or twelve Spaniards who were on their way by the road which passes there from Vera Cruz to the capital.

Although the province of Tepeaca is very large, I pacified many cities and provinces subject to it in about twenty days, and the lords and chiefs of it came and offered themselves as vassals to Your Majesty. Moreover, I expelled many Culuans, who had come to help the natives against us and to keep them by fair means or foul from becoming our friends. And so I have kept busy up till now in this matter which is not yet altogether finished, for there are still some cities and towns to be pacified, which by the help of Our Lord will shortly be like these others, subject to the royal dominion of Your Majesty.

In that part of this province where they killed those ten Spaniards, I made a number slaves, of whom I gave a fifth part to the officials of Your Majesty. I did this especially as, in addition to their having killed the Spaniards and rebelled against the service of Your Highness, they eat human flesh, a fact so notorious that I do not send proofs of it to Your Majesty. I was also moved to make them slaves in order to strike terror into the Culuans, and also because there are many who will never mend themselves until great and severe punishment is inflicted upon them. We entered upon this war with the aid of the natives of Tlascaltecal, and Churultecal, and Quasucingo, by which our friendship has been well confirmed; and we are convinced that they will always serve Your Majesty as loyal vassals.

Having pacified and subjugated to the royal service of Your Highness all of this province, Your Majesty's officials and I conferred many times respecting the measures to be taken for its security. Seeing that the natives had first given themselves as vassals to Your Highness, and then rebelled, and that they were on the road and pass where the traffic of all the seaports had to go toward the interior, we considered that if it were left to itself as before, the natives might again be seduced into rebellion against us. The traffic would cease, especially as on the road to the coast there are two very steep and rough passes in this province, where the natives could defend themselves with little difficulty. For this as well as for other reasons, it seemed to us that a town should be founded in the best part of this province of Tepeaca, where the necessary conditions could be found for the colonists. For the purpose of carrying this out, I, in the name of Your Majesty, gave the said town the name Segura de la Frontera. I named alcaldes and municipal officers as is customary; and, for the better security of the householders of this town, materials are being brought to build a fort on the place I designated.

From what I have seen and understood concerning the similarity between this country and Spain, in its fertility, its size, its climate, and in many other features of it, it seemed to me that the most suitable name for this country would be New Spain of the Ocean Sea, and thus in the name of Your Majesty I have christened it. I humbly supplicate Your Highness to approve of this and order that it be so called.

Very High and Most Excellent Prince, may God, Our Lord, preserve the life and very royal person and the very powerful state of Your Majesty, and augment it for long time with increase of many greater kingdoms and dominions, according as your royal heart may desire.

From the town of Segura de la Frontera, of this New Spain, on the 30th October, 1520.

Your Sacred Majesty's very humble servant and vassal, who kisses the very royal feet and hands of Your Highness.

HERNÁN CORTÉS

LETTER TO CHARLES V FROM THE CITY OF CUYOACAN OF THIS NEW SPAIN
OF THE OCEAN SEA ON MAY 15, 1522

Very High and Most Powerful Prince, Very Catholic and Invincible Emperor, King and Lord: With Alonzo de Mendoza, native of Medellin, whom I sent from this New Spain on the fifth of March of the past year of 1521, I dispatched a second account to Your Majesty of everything that had happened here. I finished writing this on the thirtieth of October, 1520, but there was much delay in Mendoza's departing on account of contrary winds and the loss of three ships. One of these ships I had prepared to send with the said account to Your Majesty; the two others were to bring help from the island of Hispaniola.

In the closing part of that second letter I told Your Majesty how, after the Indians of Temixtitan had expelled us by force, I had marched against the province of Tepeaca, one of its vassals which had rebelled against us, and that, with the Spaniards who remained and our friendly Indians, I had made war on them and reduced them to the service of Your Majesty. I said that the past treachery and the great sufferings and deaths of the Spaniards were so fresh in our hearts that my determination was to return against the inhabitants of that capital who had been the cause of all. At that time I had begun to build thirteen brigantines, with which to do them all the damage I could from the lake if they persevered in their wicked intention; and while the brigantines were being made and we and the friendly Indians were preparing ourselves to return against the enemy, I had sent for reinforcements of people, horses, artillery, and arms to the island of Hispaniola. I had written to Your Majesty's officials there, sending them monies for the necessary outlay and expenses. I also assured Your Majesty that, till we were victorious, I would neither think of rest, nor would I cease to use all possible solicitude to accomplish this, regardless of what danger and hardship might overtake me; and that with this determination I was preparing to leave the province of Tepeaca.

I left Segura de la Frontera, in the province of Tepeaca, at mid-

December of 1520, placing a captain with sixty men there because the natives begged me to do so. I went that day to sleep in the city of Cholula. The inhabitants wanted me to come because many of their caciques had died of smallpox, and they wanted me to appoint others in their places. When this was done to their satisfaction, I left for Tlascaltecal, where all the Spaniards and the natives of the city met me with great rejoicing. The next day all the chiefs came to me and told me how Magiscatin, who was their principal lord, had died of the smallpox, and they knew I would be much grieved by it as he was my great friend. His son, about twelve or thirteen years old, survived, and they asked me to recognize him as his heir. I did so in the name of Your Majesty.

When I arrived in this city, I found that the master workmen and carpenters had used great diligence with the joining and planking of the brigantines, and that they had accomplished a very reasonable amount of work. I immediately sent to Vera Cruz for all the iron and nails they had there, together with the sails and tackle and other needful things. As we had no pitch, I ordered some Spaniards to make it in a neighboring forest. All provisions for the brigantines were thus ordered to be ready in time, so that, please God, on arriving in the province of Mexico and Temixtitan, I might send for them from there, a distance of sixteen leagues from where they were being built.

The second day after Christmas, I held a review and found forty horsemen and five hundred fifty foot soldiers, eighty of them crossbowmen and musketeers, with eight or nine field pieces, but very little powder. I divided the horsemen into four troops of ten each, and formed nine captaincies of sixty Spanish foot each. All being assembled for this review, I spoke to them as follows: They already knew that they and I had come to serve Your Sacred Majesty by settling in this country; and they likewise knew how all the natives of it had acknowledged themselves as vassals of Your Majesty, and how they had persevered as such, receiving good deeds from us and we from them, until without any cause all the inhabitants of Culua including the people of the great city of Temixtitan, and those of all the other provinces subject to it, had revolted against Your Majesty; yet more, they had killed many of our relatives and friends and had expelled us from their country. They should remember how many dangers and hardships we had endured, and how it was profitable to the service of God and Your Catholic Majesty to return and recover what was left, inasmuch as we had just cause and good reasons on our side. One cause was that we fought for the spread of our Faith, and against barbarians; another was that we served Your Majesty; another was for the security of our lives; and another that we had many natives, our friends, to help us. All these were strong motives to animate our hearts. For the same reasons I told them to cheer up and be brave.

The men all declared that they would very gladly die for our Faith and Your Majesty's service, or return to recover the loss and revenge so great a treachery as had been done by the people of Temixtitan and their allies. I, in the name of Your Majesty, thanked them for it. On the day after the review we returned to our camp in good spirits.

The next day I had all the chiefs assembled, and told them that they already knew I was about to leave the following day to enter the country of our enemies; that they must see that the city of Temixtitan could not be captured without the brigantines, and so I prayed them to furnish everything necessary to the workmen. I said also that whenever I should send from Texcoco for the joinings, planks and other materials for the brigantines, they should be ready to send them. They promised to do so, and they also wished to send some warriors with me at once, declaring that when the brigantines moved, they would go with all their people, for they wished to die where I died, and to revenge themselves on the Culuans, their mortal enemies.

I left the next day with all my people in good order, and we marched six leagues to a town called Tezmoluca, where the natives have always been friendly. There we rested that night.

I had been informed that the natives of Mexico and Temixtitan were preparing many arms, constructing earthworks and fortifications, and gathering forces for resisting our entrance into the country; for they already knew I intended to return against them. Knowing how dexterous and crafty they were in matters of war, I many times pondered how we could surprise them. They knew we had information of three roads or entrances by which we might advance into their country. I determined to enter by the road of Tezmoluca, because its pass is the roughest and steepest of all, and I felt sure that we would not encounter much resistance there nor would they be so much on their guard.

The next day, having heard Mass and recommended ourselves to God, we left Tezmoluca, I leading the vanguard. We pursued our road four leagues leading up to the top of the pass which is already within the limits of Culua. Although it was very cold, we made ourselves comfortable that night with large quantities of wood we found there. The next morning, a Sunday, we set out to follow our road, descending the pass to the plain.

When all the people had descended, I told them that all should give thanks to Our Lord, Who had brought us safely thus far, where we could first behold all the provinces of Mexico and Temixtitan. Although we were glad at seeing them, we felt some sorrow, remembering the losses we had sustained, and we all vowed never to quit the country without victory, even if we died there. With this determination, we all advanced as merrily as if it were a pleasure party. The enemy, already having observed us, instantly made many and great smoke signals all over the country, so I again cautioned the Spaniards that they should march in good order close together.

The Indians began to yell at us from hamlets and small towns, calling on the entire land for the people to assemble and attack us at some bridges and difficult places near there. We met some squadrons of Indians, and I ordered fifteen horsemen to break through them, which they did without any loss to ourselves, killing some of them with their lances. We followed on our road to Texcoco, which is one of the greatest and finest cities to be found in all these parts. As those on foot were somewhat tired, and it was getting late, we slept in a town called Coatepeque, which we found deserted.

The following day, which was Monday, the last of December, we proceeded in the usual order, discussing with each other whether the Texcocans would be hostile or friendly, rather believing the former. Four Indian chiefs met us on the road, bearing a banner of gold on a pole, which weighed about four marks of gold. They told us to understand by this sign that they came peaceably. God only knows how much we desired peace and stood in need of it, being so few and cut off from help in the midst of our enemies. When I saw the four Indians, one of whom was known to me, I halted our people. After we had greeted one another, they said they came on the part of the chief of that city and province. They besought me, on his part, to do no injury to his country; the people of Temixtitan were to blame for the past injuries I had sustained and not they. They wished to be Your Majesty's vassals and my friends. They invited us to enter the city, where by their deeds we should recognize their sincerity.

I answered that I rejoiced in their peace and friendship. However, though they excused themselves for the war waged on me in Temixtitan, they also well knew that five or six leagues from Texcoco they had killed five horsemen, forty-five of my foot soldiers, and had taken much gold, silver and other things from them. Inasmuch as they could not excuse themselves from this fault, the penalty would be the restoration of our property. On this condition, although they well deserved death for having killed so many Christians, I told them I would make peace with them, but otherwise I would have to treat them with the utmost severity.

We entered Texcoco about noon on New Year's Day, and did not see one tenth of the people usually in the city. This was an alarming sign.

Toward evening a few Spaniards mounted some lofty terraces from which they could observe the whole town. They saw that all the natives were abandoning it, some by canoes on the lake and others going up into the hills. And so the chief of the city, whom I longed as for my salvation to have in my hands, escaped with many of the other chiefs to Temixtitan, taking away all their possessions. Those messengers had been sent to delay me somewhat, so that upon entering the city I might do them no harm. That night they abandoned not only us but also their city.

Three days elapsed in this city without any encounter with the Indians, for they neither dared to attack us nor were we disposed to go out far searching for them. At this time some neighboring lords came weeping to ask me to pardon them for having absented them-selves from their country, and promising hereafter to do everything that I might order them in the name of Your Majesty.

When the lord of Mexico and Temixtitan, and all the other lords of Culua—when this name of Culua is used, it must be understood as meaning all the country and provinces of these parts subject to Temixtitan—knew that the neighboring lords had offered themselves as vassals of Your Majesty, they sent messengers to tell them they had behaved very badly. They said that if they had acted from fear, they should realize that the Culuans were many, and had sufficient power to kill me and all the Spaniards and all the Indians of Tlascal-tecal, which indeed they would very soon accomplish; but if they had done it to save their lands, they should abandon them and come to Temixtitan, where they would receive larger and greater towns for their residence. The chiefs bound these messengers and brought them to me.

They immediately confessed that they had come from the lords of Temixtitan, but that it had been to ask those chiefs who were my friends to act as mediators in making peace between them and myself. The chiefs who wanted to be friendly denied this, and said that the people of Mexico and Temixtitan desired nothing but war.

Although I believed they spoke the truth, I wanted to entice the people of Temixtitan into friendship with us. I told them to have no fears, for I would send them again to Temixtitan. I prayed them to tell those lords that I did not want war with them, although I had good reason, but rather to be friends as we had been before.

In order to assure them still more and to win them over to the service of Your Majesty, I sent them word that I well knew that the principal persons who had led them into the past war were already dead; that the past was the past and that they ought not to provoke the destruction of their lands and cities, as I would be much distressed by it. With this I set the messengers free, and they went away promising to bring me the answer. The lords of the neighboring provinces and I remained better friends than before on account of this good action, and I pardoned them their past errors, and thus they left well satisfied.

Having been seven or eight days in Texcoco, and seeing that the natives did not attack me, I sallied out from the city with two hundred Spaniards, including eighteen horsemen, thirty archers, ten musketeers and with three or four thousand friendly Indians. I followed the shore of the lake till we reached the city of Iztapalapa, which is two leagues by water from Temixtitan and six from Texcoco. It contains about ten thousand households, and half or even two-thirds of it is built on the lake. Its lord, Montezuma's brother, whom the Indians after the latter's death had selected as sovereign, had been the leader in making war on us and expelling us from the city. For this reason, and because I had heard that the people of Iztapalapa were very badly disposed toward us, I determined to march against them.

When their people perceived me, from about two leagues away, some warriors immediately appeared on land and others in canoes on the lake. And so we advanced over those two leagues, fighting both with those on land and those on water, till we reached the city. Almost two-thirds of a league outside the town, they had opened a causeway which was like a dyke between the fresh and salt-water lakes, as Your Majesty may see from the map of Temixtitan I have sent. When the dyke was opened, the water of the salt lake began to rush with great force into the fresh-water lake, although the two lakes are more than half a league apart. Not noticing the trap in our eagerness for victory, we passed on and continued our approach, until we entered, fighting the enemy, into the city. As the populace had already been warned of our approach, all the houses on land were deserted and the people took refuge with their property in the houses on the lake, fighting us very stoutly. But we drove them into the water, and more than six thousand souls—men, women and children—perished, because our Indian allies, seeing the victory which God gave us, had only one thought—to kill right and left.

As night came on, I collected my people and set fire to some of the houses. While they were burning, it seemed that Our Lord inspired me and recalled to my mind the dyke I had seen on the road, and I realized what a great danger it was. I decided to leave the city, it being already quite dark.

When I reached the water, it was so deep and flowed with such force that we passed it running full tilt, but some of our friendly Indians were drowned, and all the plunder that had been taken in the city was lost. I assure Your Majesty that if we had waited three hours more, none of us would have escaped. We should have been surrounded by water, without having any outlet anywhere.

On arriving at Texcoco, I found the people I had left there all safe. They were very glad at our coming and our victory. The day after we returned, a Spaniard who had been wounded, died—the first white man the Indians had killed in this campaign.

In the other account, Very Fortunate and Most Excellent Prince, I told Your Majesty that when they routed and expelled me from Temixtitan, I took with me the son and two daughters of Montezuma, Cacamacin, his two brothers, and many other chiefs whom I held prisoners. All of them had been killed by the enemy except two brothers of Cacamacin, who by a happy chance were able to escape. When I reached Tlascaltical one of these two brothers, called Cucascacin, whom I had already appointed lord of Texcoco and the province of Aculuacan, escaped and returned to Texcoco, where they had already elected for chief another of his brothers called Guanacacin. On his arrival in Texcoco, the guards seized Cucascacin and informed Guanacacin their lord, who communicated the news to the lord of Temixtitan. The latter could not believe that he had escaped from us, but suspected he must have gone there to furnish us some information; so he immediately sent word to Guanacacin to kill Cucascacin, his brother. Guanacacin obeyed without delay. The younger of the two brothers still remained with me. As he was quite a lad, our conversation made more impression on him, and he became a Christian, taking the name of Don Fernando. When I left Tlascaltecal for Mexico and Temixtitan, I left him there with certain Spaniards.

The day after my return from Iztapalapa to Texcoco I sent Gonzalo de Sandoval, aguacil mayor of Your Majesty, in command of twenty horsemen, two hundred foot soldiers, musketeers, archers and shield bearers, for two very necessary objects: first, to escort messengers I was sending to Tlascaltecal to learn the state of the thirteen brigantines, and second, to make sure of that region so that the Spaniards might come and go in safety; for at that time, we could neither go out of the province of Aculuacan without passing through the enemy's country, nor could the Spaniards in Vera Cruz come to us without danger.

Having assured the security of the road, the alguacil mayor returned to Texcoco, bringing Don Fernando with him. The sovereignty of the city belonged to him, although there were other brothers.

For this reason, and because the province was without a ruler inasmuch as his brother Guanacacin had deserted it and gone to Temixtitan, and also because Don Fernando was a very good friend of the Christians, I, in Your Majesty's name, caused him to be acknowledged as ruler. The inhabitants of this city, although at that time there were very few left in it, elected him, and thenceforward obeyed him.

Many others who were absent or had fled began to return, and they obeyed and served Don Fernando. The city began to be rebuilt and well populated.

The next day I learned that some of the enemy were moving about the borders of the lake, hoping to surprise and capture some of the Tlascalans coming and going for the camp service. They had confederated with two towns, subject to Texcoco, which are near the water, and had fortified themselves with barricades, ditches and other works. When I learned this, I took twelve horsemen and two hundred foot soldiers and two small field pieces, and went to the place where they were, about a league and a half from the city. We set fire to a part of those towns and returned to our quarters victorious and happy. The next day three chiefs of those towns came to ask pardon for what had passed, beseeching us not to destroy them and promising me not to receive those of Temixtitan any more in their town. As they were persons of no importance, and vassals of Don Fernando, I pardoned them in Your Majesty's name.

The people whom I had left making the brigantines in Tlascaltecal were informed that a ship had arrived at the port of Vera Cruz with thirty or forty Spaniards—besides the sailors—and eight horses, cross-bows, muskets and powder. We were very glad of the news, as we were in extreme need of relief.

Three days later, when we knew that the brigantines had been completed and that the people who were to bring them were ready, I sent Gonzalo de Sandoval, alguacil mayor, with fifteen horsemen and two hundred foot soldiers to escort them to me. I gave orders to destroy and raze a large town, subject to Texcoco, which borders on Tlascaltecal, because its natives had killed five horsemen and forty-five foot soldiers who were coming from Vera Cruz to Temixtitan when I was besieged there, ignorant at the time that such a great treachery had been practiced against us.

When we entered Texcoco this time, we found in their places of worship or mosques the skins of five horses with their hoofs and shoes. They had offered these to their idols in token of victory, together with much wearing apparel and other things belonging to the Spaniards. We found the blood of our brothers and companions spilled and sacrificed all about these towers and mosques, a thing which filled us with grief, for all our past tribulations were thus revived. The traitors of that and the other neighboring towns had placed themselves in ambush on each side of a difficult pass, attacking those Christians as they were descending a slope on foot and leading their horses behind so that they were unable to use them. They executed upon them the greatest cruelty that has ever been done, killing some, while others, whom they captured alive, they brought to Texcoco and sacrificed, tearing out their hearts before the idols.

That it happened thus is proved by the fact that, when the alguacil mayor passed there, some of his men found in a house of a village which is between Texcoco and the place where they captured and killed the Christians, a white wall on which the following words were written in charcoal: "Here the unhappy Juan Yuste was kept a prisoner"—a thing fit to break the hearts of those that saw it. He was a gentleman, one of the five horsemen.

When the alguacil mayor arrived at that town, the natives, conscious of their great guilt, fled, and the horsemen and Spanish foot soldiers and the friendly Indians pursued and killed many and captured many women and children who were declared slaves. However, moved by compassion, he did not kill and destroy all, and before he left there he even collected those who survived and restored them to their town, so it is now populated again and repentant of the past.

The alguacil mayor proceeded five or six leagues toward the town in Tlascaltecal which is nearest to the borders of Culua, and there he met the Spaniards and the people who were to bring the brigantines. The day after he arrived they left there with the planks and cross timbers, all of which were carried in the most perfect order by eight thousand men. It was a marvelous sight to see and, it seems to me, even to hear of—the bringing of thirteen small ships overland a distance of about eighteen leagues. I assure Your Majesty that from the vanguard to the rear was a distance of two leagues.

When they set out, they took eight horsemen and a hundred Spaniards with the van, and more than ten thousand warriors on the flanks, having as captains Yutecad and Teutipil, two chiefs among the nobles of Tlascaltecal. In the rear guard came another hundred-odd Spaniards and eight horsemen, and another ten thousand warriors with Chichimecatecle, one of the principal lords of that province, as their captain. These captains also brought two thousand Indians carrying provisions.

When they started out, Chichimecatecle escorted the van with the planking, and the other two captains brought up the rear with the joinings. But when they entered the country of Culua the masters of the brigantines reversed this order, as the plankings would cause the most hindrance should any disturbance happen, which would most likely occur in the front. Chichimecatecle, who brought the planking and until now had led his warriors at the head of the vanguard, took this change in position as an affront, because he wished to meet any danger that might present itself. When after some trouble he finally agreed to the change, he nevertheless did not want any Spaniards in the rear guard, because he was very brave and wanted the honors himself.

In this order and agreement, they marched three days, and on the fourth they entered this city with much rejoicing and noise of kettledrums when I went out to receive them. The peoples were so spread out that from the entrance of the first until the last had arrived we spent six hours without the line of people once being broken. When I had thanked the chiefs for the good service they had done us, we assigned them their quarters and provided them the best we could. They told me they wished to meet the Culuans and that I should see when I commanded it that they and their people were desirous of avenging themselves or dying with us. I told them to rest and that very soon I would give them plenty to do.

When those warriors of Tlascaltecal, who were certainly for hereabouts very dashing men, had rested in Texcoco three or four days, I prepared twenty-five horsemen, three hundred foot soldiers, five hundred archers and musketeers, and six small field pieces, and without telling anyone where we were going, I left the city at nine o'clock in the morning. With me were the captains already named, with more than thirty thousand in their divisions, well organized after their fashion. It was getting late when we met a body of the enemy's warriors four leagues from the city. Our horsemen broke through them and scattered them and, as the warriors of Tlascaltecal were very fleet, they followed, and we killed many of our enemy. That night we slept in the field, keeping strict watch.

The next morning we continued our march, and still I had not revealed where I intended to go. I distrusted some of the people of Texcoco who were with us and feared they might give information to the people of Mexico and Temixtitan. We arrived at a town called Xaltoca, which is situated in the midst of the lake and is surrounded by so many trenches full of water that the horsemen could not enter. Our adversaries yelled a great deal, discharging darts and arrows at us, but the foot soldiers entered, although with some difficulty, and expelled them, burning a great part of the town. That night we slept a league from there, and as day broke, we continued our march, coming to a great and beautiful city called Guaticlan. Finding it deserted, we lodged in it that night.

The next day we advanced to another city, called Tenainca, where we encountered no resistance, and without halting we went on to another called Acapuzalco. Both are on the borders of the lake. We did not stop there either as I wished very much to reach another city nearby, called Tacuba, which is very close to Temixtitan. Upon nearing it, we found that here also they had made many trenches filled with water, and that the enemy was alerted. As soon as we saw them, we and our friends attacked them briskly and entered the city, killing some and expelling the other inhabitants from it. As it was already late then, we did nothing else that night but lodged in a house so large that we easily had room for everybody.

At daybreak, our friendly Indians began to pillage and set fire to the whole city except our quarters, and they put such diligence into it that a fourth of the place was burned. This was done because, when we were routed the other time in Temixtitan and passed through this city, its inhabitants joined those of Temixtitan and fought us cruelly, killing many Spaniards.

Of the six days we remained in the city of Tacuba, none passed on which we had not some encounters and skirmishes with the enemy. The captains of the Tlascalans, and some of their men, exchanged many challenges with those of Temixtitan and would fight most beautifully one with the other. Many arguments passed between them, with mutual threats and insults, which was a sight to see. During all this time, many of the Indians were killed, but none of our people were injured, though we often entered by the causeways and bridges of the city where they had many defenses and resisted us stoutly. Frequently they would give us a chance to enter, saying: "Come and enjoy yourselves," and at other times they would say: "Do you think there is now another Montezuma, so that you can do as you please?"

Once, while these speeches were passing, I placed myself near one of the bridges and signaled to our people to remain quiet; and they also, when they saw that I wished to speak to them, silenced their people. I then asked them why they were so foolish as to court destruction, and if there was among them any principal chief, because I wished to speak to him. They answered that the whole multitude of warriors I saw there were chiefs so that I might say whatever I wished. As I did not make answer, they began to insult me. One of our men, I do not know who, then called to them that they would die of hunger, for we would not allow them to come out to seek food. They retorted that they needed none and that when they did they would eat us and the Tlascalans. One of them took some loaves of maize bread and threw them toward us saying: "Take it and eat it if you are hungry, for we are not." Then immediately they began to yell and attack us.

My coming to Tacuba had been principally to speak with those of Temixtitan and to learn their intention. As my being there profited nothing, I decided, at the end of six days, to return to Texcoco and hasten the construction of the brigantines, so as to surround the enemy by water and land.

As the road between Vera Cruz and this city of Texcoco was safe for traveling back and forth, the people of that city had news of us every day and we of them, which before was not possible. They sent me some crossbows and muskets and powder which pleased us greatly. Two days later they sent a messenger to tell me that three ships had arrived at the port bringing many people and horses, whom they would immediately send on to me—aid which God miraculously sent us in proportion to our need.

I have always sought, Most Powerful Lord, to win the people of

Temixtitan to our friendship by every way and means I could; on the one hand because I did not wish them to provoke their own destruction, and on the other in order to rest from the hardships of all the past wars; but principally because I knew it would conduce to Your Majesty's service. Whenever I could lay hold of anyone from the city, I would send him back and admonish the inhabitants to come to terms of peace.

On Holy Wednesday, the twenty-seventh of March, 1521, I had brought before me some chiefs of Temixtitan who had been captured. I asked if any of them would go to the city and speak on my part to its lords to ask them to stop fighting and give themselves as vassals of Your Majesty as before; for I did not wish to destroy them but to be their friend. Although they took it badly, fearing they would be killed for bringing that message, two of the prisoners determined to go, and asked me for a letter. Though they did not understand what was in it, they knew that among us it was customary, and that with it the people of the city would believe them. I explained also through the interpreters what I wrote in the letter, which was what I had told them. So they left, and I ordered five horsemen to accompany them till they were in safety.

On the fifth of April, I left this city of Texcoco, with the thirty horsemen and three hundred footmen who had been equipped, leaving in it twenty other horsemen and three hundred footmen under the command of Gonzalo de Sandoval, the alguacil mayor. More than twenty thousand men of Texcoco went with me.

Since the Calcans became our friends, they have kept a strong fort and garrison there, for it is on the Culuan frontier. When we arrived at Calco, where the natives were our allies, we did not stop except to tell the chiefs of my intention to make a tour around the lakes. I believed that after accomplishing this march, which was important, the thirteen brigantines would be complete and ready to be launched.

Leaving Calco, I was joined by forty thousand friendly warriors. And so we marched in my tour of the lakes, fighting many battles and winning many victories for the service of Your Majesty. Nor was this without great trouble and danger and much killing of hostile Indians, for they were collected in each town in great multitudes, and very well fortified. A few of the Spaniards died, for a day did not pass that we did not have to fight fiercely to continue on our road.

At one town called Suchmilco, built on the fresh-water lake, the horse I rode fell from sheer fatigue. Some of the enemy saw me on foot and rushed upon me. While I defended myself with my lance, an Indian of Tlascaltecal rushed to help me, and he and a servant of mine helped me raise the horse.

Continuing thus around the lakes, we arrived in the city of Cuyo-acan, which is near Temixtitan and many other cities, the farthest being about a league and a half distant. We found it deserted, and rested there two days.

Since I was to lay siege to the great city of Temixtitan as soon as the brigantines were finished, I wished first to see its port, and the entrances and exits, and where the Spaniards might attack or be attacked. Therefore, the day after we arrived, I took five horsemen and two hundred foot soldiers and went by a causeway leading into Temix-titan to the lake which was very near. Here we saw an infinite number of canoes on the water with countless warriors in them. We reached a barricade they had erected across the causeway, and the foot soldiers began to attack it. It was very strong, and stout resistance was offered. Ten Spaniards were wounded, but we finally won it. From this place, we saw how this causeway led directly through the water until it entered Temixtitan, a full league and a half distant, and that likewise on the other causeway, which goes to Iztapalapa, there were crowds of people.

When I had considered all that it was necessary to observe (for it was likely that a garrison of horsemen and foot soldiers would have to be established here in this city), I ordered our people to retire and we returned to the town, burning their houses and the towers of their idols.

We departed the next day to go to Tacuba, two leagues from here, using our lances in one place and another along the way.

Thus, in three days' march and using our lances from time to time, we returned to Texcoco. The Spaniards rejoiced at our coming as if it were their salvation, because after I had left them they had heard nothing of me till the day we arrived. They had suffered various alarms in the city, and the inhabitants had been daily telling them the men of Mexico and Temixtitan would fall on them while I was absent. And so, with God's help this expedition was concluded, and it was a very great enterprise in which Your Majesty received great service.

When I came for the first time to the city of Temixtitan, I ordered, as I made known to Your Majesty, that certain plantations should be established for Your Majesty in two or three of the most desirable provinces. I sent two Spaniards to one of them called Chinantla, which is not subject to the Culuans. In the others, which were subject, the Culuans killed those who were at the plantations when they made war on me in Temixtitan, and took everything they had, which was a very considerable sum according to the estimates of this country. During almost a year I could learn nothing about the Spaniards who settled in Chinantla nor, while all those provinces were in revolt, could they hear anything from us. The natives of Chinantla, being vassals of Your Majesty and enemies of the Culuans, told those Christians that the Culuans had made fierce war upon us, and believing few or none of us had come out alive they would not allow the Spaniards to leave the country. Thus these two stayed there. One of them, a youth and a soldier, they made their captain, and at this time he went out with them to fight their enemies, over whom he and they were victorious most of the time.

When it pleased God they should afterward return and reorganize, the people of Chinantla told those Christians that they knew there were Spaniards in the province of Tepeaca. If they wished to learn the truth, the Indians would risk sending two of their people who, although they had to pass through much hostile country, could travel at night and off the highway till they reached Tepeaca.

The better man of the two Spaniards sent a letter by those two Indians, the tenor of which was as follows: "Noble Sirs, I have written Your Worships two or three letters, but I do not know if they have reached you or not as they have had no answer, so I doubt whether this will obtain one. I make it known to you, Sirs, that all the natives of this country of Culua are up in arms and have attacked us many times; but always—praise be to Our Lord for it—we have been victorious. We have also had daily war with the natives of Tuxtepeque, for they are allies of Culua. Those who have remained in the service of Their Highnesses as their vassals are the seven towns of Tenez; and Nicolas and I have always stopped in Chinantla, which is the capital.

"I would like very much to know where the captain is, in order to write to him and make known what has happened here. If perchance you can write me where he is, and will send twenty or thirty Spaniards, I would go there with two of the chiefs from here who wish to see and speak with the captain. It would be well for them to come now because it is the largest time for cacao, and the Culuans hinder it by making war. May the Lord guard the noble persons of Your Worships, according to your desire.

"From Chinantla, I know not what date of the month of April, of the year 1521. At the service of Your Worships, Hernando de Barrientos."

When the two Indians arrived with this letter in the province of Tepeaca, the captain I had left there sent it immediately to me at Texcoco. We all rejoiced greatly at receiving it, because though we had always confided in the friendship of Chinantla, sometimes the thought occurred to us that they might confederate with Culuans and kill the two Spaniards. I immediately wrote, giving them an account of what had happened, and telling them to have hope, for though they were surrounded on every side by enemies, they would, by God's pleasure, very soon find themselves free and able to come and go in safety.

After having made the circuit of the lakes, during which I gathered much important information for laying siege to Temixtitan by land and water, I stopped in Texcoco, strengthening myself as best I could with people and arms, hastening to get the brigantines finished and making a canal to take them to the lake. This canal was begun immediately after the planks and joinings of the brigantines had been brought, and extended from one side of our camp to the lake. From the place where the brigantines were being joined there was quite a half league's distance to the lake. More than eight thousand natives of Aculuacan and Texcoco were employed daily for fifty days; for the channel of the canal was more than twelve feet deep and as many in width, all staked and walled. Thus, the water which flows through it would by its own force carry them to the lake, so that we could take the smaller vessels without danger and with little labor to the water. It certainly was a very great work, worthy of admiration.

As soon as the brigantines were finished and put in the canal on the twenty-eighth of April, 1521, I made a review of all my people and found eighty-six horsemen, a hundred and eighteen bowmen and musketeers, seven hundred and odd foot soldiers with swords and shields, three heavy iron guns, fifteen small bronze field pieces, and ten hundredweight of powder. Having finished the review, I charged and commended all the Spaniards to obey and comply with the ordinances which I had made respecting the conduct of the war, and to be merry and keep up their courage inasmuch as they saw how Our Lord was leading us to victory over our enemies. For they well knew that when we entered Texcoco we had brought only forty horsemen, but God had helped us even more than we had thought, for a ship had arrived with horses, men and arms, as they had seen.

I said principally that the fact that we were fighting to promote the spread of our faith and for the reduction to Your Majesty's service of so many revolted provinces, should fill them with courage and zeal to conquer or die. They all answered, demonstrating a willingness and desire for this. We passed the day of the review in great rejoicing, longing to see ourselves already engaged in the siege and to bring this war to an end, on which the peace of these parts so much depended.

The next day I sent messengers to the provinces of Tlascaltecal, Guajucingo, and Churultecal, to let them know that the brigantines were ready, and that I and all my people were about to surround the great city of Temixtitan. Therefore I begged them, that as many of their people and as well armed as possible set out and join me here in Texcoco, where I would wait ten days for them. They should be no longer because it would disarrange everything that had been planned. When the messengers arrived, the people of those provinces were already prepared and eager to meet the Culuans. Those from Guajucingo and Churultecal came to Calco as I had ordered, for the siege was to be begun near that place. The captains of Tlascaltecal arrived in Texcoco with very brilliant and well-armed forces, five or six days before the Feast of the Holy Ghost, which was the time I had designated to them. When I learned on that day of their approach, I went out to meet them with great rejoicing, and they came so gladly and so well disciplined that things could not have been better. According to the account the captains made, there were more than fifty thousand warriors, who were well received by us and given quarters.

The second day after the Feast, I ordered all the foot soldiers and horsemen to assemble in the square of the city of Texcoco so that I might divide them and assign them to the captains, who were to lead them in three divisions to be stationed in three cities which are around Temixtitan. I made Pedro de Alvarado captain of one division, assigning him thirty horsemen, eighteen archers and musketeers, and one hundred fifty foot soldiers with swords and shields, and more than twenty-five thousand warriors of Tlascaltecal. These were to make their headquarters in Tacuba. I made Cristobal de Olid captain of another division, to which I assigned thirty horsemen, eighteen archers and musketeers, and a hundred sixty foot soldiers with swords and shields, and more than twenty thousand warriors of our allies. These were to make their headquarters in Cuyoacan. I made Gonzalo de Sandoval, alguacil mayor, captain of the third division, assigning him twenty-four horsemen, four musketeers, fifteen archers, and a hundred fifty foot soldiers with swords and shields, fifty of whom were chosen among those I had brought in my company, and more than thirty thousand men of the people of Guajucingo, Churultecal and Calco. This division was to go to Iztapalapa to destroy it, and afterward to advance over a causeway in the lake, protected by the brigantines, in order to join with the garrison at Cuyoacan, so that after I entered the lake with the brigantines the alguacil mayor might fix his headquarters wherever it seemed most convenient to him. For the thirteen brigantines I left three hundred men, almost all of whom were sailors and well drilled, so that in each brigantine were twenty-five Spaniards and each small vessel had a captain, a pilot and six archers and musketeers.

According to the foregoing order the captains who were to command the forces in Tacuba and Cuyoacan, after receiving instructions as to what they were to do, left Texcoco on the tenth of May. Three days later, after passing through many deserted towns and villages, they entered Tacuba, which they also found deserted. They made their quarters in the houses of the chief, which are very beautiful and large. Although it was already late, the warriors of Tlascaltecal made an inspection of the entrance of two causeways leading to the city of Temixtitan and fought bravely for two or three hours with the people of the city until night separated them, when they returned safely to Tacuba.

The next morning the two captains agreed, as I had commanded them, to cut off the aqueducts which supplied Temixtitan with fresh water. One of them went with twenty horsemen and some archers and musketeers to the source of the water, about a quarter of a league from there, and broke the pipes of wood and mortar and stone, fighting valiantly with those of the city who defended the spring by land and water. At last he routed them and accomplished his purpose, cutting off the fresh water from the city—a very politic stratagem. The same day the captains repaired certain dangerous passes, bridges and aqueducts in the neighborhood of the lake so that the horsemen might more easily gallop from one part to another.

Captain Cristobal de Olid departed with the people who were to be garrisoned in Cuyoacan, two leagues from Tacuba, and Captain Pedro de Alvarado stayed with his people in garrison at Tacuba, where he had daily skirmishes with the Indians. The same day that Cristobal de Olid left for Cuyoacan, he and his men arrived at ten o'clock in the morning and lodged in the houses of its chief. The city was deserted.

The next morning with about twenty horsemen, some archers and some six or seven thousand warriors of Tlascaltecal, they went to take a look at the causeway leading to Temixtitan. They found the enemy well prepared, the causeway broken up, and many barricades erected. They engaged the enemy, and the archers wounded and killed some of them. This was repeated for six or seven days, on each of which there were many encounters and skirmishes. As our people were distributed in so many places the garrisons longed, as for their salvation, for my arrival with the brigantines. During those six days they would meet from both headquarters daily, as they were near each other. The horsemen scoured the country, killing many of the enemy and bringing into the headquarters from the mountains great quantities of maize, of which is made bread, the principal food of these parts, and much superior to that of the Islands.

I remained in Texcoco with three hundred men and thirteen brigantines. As soon as I knew the divisions were in the places assigned for their camps, I could embark and take a look at the city and do some damage to the canoes. I very much wished to go by land, to give directions in the camps, but the captains were persons who could be trusted with what they had in hand, while the affair of the brigantines was a matter of great importance requiring stern discipline and attention. So I determined to embark in them because we calculated to have the greatest risk and adventure by water. The principal persons of my company, however, *required* me in due form to go with the garrisons, as they believed that they were to undertake the most dangerous part. The day after the Feast of Corpus Christi, Friday at dawn, I ordered Gonzalo de Sandoval, alguacil mayor, to go with his people directly to Iztapalapa, about six short leagues from there. Shortly after mid-day they arrived there and began to burn it and to fight with its people, who, when they saw the great force of the alguacil mayor—for more than thirty-five or forty thousand of our allies had gone with him—retreated to their canoes. The alguacil mayor with all the people accompanying him lodged in that town, and remained there that day awaiting my orders and what might happen to me.

Immediately after I had dispatched the alguacil mayor I embarked in the brigantines and we started with sails and oars. While the alguacil mayor was fighting and burning the city of Iztapalapa, we came in sight of a very large and strong hill near that city, all surrounded by water, where many people had collected from the towns round about the lake as well as from Temixtitan.

They well knew that our first encounter would be with those of Iztapalapa, and they were there for their own defense and also to attack us if possible. When they saw the fleet coming they began to shout and make great smoke signals so that all the cities of the lake might know and be prepared. Although my intention was to attack that part of Iztapalapa which is on the water, we retraced our course to that hill or knoll and I leaped on it with one hundred fifty men. It was very steep and high and we began to ascend it with much difficulty. We stormed their trenches on the top, and not one of them escaped except the women and children. In this fight they wounded twenty-five Spaniards, but it was a beautiful victory.

As the people of Iztapalapa had made smoke signals from some towers of their idols which stand on a very high hill near their city, Temixtitan and the other cities on the water knew that I had already entered the lake with the brigantines. They quickly assembled a very great fleet of more than five hundred canoes to attack us and discover what sort of things the brigantines were.

When I saw that their course was straight toward us, I and the people who had disembarked on that hill boarded our vessels in great haste. I ordered the captains of the brigantines not to move at all so that the canoes, believing that we did not dare to move out toward them, might decide to attack us. And so they directed their fleet against us with great force. However, at about two arrow-shots' distance they stopped and remained still.

I strongly desired the first encounter to be a great victory inspiring them with a dread of the brigantines—which held the key of the whole war—because both the Mexicans and we were exposed to the greatest damage on the water.

It pleased Our Lord that while we were observing one another a favorable land wind sprang up, enabling us to attack them. I immediately ordered the captains to break through the fleet of canoes and pursue them until they took refuge in Temixtitan. As the wind was very good, we bore down in the midst of them and they fled as fast as they could. We destroyed an infinite number of canoes and killed and drowned many of the enemy, the greatest sight to be seen in the world. We pursued them for fully three long leagues, until we shut them up amid the houses of the city. And so it pleased Our Lord to give us the best and greatest victory we could have asked or desired.

The garrison of Cuyoacan could see the movements of the brigantines better than that of Tacuba. They beheld all the thirteen sails on the water, favored by such good weather, and knocking the enemy's canoes to pieces. Afterward they assured me it was the one thing in the world which gave them the most pleasure and that they most wished for.

As I have said, they and those at Tacuba strongly wished for me to come there, and with good reason, for both garrisons were in the midst of such multitudes of enemies. But Our Lord miraculously inspired them and diminished the enemy's courage so that they could not decide to attack our camp. Had they done so, they would have done great harm to the Spaniards, although they were always well prepared and determined to conquer or die, like men cut off from all succor save what they hoped from God. When the garrison of Cuyoacan saw us pursuing the canoes, most of the horsemen and foot soldiers took the road toward the city of Temixtitan and fought very stoutly with the Indians who were on the causeway. They captured the trenches which had been made and victoriously advanced a long league on the causeway until they reached the place where I stopped with the brigantines.

We continued chasing the canoes with the brigantines for nearly three leagues. Those which escaped us took refuge among the houses of the city, and as it was already vespers I ordered the brigantines to retire. When we arrived at the causeway I determined to land with thirty men and capture two small towers of their idols, which were surrounded by a low wall of stone and mortar. They fought us very stoutly to defend them, but finally after much danger and trouble we captured them. I immediately landed and mounted three heavy iron field pieces I had brought. About half a league of the causeway between there and the city was crowded with the enemy, and on both sides of it the water was covered with canoes full of warriors. I therefore ordered one of the field pieces to be aimed and fired, which raked the causeway and did much execution among the enemy.

Although it had been my intention on first embarking in the brigantines to go to Cuyoacan and do as much damage as possible, as soon as I had landed on the causeway that day and had captured those two towers, I determined to establish my headquarters there and to keep the brigantines near the towers. I also ordered the force at Cuyoacan and some fifty of the alguacil mayor's soldiers to come there next day. We passed the night with caution, for all the people of the city gathered there on the causeway and on the water. At midnight a great multitude of people arrived in canoes and began to attack our camp. They threw us into great fear and alarm, especially as they never attacked or fought at night except when they were very sure of victory. But we were well prepared. Each brigantine carried one small field piece and we used these, and the archers and musketeers did their part. So they left off attacking us for the remainder of the night.

Next morning at daybreak there arrived at my camp on the causeway fifteen archers and musketeers, fifty men armed with swords and shields, and seven or eight horsemen from the garrison at Cuyoacan. When they got there, those of the city were fighting with us from canoes and on the causeway. The multitude was such that on land and on water we could see nothing but people, shouting and yelling so that it seemed the world was sinking. We fought with them, doing such damage with the field pieces and the horsemen that we almost shut them up amid the first houses of the city.

Many canoes were collected on the other side of the causeway, where the brigantines could not pass, and did us much harm with arrows and darts. I ordered an opening to be made in the causeway near our camp, and sent four brigantines through. The enemy did not dare to come out into the open. On the other side of the causeway the other eight brigantines fought with the canoes and burned many of the houses in the outskirts. We spent all that day fighting.

The following day Sandoval departed with his people for Cuyoacan, where there is another causeway about a league and half in length to the mainland. When I learned that the Indians had made a great breach in this causeway, which our people could not easily cross, I sent two brigantines to help them, and these were used as bridges for the foot soldiers. Once across, they went to camp at Cuyoacan, and Sandoval with ten horsemen took the causeway road to our camp. Upon his arrival he found us fighting, so he and his men joined in. The enemy pierced his foot with a dart, but although he and some others were wounded that day, we did such harm among the enemy with the large field pieces and crossbows and muskets that neither those in the canoes nor those on the causeway dared come near us. They showed more fear and less pride than they had formerly exhibited. Thus for six days we had daily combat with them, and the brigantines set fire to all the houses they could in the outskirts of the city, and penetrated to the heart of it. None of the canoes dared to come within a quarter of a league of our camp.

The next day Pedro de Alvarado, captain of the garrison at Tacuba,

reported to me that the people of Temixtitan came in and out as they
pleased by a highway which leads to some towns on the mainland,
and by another small one which joins it. He believed that if they
found themselves hard pressed, they could escape by that way. I
desired their departure more than they themselves did, as we could
more easily overcome them on the mainland than in the big fortress
they had on the water. Nevertheless, in order to shut them in completely so that they could not profit by anything from the mainland, I
ordered the alguacil mayor, even though he was wounded, to plant
his camp at a little village at the end of one of the two causeways. He
left with twenty-three horsemen, a hundred foot soldiers, eighteen archers and musketeers, leaving me fifty other soldiers for my company.
The next day he planted his camp where I had commanded him.
From then on the city of Temixtitan was surrounded on all sides
wherever they could reach the mainland by the causeways.

As we had the enemy completely surrounded and had many friendly
warriors, I decided to penetrate into the city as far as possible by the
causeway, while the brigantines covered our rear on both sides. I
ordered some horsemen and foot soldiers of the divison in Cuyoacan
to join us, and ten horsemen to remain at the entrance of the causeway
to protect our rear. It seemed best that some force should remain in
Cuyoacan, because the natives of many of the cities on the lake were
rebellious and in favor of those of the city. If they wished to take us
on our rear, we would be protected by those ten or twelve horsemen I
had ordered to guard the causeway, while many more remained in
Cuyoacan with more than ten thousand Indian allies. I likewise
ordered Sandoval and Pedro de Alvarado to attack from their positions that same day, for I wished to gain as much of the city as possible.

The enemy fought valiantly, and on both sides of the street there
was an infinite number of them fighting very stoutly from the roofs.
But when some archers and musketeers arrived and we fired with
two field pieces up the street, we did them much damage.

The Spaniards and our allies captured the court of the idols, and
remained in it and on the towers for a long while. When the inhabitants of the city discovered there were no horsemen, they turned against
the Spaniards, who were unable to withstand the force of the enemy
and had to retreat exposed to great danger. In the midst of this retreat
it pleased God that three horsemen should advance into the square.

When the enemy saw them they believed there were more, and took to flight. The horsemen killed some of them and recaptured the court and enclosure.

As it was now late, I ordered our people to collect and retire.

In the meantime Don Fernando, lord of Texcoco and the province of Aculuacan, of whom I have already made mention to Your Majesty, succeeded in winning over all the natives of his city and province to our friendship. Many chiefs and the brothers of Don Fernando daily joined him, determined to declare for us and fight against those of Mexico and Temixtitan.

One of them, Istrisuchil, who is twenty-three or twenty-four years of age, very brave and beloved and feared of all, he sent as captain. Istrisuchil arrived at the camp on the causeway with more than thirty thousand warriors very well supplied in their fashion, and another twenty thousand joined the other two camps. I received them gladly, thanking them for their good disposition and conduct. Your Caesarian Majesty may well judge how valuable was this help and friendship from Don Fernando, and how those of Temixtitan felt to see those whom they considered their vassals, friends, relatives, and even fathers, brothers and sons, marching against them.

I sent three brigantines to each of the other camps, keeping seven, and I instructed the captains that as supplies of fresh water, fruits, maize and other provisions came from the mainland on those sides, they should cruise about in turns both day and night. Moreover, they should back up our people when we planned an assault to force an entrance into the city. The allotment of these six brigantines to the other two camps was a necessary and profitable measure, for every day and night they captured many canoes and prisoners.

The captains having been instructed and the people prepared and equipped, I left our quarters next morning with twenty horsemen and three hundred Spaniards and all our allies, an infinite number. Advancing along the causeway, we found the enemy already waiting for us, three bowshots from the camp, yelling fearfully. During the three preceding days there had been no fighting, and so the Indians had undone all we had accomplished in filling up the breaches in the causeway, making them very much stronger and more dangerous to capture than before.

The brigantines accompanied us on both sides, for they could approach very near and do much damage with field pieces, muskets and crossbows. Discovering this, our men landed and captured the breastworks and the bridge. We crossed to the other side and pursued the enemy, capturing the other breastworks and bridges, although with greater trouble and danger than before, and expelling them from the street and square where the great houses of the city stand. I ordered that no Spaniard should leave there while I and our allies were filling the breaks in the causeway with stones and adobe. This was such a labor that although ten thousand Indians helped us it was the hour of vespers when we finished making repairs. During all this time the Spaniards and our allies were constantly fighting and skirmishing and preparing the ambushes in which many of the enemy perished.

I rode with the horsemen through the city for a while, and in the streets where there is no water we killed with our lances all whom we could catch, and so held them at a distance. They did not dare attack us on dry land. Seeing that they were so rebellious and showed such determination to defend themselves to the death, I inferred two things: first, that we should recover little or none of the treasures they had taken from us, and the other, that they gave occasion and forced us to totally destroy them. This last reason caused me the greater grief, for it weighed on my soul and made me reflect on what means I might employ to frighten them so that they should realize their error and the injury they would sustain from us. I kept on burning and destroying the towers of their idols and their houses. In order to make them feel it more, I ordered the great houses in the square set afire. This seemed to cause immense sorrow to the enemy as well as to their allies in the cities about the lake, for none of them ever thought our force would be sufficient to penetrate so far into the city.

After setting fire to the houses, it was already late and I collected our people to return to our camp. When those of the city saw we were retiring, an infinite number of them charged us and fell upon us furiously. As the whole street was available to the horsemen, we turned on them, lancing many every time. Nevertheless they kept on attacking our rear guard, yelling all the time. My seven brigantines also had entered that day into the city by the water streets and burned a greater part of it.

On this day the enemy felt and showed great dismay at seeing us burning and destroying their city, and our native allies fighting against them, each shouting the name of his province. In one quarter they saw those of Tlascaltecal, all showing them their countrymen cut in pieces, telling them they would sup off them that night and breakfast off them next morning, as in fact they did. We returned to our camp to rest, for we had labored much during that day.

It may seem to Your Majesty that after having gone through such danger to gain these bridges and barricades, we were negligent in not holding them, rather than be obliged every day to face so much danger and trouble. Certainly it must appear so to those who were not there. But Your Majesty should know that this could in no wise be done, because two things were required to do it: either the camp transferred from where it was to the square enclosure of the towers of the idols, or a guard placed at the bridges during the night. Neither one nor the other could be done without great danger, nor was it possible; for if we had placed the camp in the city, we should have had to fight them day and night and at every hour. They would have given us intolerable labor, attacking us on every side, they being so many and we so few. As for placing people to guard the bridges by night, the Spaniards were so weary after fighting all day that it was impossible to do this. Hence we were obliged to retake them every day when we entered the city.

During all this time the natives of Iztapalapa, Oichilobuzco, Culuacan, Mezquique and Cuitaguaca, which are on the fresh-water lake, would never seek peace, nor had we all this time sustained injury from them. As the Calcans were very loyal vassals of Your Majesty and saw that we had enough to do with those of the great city, they joined with other towns on the borders of the lake to do all the damage they could to the towns on the water. Seeing we were daily victorious over those of Temixtitan, and on account of the injury they were sustaining and might sustain from our friends, these rebellious natives determined to come to us. They arrived in our camp and besought me to pardon them the past, and to order the Calcans and their other neighbors to do them no further injury.

I told them I was pleased with this and harbored no anger against any except those of the city. That we might believe their friendship sincere, I prayed them that inasmuch as I was determined not to raise the siege till I had taken the city by peace or war, and as they had many canoes capable of aiding me, they should prepare everything they could with as many warriors as were in their towns, to aid us on the water. I also asked them, as it was the rainy season and the Spaniards had few and miserable huts, to build us as many houses in the camp as they could, and to bring adobe and beams from the houses in the city which were nearest to the camp. All this they did, and also supplied us with provisions, of which we stood in great need.

As we on our side had entered the city two or three days successively, besides three or four before, and had always been victorious against the enemy and had killed an infinite number, we thought that any hour they would move to propose peace, which we desired as our salvation; but nothing availed to bring them to this determination. To reduce them to greater straits and to try to force them to make peace, I decided to enter the city each day in three or four divisions. I therefore ordered all the people of the cities situated on the water to come in their canoes. That day there were in our camp more than a hundred thousand allies. I ordered the four brigantines, with half the canoes—as many as fifteen hundred—to go on one side, and the other three, with as many more canoes, to go on another, and overrun the greater part of the city and burn and do all the damage they could.

I entered by the principal street and found it all free up to the large houses of the square, none of the bridges having been opened. I advanced to the street which leads to Tacuba, where there were six or seven bridges. From there I ordered a captain to enter another street, with sixty or seventy men and six horsemen to protect their rear, and with them went more than ten or twelve thousand Indians, our friends. Another captain was to do the same in another street; and I, with the remaining people, advanced on the street to Tacuba.

I wished to occupy that street so that the people of Pedro de Alvarado's camp might communicate with ours and go from one camp to the other, and the brigantines the same. That day was one of great victory both on water as well as land, and some plunder was obtained from the city. In the camps of Sandoval and Pedro de Alvarado there was also great victory.

On that day and the day before, I was positive they would sue for peace, in favor of which, with or without victory, I made every demonstration I could. Nevertheless, we saw no sign of peace in them, and we retired that day to our camp very gladly although we were grieved to our very hearts to see their determination to die.

In these past days Pedro de Alvarado had also attacked them briskly and had captured many bridges. In order to hold and defend them, he placed a guard of foot soldiers and horsemen on them throughout the night, while the remainder of his people returned to camp, three-quarters of a league from there. As this labor was unendurable, he

determined to move his camp to the end of the causeway leading to
the market place of Temixtitan, which has a larger square, all surrounded by arcades. To reach it, it was necessary to capture only
two or three more bridges. As they were very broad and dangerous,
he was occupied in it some days, during which he fought constantly
and obtained victory. He got such a taste of victory that he determined
to go farther and capture a bridge where they had destroyed the causeway for more than sixty paces, and where the water had entered to a
depth of about nine feet. He crossed the water, captured the bridge
and pursued the enemy, who fled. Pedro de Alvarado hastened to
have that pass filled so that the horsemen might cross, and also because I had daily admonished him by writing and by word of mouth
not to gain a palm of ground without having the exit and the entrance
for the horsemen absolutely assured, as they in reality sustained the
war. When the enemy saw there were only forty or fifty Spaniards
and some of our friends on the other side, and that the horsemen could
not cross, they turned on them so quickly that they drove them back
and into the water. Some of our friends were killed and three or
four Spaniards captured alive. These were immediately sacrificed.

Finally Pedro de Alvarado retired to his camp, and when I arrived
in ours that day and learned what had happened, it caused me the
greatest grief in the world, as this was an event to encourage the
enemy, who might think that we would not again dare to enter.

The morning after the day of Pedro de Alvarado's disaster, I went
to his camp to rebuke him for what had happened, to see what had
been accomplished and where he had moved his camp, and to advise
him as to his security and the attack on the enemy. I was so astonished to see how far toward the middle of the city his camp was, and
the bad places and bridges he had taken, that I no longer blamed him
so much as he had seemed to deserve.

I then effected several entries into the city at the usual points. The
brigantines and canoes fought in two places, and I in four others within
the city, and we always obtained the victory, killing many of the
adversaries. I hesitated to penetrate farther into the city, on the one
hand hoping that our enemies might reconsider their determination and
stubbornness, and on the other because our entrance could not be
effected without great danger, as they were very united, strong and
desperate unto death. The Spaniards, who had fought ceaselessly for
more than twenty days, importuned me again to enter and take the
marketplace. If we gained that, they said, the enemy would have little

space left from which to defend themselves. If they did not surrender, they would die from hunger and thirst.

When I excused myself, the treasurer-accountant of Your Majesty told me that the entire camp insisted upon it and that I ought to do it. I answered him and other persons who were in favor of this plan that their object and wish were excellent, and that I desired to do it more than anybody else. I was forced by his importunity to tell him the reason why I did not do it, which was that although he and others approved of it, there might be some who, on account of the great danger, would not. Finally they forced me so much that I agreed to do what I could after first consulting the people of the other camps.

The next day I conferred with some of the principal persons of our camp, and we agreed to notify Sandoval and Pedro de Alvarado that we would enter the city on the following day and make an effort to reach the marketplace. The course they were to follow was this: Sandoval was to come with ten horsemen, one hundred foot soldiers and fifteen musketeers to Pedro de Alvarado's camp. He was to leave in his own camp ten other horsemen, to lie in ambush behind some houses at the hour of the next day's battle. He was to remove all his baggage as though he were breaking up his camp, so that when the enemy came in pursuit those in ambush would fall upon their rear. Sandoval with his three brigantines and the three of Pedro de Alvarado was to take that bad pass, where Pedro de Alvarado had been routed. They were not to advance one step beyond without having first filled it up and repaired it. If they could advance to the marketplace without any great risk or danger, they were to make every effort to do so, as I would do the same. They were to note well that although I sent to say this, I did not oblige them to advance a single step which might expose them to any defeat or mishap. This I said because I knew them, and that they would put their face to what I ordered them, even though they knew that by it they might lose their lives.

The seven brigantines, with more than three hundred canoes of our friends, left our camp next day. With twenty-five horsemen, my people, and seventy men from the camp of Tacuba, I began our march and entered the city, where I divided them. From the point we had already reached, three streets led to the marketplace. Into the principal one, I told Your Majesty's treasurer and accountant, Julian de Alderete, to enter with seventy men and more than fifteen or twenty thousand of our friends, and with seven horsemen in his rear. As they captured the bridges and barricades these should be filled up. Two narrower streets led from the streets of Tacuba to the marketplace, having more causeways, bridges and water streets. I ordered two captains to enter by the broader one, with eighty men and more than ten thousand Indians, our friends. At the mouth of the street of Tacuba I placed two heavy field pieces with eight horsemen to guard them. With eight other horsemen and one hundred foot soldiers, among whom were more than twenty-five archers and musketeers, and with an infinite number of our friends, I pursued my road, penetrating by the other narrow street as far as possible.

I halted the horsemen at the entrance of it and ordered them on no account to advance from there nor to follow after me unless I first ordered· them to do so. I then dismounted and we advanced to a barricade they had made at the end of a bridge, which we took with a small field piece. The archers and musketeers advanced by a causeway the enemy had broken at two or three different places. Besides these three battles we waged, our friends who entered by the roofs and other places were so numerous that it did not seem anything could resist us. The Spaniards took those two bridges, the barricades and the causeway. I remained with about twenty Spaniards on a small island. Meanwhile our friends advanced by the street, not taking any spoils, but fighting the enemy, who sometimes would repel them and drive them into the water. With our assistance, however, they would turn again upon them. Besides this we took care that from certain cross streets those of the city should not sally out to take at their backs the advancing Spaniards.

Our allies sent to tell me at this time that they had advanced a good distance and were not very far from the marketplace. In any case they wished to push on because they already heard the battle which Sandoval and Pedro de Alvarado were waging on their side.

I sent orders that they should on no account advance a step without leaving the bridges well filled up, so that if they needed to retreat the water would be no obstacle, for therein lay the danger. They returned to tell me that all they had gained were well repaired and I might go myself and see if it was so. Dreading that they might go astray ·and commit blunders in filling up the ditches, I went there and found that they had passed over a ditch in the street which was ten paces broad, with water flowing through it ten feet in depth, and that in passing they had thrown wood and maize and reed grass into it. As they had passed few at a time and with care, the wood and maize had not sunk. In the joy of victory they were going ahead so recklessly that they believed the work had been thoroughly done.

The moment I reached that wretched bridge I saw the Spaniards and many of our friends returning in full flight, and the enemy like dogs setting on them. Seeing the impending mishap, I began to cry, "Stop! Stop!" but when I arrived at the water I found it full of Spaniards and Indians as though not one straw had been put into it. The enemy charged so furiously that they threw themselves in to the water with the Spaniards, and their canoes came by the water streets and captured the Spaniards alive.

As the affair came about so suddenly, and I saw the people being killed, I determined to remain there and die fighting. The most that I and my men could do was lend our hands to some unlucky Spaniards who were drowning and help them out. Some came out wounded and others half drowned and others without weapons. I sent them on ahead. Such was the number of the enemy that they surrounded me and some ten or fifteen who had remained with me.

Being entirely occupied in helping those who were drowning, I had not observed or thought of my own danger. Already some Indians had grasped me and would have carried me away had it not been for a captain of fifty whom I always had with me, and a youth of my company who, after God, gave me my life, and in giving it lost his own.

Meanwhile the Spaniards who had been routed were retreating by the causeway. It was small and narrow and on a level with the water, which those dogs had intentionally prepared in this manner. As many of our own friends who had been put to rout were also going by it, the road was so encumbered and there was such a delay in advancing that the enemy had time to come up from both sides and take and kill as many as they chose. And that captain who was with me, called Antonio de Quinomes, said to me, "Let us go away from here and save yourself, as you know that without you none of us can escape." When he could not prevail upon me to go, he grasped me by the arms to force me to retire. Although I would have rejoiced more in death than in life, by his importunity and that of my other companions we began to withdraw, fighting with our swords and bucklers against the enemy who surrounded us.

In the midst of this great conflict, waiting for the people to pass that small causeway and reach safety while we held back the enemy, a servant of mine arrived with a horse. Another young servant of mine called Cristóbal de Guzman mounted a horse to bring to me, but he and the horse were killed before they reached me. His death filled the whole camp with such sadness that the sorrow of those who knew him is still fresh today. Finally it pleased God that those who were left reached the street of Tacuba, which is very broad. I collected the people and stopped in the rear, where the enemy were charging with such triumph and pride it seemed they would leave nobody alive.

Retiring as best I could, I sent word to the treasurer-accountant to retreat to the square in good order. I sent the same order to the other two captains who had entered by the street leading to the market, both of whom had fought valiantly and captured many barricades and bridges, which they completely filled up so that they were able to retreat without injury. Before the treasurer-accountant retired from the breastwork where they were fighting, those of the city had already thrown two or three heads of Christians at them, although then they did not know whether they came from Pedro de Alvarado's camp or from ours. We all gathered in the square, so many of the enemy charging on us from every side that we had enough to do to keep them off. Even in places where before this rout they would never have dared to come, they killed three horsemen and ten soldiers.

Immediately after, in one of the towers of their idols which was near the square, they offered many perfumes and incense of gums to their idols in sign of victory. Even if we had wanted to stop this, it could not be done, as almost all the people were already hastening toward the camp. In this rout, the enemy killed thirty-five or forty Spaniards and more than one thousand friendly Indians, and wounded more than twenty Christians. I came out wounded in one leg. A small field piece was lost, and many crossbows, muskets and arms.

After obtaining this victory the defenders of the city, in order to frighten Sandoval and Pedro de Alvarado, took all the living and dead Spaniards whom they had captured to Tlateloco, which is the market, and in some lofty towers there they stripped them and sacrificed them, opening their breasts and taking out their hearts to offer them to the idols. This the Spaniards in Pedro de Alvarado's camp could see from where they were fighting, and in the naked white bodies which they saw sacrificed, they recognized that they were Christians. Although they were saddened and dismayed by this, they retreated into their camp. The marketplace would have been won that day if God, on account of our sins, had not permitted so great a misfortune.

We returned to our camp sadly, somewhat earlier than we were accustomed to because we heard the brigantines were lost as the Mexicans had fallen on our rear with the canoes, though it pleased God that this should not be true. The brigantines and canoes of our friends had indeed found themselves in tight straits. A brigantine was almost lost, and the captain and the master both wounded, the captain dying eight days later.

That day and the following night the people of the city rejoiced greatly with trumpets and kettledrums so that it seemed the very world was sinking, and they opened all the streets and bridges over the water as they had been before, and lighted fires and placed night watchmen at a distance of two bowshots from our camp; for, as we were all so disordered and wounded and without arms, we needed to rest and recuperate. Meanwhile the enemy had time to send their messengers to many provinces subject to them, telling them how they had obtained a great victory and killed many Christians, and that they would soon finish all of us, and that by no means would they sue for peace with us. The proofs they carried were the heads of the two horses and some of those Christians they had killed, carrying them about and showing them wherever it seemed useful, which confirmed the rebels more than ever in their stubbornness. However, lest they should become too proud and guess our weakness, some Spaniards on foot and on horseback, with many of our friends, would go into the city to fight every day, although they never could gain more than a few of the bridges of the street before the square.

A chief of Tlascaltecal called Chichimecatecle, who had brought the timbers for the brigantines from that province, had stayed with his people since the beginning of the war, in the camp of Pedro de Alvarado. After our rout, when he saw that the Spaniards did not fight as before, he determined to make an entrance with only his own people. Leaving four hundred of his bowmen at a dangerous broken bridge he had taken, he and his people advanced with great shouts, cheering and naming their province and lord. They fought very bravely, and there were many wounded and dead on both sides. Those of the city believed they had trapped them because it is their custom, when their adversaries retire, to follow them with much persistence, taking their revenge when the adversaries cross the water, where there is some danger. To forestall this, Chichimecatecle had left the four hundred bowmen at the water pass, and his warriors threw themselves into the water and crossed under the protection of the bowmen, leaving the enemy greatly surprised at the resistance they encountered and at the daring which Chichimecatecle had displayed.

While some Spaniards fought on in the city, I had to dispatch horsemen and foot soldiers, which I could ill spare, to aid friendly Indians who came to ask me for help against vassals and allies of the Culuans. God knows the danger which attended all who went as well as all who were left. But, as it was necessary to show more valor than ever, we hid our weakness from friends as well as from foes, and went to their aid.

The citizens of Temixtitan had sent word to ask our interpreter to come because they desired to discuss peace, which, as it appeared, they wished only on the condition that we should all leave the country. Their object was to rest some days and furnish themselves with necessaries, although we never overcame their disposition to fight. While engaged in these parleys with the interpreter, our people were very near the enemy with only a broken-down bridge between them. An old man among them, in full sight of all, very slowly drew from his provision bag some things which he ate, so as to give us to understand that they were not in want, for we had told them that they would starve to death.

At this our friends assured the Spaniards that the peace was all a pretense and that they wished to fight. Through that day, no other fighting took place. That night, those of the city fell upon the camp of Alvarado at a quarter before dawn. The watchmen perceived them, and called "To arms!" and those who were ready charged on them.

When the enemy saw the horsemen they threw themselves into the water. In the meantime our people came up and fought them for three hours. From the camp we heard one of the field pieces firing and, fearing they might be routed, we ordered the people to arm themselves and enter the city so as to draw off the attack from Alvarado. The Indians found the Spaniards so courageous that they returned to the city, where we continued to fight during the day.

By this time those who had been wounded in our rout were already recovered, and the ship belonging to Juan Ponce de León, who had formerly been routed in the country or island of Florida, arrived at Villa Rica. They sent me powder and crossbows, of which we stood in extreme need, and now, thanks to God, all about here there is no province not in our favor.

Seeing that the people of the city were so rebellious, and displayed such determination to die as no race had ever shown, I knew not what means to adopt to relieve our dangers and hardships, and to avoid utterly destroying them and their city, which was the most beautiful thing in the world. It was useless to tell them that we would not raise our camps, or that the brigantines would not cease to make war on them, or that nowhere in the country was anyone left to help them, or that they could not obtain maize or wheat or fruit or water or any provisions from anywhere. The more I spoke of these things, the less sign of yielding did we see in them. Rather we found them more courageous than ever both in their fighting and scheming.

Seeing that already more than forty-five days had been spent in this siege, I determined to take measures for our security and to further straiten the enemy. This latter consisted in our gaining the streets of the city and demolishing all the houses on both sides so that henceforward we would not go one step ahead without leveling everything. What was water was made into dry land, no matter how much time it took.

I called the lords and chiefs of our allies and told them what I had determined, so that they might have their workmen bring their spades and coas, which are certain poles which they use, similar to the Spanish hoe. They answered me that they would do this willingly, for it was a very good decision. They rejoiced greatly at it, because they perceived that in this way the city would be destroyed, which is what they desired more than anything else in the world.

Three or four days passed in organizing this plan. The people of the city easily divined that we were planning some mischief against them, and they also, as it afterward appeared, were arranging what they could for their defense. Having agreed with our friends that we would attack them by land and water, the next morning after having heard Mass we took the road to the city.

When we reached the water pass and barricade near the great houses of the square, intending to attack them, the people of the city asked us to be quiet as they wished to sue for peace. I ordered my people to cease fighting and said that the lord of the city should come there to speak to me and arrange the conditions of the peace. Telling me that they had already gone to call him, they detained me for more than an hour. But in truth they did not want peace, as they immediately showed. While we were quiet they began to throw adobe and darts and stones at us. When I saw this I attacked the barricades and captured them. We found both the square and some of the streets strewn with large stones to impede the horses, which generally do the most fighting. During the rest of that day, we filled up the water street which leads out from the square, so that the Indians never opened it again. Thenceforward we began, little by little, every day, to destroy the houses, to shut up and fill in completely the streets and to level the dangerous passes as we captured them. We were accompanied into the city by more than one hundred fifty thousand warriors, some of them leveling, some burning the houses, and others fighting, while the horsemen guarded the rear of all. Thus a good deal was accomplished, and we again reached as far as the enclosure and large court where the towers of the idols are.

Each day I ascended the highest tower, so that the Indians might recognize me, for I also knew that they would be much vexed to see me mounted on the tower. From there I encouraged our friends and gave aid wherever it was necessary.

In this wise and order, we entered the city on the five or six following days. Always at the hour of retreat we would put our allies ahead and post a number of Spaniards in ambush in some of the houses, the horsemen remaining behind and feigning to retreat hastily, so as to bring them out of the square. With these and the ambushes of the foot soldiers we would kill some of them every afternoon with our lances.

One afternoon I called Sandoval by messenger to come to our camp before daybreak with fifteen of his own and Pedro de Alvarado's horsemen. He arrived the following morning, and I obtained another twenty-five horsemen from those at Cuyoacan, so that there were forty in all. Ten of them I ordered to join in the morning with our force, and in conjunction with the brigantines to go in the same order as heretofore to attack the enemy and to destroy and capture everything possible. When the time came for them to retire I would start with the other thirty horsemen. When the larger part of the city was demolished, they were to drive the enemy into their entrenchments and water streets, keeping them there until the hour of retiring. Then I and the other thirty horsemen would secretly form an ambuscade in the large houses in the square.

The Spaniards did as I ordered, and at one o'clock after mid-day I set out with the thirty horsemen and stationed them in those houses while I went to the city and mounted the high tower as usual. While I was there some Spaniards opened a sepulchre and in it found more than fifteen hundred castellanos worth of articles in gold.

At the hour of retiring I ordered the Spaniards to begin to withdraw in a compact body, and that from the first moment of leaving the square the horsemen should feign an attack, behaving as though they hardly dared to make it and choosing the time when they saw a great number of people in and about the whole square. The men posted in ambush longed for the hour to arrive because they much desired to act their part well and were already tired of waiting. I then joined them as the infantry and horsemen began retiring through the square, accompanied by the Indians our friends, who understood all about the ambush.

The enemy rushed out, yelling as if they had gained the greatest victory in the whole world, and the nine horsemen feigned to charge them across the square and then suddenly to fall back. When they had done this twice the enemy acquired such fury that they pressed up to the very croups of the horses and were thus decoyed toward the end of the street where the ambush was laid. When we saw the Spaniards had passed ahead of us and heard the shot of a gun, which was the signal agreed upon, we knew that the time to sally forth had arrived. With the cry of "Señor Santiago!" we suddenly fell upon them and rushed forward into the square with our lances, overthrowing and stopping many, whom our friends, who joined in the pursuit, were able to capture.

In this ambush more than five hundred, all the bravest and most valiant of their principal men, were killed. That night our allies supped well because they cut up and ate all those whom they had killed and captured. Such was the fright and wonder of the enemy at seeing themselves suddenly routed that there was no more shouting the whole afternoon, nor did they dare show their heads in the streets nor on the roofs except where they were entirely protected and safe.

The consternation of the enemy from this, our victory, was so great that during the rest of the war they never again dared to enter the square when we were retiring, even if only one horseman was there; nor did they ever dare to come out against an Indian or foot soldier, fearing that another ambush might spring up beneath their feet. The victory God was pleased to give us that day was one of the principal reasons why the city was taken sooner, for the natives were dismayed by it and our friends doubly encouraged. We returned to our camp, intending to hasten on the war and, until we finished it, not to let a single day pass without entering the city.

We already knew that the Indians of the city were much discouraged, and two poor creatures who came out by night to our camp because they were starving told us that during the night they came to hunt among the houses and search in those parts we had already captured, looking for herbs and wood and roots to eat.

The next morning we again entered the city. As our friends had observed the systematic order we followed in the destruction of it, the multitude which daily came with us was beyond all reckoning. We finished taking the whole street of Tacuba that day and filling up the bad places in it, so that the people from Pedro de Alvarado's camp could communicate with us through the city. We won two other bridges on the principal street leading to the marketplace, and we burned the houses of the lord of the city, who was a youth of eighteen called Quatamucin, the second ruler since the death of Montezuma. Three of the four quarters of the city were already ours, and the Indians could only retreat to the strongest part of it, which comprised the houses farthest out in the water.

While preparing to return to the city about nine o'clock two mornings after the feast of the Apostle Santiago, July 25, we observed from our camp that smoke was rising from the two highest towers. This we could not understand, for it seemed something more than the incensing which the Indians usually made to their idols. We suspected that Pedro de Alvarado's men had arrived there, and although this was the fact we could not believe it. Pedro de Alvarado's men certainly behaved very valiantly, for there were many bridges and barricades to capture and the greater part of the enemy always came to defend them. But he saw that on our side we were hedging the enemy in, and he did everything he could to enter the marketplace, where their whole strength was centered. However, he could arrive only within sight of it and capture those towers and many others which adjoin the same marketplace, forming an enclosure almost like that of many of the towers in the city. The horsemen had hard work and were forced to retreat to their camp with their horses wounded.

On the morning after this we encountered no obstacle before reaching the marketplace except a water course and a barricade near a small tower. This we attacked. The standard bearer and two or three other Spaniards threw themselves into the water, so the defenders immediately abandoned the pass, which we filled and made passable for horsemen.

While we were repairing it, Pedro de Alvarado arrived by the same street with four horsemen, to our mutual satisfaction, for this was the way speedily to finish the war. We reconnoitered the square for a short time, inspecting its arcades whose roofs were full of the enemy. I ascended that large tower which adjoins the marketplace, in which, and in others also, we found the heads of the Christians they had killed and offered to their idols. I saw from that tower that we had without doubt captured seven-eighths of the city.

In such straits the enemy could not possibly hold out. Those houses left them were far too small for such large numbers, and above all a great famine prevailed among them, for we found the gnawed roots and bark of trees in the streets.

I determined to suspend fighting for a day and devise some measure to save this multitude of people from perishing. The harm done them caused me such compassion and distress that I continually importuned them with offers of peace, but they answered that in no wise would they surrender, but that if only one man were left, he would die fighting. All they possessed we could never obtain, for they would burn it and throw it into the water. Not wishing to return evil for evil, I dissembled and refrained from fighting.

As very little powder was left to us, we had in the last fifteen days discussed making a catapult. Though there was no first-class masterworkman who knew how to do it, some carpenters offered to make a small one. Although I believed that we could not succeed in this work, I consented that they should make it while we had the Indians cornered. It was finished and taken to the marketplace. Three or four days were occupied in placing the catapult and the friendly Indians threatened those of the city with it, telling them that with this engine we would kill them all. It was useless. The deception was a double one because the carpenters did not fulfill their design, and the defenders of the city did not surrender. I disguised the failure of the catapult by pretending that, moved by compassion, we forbore to kill them all.

The day after placing the catapult, we returned to the city. Three or four days had passed without any fighting, and we found the streets full of women and children and other miserable people who came out so emaciated and thin that it was the greatest pity in the world to behold them. I ordered our friends not to hurt them. But none of the warriors appeared where any harm could reach them, though we saw them on the tops of their roofs. They were prepared to fight with us, and I ordered Pedro de Alvarado to enter with all his people through a large quarter which the enemy held. I, with those of our camp, came on foot from another side, because we could not avail ourselves of the horsemen. The first encounter between us and our enemies was very stubborn, but finally we won that whole quarter. Such was the slaughter committed upon our enemies that between killed and wounded there were more than twelve thousand.

Our allies handled the enemy most cruelly, for they would in no wise spare any life, although they were reproved and punished by us.

In the city next day I ordered that no fighting should take place nor any harm be done to the enemy. When they saw such a multitude of people, and their own vassals and subjects arrayed against them, and saw their extreme necessity which left them not even a place to stand save upon the bodies of their own dead, they said they all desired to be out of it and asked us why we did not put an end to them. Then suddenly they told my people to call me as they wished to speak to me. All the Spaniards wished that this war might finally end, and pitying such misery they rejoiced, believing that the Indians wanted peace. So they came gladly to importune me to come to a barricade where certain chiefs wished to speak to me. I thought that little profit would come of my going, but I went. I knew, however, their not surrendering depended only on the sovereign and some three or four other chiefs of the city.

When I arrived at the barricade, it was as I had thought. They begged me to finish killing them speedily and save them from so much suffering, because they wished to die and go to heaven to their Ochilobus, the idol which they hold in greatest reverence. I tried without success to persuade them to surrender.

In order to win them from their evil determination to die, I spoke to one of their noble chiefs, the uncle of Don Fernando, lord of Texcoco, who had been captured fighting in the city and whom we held prisoner. Although badly wounded, I asked him if he wished to return to the city, and he answered "yes." When we entered it the next day, I delivered him to the people of the city who received him with much deference as a nobleman. They took him before Quatamucin, their sovereign, and he began to speak of peace. It is said they immediately ordered him to be killed and sacrificed, and they gave us the answer we were awaiting with great yells, saying that they wanted nothing but death.

The next day we did not care to fight with our adversaries but only moved about in their city, because every hour and every moment we believed they would come to surrender.

Two days later some chiefs came to our camp very early in the morning and asked me to come to the square of the market of the city, because their sovereign wished to speak to me. Believing it was true, I mounted my horse and awaited him where it had been agreed for more than three or four hours, but he never chose to appear before me. I saw the mockery and sent for the Indians, our friends, who had been left at the entrance of the city almost a league from where we were. I had ordered them not to advance beyond there because the people of the city had asked me that, while treating for peace, none of them should be inside it. Neither they nor those of Pedro de Alvarado's camp delayed in coming, and when they arrived we attacked some of the barricades and water streets.

Before leaving the camp I had ordered Gonzalo de Sandoval to proceed with the brigantines to the place where the Indians had fortified themselves in the houses, thus holding them surrounded but not attacking them until he saw us begin to fight. And so they had no place to go except among the dead and on the roofs which were left them. They had neither arrows nor darts nor stones with which to hurt us. Our friends accompanied us, armed with swords and shields, and such was the slaughter done that day on water and land that, with prisoners taken, they numbered in all more than forty thousand men; and such were the shrieks and the weeping of the women and children that there was none whose heart did not break.

We had more trouble preventing our allies from killing and inflicting tortures than we had in fighting with the Indians, for no such inhuman cruelty as the natives of these parts practice was ever seen. Our allies obtained very great plunder, which we could not prevent, because we were about nine hundred Spaniards and they more than one hundred fifty thousand men. No attention or diligence was sufficient to prevent them from robbing, although we did everything possible to stop it. One of the reasons why I refused to go to extremes in those previous days was that, by taking them by assault, they would probably throw what they had into the lake, and if they did not do so, our allies would steal everything they found. For this reason, I feared that only a small part of the great wealth existing in the city, as shown by what I had before obtained for Your Highness, would be secured for Your Majesty. As it was already late and we could no longer endure the stench of the dead which had lain for many days in those streets—the most pestilential thing in the world—we returned to our camps.

When the next day had dawned I had our whole force prepared and the large field pieces brought out. The day before, I had ordered Pedro de Alvarado to await me in the square of the marketplace and not to begin fighting until I arrived. All being assembled, and the brigantines ready for action behind the houses on the water where the enemy were gathered, I ordered that on hearing a musket shot the land force should enter the small part which was still to be captured, and force the enemy toward the water where the brigantines would be awaiting them. I cautioned them particularly to look after Quatamucin and endeavor to take him alive, because then the war would stop.

I mounted the top of a roof and before the fight began spoke with some of the chiefs of the city whom I knew, saying that they ought not to be the cause of all perishing. I told them to call their lord and assured them that nobody need be afraid.

Two of those chiefs went to call him. After a short time they returned with one of the highest chiefs of all of them, who was called Ciguacoacin, captain and governor of them all, whose counsel was followed in everything concerning the war. I showed a very good disposition toward him so that he might be reassured and have no fears. Finally he told me that the sovereign would in no way appear before me, and that he preferred to die where he was. He himself was much grieved at this decision, but I could do as I pleased. Recognizing by this his determination, I told him to return to his own people. He and they might prepare themselves as I was determined to attack them and finish destroying them. And so it happened.

More than five hours had passed in these parleyings, and the inhabitants of the city were all treading on the dead. Others in the water were swimming, and others drowning themselves in the large lake where the canoes were collected. Such was their plight that no understanding could conceive how they could endure it. An infinite number of men, women and children kept coming toward us. In their haste they pushed one another back into the water and were drowned amid the multitude of dead. It appears they had perished to the number of fifty thousand from the salt water they drank, or from starvation and pestilence.

All these bodies, in order that we should not understand their extremity, were neither thrown into the water lest the brigantines should come across them, nor were they thrown outside their boundary, lest we should see them in the city. Thus, in the streets they occupied, were found heaps of dead, so that nobody could step without trampling them.

As the people of the city came toward us, I ordered Spaniards to be stationed in all the streets to prevent our allies from killing these unhappy creatures who were beyond number. I also ordered the captains of our allies not to allow those fugitives to be killed. But they were so many, it was not possible to prevent it that day, and more than fifteen thousand persons were massacred.

Meanwhile some of the chiefs and warriors of the city were brought to bay on some roofs and in the water, where they could no longer stop, or hide from us all their disasters and their weakness.

Seeing that the afternoon was coming on us, and that they would not surrender, I had two large field pieces directed against them to see whether they would surrender then. As this also brought no result, I ordered the signal of the musket to be fired, whereupon the corner they still held was immediately taken, and those who were in it were forced into the water. Others, who had not fought, surrendered. The brigantines swiftly entered that lake and broke into the midst of the fleet of canoes, and the warriors no longer ventured to fight.

It pleased God that the captain of a brigantine, called Garci Holguin, overtook a canoe in which there were some distinguished people. He had two or three crossbowmen in the prow of the brigantine, and, as he was crossing in front of the canoe, they signaled to him not to shoot because their sovereign was there. The canoe was quickly captured, and they took Quatamucin, and the lord of Tacuba, and the other chiefs who were with him. The captain immediately brought the sovereign and the other chief prisoners to the terrace where I was, which was near the lake. When I invited them to sit down, not wishing to show any rigor, he approached me and said to me in his language that he had done all he was bound to do to defend himself and his people, until he was reduced to that state, and that I might now do with him as I chose. Placing his hand on a dagger which I wore, he bade me stab him with it and kill him. I encouraged him, and told him not to be afraid.

This lord having been made prisoner, the war immediately ceased, which God Our Lord was pleased to bring to its end on this day, the Feast of San Hipolito, which was the 13th of August in the year 1521. So that from the day when we laid siege to the city, which was the 30th of May of the said year, until it was taken, seventy-five days passed, in which Your Majesty may perceive the hardships, dangers, and cruelties, which these, your vassals, suffered, and in which they so exposed themselves that their deeds will bear testimony of them.

With the city in his hands, Cortés turned his attention to the treasure he had left behind that fateful night over a year before. A search through the rubble revealed nothing. Torturing the ex-emperor Guatemoc uncovered the fact that some of the gold had been thrown into the lake, but divers scouring the bottom found none.

The soldiers who through the long siege and longer conquest had comforted themselves with hopes of riches were disgusted. Many of the officers turned their anger on Cortés. But he knew he had more than his men to worry him. He lacked the treasure to convince Charles the conquest had been justified without royal approval. He prepared his third letter describing the conquest, gathered all of the treasure he could find and sent it on to Spain. But he was dealing with a situation more serious than he suspected. While Cortés was conquering Mexico, his enemies were working effectively against him at home.

Two years earlier when he had sent that last ship to Spain before destroying the fleet at Vera Cruz, he had directed the master not to stop at Cuba. But his order had been ignored. The boat had put in to harbor, and Velásquez quickly had heard of Montezuma's gifts. Velásquez wrote to Spain, where he had the most powerful ally— Fonseca, the Bishop of Burgos, who ruled the Council of the Indies. The Bishop was not only a warm friend of Velásquez but was about to become a relative through marriage. He blocked the treasure from reaching the king for six months, and, possibly, prevented the first letter of Cortés from getting through.

With the Bishop's help, Velásquez obtained an order for an inquiry into Cortés' activities as well as a right of seizure of his person. However, the man sent to accomplish these things accepted the conquistador's bribe and departed. Finally, after a year of confusion, a board was formed to hear the accusations against Cortés. He was quickly cleared, and Velásquez was forbidden to interfere again.

A year after the conquest, Cortés was confirmed in the rank for which he had been fighting. He was appointed governor, captain-general and chief justice. But he had not spent the year waiting for recognition. The new Mexico City was already rising. A cathedral was being built on the site of the temple of the Aztec war god. A viceroy's palace of rough stone was taking shape as well as a fortress for the city. An expedition to the Pacific had founded the town of Zacatula, build a dock yard and started constructing four ships which would be used to explore the Pacific shoreline.

Cortés wrote the king that he intended to locate the strait from the North to the South Sea so that there would be a direct route to the Spice Islands. The energies of the conquerors were almost uncontrollable. Some of them even considered creating the strait if it did not exist. After Alvarado departed south for further conquest,

Cortés himself left the control of his capital in the hands of friends and set out through the swamps, rivers and jungle for Honduras, where one of his captains had mutinied. Cortés took the ex-emperor with him on his journey, and when he heard a rumor that the Indians were going to rise against him, he hanged Guatomoc and seven of his followers out of hand.

The captain-general and those with him converted the Indians they met with such energies and enthusiasm that one Indian chief who accepted the holy faith was given a horse as a gift. A century later two Franciscan padres journeying through the same country realized that the confusion left by Cortés was such that the Indians were worshiping an image of the horse.

When Cortés arrived in Honduras, the mutiny was already quelled and he had to rush home because the situation in Mexico City was chaotic. Those he had made his deputies had become his enemies. Rumors had been spread about his death. The city was being plundered, and his friends maltreated. Sailing to Vera Cruz, he arrived home in June, but the damage had already been done. The name of the conquistador had been badly smeared in every dispatch to Spain: Cortés poisoned his wife; Cortés pilfered the treasure; Cortés plots independence from Spain.

The threat of Cortés' power was enough to frighten Charles. The king appointed a successor to Cortés, but the successor died as did the next he named. Again the slander that Cortés had poisoned them. By the spring of 1528 the situation was untenable, and Cortés at the age of forty-three returned to the Spain he had not seen since he had left it as a boy of nineteen. But the edge was taken off the victorious homecoming. His father died that same spring and so did his most loyal friend—Sandoval, who had stood beside him throughout the conquest.

Charles treated the hero kindly. He granted him the title Marqués del Valle, gave him permission to explore the Pacific coastal area, raised him to the Order of Santiago and even visited him when he was ill. But Charles never gave Mexico back to Cortés, and on his return to New Spain Cortés was not permitted entry into his capital.

The conquistador withdrew to his home in Cuernavaca and threw his great energies into new breeds of cattle, new plants, hospital construction, church construction, new schools, and orphanages. But he became bored and turned again to the Pacific. By 1535 he had lost three ships, had visited Lower California and had discovered that the Viceroy Mendoza was blocking everything he attempted. Most of his fortune was gone, his title of captain-general empty. Finally, in despair, he went home to Spain for the last time.

He briefly took part in a foolish expedition to Algiers, where he watched Charles throw away opportunities for victory. He visited his children and wandered from place to place trying to get a hearing that would clear his debts, free his properties in New Spain for his use and let him return to his wife. He petitioned Charles for relief as his monies were being withheld for no reason other than the court's desire.

Sacred Catholic Caesarian Majesty:

I thought that the labor of my youth would have procured me repose in my old age, and thus for forty years I have given myself to God's service, deprived of sleep, eating poorly, and even at times not eating at all, with my arms always at my side, myself exposed to dangers and my fortune sacrificed to bring into His fold the sheep of a distant and unknown hemisphere, of which we even had no record, and to magnify the name and extend the patrimony of my King by conquering and bringing under his royal yoke and scepter the great kingdoms and dominions of barbarious people. And this I have done at my own expense, unaided in any way—nay, even hindered by emulous rivals, who like leeches have sucked my very blood.

Your Majesty has such a good memory you will not have forgotten that besides the words and promises your Majesty made me, I possess still more and greater ones in Your Majesty's letters. I do not know wherefore the promised benefits are withheld, nor why I am deprived of those I possessed.

I am old and poor, with more than twenty thousand ducats of debts in the kingdom, besides a hundred more which I brought or were sent after me, of which I also owe something for they were borrowed to be sent to me.

May your Majesty be pleased to order the judges to give their decision within a certain time Your Majesty shall fix without delay. This will be a great grace to me, for waiting is my loss, as I must return home being now no longer of an age to travel from inn to inn, but rather to withdraw and settle my account with God, for it is a long one, and little life is left me to discharge it; better to lose my estate than my soul.

May God our Lord grant the Royal Person of Your Majesty with the extension of your Kingdoms and glory as Your Majesty may desire. From Valladolid, the 3rd of February, 1544.

THE MARQUÉS DEL VALLE

No Reply Necessary is said to be written at the bottom of this letter, which lies in the archives.

Soon after the marriage of his daughter was broken off because he could not pay the dowry money, the old conquistador asked permission to return to Mexico. He died December 2, 1547, on his way to the harbor of Seville.

Alvarado
Wins
Guatemala

CARIBBEAN SEA

CARIBBEAN SEA

SOUTH SEA

Quezaltenango

Utatlan

Guatemala

Atiepac

Pasaco

Acatepeque

Cuzcaclan

Malalaca

Choluteco

ALVARADO

WINS

GUATEMALA

1523 — 1525

W E

0   50   100   150

4

Alvarado Wins Guatemala

IF THERE was a Golden Boy among the conquistadores, it was Pedro de Alvarado, a tall, absolutely ruthless, red-haired giant whom the Indians called Tonatiuh, which in Tlascalan meant "the Sun." Born in Badajoz, Estremadura, the same year as Cortés, Alvarado left Spain for Santo Domingo in 1510 with his five brothers. After eight years of dull plantation life, much of which was spent loafing in the company of Don Luis Colón, nephew of the Admiral, Alvarado joined the Grijalva expedition as one of five captains. Francisco de Montejo was another captain of the group. With a rashness that was to become evident in everything he did, Alvarado pressed ahead of the fleet, exposing both his ship and his men to the Indians. Although Grijalva reprimanded him for his rashness, the first treasure located was placed aboard Alvarado's vessel and rushed back to Cuba. By the time Grijalva returned, Governor Velásquez was already organizing the Cortés expedition.

Alvarado was named second in command with seventy Spaniards including Bernal Díaz del Castillo, the future chronicler, in his personal company. When the city of Vera Cruz was founded, Alvarado was named alcalde, and he was among those who requested that Cortés resign the commission granted him by Velásquez and lead the expedition to Mexico.

In the years that followed, Cortés leaned heavily on Alvarado, though there were times when the impetuous officer must have tried the captain-general. Alvarado was in command of the capital when Cortés went to the coast to deal with Narváez; and it was the blunder he made then which brought about the Night of Sorrows and the deaths of at least two hundred Spaniards. The exact details of this blunder have never been clear. With Cortés away, the Indians held a religious service. Whether they did so with the permission of Cortés or without it, and whether they intended human sacrifice or not, has never been clear, but Alvarado massacred the priests and chiefs who were attending; and this mass murder brought about the uprising that ended only with the total destruction of the city on the lake. Whatever responsibility Cortés laid to Alvarado for this, he protected his subordinate by ignoring the reason for the uprising in his own letter to the king.

Alvarado commanded the rear guard during the famous Night of Sorrows when Cortés retreated down the causeway with his men and plunder. As the main body passed, Alvarado is reported to have been left alone with an unbridged gap separating him from Cortés and his companions. According to the legend, the Aztecs became silent as they lowered their spears and approached him—the man they blamed for the massacre. Alvarado picked up a long lance lying at his feet, paused for one instant to face his enemies and then, rushing at the abutment, planted his lance on a piece of floating wreckage and vaulted to the far side. The Indians watched in astonishment and disbelief at what has become known as "Salto de Alvarado"—Alvarado's Leap.

In the process of retaking the city, Cortés destroyed it building for building, and when the conquest was complete he assigned Alvarado the task of constructing the new city. The restless conquistador labored for several months, but this was not the kind of work he could do. And so by the middle of 1521 he was sent to complete the pacification of the Aztecs. He subdued the Indians of Oaxaca Valley, and his reports of the place were so glowing that Cortés requested the valley as his own. From this he drew his title: Marquis of the Valley of Oaxaca.

The loyalty between the lieutenant and captain was such that, when Cortés asked that whatever gold Alvarado had found be sent at once to replace the shipment captured by the French, Alvarado sent on all he had without questions, even though he was forced to put down a mutiny and hang two of his followers.

In the months that followed, Mexico was in complete chaos. Small bands of Spaniards, hungry for the gold which the conquest had failed to uncover, began to plunder the country without regard for the life of anyone. Alvarado put down both the Indian and Spanish rebellions with an equally ruthless hand until he finally received the assignment which was to occupy him for years—the conquest of Guatemala.

Shortly after the conquest of Mexico, Cortés sent two scouts far to the south to learn what they could about the country. The reports which they brought back were enough to attract the attention of the gold-hungry Spanish. The Guatemalans had a civilization in many ways as high as that of the Aztecs. Of Mayan stock intermingled with Aztec, Toltec and that of other northern races, the Guatemalans were divided into three nations: Quiches, Cakchiquels, and Tzutuhils. The former two were almost constantly at war with each other and had been for centuries. The Guatemalans were an intelligent and energetic people. And the Quiches had built in Utatlan a capital city which was almost impregnable, erected in a deep canyon with a four-story fortress to protect it.

The conquest was not going to be a simple one. There was no road from Mexico to Guatemala, though the two countries had been in contact with each other over the years.

In a series of four letters Alvarado reported directly to Cortés, keeping his superior informed of what was taking place. Two of those letters were lost, but the ones of April 11, 1524, and July 28, 1524, exist. In the first, Alvarado is clearly the lieutenant of Cortés, but in the second letter he protests a lack of attention and begins to emerge his own man and a captain-general in his own right.

Bernal Díaz, who served under Alvarado, describes how the expedition began.

AN ACCOUNT GIVEN BY BERNAL DÍAZ DEL CASTILLO

Cortés always had lofty thoughts, and in his ambition to command and rule he wished in every way to copy Alexander of Macedon. He always had excellent captains and accomplished soldiers about him, among them Pedro de Alvarado.

After Cortés had established the great cities of Mexico, Oaxaco, Zacatula, Colima, la Vera Cruz, Panuco, and Coatzacoalcos, he received news that in the province of Guatemala there were strong towns with large populations, and that there were mines there. He had already sent messengers there to beg the people to come in peaceably, but they would not come. He decided, therefore, to send Pedro de Alvarado to conquer and settle that province. For that expedition he gave Alvarado over three hundred soldiers, including one hundred twenty musketeers and crossbowmen. In addition, he gave him one hundred thirty-five horsemen, four cannon and much powder, and over two hundred Tlascalans and Choluans as auxiliaries.

Cortés instructed Alvarado as follows: He should endeavor with the greatest care to bring the people to peace without making war on them, and to preach our holy faith through interpreters and ecclesiastics whom he took with him. He was not to permit sacrifices or sodomy or the robbing of one another. When he met with prisons and cages in which it was the custom to keep Indians confined in order to fatten them for food, he should break them down and liberate the captives. He should bring the people, with kindness and good will, to render obedience to His Majesty, and should treat them well in all respects.

After Pedro de Alvarado had said good-bye to Cortés and his friends in Mexico, he set out from that city on the thirteenth day of November in 1523.

Cortés ordered him to go by certain rocky hills in the province of Tehuantepec, which were near his road, and where the people were in revolt. Alvarado brought the inhabitants of these rocky hills to peace. The hill was known as the Penol de Guelamo because it was then in the encomienda of a soldier named Guelamo.

From there he went to Tehuantepec, a large pueblo of the Zapotecs, where they received him very well for they were at peace. They had already gone to Mexico and given their fealty to His Majesty and had taken a good present of gold to Cortés.

From Tehuantepec he went to the province of Soconusco, which at that time had more than fifteen thousand inhabitants. They also received him peaceably and gave him a present of gold and surrendered themselves as vassals to His Majesty. From Soconusco he arrived near to another group of villages named Zapotulan.

LETTER FROM PEDRO DE ALVARADO TO HERNÁN CORTÉS

Sir: From Soconusco I wrote to Your Grace all that had happened to me as far as that place. After having sent messengers of their own people to this country, informing them that I was come to conquer and pacify the provinces in behalf of His Majesty, I asked their favor and assistance in passage through their country. I informed them that by so doing they would act as good and loyal vassals of His Majesty. However, if they did not, I threatened to make war on them as on traitors and to make slaves of all those who should be taken alive in the war.

Having done all this and reviewed my men, I set out in search of their land. After three days' march through uninhabited forest, we pitched our camp. The scouts I had sent out captured three spies from a town named Zapotulan. I asked them what they came for, and they told me they were collecting honey. It was obvious they were spies, but as I wished to treat them reasonably I gave them another command and requirement as before and sent them to their chiefs. To none of my requests did I receive an answer.

Arriving at the town, I found all the roads open, the highway as well as the crossroads. But the roads that ran to the principal streets were obstructed. I then understood their evil intentions and that all was arranged to fight us. A few of them told me, from a distance, that I should lodge in the town, that they might fight us at their convenience. But I camped near the town until I could reconnoiter the country and see their plans. Later that afternoon they killed and wounded some Indians of my army.

The next day I went to examine the road by which we had to advance, and saw many warriors. The country was so thickly wooded, covered with trees and cocoa plantations, that it was very favorable for them and not for us, so I returned to camp. Next day I left with all my men to enter the town. The Indians had taken their position at a river which was difficult to cross, but after a struggle we defeated them. I waited for the stragglers on a high bank of the river, because the way was very dangerous, although I carried the best outfit that could be had. While I was waiting, they assaulted me again from the woods, and we resisted them for a long while until we had carried all our baggage across. After entering the houses we struck down the people and continued the pursuit as far as the market place and half a league beyond, returning to the market place to camp. We spent two days here reconnoitering the country. Then I left for another town called Quezaltenango.

That day I crossed two rivers with very steep, rocky banks, and started to climb a mountain pass that was six leagues in length. That night I made camp half way up. The pass was so rough that the horses could scarcely climb. Next morning I continued, and above a gully I found a woman and a dog sacrificed. This, my interpreter informed me, was a challenge. We had just got through the pass with the archers and infantry in front of me, as the horses had not been able to keep up with us, when there appeared three or four thousand warriors above a ravine and struck at the contingent of our friends, causing them to retreat. While up there rallying the people, I saw more than 30,000 men coming toward us. I thanked God that we found some plains there. Although the horses were tired from the pass, we waited for the Indians to arrive within arrowshot, and then attacked them. As they had never seen horses, they showed much fear. We made a very good advance and scattered them, killing many.

Then we waited for all our people and went to camp a league away near some springs, because we were suffering greatly from thirst. As we were very tired, any place was a good site to camp. The country was flat and I took the lead with thirty horsemen. Many of us had taken along a relay of horses. The rest of the men came in a body, and then I dismounted to drink the water. While dismounted and drinking we saw many warriors approaching. As they came over very wide plains, we allowed them to draw near and then defeated them. We continued the pursuit for a full league and they brought us to a mountain where they faced us. I put myself in flight with some of the horsemen to draw the Indians to the plains, and they followed us until reaching the horses' tails. I then turned on them, inflicting severe punishment. In this affair one of the four chiefs of the city of Utlatan was killed. He was the captain-general of all this country. I returned to the spring, greatly fatigued, and with several Spaniards and horses wounded.

The next morning I left for Quezaltenango, a league away. After yesterday's punishment I found it empty—not even a single person there. I camped and reorganized and reconnoitered the country. It is as thickly populated as Tlascala, equally cultivated and excessively cold.

Six days later a great multitude of people appeared on many sides. According to what I learned from them, 12,000 were from this city and surrounding towns, and the others they said could not be counted. I put my men in order and went out to give them battle with ninety horsemen, in the middle of a plain three leagues long. I left men in the camp to guard it, and at a gunshot from the camp we commenced to crush them. We scattered them in all directions and followed them in pursuit for two and a half leagues until all of them were routed. Later we returned against them, and our friends and the infantry made the greatest destruction in the world. They surrounded a bare mountain where the Indians had taken refuge, pursued them to the top, and took all that had gone up there. That day we killed and imprisoned many people, many of whom were captains and chiefs and people of importance.

When the chiefs of this town found that their people were defeated, they took counsel with all the land and called many other provinces to them. They even gave tribute to their enemies and induced them to join them so that all might come together and kill us. They sent to tell us that they wished to be friends and give obedience to our Lord the Emperor, so that I should enter the city of Utlatan. They thought they would lodge me there and then set fire to the town and burn us all in it. And in truth their evil plan would have come to pass but that God did not see good that these infidels should be victorious over us.

For this city is very, very strong, and there are only two ways of entering it. One way was over thirty steep stone steps. The other was by a causeway made by hand, much of which was already cut away so that they might finish cutting it that night and no horse could then have escaped into the country. As the city is very closely built and the streets very narrow, we could not have stood it without either suffocating or else falling headlong from the rocks when fleeing from the fire.

As we rode up, I could see how large the stronghold was, and that we could not avail ourselves of the horses because the streets were so narrow and walled in. I determined at once to clear out of it onto the plain, although the chiefs of the town invited me to seat myself and eat before I departed, so as to gain time to carry out their plans. But I knew the danger we were in, and I at once sent some men ahead of me to take possession of the causeway and the bridge. The causeway was already in such a condition that one could hardly get over it on horseback.

There were many warriors outside the city, and as they saw me pass out on to the plain they retreated, but not so much that I did not receive much harm from them. But I concealed it all so that I might capture the chiefs who were taking to flight. By the cunning with which I approached them and the presents I gave them, I took them captive and held them prisoners in my camp. Nevertheless, their people did not cease fighting against me in the neighborhood, and they killed and wounded many Indians who had gone out to gather grass. One Spaniard was slain by a stone rolled down the hill. This land is very full of deep gullies, and because of them one cannot carry on war and punish these people as they deserve.

Seeing that I might bring these people to the service of His Majesty by fire and sword, I determined to burn the chiefs. At the time I wanted to burn them, they told me, as it will appear in their confessions, that they were the ones who had ordered the war against me and they were the ones also who made it. I knew them to have a bad disposition towards the service of His Majesty, and to insure the good and peace of this land, I burnt them, and sent to burn the town and destroy it, for it is a very strong and dangerous place, that resembles a robbers' stronghold more than a city. To enable me to hunt out these people, I sent to the city of Guatemala, which is ten leagues distant, and ordered them on the part of His Majesty to send me some warriors, which I did to find out their disposition as well as to strike terror into the land. They were well disposed toward me and sent me four thousand men. With these men and those that were already with me, I chased them and threw them out of the entire country.

Seeing the damages which they had suffered, they sent me messengers to tell me that now they wished to be good, and that if they had erred, it had been at the order of their chiefs. Now that their chiefs were dead, they prayed me to pardon them. I spared their lives and ordered them to return to their houses and live as they had before. This they did, and at the present time I have them in the same condition as they were formerly, at the service of His Majesty. And for greater security I gave liberty to two sons of the chiefs whom I placed in their fathers' positions. I believe that they will carry out faithfully all that tends to the service of His Majesty and the good of his lands.

As for the war, I have nothing more to relate at present, except that all the prisoners of war were branded and made slaves. I gave His Majesty's fifth part to the treasurer, Baltazar de Mendoza, which he sold by public auction so that the payment to His Majesty should be secure.

I wish Your Grace to know that the country is healthy and the climate temperate. It is well populated, with many strong towns, and this city is well built and wonderfully strong. It has much corn and many people subject to it. This with all the subject towns and neighborhoods I have placed under the yoke and in the service of the royal crown of His Majesty.

In this country there is a mountain range of alum, another of copperas and another of sulphur, the best I have yet seen. They brought me a piece of it, and without refining or any such process I made half an arroba of very good gunpowder.

On Monday, April 11, I am leaving for Guatemala, where I mean to stop but a short time. There is a town there, situated on the water, named Atitlan. It is at war and has killed four of my messengers, and I think with the aid of our Lord to subdue it soon to the service of His Majesty.

I have much to do in the future and I am therefore in haste to winter fifty or one hundred leagues beyond Guatemala, where they tell me of marvelous and large buildings and wonderful cities. They also tell me that twenty-five days' journey from here, beyond a large city, is the end of this country, and they confirm it. If it is so, I am certain it is the strait connecting with the South Sea. May it please God to bring me victory over these infidels so that I may bring them to His service or that of His Majesty.

The Spaniards of my company, both horse and foot, have conducted themselves so well in the war that they are worthy of great thanks. At present I have nothing more of importance to say except that we are in the wildest country and people ever seen. So that our Lord may give us victory, I supplicate Your Grace to ordain that a procession be held in your city of all the priests and friars so that the Lord may help us. We are so far from help that if He does not help us, nobody can. Also be sure to inform His Majesty how we have served him with our persons and our properties at our own cost, for your own conscience' sake and so that His Majesty may grant us privileges. May our Lord protect the very magnificent person of Your Grace for so long a time as you desire. From this city of Utlatan, April 11.

As I am on a long voyage and think I will lack horseshoes, if, during the coming summer, Your Grace could provide me with same, it would be very well, and His Majesty will be served by it. They are now worth here 190 pesos a dozen and so we are trading them and paying for them in gold.

I kiss the hands of Your Grace.

PEDRO DE ALVARADO

ANOTHER ACCOUNT GIVEN IN A LETTER BY PEDRO DE ALVARADO
TO HERNÁN CORTÉS

Sir: I have given a long account to Your Grace of the things that had happened to me up to Utlatan. Now I wish to give you an account of all the lands that I have traveled and conquered, and of the other things that have happened to me.

I left Utlatan and came in two days to this city of Guatemala, where I was very well received by its chiefs. I could not have been better off in our parents' house. After eight days, I learned from the chiefs that seven leagues from there was another city on a very large lake which made war against Guatemala and Utlatan. They are very strong on account of the lake and their canoes, coming out at night to make raids. The people of Guatemala told me that they did not wish to make war against them without my permission and prayed that I should help them. I replied that I would send for them on the part of our Lord the Emperor. If they came, I would command them not to make war or do anything wrong. If they did not come, I would go with them to make war and punish them. I therefore sent two messengers, natives of this city, whom they killed without fear.

When I saw their wickedness, I went against them with sixty horsemen and a hundred fifty foot, in company with the chiefs and people of this land, arriving in the enemy's land the same day. No one came out to receive me, in peace or otherwise. I started out with thirty horsemen to the shores of the lake and came to an inhabited rock which stood out in the water. There I saw a company of men and we attacked them.

They got on to a very narrow causeway which led to the rock, where we could not follow on horseback. I and my companions dismounted and followed on foot at the heels of the Indians, so that we reached the rock before they could break down the bridges. We gained possession of the rock, which was thickly inhabited, but all the people threw themselves into the water to swim to another island. Many of them escaped because my allies, who were bringing three hundred canoes across the lake, did not arrive soon enough. That afternoon I left the rock with all my men and we camped in a maize field.

The next day we commended ourselves to God and set out for the town ahead of us, which was very strong because of the many rocks and palisades about it. We found it deserted. Having lost their fortress on the lake, they did not dare face us on land, although a few of them waited for us at the end of the town. But owing to the roughness of the ground, no more people were killed. We began to reconnoiter the country and captured some of the native Indians. I sent off three of them as messengers to their chiefs, advising them to come and submit themselves to the Imperial crown and to me in His Majesty's name. Otherwise I should still carry on the war and seek them out in the mountains. These chiefs replied to me that hitherto their land had never been broken into nor entered by force of arms. Since I had forced an entrance, they would be glad to serve His Majesty in any way I might direct them. Soon afterward they came to place themselves at my orders.

I gave them to understand the greatness and power of our Lord the Emperor, and that they should appreciate that I, in His Royal name, would pardon them for all that had passed. From now on, I said, they should behave themselves and not make war against anybody in the neighborhood, as all were now vassals of His Majesty. I dismissed them, leaving them safe and peaceful, and returned to this city.

Three days after my return, all the chiefs, principal people and captains of that lake came to me with presents and told me that now they were our friends, and considered themselves fortunate to be vassals of His Majesty and relieved of hardships, wars and differences among themselves. I received them very well, and gave them some of my jewels and sent them back to their country with much affection. They are now the most pacific in this land.

While I was in this city, there came to me many chiefs of other provinces of the south coast to give obedience to Their Majesties. They said that they wished to be their vassals and did not wish to make war with anybody, and that therefore I should receive them as such, and favor them and maintain them in justice. I received them very well, as was proper, and told them that they would be favored and helped by me in the name of His Majesty.

They told me of another province called Yscuintepeque, somewhat more inland, that would not allow them to come and give obedience to His Majesty. Not only this, but other provinces of that part of the land were well disposed and wished to come in peace; but those people would not allow them to pass, saying they were crazy and they should allow me to go there and then all would make war on me.

As I was assured that this was so, I left with all my people, both foot and horse, and remained encamped for three days in a desert. Next morning we entered the outskirts of that town. It is very heavily wooded, and we found all the roads closed and very narrow—really only pathways—because they did not trade with anybody and had no open road. Since the horsemen could not fight there because of the many marshes and thickets, I sent the crossbowmen ahead. It had rained so much that their watchmen and spies had returned to the town. They did not think I would arrive among them that day and they were somewhat careless. Consequently they did not know of my sally until I was in the town among them. When I entered, all the war-riors were huddled together in houses because of the rain, and they had no time to form, although some of them wounded some Spaniards and many of the friendly Indians. Because of the thick woods and rain, they escaped into the forest, so that I had no opportunity to do them any damage except to burn their town. Then I sent messengers to the chiefs, telling them to come to give obedience to Their Majesties and to me in their name. If not, I would do great damage to their land and lay waste their maize fields. They came and gave themselves as vassals of His Majesty, and I ordered them to be good in the future. I remained in this town eight days, and received many people from other towns and provinces, who came in peace and offered themselves as vassals of our Lord the Emperor.

Since I wished to explore the country and know its secrets so that His Majesty may be better served and rule more lands, I determined to leave here, and went to a town called Atiepar. There I was received by the chiefs and natives, who are of a different language and race. At sunset, without any reason, it was suddenly depopulated. In order to prevent the rigors of winter catching me there and impeding my journey, I left them and passed on without stopping, desiring to ex-plore for a hundred leagues further and to pacify them on the return. The following day I left and went to another town called Tacuylula where they did the same as the people of Atiepar, receiving me in peace and hiding an hour afterward. I then went to another town called Taxisco, which is very strong and has many people. Here I was received as by the previous ones. Next day I left for another very large town, Nacendelan. Not understanding these people and being fearful, I left ten horsemen as a rear guard and ten more with the baggage, and continued my march.

I might have gone two or three leagues from Taxisco when I heard that warriors had attacked the rear guard and killed many friendly Indians and taken a large part of the baggage, including all the strings of the bowmen and all the iron that I carried for the war. I immediately sent Jorge de Alvarado, my brother, with forty or fifty horsemen, to look for all they had taken. He found many armed peo-ple in the fields and he defeated them. But he could recover nothing that had been lost because the clothes had already been torn to pieces and each one wore a loin cloth of it. Having reached Nacendelan, Jorge de Alvarado returned because all the Indians had fled to the mountains. I sent Don Pedro with foot soldiers to search the moun-tains, but nothing could be done because of the great thickness of the forests, and so he returned. Then I sent Indians of their own country to them as messengers, with requirements and orders, warning them that if they did not come, I would make them slaves. With all this they did not wish to come, neither the messengers nor themselves.

After eight days in Nacendelan, there came in peace a people called Pasaco, which was on the road by which we had to go. I received them and gave them of what we had and entreated them to be good. The next morning I left for this town, and at the entrance found the roads closed and many stakes thrust in. When I was entering into the town, I saw some Indians cutting a dog in quarters in the manner of a sacrifice. We saw a great multitude of people and we attacked them, breaking them up until we drove them from the town.

From here I left for another town called Mopicalco and was received in exactly the same way as in the others. When I arrived in the town I did not find a living person. From here I left for a town called Acatepeque where I found nobody.

Following my plan to explore the said hundred leagues, I left for Acaxual, which is on the coast of the South Sea. Within half a league of this town I saw the fields full of warriors with their plumage and insignias and with their offensive and defensive arms. They awaited me in the middle of a plain. Arrived within bowshot of them, I waited until all my people had gathered. There was no movement among the warriors that I could tell, and it seemed to me that they were somewhat near to a woods where they could take shelter from me. I therefore ordered my people to retreat, while I remained in the rear guard. The pleasure they had on seeing me retire was so great that they followed me, even up the horses' tails, so that the arrows they shot passed in front of us. All this took place on a plain where neither for them nor for us was there anything to stumble over.

When I had retreated a quarter of a league, I turned on them with all my people and broke through their ranks. The destruction we made was so great that in a short time none were left alive. They came so heavily armed that those who fell to the ground could not get up. Their arms are corselets of cotton three fingers thick, reaching to their feet, and they had arrows and long lances, so that when they fell, the foot soldiers killed all of them. In this encounter many Spaniards were wounded, including myself. An arrow passed through my leg and entered my saddle. I remained lame from this wound, one leg being a good four fingers shorter than the other. And I was forced to remain five days in this town to cure our wounds.

I sent Don Pedro and other companions as scouts to another town called Tacuxalco. They caught two spies who told us that there were many warriors of that town ahead. At this time Gonzalo de Alvarado arrived with forty horsemen and made front until we had all arrived. I mounted a horse as best I could to arrange the attack. I saw that they had a body of warriors ready and formed in battle, and I sent Gómez de Alvarado with thirty horsemen on the right hand, and Jorge de Alvarado to attack them with the rest of the army. To see them from afar was terrifying, because most of them had lances thirty palms long, all raised high. I mounted a hill to see better what was happening and I saw that all the Spaniards arrived at within a quoit's length of the Indians and that neither the Indians fled nor the Spaniards attacked, so that I was afraid of the Indians who so dared to wait. The Spaniards had not attacked because they thought the field that lay between them was a marsh. After they saw it was firm and good, they attacked the Indians and defeated them, following them in pursuit through the town and making a great massacre and punishment. As the people thereafter saw that we defeated them in the plain, they determined to hide and leave us the towns.

After two days' rest, I left for a town called Miaguaclam, where they left for the woods like the others. And from here I left for another town called Atehuan, where the chiefs of Cuxcaclan sent me their messengers to give obedience to Their Majesties. I received them, thinking they would lie like the others.

Arriving at Cuxcaclan, I found the town empty, all having gone to the hills. I sent my messengers to the chiefs to tell them that they behaved badly. I assured them that if they came, I would not make war against them nor take their property, but merely bring them to the service of God and His Majesty. They sent me word that they did not know either of them, and that if I wanted anything, they were there waiting with their arms. When I saw their evil intentions, I sent them an order and requirement on the part of the Emperor, that they should not break the peace nor revolt, as they had already given themselves as his vassals. If not, I would make war against them as rebellious traitors, and all taken alive would be branded as slaves. If they were loyal they would be protected and favored by me as vassals of His Majesty. To this there was no answer, neither did the messengers return.

Seeing their wickedness, and because that country should not remain without punishment, I sent the army to the woods and mountains to look for them. They found the warriors and fought with them, making prisoner a principal of this city. For greater justification I returned him with another order, and they answered the same as before. Owing to their rebelliousness, the proceedings were closed, and I sentenced them, as traitors, to death. Both the chiefs of these provinces and all the others that had been taken or might henceforth be taken in the war should be slaves and branded. And from their value as slaves they should pay for eleven horses that had been killed in conquering them, and all those that might thereafter be killed, and for the arms and other necessary things for such a conquest. I was after these Indians of Cuxcaclan for seventeen days and was never able to attract them by the expeditions I ordered and the messengers I sent them, because of the great thickness of the woods and the great mountains and broken ground and other great powers they had.

Here I learned of very great countries inland, of cities of stone and mortar, and that this land has no end, and to conquer it much time is required. Because the rigorous winter was beginning, I did not go farther to conquer but decided rather to return to this city of Guatemala and to pacify, while returning, the country I had left behind.

So I did, and labored with them, but never could attract them to the service of His Majesty, because all this southern coast is densely wooded and mountains are near, affording them refuge. So it is that I am come to this city. For the better conquest and pacification of this land, so great and so thickly inhabited, I made and built here in the name of His Majesty a Spanish city which is called the city of our lord Santiago. This is the center of all the country, and there are more and better arrangements for conquest and pacification, and to populate the surrounding country. I elected two Alcaldes Ordinarios and four Regidores, as Your Grace will see by the election.

At the end of these two coming winter months, which are the most rigorous of all, I will leave from this city in search of the province of Tepalan, fifteen days' journey towards the interior. According to my information, it is as large as Mexico, of large buildings of rough stone and mortar, and flat roofed. Apart from this there are many others. Four or five of them have come here to me to give obedience to His Majesty, and they say that one of them has thirty thousand inhabitants. This coming summer, God willing, I expect to go forward two hundred leagues, where I think His Majesty will be well served and his estate augmented. And Your Grace will have news of other new matters. From the city of Mexico to where I have traveled and conquered there are four hundred leagues, and, believe it Your Grace, that this land is more populated and has more people than all the lands that Your Grace has governed up to now.

In this country we have found a mountain range where there is a volcano, the most terrifying thing ever seen. From its mouth it throws stones as large as a house, burning in living flames and covering the mountain with fire when they fall and break in pieces.

Sixty leagues beyond this we saw another volcano which threw out terrifying smoke that rose to the sky and which has a width of half a league. Nobody can drink the waters of any of the rivers that come down from there because they are sulphurous. There is one large river which comes from there, very beautiful, and so hot that it could not be crossed.

Of the things in these parts there is not more to advise Your Grace, except that the Indians tell me that from this southern sea to that of the north there is a winter's and a summer's travel. As the Indians say so, it is of course to be understood that the journey is made on foot.

Your Grace gave me the honor of the lieutenancy of this city, and I helped to gain it and defended it when I was there, with the danger and suffering that Your Grace knows. For what I have served His Majesty he would have confirmed me in it and granted me other favors, if I might have gone to Spain. They tell me that His Majesty has disposed of it, which does not surprise me, as he has no notice of me. For this, nobody is to blame but Your Grace, for not having given an account to His Majesty of how I have served him since you sent me here. I pray Your Grace to give him an account of who I am and of how I have served His Majesty in these parts. Pray tell him where I am and what I have conquered recently, and the will that I have to serve him, and will have in the future, and how, in his service, I am lamed in one leg. Pray tell him also how little return I and these hidalgos in my company have received up to the present and the little profit that we have made so far.

May our Lord prosperously increase the life and very magnificent estate of Your Grace for a long time.

From this city of Santiago, the 28th day of July of 1524.

PEDRO DE ALVARADO

In addition to the reports of Alvarado, another account exists. Written in a strange and almost uncomprehensible language, it tells the story of the conquest of Guatemala from a completely different point of view—that of the conquered. The Cakchiquel Annals describe the arrival of Alvarado or Tunaituh and the years of war that followed not only with the Spanish but between the Guatemalan nations as well. It was internecine violence and hatred which made Alvarado's conquest possible in a hundred bloody days. In some details the Indian account does not agree with Alvarado. The Spaniard claimed the Cakchiquels sent him four thousand men. The Indians report four hundred.

THE CAKCHIQUEL ANNALS

On the day 5 Ah was the eighth year of the first cycle.

It was during this year that the Castilians arrived. Forty-nine years have passed since the Castilians came to Xepit and Xetulul. On the day 1 Ganel the Quiches were destroyed by the Castilians. Tuniatuh Avilantaro, as he was called, conquered all the towns. Their countenances were previously unknown and the people rendered homage to sticks and stones.

On their arrival at Xelahub, the Quiche nation was routed and destroyed. All of them had hastened there to oppose the Castilians; and there the Quiche nation was destroyed, in front of Xelahub.

He then went to the city Gumarcaah, and there came before him the chiefs, the king, and the next in rank, and tribute was paid by the Quiche; and the chiefs suffered many torments from Tuniatuh.

On the day 4 Qat three chiefs, the king and the next in rank were burned alive by Tuniatuh, nor was the heart of Tuniatuh satisfied with war. Soon a messenger from Tuniatuh came to the chiefs that they should send him warriors: "Let the warriors of the Ahpozotzils and Ahpoxahils come to the slaughter of the Quiches!" So spoke the messenger of Tuniatuh to the chiefs. Immediately the words of Tuniatuh were published, and 400 men went forth to the slaughter of the Quiches; but they were only those of the city, the other warriors refusing to obey the chiefs. Only three times did the warriors go forth to enforce the tribute on the Quiches; then we also were taken by Tuniatuh.

It was on the day 1 Hunahpu when the Castilians arrived at Iximche with their chief Tuniatuh. The people went forth to meet Tuniatuh with the chiefs Belehe Qat and Cahi Ymox. Good was the heart of

Tuniatuh when he entered the city with the chiefs. There was no fighting and Tuniatuh rejoiced when he entered Iximche.

But it was a fearful thing when the Castilians entered; their faces were strange, and the chiefs took them for gods. We, even we, your father, saw them when they first set foot in Iximche, at the palace of Tzupam where Tuniatuh slept. The chief came forth, and truly he frightened the warriors; he came from his chamber and called the rulers: "Why do you make war with me, when I can also make it?" said he.

"Not at all. Why should so many warriors find their death? Do you see any pitfalls among them?" replied the chiefs.

He went to the house of the chief Chicbal.

The Tuniatuh agreed to join the chiefs in their wars, and the chiefs said to him: "O thou God, we have two wars, one with the Tzutuhils, one at Panatact."

Only five days after, Tuniatuh went forth from the capital. Then the Tzutuhils were conquered by the Castilians. It was the day 7 Camey that the Tzutuhils were destroyed by the Castilians.

Twenty-five days afterward Tuniatuh went forth from the capital to Cuzcatan going there to destroy Atacat. On the day 2 Queh, Atacat was slain by the Castilians, with all his warriors. There went with Tuniatuh all his Mexicans to this battle.

On the day 10 Hunahpu he returned from Cuzcatan. He had been absent only forty days to make the conquest at Cuzcatan when he returned to the capital. Then Tuniatuh asked for a daughter of one of the chiefs, and she was given to Tuniatuh by the chiefs.

Then Tuniatuh began to ask the chiefs for money. He wished them to give him jars full of precious metals, and even their drinking cups and crowns. Not receiving anything, Tuniatuh became angry and said to the chiefs: "Why have you not given me the metal? If you do not bring me the precious metal in all your towns, choose then, for I shall burn you alive and hang you."

Then Tuniatuh cut from three of them the gold ornaments they wore in their ears. The chiefs suffered keenly from this violence, and wept before him.

But Tuniatuh was not troubled, and said: "I tell you that I want the gold here within five days. Woe to you if you do not give it. I know my heart."

The word was then given. The chiefs gathered together all their metals, those of the parents and children of the king, and all that the chiefs could get from the people.

While they were gathering the gold for Tuniatuh, a priest of the Demon showed himself. "I am the lightning; I will destroy the Castilians. I will destroy them by fire. When I beat the drum, let the chiefs come forth and go to the other bank of the river. This I shall do on the day 7 Ahmak."

Truly the chiefs thought that they should trust in the words of this man. It was when they were gathering the gold that we went forth.

The day 7 Ahmak was that of the going forth. They deserted the city of Iximche on account of the priest of the Demon, and the chiefs left it.

"Yes, truly, Tuniatuh shall die," they said. "There is no more war in the heart of Tuniatuh, as he now rejoices in the gold given him."

And so our city was abandoned on the day 7 Ahmak on account of a priest of the Demon.

But what the chiefs did was soon known to Tuniatuh. Ten days after we had left the city, war was begun by Tuniatuh. On the day 4 Camey our destruction began. We scattered in the forests. All our towns were taken. We were slaughtered by Tuniatuh. When the Castilians entered the city they arrived as to a deserted spot. From that time the Castilians were hated by the Cakchiquels. They made trenches, they dug pitfalls that the horses might be killed, and their men waged war. Many men of the Castilians were slain, and many horses killed in the pitfalls. The Quiches and Tzutuhils were destroyed and all their villages ruined by the Cakchiquels. Only in this way did the Castilians let them live. One hundred and eighty days after the desertion of the city of Iximche was completed the ninth year (of the second cycle).

On the day 2 Ah was completed the 29th year after the Revolt.

During the tenth year the war continued with the Castilians. But the Castilians having received aid in this tenth year at Xepau, carried on the war with such vigor that they destroyed the forces of the nation.

Tuniatuh then went forth from Xepau and so harassed us that the people would not come before him. There were lacking one hundred and twenty days to complete two years since we had abandoned the capital, now deserted, when Tuniatuh came there on his march in order to set fire to the city. On the day 4 Camey, two years less six months after the beginning of the war, he set fire to the capital and returned.

On the day 12 Ah was completed the 30th year after the Revolt.

When the conquest was essentially complete, Alvarado established his capital, levied a gold tax on the Indians and then spent almost a year in the field trying to pacify the country he had conquered. Indian rebellions were almost constant and he was barely able to hold what he had taken. Cortés sent him two hundred additional Spaniards in 1525, but the wars with the natives had kept his men in the field so long that many of them rebelled and fled to Mexico where they reported Alvarado's violence. The conquistador decided to go to Mexico City himself and he left his brother Jorge in command in Guatemala.

He was well received in the capital, but the old enemies of Cortés and himself were so active that to protect his conquest he went directly to Spain to report in person to the king. On his arrival in Spain, he was called before the Council of the Indies and fined 15,000 ducats on charges that came down to his having conquered Guatemala.

In anger and disgust, Alvarado appealed directly to the king. In his appeal he had the support of the most powerful families in Spain as he had just married the beautiful and wealthy Doña Francisca de la Cueva, niece of the Duke of Albuquerque.

Charles was more generous than usual. He knighted the red-headed conquistador, gave him the title of Adelantado, and the Cross of the Order of Santiago. And on December 18, 1527, he appointed Alvarado governor and captain-general of Guatemala, subject only to the crown. After six months, Alvarado returned to Vera Cruz, but before he could set out for Guatemala, his bride died of fever. He returned bewildered and depressed to Mexico City, where he was immediately charged by the Audiencia of Mexico with every crime that could be listed against him. The enemies of Cortés were not satisfied with destroying the conqueror of Mexico. They were after all of those who were friendly to him, and they had no intention of permitting Alvarado to escape their fury. With vivid imaginations, they set down thirty-four charges against Alvarado. Some of them were interesting. Most of them were false.

TRIAL OF PEDRO DE ALVARADO

1529

FROM THE LIST OF CHARGES AS DRAWN BY THE AUDIENCIA OF MEXICO

1. That when the said Pedro de Alvarado came with Don Hernán Cortés to New Spain to conquer and populate the same, that being captain of one of the ships of the fleet of the said Cortés, he came ahead of the fleet to the island of Cozumel where the Indians received him in peace and gave him that which they had. Not being content therewith he entered into the country with certain of his people, burning and robbing certain towns without cause or reason. Whereupon the Indians of the island fled to the jungle and the said Pedro de Alvarado made war upon them.

3. And the said Pedro de Alvarado is accused: when the Spaniards first came to this city, he being captain of a certain party of them, of seizing secretly large quantities of gold, feathers, jade, cloth, cacao and many other things which in our secret investigation appears to have been proven and of which the gold alone was worth at least thirty thousand pesos, and that of the same he did not pay the Royal Fifth nor give any part thereof to his companions as he was obligated to do.

4. As the said Pedro de Alvarado is accused of: at the time that the Spaniards came to this city and captured Montezuma, they also took one Camazin, nephew of the said Montezuma, who was in his own right a great Lord in this country; and the said Camazin said to Hernán Cortés that if he would send a captain with him to his domain, he would give him all the gold and jewels that he had; and the said Hernán Cortés sent with him Pedro de Alvarado to the city of Tuzcuco, where the said Camazin lived; and because the said Camazin did not give him all the gold and treasure which he wished, he ordered the said Camazin tied hand and foot to a pole and being bound thus burning, resin was thrown upon him in such a way that his body was burned in all parts and that he was on the point of death, and this was done in order that he should give them more gold and without any other reason or motive whatsoever.

5. And the charge is made against the said Pedro de Alvarado that at the time the said Hernán Cortés left this city to proceed against Pánfilo de Narváez, he left the said Pedro de Alvarado to guard this city and in his power, Montezuma, the Lord thereof, together

210 • THE GOLDEN CONQUISTADORES

with all of the gold and treasure which up to that time had been accumulated, which was a great quantity; and at the time of departure, Montezuma asked permission of Cortés to hold certain feasts and dances which his people were accustomed to celebrate at such time of the year, and the said Cortés gave the requested permission; and the time having come for the said feasts and dances, Montezuma ordered them held; and there being one day in the house of Montezuma a great number of Indians dancing and celebrating their feast, Pedro de Alvarado, together with the Spaniards under his command, entered into the house where Montezuma was prisoner, together with many Lords and principal chiefs and their servants; and entering into the patio where all were dancing, without any cause or reason whatsoever, fell upon the Indians and killed all of the Lords captive with Montezuma and four hundred principal chiefs who were present and three thousand Indians who were dancing; for which reason the tribes rose in arms because their fellows had been killed without reason; and because of this war, more than two hundred Spaniards died at the hands of the Indians, many horses were lost and more than four hundred thousand Indians were killed in the said war. Much gold was lost, much of which belonged to His Majesty and to the soldiers. All of which is a charge against Pedro de Alvarado because he killed Indians who were dancing in a state of peace by license of Cortés.

6. And the further accusation is made against Pedro de Alvarado that being Captain as aforesaid and commanding the rear guard with many horses and foot-soldiers at the time when the army evacuated the capital, the said Pedro de Alvarado arrived at one of the gaps which existed in the causeway there being one beam remaining across the gap on which the Spaniards must pass, Pedro de Alvarado vaulted the gap leaving his people without a Captain while the enemy came behind them. And Alvarado on his horse galloped to the head of the column where Hernán Cortés was, and when he arrived Cortés asked him if all his people had passed, and Pedro de Alvarado replied that they had, which was not true since they did not have a Captain to animate them and encourage them to kill the Indians, and because of the absence of Pedro de Alvarado, a quantity of gold belonging to His Majesty was lost. All of which is a charge against the said Pedro de Alvarado.

8. And the said Pedro de Alvarado is accused, while he was lieu-

tenant at Villa Rica, of taking from the Indian chief at Papolo against his will, two handsome women that he had. And because the chief did not want to deliver them willingly, Pedro de Alvarado caused him to be imprisoned, whereupon he died of the treatment received from Pedro de Alvarado.

9. And the further accusation is made against Pedro de Alvarado that at the time of the conquest of this city, he being captain at Tlatelulco, he as captain should strive to animate and enthuse the people under his command in as much as they were in great peril, but he left many nights and went to the town of Tlacopan, and it was public among all his soldiers or most of them that he went there to sleep with an Indian woman whom he kept as mistress, using as a pretext that he went to Tlacopan to obtain reinforcements and supplies.

19. And it is further charged against the said Pedro de Alvarado that while Captain of the said Province of Guatemala, the Indian Lords came in peace and gave him presents of gold, silver and jewels and treated him very well. It being known by Pedro de Alvarado that a Prince of the Province had a very beautiful wife, he seized her and kept her prisoner until the husband offered jewels and gold and silver and slaves and begged Pedro de Alvarado to give back his wife and take his possessions. Pedro de Alvarado took all of the gold and slaves but kept the woman.

27. And the accusation is made against Pedro de Alvarado that upon his return to Guatemala he stated to the Lords of the country that he desired to found a city which they thought well of and thereupon Pedro de Alvarado commanded them to deliver to him within a certain period of time one thousand sheets of gold of a value of fifteen pesos per sheet, and the Lords set to work to collect the gold in order to please Pedro de Alvarado, and they gave him eight or nine thousand pesos and said that in view of the short period of time they did not have enough to make up for that required by Alvarado because the latter would only take pure gold; and remembering his cruelty such as the time he had taken the wife of the Prince as his mistress, they rose in arms and the war continued for a long time; and the same thing occurred in other parts of the Province, and the Indian King said that while Pedro de Alvarado was Captain of the Province, there would be no peace for Christians, even though all the Indians died in war, for which reason His Majesty lost much gold.

33. And the further charge is made against Pedro de Alvarado that

when he left for Spain he took with him gold, silver, jewels, etc., without paying the Royal Fifth, and particularly a large jewel which was worth five thousand pesos of gold, and that the Royal Fifth of the value of these treasures was not paid to the Royal Treasurer.

34. And finally it is charged against Pedro de Alvarado that not being a Knight of the Order of Santiago and having no right to wear the Red Cross that the Knights of the order wear, that with much daring and contempt for the order he publicly wore the habit of the Knights of Santiago with a red cross thereon in the city of Santo Domingo and on the Island of Cuba as well as in New Spain; and to further injure the order he wore the cross turned inside out; and when the Admiral Diego Columbus saw this and asked him why he wore the cross in such a manner, Pedro de Alvarado said to him that although a Knight of the Order of St. James, he was ashamed to wear it openly because he was poor; whereupon the said Admiral reprimanded him and told him not to be ashamed of wearing it in public, and thereafter he signed himself falsely as a member of this Order.

To the surprise of everyone concerned, Alvarado made a point of answering the charges one by one. Those raised concerning his actions during the conquest of Mexico were not considered the most damning, even though the ghost of the massacre in Mexico City was raised to haunt him. Charge 6 had been raised to discredit the legend of the leap. Concerning Charge 8, Alvarado said the woman was old, almost fifty, and he had taken her to learn about the South Sea coast area from which she had come. Besides, he insisted, she was a slave and not a princess; for if she had been young and a princess, as his enemies claimed, he would not have had to kidnap her, for she would have come to him of her own free will. Charge 13, he claimed, resulted from an incident that happened when he was a much younger man. The coat had been his father's and the Cross of Santiago had been removed, leaving the markings still on the velvet.

However, the most serious charges against Alvarado were his failure to deliver the king's fifth and his having stolen jewels which rightfully belonged to the king. To this charge Alvarado had a simple reply: he delivered the receipt of his payment along with his answers. The king had not only received the jewels but had returned some of them to Alvarado at the time of the conquistador's marriage.

While the Audiencia was trying Alvarado, the Secretary of the Audiencia appeared in Guatemala with papers from Mexico naming him governor, captain-general, mayor and judge. Jorge de Alvarado yielded up his authority and the plundering of Alvarado's friends began. The Indians revolted, and Pedrárias to the south moved in to claim some of the province for himself.

In April 1530, Alvarado was freed of the charges against him. He returned home, showed his grants from the king and scheduled the trial of the Secretary of the Audiencia, who fled into Mexico. The affairs of government in hand, Alvarado set out to put down the Indians again, and by August the Cakchiquel kings surrendered. For the first time now he could turn his attention to a conquest which had interested him for years: the conquest of the Spice Islands of the South Sea.

But as he was preparing to organize for this venture, he heard of the success that Pizarro was having among the Incas. Alvarado quickly raised an army, equipped it and set out for Peru. However, on his arrival he met with Almagro, Pizarro's partner, and allowed himself to be bought off for immediate cash. He was back in Guatemala, bored and restless, by 1535. At the request of the colonists of Honduras he marched in and established a government. But no sooner had he left than Francisco de Montejo arrived from Spain with credentials naming him governor-elect. Montejo and Alvarado were old adversaries and companions. They had sailed as captains together under Grijalva and had fought as captains under Cortés. They had both traveled far since those days and neither was prepared to yield to the other now.

On May 10, 1536, a government lawyer arrived in Guatemala to try Alvarado, and in the captain-general's absence he seized his properties and with the help of Fray Bartolomé de Las Casas began proceedings. Alvarado, no longer able to withstand the constant harassment, departed a second time for Spain. Charles confirmed the conquistador's appointment for another seven years and nullified all proceedings against him from any source.

Relieved of the legal pressures, Alvarado married the sister of his late wife and returned to Honduras to settle accounts with Montejo. On the king's orders, the local bishop interceded between the two captain-generals. Alvarado traded the Province of Chiapa for Honduras, agreed to give Montejo his estate in Mexico and stand good for two thousand pesos of indebtedness the other captain had incurred. As soon as Alvarado left, Montejo protested to the king that the entire transaction had been carried on under duress and should be considered null and void.

Meanwhile Alvarado rushed back to Guatemala to deal with the lawyer sent to try him. In a matter of days he re-established himself and was again ready to turn his attentions to the Spice Islands which had held his imagination for so long. Cortés had already attempted to locate them, and his ships, prowling about the South Sea, discovered Lower California.

Alvarado began to prepare on his own. He spent his own money to build a fleet of thirteen ships and hauled the ironware six hundred miles overland from Vera Cruz to the South Sea coast. He sailed on June 4, 1540, with eight hundred fifty men-at-arms and sailors whom he equipped at his own expense. He paused in Mexico to meet with Viceroy Mendoza, who persuaded him to join the search for the Seven Cities of Cíbola. On November 29, 1540, they drew up a contract dividing the unfound cities between them.

Putting aside his plans for the Spice Islands, Alvarado returned to Mexico City with the viceroy and remained there until May 1541. He was ready to leave when word reached Mexico City that Cristóbal de Oñate, one of the three silver kings of northern Mexico, was besieged by natives. Oñate, the father of the colonizer of New Mexico, was not only one of the wealthiest men in the empire but he was also a friend. Alvarado rushed north to help him. In the captain-general's first battle with the Indians, a scribe named Montoya lost control of his horse and the beast, stumbling about, rolled over on Alvarado, crushing him. Furious with himself, the conquistador said: "What happened could not be helped. It should happen to anyone who takes people like Montoya with him."

Alvarado ordered his men to withdraw to a village near by and dictated a brief will.

. . . and I am very tired from my wounds and as the said Bishop of Guatemala knows the persons to whom I am indebted, be it little or much, because I have many times discussed my debts with him, I hereby give him full power in order that he and Juan de Alvarado, resident of the City of Mexico, shall make and carry out my will according as may seem best and in accordance with instructions which I have herein above given and may they discharge it as though to clear my conscience of debts.

He signed the document and died.

In September that same year Doña Beatrice de Alvarado, his wife, forced the people of Guatemala to recognize her as their governor and captain-general. However, her time in office was very brief, as she and six hundred Spaniards died the next day in a flood which destroyed Alvarado's capital. It was never rebuilt.

5

Cabeza de Vaca

Becomes Shipwrecked

and Crosses a Continent

Ures
Matape
Monclava
Culiacán
Alpine
Rio Grande
Mobile
Apalache
Bad Luck I.
Tampa Bay
Matanzas
CUBA
YUCATAN
SOUTH SEA

CABEZA de VACA
CROSSES A CONTINENT
September 1528 - April 1536

W E

0   200   400

5

Cabeza de Vaca Becomes Shipwrecked
and Crosses a Continent

THE STORY of Álvar Núñez Cabeza de Vaca is the tragedy of a man who tried to live up to a family tradition. Cabeza de Vaca's grandfather was the conquistador of the Grand Canary and his contemporaries were ruthless realists, but Cabeza de Vaca himself possessed a completely different personality. He was a man out of his times and most certainly in the wrong profession. There is little question, however, that as a humanitarian he would have made one of the great missionary-explorers of the nineteenth century in the tradition of Livingstone or even the earlier Mungo Park.

But the different quality of Cabeza de Vaca was not easily seen. He was born in Jerez de la Frontera, in the sherry wine country of Southern Spain, about 1490, and grew up along the coast only twelve miles from Cadiz. When he was just a boy, his grandfather lived with him for about eight years. This Pedro de Vera Mendoza was one of the most famous men of his time, and it was he who helped set the pattern of the conquistador in his conquest of the Canaries. But for reasons he never recorded, the young boy took the name of his maternal ancestors, who earned it by leading an early thirteenth-century Spanish army to victory by guiding them through the mountain passes with the skull of a cow—*cabeza de vaca*.

The young Cabeza de Vaca followed the family tradition. He became a soldier in 1511 and fought in Naples and Ravenna. He survived the bloody battle of Ravenna in which twenty thousand were killed, and he was placed in command of the city of Gaeta near Naples. By 1513 he was back in Spain as steward for the Duke de Medina Sidonia, combining administrative talents with military. He fought in the uprising of the Comuneros in 1520, participated in the battle of Tordesillas, and after the uprising was suppressed, he fought

in Navarre against the French. In the years that followed, he married
and settled down. He might have remained in obscurity except for
the expedition of Pánfilo de Narváez.

Narváez, ten years or more Cabeza de Vaca's senior, had gone to
the Indies about 1500, probably in one of the Columbian voyages.
In 1510 he had become chief captain under Diego de Velásquez in
the conquest of Cuba and had come under severe criticism from Las
Casas, the conscience of the Indies. In 1518 Narváez returned to
Spain to represent Velásquez, and soon afterward he led the expedition against Cortés. He became for three years the prisoner of the
captain-general and conquistador of Mexico. At the request of Narváez' wife, Cortés released her husband.

Humiliated and defeated, and blinded in one eye, Narváez returned
to Cuba and his plantation. But he had visions of his own Mexico.
And there was a restlessness in the times. The Island of Beminy—
Florida—had been discovered by Juan Ponce de León in 1513, and
four times in the next thirteen years unsuccessful expeditions had
attempted to colonize Florida. On November 17, 1526, the King
gave Narváez the chance to "discover, conquer and people" the area
from Rio de las Palmas in northeast Mexico to the island of Florida.
The conquistador was to pay all of his own expenses and establish
two colonies of one hundred men each.

By this time Narváez had spent twenty-six years in the Indies, and
he had every reason to believe he was as able as any of his contemporaries. He spent the winter enlisting soldiers for the venture. The
flood of men out of the Islands to the mainland had already begun
to worry the crown, and every effort was made to recruit men from
Castile itself. On February 15, 1527, Narváez signed an agreement
with Cabeza de Vaca to join the expedition as treasurer, responsible
for the King's Fifth. The new treasurer placed a bond for two
thousand ducats and sailed as commander of one of the five caravels.

One of the most interesting accounts of all the Spanish conquistadores, Cabeza de Vaca's is also one of the most frustrating for scholars. He describes in detail his relationships to the natives and what
happened to him and his companions, but he is extremely vague on
distances and directions, leaving his exact route in doubt. The most
educated guesses take him from Galveston Bay westward to the Colorado River in Texas, then north to Big Spring through the Pecos to
Carlsbad, New Mexico, and north into Zuñi country and south again
to El Paso, and from there north through Arizona and south again

through Mexico past the Rio Sonora paralleling the Pacific coast to Culiacan. He crossed the southern United States and Mexico from sea to sea, spending eight years as a castaway, slave and wanderer, and in this time his character emerged as one almost incomprehensible to his fellow countrymen. The difference became clear near the end of his journey when he attempted to prevent his Indian companions from being taken as slaves.

The castaways of the Spanish voyages left their mark on Spanish history in the New World. Gerónimo de Aguilar, cast ashore from a Darien voyage, served as an early intepreter for Cortés. A companion of Aguilar remained with the Mayans in Yucatan because he had been accepted into the tribe, and because he had been tattooed. This same unfortunate caught between two worlds eventually led the Indians against the Spanish incursion of Yucatan. And Cabeza de Vaca on his visit to Mexico began the train of events that led to the expeditions of Fray Marcos and Coronado.

The voyages along the coasts were numerous and almost impossibly dangerous in the small vessels built in Spain. They were foolhardy in a fleet like the one built by Narváez and Cabeza de Vaca. But the tradition of shipbuilding in the colonies came early. Alvarado built his fleet on the West Coast, preparing to sail for the Spice Islands. Before him Cortés had financed four ships to be used in South Sea exploration. Cortés had a fleet built and carried overland for the conquest of Mexico. Balboa had carried the timbers for his ships across the Isthmus and was probably executed by Pedrarias as much to gain those two ships as for any other reason. And Orellana, the captain who marched with the Pizarros, built a ship at the headwaters of the Amazon in the same fashion as Narváez and sailed the length of that great river. This, as well as the ruthlessness for which they are most remembered, is also a part of the conquistador tradition.

What happened to the Narváez expedition, Cabeza de Vaca himself tells in a *Relación* first printed in 1542. It was paraphrased into English by 1613, and in 1621 an Austrian monk wrote a protest against such persons as Cabeza de Vaca performing miracles.

THE NARRATIVE OF CABEZA DE VACA

Relation that Álvar Núñez Cabeza de Vaca gave of what befell the armament in the Indies whither Pánfilo de Narváez went for Governor from the year 1527 to the year 1537, when with three comrades he returned and came to Seville.

PROEM

Sacred Caesarian Catholic Majesty:

Among the many who have held sway, I think no prince can be found whose service has been attended with the ardor and emulation shown for that of your Highness at this time. The inducement is evident and powerful; men do not pursue together the same career without motive, and strangers are observed to strive with those who are equally impelled by religion and loyalty.

Although ambition and love of action are common to all, there great inequalities of fortune as to the advantages that each may gain, the result not of conduct, but only accident, coming in the providence of God and solely by His will. Hence to one occur deeds more signal than he thought to achieve; to another the opposite occurs, so that he can show no higher proof of purpose than his effort, and at times even this is concealed.

As for me, I can say that in undertaking the march I made on the main by the royal authority, I firmly trusted that my conduct and service would be as evident and distinguished as were those of my ancestors. Yet neither my counsel nor my constancy availed to gain the goal we sought. None of the many expeditions that have gone into those parts has found itself in straits so great as ours, or comes to an end alike forlorn and fatal. To me only one duty remains; to tell of what was seen and heard in the ten years I wandered lost and in privation through many and remote lands. Rather than to exaggerate, I have understated all things, and it is enough to say this tale is offered to your Majesty as truth. I beg it may be received in the name of homage, since it is the most that one could bring who returned from there naked.

On the seventeenth day of June, in the year 1527, the Governor Pánfilo de Narváez left the port of San Lúcar de Barrameda, authorized and commanded by your Majesty to conquer and govern the provinces of the main, extending from the River Palmas to the cape of Florida. He took five ships, in which went six hundred men. The officers—for we shall have to speak of them—were these, with their rank: Cabeza de Vaca, treasurer and high-sheriff; Alonso Enriquez, comptroller; Juan Xuarez, a friar of Saint Francis, commissary; and four more friars of the same order.

We arrived at the island of Santo Domingo, where we delayed nearly forty-five days getting some necessary supplies, particularly horses. Here we lost more than one hundred forty men, who wished to remain, seduced by the advantages held out to them by the people of that country.

We sailed from the island and arrived at Santiago, a port of Cuba, where the Governor supplied himself with more men, arms and horses. The Governor sent me with two ships to Trinidad for some supplies which had been offered by Vasco Porcallo de Figueroa of that city. While I was ashore on this business, a terrible tempest arose. The two ships were lost, and with them sixty persons and twenty horses. We struggled for many days with hardship and hunger, for the provisions and subsistence were destroyed.

On the fifth of November the Governor arrived with four ships, which had survived the great storm, having run into a place of safety in time. Our people were so frightened by what had happened that they begged the Governor to spend the winter there. Since it was also the wish of the townspeople, he gave the ships and people into my charge to pass the winter at the port of Xagua, twelve leagues from there, where I remained until the twentieth day of February.

At this time the Governor arrived with a brigantine bought in Trinidad, and brought with him a pilot named Miruelo, who said he knew the position of the River Palmas and had been there, and was a thorough pilot for all the coast of the north. The Governor had also purchased and left in Havana another vessel, in the charge of Alvar de la Cerda, with forty infantry and twelve cavalry.

The second day after his arrival the Governor set sail with four hundred men and eighty horses, in four ships and a brigantine. The pilot put the vessels among the shoals they call Canarreo, and on the following day we were struck. There we remained fifteen days, the keels of our vessels frequently touching bottom. At the end of this time a tempest from the south threw so much water on the shoals that we got off, although not without danger. We arrived at Guan-iguanico, where another storm overtook us and we were nearly lost. At Cape Corrientes we had still another storm which delayed us for three days. Finally we doubled Cape San Antonio, and sailed with head winds until we were within twelve leagues of Havana. Standing in the next day to enter the harbor, a wind came from the south which drove us from the land toward the coast of Florida. We came in sight on Tuesday, the twelfth day of April, and sailed along the coast. On Holy Thursday we anchored near the shore in the mouth of a bay [just west of Tampa] at the head of which we saw some Indian villages.

On the same day the comptroller, Alonzo Enriquez, landed on an island in the bay. The following day, which was Good Friday, the Governor debarked with as many people as the boats could hold. The day after, he raised ensigns for your Majesty and took possession of the country in your royal name. He made known his authority and was obeyed as Governor, as your Majesty had commanded. At the same time we laid our commissions before him and he acknowledged them according to their tenor. Then he ordered that the rest of the people and the horses should land. Only forty-two of the beasts were left, the rest having died because of the great storms and the length of time at sea. These few remaining were so weak and lean that for the time we could have little service from them.

The following day the Governor began to explore the land. We went north until evening, when we arrived at a very large bay that appeared to stretch far inland [the western arm of Tampa Bay]. The next day we returned to our ships and people. The Governor ordered the brigantine to sail along the coast of Florida and search for the harbor that Miruelo, the pilot, said he knew, though as yet he had failed to find it and could not tell us where we were. If the port were not found, the brigantine should steer for Havana and find the ship in the command of Alvar de la Cerda, and taking provisions they should both come to look for us.

After the brigantine left we returned to enter the land. Keeping along the shores of the bay, we captured four Indians. We showed them maize, to see if they had knowledge of it, for up to that time we had found none. They said they could take us to where there was some, and brought us to their town near the head of the bay, showing us a little corn not yet fit for gathering.

There we saw many cases such as are used to contain the merchandise of Castile, in each of them a dead man, and the bodies were covered with painted deerskins. This appeared to the commissary to be a kind of idolatry, and we burned the cases with the bodies. We also found pieces of linen and of woolen cloth, and bunches of feathers which appeared like those of New Spain. There were also traces of gold. We asked the Indians by signs where these things came from, and they motioned to us that very far from there was a province called Apalachen, where there was much gold and abundance of everything we desired.

On the first of May, the Governor called aside the commissary, the comptroller, the assessor, myself, a sailor named Bartolomé Fernández, and a notary named Hieronymo Alaniz. He said that he wished to penetrate the interior, and that the ships ought to go along the coast until they came to the port which the pilots believed was very near on the way to the River Palmas. He asked us for our opinions.

I said that under no circumstances ought we to leave the vessels until they were in a secure and peopled harbor. The pilots were not confident. They did not agree in any particular, nor did they know where we were. Also, the horses were in no condition to serve us in any emergency that might occur. Above all, we could not communicate with the Indians without an interpreter. We were about to enter a country we knew nothing about, not even who lived in it. Besides all this we had no food for wandering we knew not where. My opinion was that we should embark and seek a harbor and a soil better than this to occupy, since what we had seen of it was desert and poor.

The commissary, Fray Juan Xuarez, held other views. He thought we ought not to sail but that, always keeping to the coast, we should march in search of the harbor, which the pilots stated was only ten or fifteen leagues from there on the way to Panuco. He said it was not possible, marching always by the shore, that we could miss finding the harbor, because they said it stretched inland a dozen leagues. To embark, he said, would be to brave the Almighty after so many storms and the great losses of men and ships sustained in reaching here. For these reasons we should march along the coast until we reached the harbor, and the ships should take a like direction until they arrived at the same place.

The Governor followed his own judgment and the counsel of most of the others. Seeing his determination, I required him in behalf of your Majesty not to quit the ships before putting them in port and making them secure. And I asked a certificate of this under the hand of the notary. The Governor responded that he only abided by the judgment of the commissary and of the majority of the officers, and that I had no right to make these requirements of him. He then asked the notary to give him a certificate that inasmuch as there was no subsistence in that country for the maintenance of a colony, nor haven for the ships, he broke up the settlement he had placed there, taking its inhabitants in quest of a port and land that should be better. He said to me in the hearing of those present that since I so much discouraged and feared entering the land, I should sail in charge of the ships and the people in them and form a settlement, should I arrive at the port before him; but from this proposal I excused myself.

The Governor asked me the cause of my reluctance, and I answered that I rejected the responsibility because I felt certain that he would never find the ships again, nor the ships him, with the small amount of supplies and equipment we had for entering the country. I preferred to expose myself to the danger which he and the others adventured than to take charge of the ships and allow it to be said that I had opposed the invasion and remained behind from timidity, and so have my courage called into question. I chose rather to risk my life than put my honor in such a position. Seeing that he could not change my mind, he begged others to reason with me. I answered them in the same way I had him; so he appointed for his lieutenant of the ships an alcalde whose name was Caravallo.

That same day the Governor gave to each man going with him two pounds of biscuit and half a pound of bacon; with these supplies we took up our march into the country. There were three hundred men including the commissary and another friar, Juan de Palos, three clergymen, and the officers.

On the allowance we had received, we traveled fifteen days without finding anything to eat except palmitos. In all that time we did not see an Indian, a village or a house. Finally we came to a river, which we passed with great difficulty because of the very strong current. On the other side some two hundred natives appeared. Conversing by signs, they so insulted us with their gestures that we were forced to break with them. We seized five or six, who took us to their houses half a league off. Near by we found a large quantity of maize that could be gathered. We gave infinite thanks to our Lord for having succored us in this great extremity, for we were yet young in trials, and besides our weariness we were exhausted from hunger.

Again we asked the Governor to seek the sea and a port. He said it was remote, but since I insisted so, he told me to take forty men on foot and find a harbor. We found some sea sands that appeared to be a good way inland, and we followed the river down toward the sea. It led to a bay where the water was no higher than the knee, and over which five or six canoes of Indians were seen passing from one shore to the other.

With this information we left the next day, still in search of Apalachen. On the seventeenth of June a chief approached, borne on the back of another Indian and covered with a painted deerskin. A great many people attended him, some walking in advance playing on flutes of reed. By signs we told him that we were going to Apalachen. It appeared that he was an enemy to its people and would go to assist us against them. We gave him beads and hawk-bells and other articles of barter. He gave the Governor the skin he wore, and left. We followed in the road he took.

We arrived at the town of the chief, who sent us maize. During the night one of our men was shot at, and the next day we left. We went through a very difficult country that was wonderful to look upon. In it are vast forests with astonishingly high trees. So many had fallen on the ground that we advanced only with the greatest difficulty. Many of the standing trees were riven from top to bottom by bolts of lightning which fall in that country of frequent storms and tempests.

We labored on until the day after Saint John's, when we came in view of Apalachen without the inhabitants being aware of our approach. We gave many thanks to God at seeing ourselves so near, for we believed what had been told us of this land, and that there would be an end to our great hardships caused as much by the length and badness of the way as by our great hunger. Having come to where we had been informed there were much food and gold, we already felt recovered in part from our sufferings and fatigue.

When we came in view of Apalachen, the Governor ordered me to take nine cavalry with fifty infantry and enter the town. After a slight skirmish we entered the town and found a large quantity of growing maize and a large store of dried; also many deerskins, and among them some mantelets of thread, small and poor, with which the women partially cover their persons. The town consisted of forty small thatch houses.

Two hours after our arrival at Apalachen, the Indians who had fled came to us in peace, asking for their women and children whom we had captured, and we released them. However, the Governor had detained a cacique. Because of this, they attacked us the next day and set fire to the houses we were in. When he sallied forth, they fled to the lakes near by and to the large maize fields, so that we could do them little harm. The following day others came against us from a town on the opposite side of the lake. They attacked and escaped the same way.

We were in the town twenty-five days, in which time we made three incursions and found the country very thinly peopled and diffi-

cult to travel in. We asked the cacique we kept and the natives we
brought with us, who were the neighbors and enemies of these Indians. We asked about the nature of the country and its people, of the
food and all other matters concerning it. Each native answered, apart
from the rest, that the largest town in all that region was Apalachen;
the people beyond were less numerous and poorer, the land little occupied, and the inhabitants very scattered; that from here on were great
lakes, dense forests, immense deserts and solitudes. We then asked
about the region toward the south. They said that in nine days' journey there was a town called Aute which had much maize, beans and
pumpkins, and being near the sea had fish, and that those people
were their friends.

In view of the poverty of the land and the unfavorable accounts of
the population, the Indians making continual war upon us, shooting
from the lakes where we could not retaliate, we decided to leave that
place and go in search of the sea and the town of Aute. After the
first day we reached a lake full of logs where the water reached to
the paps. We crossed it only after great difficulty and constant attacks by Indians who wounded many men and horses. The good
armor some of our men wore did not help. There were those who
swore that they had seen two reed oaks, each the thickness of the
lower part of the leg, pierced through from side to side by arrows. I
myself saw an arrow that had entered the butt of an elm to the depth
of a span.

The Indians we had seen so far in Florida are all archers. They go
naked, are large of body, and appear at a distance like giants. The
bows they use are as thick as the arm, eleven or twelve palms in
length. They discharge them at two hundred paces with great precision, and miss nothing.

With much fighting and great danger, we traveled eight days. On
the ninth day we reached Aute. All the inhabitants had gone and
the houses were burned. There were maize, beans and pumpkins in
quantity, all fit for harvest. After two days' rest, the Governor begged
me to go and look for the sea, which the Indians said was near, and
which we had discovered, while on the way, from a very large stream
to which we had given the name of River of the Magdalena.

I set out the next day and traveled until the hour of vespers, arriving
at a road or entrance of the sea. Oysters were abundant, and we rejoiced. The following morning I sent twenty men to explore the coast.
They returned the next night, reporting that the creeks and bays were

large and lay so far inland that it was difficult to examine them, and
that the seashore was very distant.

We went back to the Governor and found him and many others
sick from a malady that had come upon them. The Indians had
assaulted them the night before, and they had been hard pressed.
One of the horses had been killed. I gave a report of what I had done
and of the strange nature of the country. We remained there that day.

The next morning we left Aute and traveled all day before coming
to the place I had visited. The journey was extremely difficult. There
were not enough horses to carry the sick, who increased in numbers
day by day, and we knew of no cure for them. It was piteous and
painful to witness our confusion and distress. There was nowhere to
go; and if there had been, the people were unable to move on because
most of them were ill. Worse than all of our other problems, most of
the mounted soldiers began secretly to plot a better fate for themselves
by abandoning the governor and the sick, who were weak and pros-
trated. But among them were many hidalgos and persons of gentle
condition who would not permit this to go on without informing the
Governor and the officers of your Majesty. Given the choice of desert-
ing their captain and those who were ill and feeble and above all diso-
bedient to the orders of your Majesty, they decided to remain, so that
whatever might happen to one should be the lot of all.

It was clear that we could leave this terrible land only by dying.
After considering many plans, we agreed on one that was extremely
difficult to put in operation. That was, to build vessels in which we
might leave. This appeared impossible to everyone. We did not know
how to build them, nor were there tools, iron, forge, tow, resin, rigging,
or many other necessary things. Nor was there a man among us with
any knowledge of their manufacture. Above all, there was nothing
to eat, while building, for those who should labor.

The next day one of the company came saying that he could make
pipes out of wood, which with deerskins might be made into bellows.
This was a time when anything that had the semblance of relief appeared important, and we told him to set to work. We agreed that
the nails, saws, axes and other tools should be made from the stirrups,
spurs, crossbows and the other things of iron we had. While the work
was going on, we would make four entries into Aute, with all the
horses and men that were able to go, and on every third day a horse
should be killed to be divided among the sick and those who worked
on the boats. We brought back four hundred fanegas of maize from

Aute after many clashes with the Indians. We collected palmitos for the woof or covering, twisting and preparing it for use in place of tow for the boats.

We started building the boats on the fourth, with the only carpenter in the company, and we proceeded with such great effort that on the twentieth of September five boats were finished, twenty-two cubits in length, each caulked with the fiber of palmito. We pitched them with a resin made from pine trees by a Greek, named Don Theodoro; from the same husk of the palmito and from the tails and manes of the horses we made ropes and rigging; from our shirts we made sails; and from the savins growing there we made the oars. The country into which our sins had cast us was such that only by very great search could we find stone for ballast and anchors. We flayed the horses, taking the skin from their legs entire, and tanned them to make bottles to carry water.

Meanwhile some men gathered shellfish in the coves and creeks. The Indians attacked them twice and killed ten men in sight of the camp without our being able to help. We found their corpses pierced from side to side with arrows. Even though some had on good armor, it did not give adequate protection against the powerful archery of which I have spoken.

Before we embarked, more than forty men died of disease and hunger, without counting those killed by the Indians. By the twenty-second of September, all the horses but one had been eaten. We embarked that day in the following order: in the boat of the Governor went forty-nine men; in another, which he gave to the comptroller and the commissary, went as many others; the third he gave to Captain Alonzo del Castillo and Andres Dorantes, with forty-eight men; and another he gave to two captains, Tellez and Penalosa, with forty-seven men. The last was given to the assessor and myself, with forty-nine men. After the provisions and clothes had been taken in, not over a span of the gunwales remained above water. The boats were so crowded that we could not move. Desperation drove us to hazard our lives in this way—running into a turbulent sea without a single one of us having a knowledge of navigation.

We moved along the coast in the direction of the River Palmas, our hunger and thirst continually increasing. Our scant subsistence was nearly gone. The water was out, and the bottles made from the legs of the horses soon rotted and were useless. Sometimes we entered coves and creeks that lay far in, and found them all shallow and dangerous. And so we journeyed for thirty days, occasionally finding some Indian fishermen—a poor and miserable lot.

At this time we saw a small island and stopped for water, but there was none. While lying there at anchor, a heavy storm came on that detained us six days. Our thirst was now so great that we went so far as to drink salt water. Some of the men became crazed and three or four suddenly died.

Although the storm had not ceased, we resolved to commend ourselves to God our Lord, and adventure the peril of the sea rather than await the end which thirst made certain. We were overwhelmed by the waves many times and were in such jeopardy that death seemed inevitable. Thanks be to Him that in the greatest dangers He was wont to show His favor; for at sunset, doubling a point made by the land, we found shelter and calm.

Many canoes came with Indians, and we followed them to their houses near by, at the edge of the water, and jumped on shore. Before their dwellings were a large quantity of cooked fish and many clay pitchers with water.

Governor and then took him to his house. On entering, the cacique gave us fish, and we gave him of the maize we brought and many trinkets. At midnight the Indians suddenly fell upon us and on those who were very sick, scattered along the shore. They also attacked the house where the Governor was, and struck him in the face with a stone. Those of our comrades present seized the cacique; but his people liberated him, leaving in our hands a robe of civet-marten.

These skins are the best, I think, that can be found; they have a fragrance that can only be equaled by amber and musk, and even at a distance is strongly perceptible.

We put the Governor in his boat, and had the others go to their boats also, leaving some fifty men to withstand the natives. None of us escaped injury. I was wounded in the face. In the last attack, the Captains Dorantes, Penalosa and Tellez put themselves in ambuscade with fifteen men and fell upon the enemy rear, and the Indians fled.

The next morning I broke up more than thirty canoes for fuel, for we were suffering severe cold. When the sea subsided, we again left and sailed on for three days. As we brought little water and the vessels were few, we were reduced to desperation. Entering an estuary, we saw Indians approaching in a canoe. The Governor asked for water, which they agreed to give, asking for something in which they might bring it. Dorotheo Theodoro, the Greek mentioned before, said that he wished to go with them. The Governor and others tried to dissuade him, but he was determined to go, whatever might happen. He took with him a Negro, two of the natives remaining as hostages. At night the Indians returned with the vessels empty and without the Christians. Our two hostages tried to plunge into the sea, but we detained them. Thereupon the Indians in the canoe fled, leaving us sorrowful and much dejected for our loss.

We sailed the next day until the middle of the afternoon, when my boat, which was the first, discovered a point made by the land. Against a cape opposite passed a broad river [the Mississippi]. I cast anchor near a little island forming the point, to await the arrival of the other boats. When we came together, we took fresh water from the sea, the stream entering it in freshet. To parch some of the maize we brought with us, we went to an island, but finding no wood we agreed to go on the river beyond the point, one league off. The current was so violent that we could not get there. And the north wind, which came from the shore, began to blow so strongly that it forced us to sea.

We sounded half a league out, and found we could not get bottom with thirty fathoms. Fighting to reach land, we navigated three days, and at the end of this time, a little before the sun rose, we saw smoke in several places along the shore. Attempting to reach there, we found ourselves in three fathoms of water, and in the darkness we dared not land. We decided to stop until morning.

When day came, the boats had lost sight of each other. Keeping my course until the hour of vespers, I sighted two boats and, drawing near, I found that the first was the Governor's. He asked me what I thought we should do. I told him we ought to join the boat which went ahead and not to leave her, and the three of us together must keep on our way to where God should be pleased to lead us. He said this could not be done, because the boat was far to sea and he wished to reach the shore; that if I wished to follow him, I should order the men in my boat to take the oars and work, for it was only by strength of arm that the land could be gained. We rowed until near sunset, but the Governor had the healthiest of all the men and we could not keep up with his boat. I asked him to pass me a rope so that I could keep up with him; but he refused, saying that he himself would have all he could do to reach the land that night. I said to him that since he saw we did not have the strength to follow him, he must tell me what he wished me to do. He answered that it was no longer a time for one to command another, but that each should do what he thought best to save his own life; and this was what he intended to do. Saying this, he left with his boat.

As I could not follow him, I steered to the other boat at sea, which waited for me. It was the one commanded by the Captains Penalosa and Tellez.

We continued in company, eating a daily allowance of half a handful of raw maize, for four days, when we lost sight of each other in a storm. It was only by God's favor that we did not all go down.

Because of the winter and its inclemency, the many days we had suffered hunger, and the heavy beating of the waves, the people began to despair. All the people in my boat had collapsed one on another, so near to death that there were few in a state of sensibility. Of the whole number not five men were on their feet; and when night came, only the master and myself were left to work the boat. Two hours after dark, he said I must take charge of her as he was in such condition he believed he was going to die that night. I took the paddle, and after midnight I went to see if the master was alive. He said he was better and would take charge until day. In that hour I would more willingly have died than seen so many people before me in such condition. After the master took command of the boat, I lay down a little but could not rest, for nothing at that time was farther from me than sleep.

Near dawn, it seemed to me I heard the tumbling of the sea. The coast was low, it roared loudly. Surprised, I called the master, who said he believed we were near the land. We sounded and found ourselves in seven fathoms. He advised that we should keep to sea until sunrise, and so I took an oar and pulled on the land side until we were a league away, when we gave her stern to the sea. Near the shore a wave took us and knocked the boat out of water the distance of the throw of a crowbar. From the violence with which she struck, nearly all the people, who had seemed dead, were roused to consciousness. Finding themselves near the shore, they began to crawl on hands and feet to land, into some ravines. There we made fire, parched some of the maize we brought, and found rainwater. From the warmth of the fire the people recovered and began to arouse themselves. This was the sixth of November, 1528.

After the people had eaten, I ordered Lope de Oviedo, who had more strength than any of the rest, to climb a near-by tree to look about and try to gain knowledge of the country. It appeared that we were on an island, and that the land was pawed up like ground where cattle range.

Exploring further, he found some huts whose tenants had gone into the field. He took from these an earthen pot, a little dog, some few mullets, and returned. Three Indians with bows and arrows followed and were calling to him, while he in the same way was beckoning them on. When he arrived where we were, the natives remained a little way back, seated on the shore. Half an hour later, they were joined by one hundred other Indian bowmen, who, if they were not large, our fear made giants of them. They stopped near us with the first three. It was idle to think that we could make any defense for there were not six of us who could rise from the ground. We tried the best we could to make friends with them. We gave them beads and hawk-bells, and each of them gave me an arrow, which is a pledge of friendship. They told us by signs that they would return in the morning and bring us something to eat, as they had nothing with them.

At sunrise the next day the Indians returned and brought us fish, and some roots. They sent their women and children to look at us, and they went back rich with the hawk-bells and beads we gave them. Finding that we had provision, fish, roots, water and other things we asked for, we decided to sail on. We dug out our boat from the sand, stripping off our clothes to launch her.

At the distance of two crossbow shots in the sea, we shipped a wave that soaked us. As we were naked and it was very cold, the oars loosened in our hands, and the next blow of the sea capsized the boat. The assessor and two others held fast to her but the boat carried them over, and they were drowned under her. As the surf near the shore was very high, a single roll of the sea threw the rest of us into the waves and upon the shore of the island half-drowned. The survivors escaped naked as the day they were born, with the loss of all they had. It was November and the cold was severe. Our bodies were so emaciated that the bones could be counted, and we looked like the perfect figures of death.

At sunset the Indians, thinking that we had not gone, came to seek us and bring us food. When they saw what had happened to us, and our state of suffering and melancholy destitution, they sat down among us and began to lament so earnestly that they might have been heard at a distance. It was strange to see these men, wild and untaught, howling like brutes over our misfortunes. It caused in me, as in others, an increase of feeling and livelier sense of our calamity.

When the cries ceased, I said to the Christians that if they agreed I would beg these Indians to take us to their houses. Some who had been in New Spain replied that we should not think of it, for they would sacrifice us to their idols. But I saw no better course, and asked the Indians to take us to their dwellings. They signified that it would give them delight.

Presently thirty men loaded themselves with wood and started for their houses, which were far off, and we remained with the others until evening. Then, holding us up, they carried us with all haste. Because of the extreme cold they had made four or five very large fires at intervals along the way, and at each they warmed us. When we had regained some warmth and strength, they took us to the next fire so swiftly that they hardly let us touch our feet to the ground. In this manner we went as far as their habitations, where we found that they had made a house for us with many fires in it. An hour after our arrival they began to dance and hold great rejoicing, which lasted all night, although for us there was no joy, festivity or sleep, awaiting the hour they should make us victims. In the morning they again gave us fish and roots, showing us such hospitality that we were reassured and lost somewhat the fear of being sacrificed.

That day I saw a native with an article of traffic I knew was not one we had given them. I was told by signs that it had been given by men like ourselves. Hearing this, I sent two Indians, and with them two Christians, to meet with these persons. They met near by, as the men were coming to look for us; for the Indians of the place where they were had given them information about us. They were Captains Andres Dorantes and Alonzo del Castillo, with all the persons of their boat.

They related that on the fifth day of that month their boat had capsized a league and a half from there, but they had escaped without losing anything.

Most of us were naked, and the weather so violent we could not consider traveling and crossing rivers and bays by swimming, and we were without provisions or the means of carrying any. Therefore we yielded to necessity and decided to pass the winter where we were. We also agreed that four of the most robust men should go on to Panuco, which we believed to be near. If by Divine favor they should reach there, they could give information of our remaining on that island and of our sorrows and destitution. These men were excellent swimmers. One of them was Alvaro Fernandez, a Portuguese sailor and carpenter; the second was named Mendez; the third Figueroa, who was a native of Toledo; and the fourth Astudillo, a native of Cafra. They took with them an Indian of the island of Auia.

After the four Christians had left, the weather became so cold and tempestuous that the Indians could not pull up roots. The cane weirs in which they took fish no longer yielded anything and, the houses being very open, our people began to die. Five Christians, quartered on the coast, went so far as to eat their dead. Finally, of eighty men who arrived in the two boats, only fifteen remained alive.

To this island we gave the name Malhado. The people we found there are large and well formed. They have no other arms than bows and arrows, which they use well. The men have one of their nipples bored from side to side, and some have both, wearing a cane in each, the length of two palms and a half, and the thickness of two fingers. They have the underlip also bored, and wear in it a piece of cane the breadth of half a finger. Their women are accustomed to great work. They stay on the island from October to the end of February, during which time they live on roots which they get from under the water in November and December. They have weirs of cane and fish only in this season; afterward they live on the roots. At the end of February they go elsewhere for food, for by then the root is beginning to grow and cannot be eaten.

For three months in the year they eat only oysters and drink very bad water. The houses are of mats set up on masses of oyster shells, which they sleep upon, and in skins, should they accidentally possess them. We lived in this way until April 1529, when we went to the seashore. There we ate blackberries for a month while the Indians observed their festivities.

On this island of Malhado they wished to make us physicians without examination or inquiring for diplomas. They cure the sick by blowing, and with that breath and laying on of hands they cast out infirmity. They demanded we do this, too, and be of use to them in some way. We laughed at what they did, telling them it was foolish, that we did not know how to heal. In consequence, they withheld food from us until we did what they wanted. At last, finding ourselves in need, we agreed—but not without fear that we would be blamed for any failure or success.

Their custom, on finding themselves sick, is to send for a physician. After he has applied the cure, they give him not only all they have but ask their relatives for more to give. The practitioner scarifies over the seat of pain and then sucks about the wound. They make cauteries with fire, which I have tried on myself and found it helps. They afterwards blow on the spot, and the patient believes he is cured.

Our method was to bless the sick, breathing upon them, and recite a Pater Noster and an Ave Maria, praying with all earnestness to God our Lord that he would give health and influence them to make us some good return. In His clemency He willed that all those for whom we supplicated should tell the others that they were sound and in health, directly after we made the sign of the blessed Cross over them. For this the Indians treated us kindly; they deprived themselves of food to give it to us, and they made us gifts of skins and some trifles.

So protracted was our hunger that many times I was three days without eating. The natives endured as much; and it appeared to me impossible that life could go on, although afterward I found myself in far greater hunger and necessity.

The Indians who had Alonzo del Castillo, Andres Dorantes, and the others that remained alive, were of a different tribe and went to the opposite shore of the main two leagues away to eat oysters, where they remained until the first day of April. This island is half a league in breadth and five leagues in length.

After Dorantes and Castillo returned to the island they brought together the Christians, and found fourteen survived. As I have said, I was on the opposite shore where my Indians had taken me; I was very sick with very little hope of life.

When the Christians heard of my condition, they gave an Indian the cloak of marten skins we had taken from the cacique in exchange for transportation to where I was. Twelve of them crossed; for two were so feeble that their comrades could not bring them. When they reached the mainland, they found another of our company named Francisco de León. The thirteen together followed along the coast. As soon as they had come over, my Indians informed me, but sickness prevented me from going with my companions or even seeing them.

I was obliged to remain with the people of the island more than a year. I resolved to flee from them because of the hard work they put upon me, and the harsh treatment, and go to Charruco on the main. And so I began to plan. I set to trafficking, and tried to make my employment as best I could, and by that means I got food and good treatment. The Indians would beg me to go from one quarter to another for things they needed; for because of constant fighting, they could not cross the country or make many exchanges. With my merchandise and trade I went into the interior as far as I pleased and traveled along the coast forty or fifty leagues. The principal wares were sea beads, cones and pieces of seasnail, conchs used for cutting, and bean-like fruit of highest value among them, which they use as a medicine and in their dances and festivities. I carried these into the interior, where I bartered them for skins, ochre with which they rub and color their faces, hard canes for arrows, sinews, cement and flint for the heads, and tassels of the hair of deer which they dye red.

My work suited me well, for the travel allowed me to go freely where I wished. I was not obliged to work and was not a slave. Wherever I went I received fair treatment, and the Indians gave me food for my trade goods. My main purpose, while journeying in this business, was to find out the way I could leave, and I became well known. The Indians were pleased when they saw me and I brought them what they wanted; and others who did not know me tried to find me for my reputation. I underwent terrible hardships of peril and privation as well as of storms and cold. Often they overtook me alone and in the wilderness; but I came forth from them all by the great mercy of God our Lord. Because of them I avoided doing business in winter, a season in which the natives themselves retire to their huts and ranches, torpid and incapable of exertion.

I was in this country nearly six years, alone among the Indians and naked like them. I remained so long because I wished to take with me the Christian Lope de Oviedo, who was one of those two who had remained on the island. His companion, Alaniz, had died soon after the departure of the others. I went over to the island every year and pleaded with him to join me in search of Christians. He put me off every year, saying that he would come in the next crossing. At last I got him off, crossing him over the bay and over four rivers in the coast, as he could not swim.

We went on with some Indians to a bay a league in width, and deep everywhere. From its appearance we supposed it to be that which is called Espiritu Santo. We met some Indians on the other side of it, coming to visit ours, who told us that beyond them were three men like us, and gave their names. We asked for the others and were told they were all dead of cold and hunger; that the Indians farther on, for their diversion, had killed Diego Dorantes, Valdeviseo and Diego de Huelva, because they left one house for another; and that other Indians, their neighbors with whom Captain Dorantes now was, had killed Esquivel and Mendez. We asked how the living were, and the Indians said they were very ill used. The boys and some of the Indian men, being very idle, gave them many kicks, cuffs and blows with sticks.

We asked about the country ahead and the food: they said there was nothing to eat and that there were only a few people, who suffered from cold, having no skins or other things to cover them. They told us also that if we wished to see those three Christians, the Indians who had them would come in two days to eat walnuts a league from where we were. And so that we might know what they told us of the ill usage was true, they slapped my companion and beat him with a stick, and I was not left without my share. Many times they threw lumps of mud at us, and every day they put their arrows to our hearts, saying that they were inclined to kill us in the way they had destroyed our friends. Lope Oviedo, my comrade, said in fear that he wished to go back with the women of those who had crossed the bay with us. I protested strongly against his returning, but in no way could I prevent it. So he went back and I remained alone with those savages.

Two days after Oviedo left, the Indians who had Alonzo del Castillo and Andres Dorantes came to the place of which we had been told to eat walnuts.

An Indian told me of the arrival of the Christians, and he and some of his kinsmen took me with them. When I arrived, Andres Dorantes came out to see who it could be, for the Indians had told him that a Christian was coming. His astonishment was great when he saw me, as they had long considered me dead and the natives had said that I was. We gave many thanks at seeing ourselves together, and this was a day of the greatest pleasure in our lives. Dorantes said that for a long time he had entreated Castillo and Estevanico, the Negro, to move on; but they had not dared because they did not know how to swim and were afraid of the rivers and bays they should have to cross.

And so the Almighty had been pleased to preserve me through many trials and diseases, conducting me in the end to the fellowship of those who had abandoned me, that I might lead them over the bays and rivers that obstructed our progress. They advised me on no account to let the natives suspect my desire to go on because they would destroy me, and that for success it would be necessary for me to remain quiet until the end of six months, when the season comes for these Indians to go to another part of the country to eat prickly pears. People would arrive from farther on, bringing bows to barter and exchange. After making our escape, we should be able to go with them on their return. They agreed to this plan, and I remained. The prickly pear is the size of a hen's egg, vermilion and black in color, and of agreeable flavor. The natives live on it three months of the year.

I was given as a slave to the same Indian as Dorantes was. The Indian was blind in one eye, as were also his wife and sons, and likewise another who was with him; so that of a fashion they were all blind. Castillo was with a neighboring tribe.

When the six months were over, the Indians went after the prickly pears to a place thirty leagues off. When we approached the point where we planned to escape, the Indians we were with quarreled about a woman. After striking with fists, beating with sticks and bruising heads in great anger, each took his lodge and went his way, which made it necessary for the Christians to also separate, and it was another year before we could come together again.

In this time I passed a hard life, hungry and ill used. Three times I was obliged to run from my masters, and each time they came after me and tried to kill me. But God in His mercy chose to protect me; and when the season of prickly pears returned, we came together again in the same place. After we had arranged our escape and appointed a time, that very day the Indians separated and all went back. I told my comrades I would wait for them among the prickly-pear plants until the moon was full. This day was the first of September, 1534, and the first of the moon; and I said that if in this time they did not come as we had agreed, I would leave and go alone. So we parted, each going with his Indians. I remained with mine until the thirteenth day of the moon.

At this time Dorantes arrived with Estavanico and told me that they had left Castillo with other Indians near by. The next day our Indians planned to move to where Castillo was. They were going to unite with those who held him and become friends, having been at war until then, and in this way we would recover Castillo.

These Indians told us that there was another people next in advance of us, living toward the coast. They had killed the people who came in the boat of Penalosa and Tellez, for they arrived so feeble that they could not resist. We were shown their clothes and arms and were told that the boat lay stranded. This, the fifth boat, had remained until then unaccounted for. The boat of the Governor had been carried out to sea, and that of the comptroller and the friars had been cast away on the coast. We have already told how the two boats in which Castillo, I, and Dorantes came, foundered near the Island of Malhado.

The second day after we had moved, we commended ourselves to God and set forth with speed. Hurrying on in great fear lest the Indians should overtake us, we saw some smokes. We took that direction and arrived there after vespers. We found an Indian who guided us to the houses of those who had made the fires. The inhabitants seemed pleased with our company and took us to their dwellings. Dorantes and the Negro were lodged in the house of a physician; Castillo and I in the house of another.

The community directly brought us a great many prickly pears, having heard of us before, of our cures, and of the wonders Our Lord worked by us. Although there had been no other wonders, these were adequate to open ways for us through this poor country, keeping us alive, sustaining us in great want, and putting into these nations the heart of kindness.

The night we arrived, some Indians came to Castillo and told him they had great pain in the head, and begged him to cure them. After he had made the Sign of the Cross over them, and commended them to God, they instantly said that all the pain had left, and went to their houses bringing us prickly pears, with a piece of venison, a meat little known to us. As the report of Castillo's cures spread, many sick came to us that night that we should heal them, each bringing a piece of venison, until the quantity became so great we did not know where to put it. We gave many thanks to God, for every day went on increasing His compassion and His gifts. After the sick were attended to, they began to dance and sing until sunrise; and because of our arrival the rejoicing was continued for three days.

When the festivities ended, we asked the Indians about the country farther on, the people we should find in it, and of the subsistence there. They answered us that throughout all the region prickly pears abounded; but the fruit was now gathered and all the people had gone back to their houses. They said the country was very cold, and there were few skins. Since it was already winter, we decided to pass the season with these Indians.

Five days after our arrival, all the Indians went off, taking us with them to gather more prickly pears, to a place where there were other peoples speaking different tongues. After walking five days in great hunger, we came to a river and put up our houses. We then went to seek the product of certain trees, which is like peas. As there are no paths in the country, I was detained some time. The others returned, and coming to look for them in the dark I got lost. Thank

God I found a burning tree, and in the warmth of it I passed the cold of that night. In the morning, loading myself with sticks and taking two brands with me, I returned to search for them.

I wandered, naked as I was born, for five days with my fire and load; for this was all the protection I had against the cold. Going to the low woods near the rivers, I prepared for the night. I made a hole in the ground and threw in fuel from trees that were fallen and dry. I made four fires, in the form of a cross, around the hole. I also gathered some coarse straw with which I covered myself in the hole. In this way I was sheltered at night from the cold. On one occasion while I slept, the fire fell on the straw, and began to blaze so rapidly that despite the haste I made to get out of it, I carried some marks on my hair. During all this time I could not find anything I could eat. My feet were bare and bled a good deal. Through the mercy of God, the wind did not blow from the north in all this time, or I would have died.

At the end of the fifth day I arrived on the margin of a river where I found the Indians, who, with the Christians, had considered me dead, supposing that I had been stung by a viper. All rejoiced to see me, and especially so my companions.

The next morning many Indians came and brought five persons who had cramps, so that Castillo might cure them. Each offered his bow and arrows, which Castillo accepted. At sunset he blessed them, commending them to God our Lord, and we all prayed to Him the best we could to send health. In the morning all got up well and sound, and were as strong as though they had never had a disorder. This caused great admiration, and inclined us to render many thanks to God our Lord, Whose goodness we now clearly beheld, giving us firm hopes that He would liberate us and bring us to where we might serve Him.

The Indians left and took their friends with them in health, and we departed for a place at which others were eating prickly pears. Through all the country they talked only of the wonders which God our Lord worked through us, and persons came from many parts that we might cure them. At the end of the second day after our arrival, some other Indians, of the Susolas, came to us and beseeched Castillo to go with them to cure one wounded and several sick. They also said that among them was one very near his end. Castillo was a timid practitioner, particularly in serious and dangerous cases, believing that his sins would weigh and some day hinder him in performing cures. The

Indians told me to go and heal them, as they liked me. So I had to go with them, and Dorantes accompanied me with Estevanico.

Coming near their huts, I saw that the sick man we had come to heal was dead. Many persons were around him weeping, and his family was prostrate, a sign that the one who had dwelt in the house was no more. When I arrived, I found his eyes rolled up and the pulse gone. He had all the appearances of death. I removed a mat with which he was covered, and supplicated our Lord as fervently as I could to give health to him, and to the rest that might have need of it. After he had been blessed and breathed upon many times, they brought me his bow and gave me a basket of pounded prickly pears.

The natives took me to cure many others who were sick of a stupor, and presented me with two more baskets of prickly pears, which I gave to the Indians who accompanied us. Those to whom we gave the fruit tarried, and returned at night to their houses, reporting that he who had been dead had arisen whole and walked, had eaten and spoken with them, and that all to whom I had ministered were well and happy. This caused great wonder and fear, and throughout the land the people talked of nothing else. All to whom the fame of it reached came to seek us to cure them and bless their children.

When the Cuthalchuches, who were in company with our Indians, were about to return to their own country, they left us all the prickly pears they had, without keeping one. They gave us flints of very high value there, a palm and a half in length, with which they cut. They begged us to remember them and pray to God that they might always be well, and we promised to do so. They left, the most satisfied beings in the world.

For eight months, reckoned by the number of moons, people came to us from many places, and said that most truly we were children of the sun. Dorantes and the Negro up to this time had not attempted to practice; but because of the great solicitation made by those coming from different places to find us, we all became physicians, although I was the most venturous and bold, willing to attempt the performance of any cure. Everyone we treated told us he was well; and so great was the confidence that they would become healed if we administered to them, they even believed that while we remained none of them would die.

For six of the eight months we were among this people, we were in great want. When the prickly pears began to ripen, I and the Negro went, without these Indians knowing it, to others, the Maliacones, a day's journey distant. Three days later I sent him to bring Castillo and Dorantes, and we all set out with the Indians to get the small fruit of certain trees on which they support themselves ten or twelve days while the prickly pears are maturing.

I have already stated that throughout all this country we went naked. As we were unaccustomed to this, twice a year we cast our skins like serpents. The sun and the air produced great sores on our breasts and shoulders, giving us sharp pain; and the large loads we carried caused the cords to cut into our arms. The country is so broken and thicketed that often, after getting our wood in the forests, the blood flowed from us in many places because of the thorns and shrubs that tore our flesh wherever we went. In this work my only solace and relief was the thought of the sufferings of Our Redeemer, Jesus Christ, and in the blood He shed for me, and in considering how much greater must have been the torment He sustained from the thorns.

After eating two dogs we had bought, we had some strength to go forward. We took leave of the Indians, who showed us the way to others near by who spoke their language. We traveled all day and found other houses whose inhabitants told us that food was very scarce with them. They were astonished at our appearance and were very frightened. After becoming somewhat accustomed to us, they reached their hands to our faces and bodies, and passed them in the same way over their own.

We stayed there that night, and in the morning the Indians brought us their sick, beseeching us to bless them. They gave us what they had to eat, the leaves of the prickly pear and roasted green fruit. They did this with such kindness and good will and were so happy to be without anything to eat, giving us their food, that we remained several days. While there, others came from beyond, and when they were about to depart we said that we wished to go with them. Our hosts pressed us warmly to stay. However, we took our leave despite their weeping.

After parting with those we left weeping, we went with the others to their houses and were well received. They brought their children to us that we might touch their hands, and gave us a great quantity of flour.

When we proposed to leave them, some women of another people who lived farther along came there. We went on, taking them for guides, and passed over a river toward evening, the water reaching to the breast. It might be as wide as that at Seville and its current was very rapid.

At sunset we reached a village with a hundred Indian homes. All the people came out to receive us, yelling and striking the palms of their hands violently against their thighs. They brought us gourds bored with holes and with pebbles in them, an instrument for the most important occasions, produced only at the dance or to effect cures, and which none dare touch but those who own them. We were so crowded that we went into the houses they had made for us. They passed the night singing and dancing, and the next day they brought us all the people of the town so that we could touch and bless them. After this they presented many arrows to some women of the other town who had accompanied theirs.

We moved from one place to another, in each one better received than in the last. They brought us their sick, and after we had blessed them, they declared they were sound. The cures we effected gave us control throughout the country over everything the inhabitants believed of any value. Wherever we went, we were accompanied by a host of Indians who plundered those by whom we were received. But there was no anger in this, for those who received us went with us to the next village, where in their turn they plundered their neighbors.

After some days we began to see mountains. According to the information the Indians gave us, they rise fifteen leagues from the North Sea. We went toward them, traveling inland, for the Indians of the interior are better provisioned.

Frequently we were accompanied by three or four thousand persons. As we had to breathe upon and sanctify the food and drink for each, and grant permission to do the many things they would come to ask, it may be seen how great was the annoyance.

In company with these, we crossed a great river coming from the north. Passing over some plains thirty leagues in extent, we found many persons coming a long distance to receive us. They met us on the road over which we were to travel, and welcomed us in the manner of those we had left.

From this place on there was another method of receiving us. Those who came out to bring us presents were not plundered; but on our coming into their houses they themselves offered us all they had as well as the houses. We gave the things to the chiefs who accompanied us, so that they should divide them. Those who were despoiled always followed us until coming to a populous country where they might replace their loss. They would tell those among whom we came not to hide anything, as nothing could be done without our knowledge and we might cause them to die, for the sun revealed everything to us.

They guided us through more than fifty leagues of desert, over rough mountains which were dry and without game, and we suffered greatly from hunger.

Finally we forded a very large river. From this place many of the people began to sicken from the great privation and labor they had undergone in the passage of those ridges. They conducted us to some plains at the base of the mountains, where people came to meet us from a great distance and received us as the last had done. They gave so many goods to those who came with us that half were left behind because they could not be carried.

We told these people that we desired to go where the sun sets, and they said that inhabitants in that direction were very distant. We commanded them to send and make known our coming; but they tried to excuse themselves, because those people were their enemies. But they did not dare disobey, and sent two women, one of their own, the other a captive from that people; for the women can negotiate even though there is war. We followed them and stopped at a place where we agreed to wait. They were gone five days, and the Indians said they could not find anybody.

We told them to take us north and they answered as before, that except for a great distance there were no people in that direction and nothing to eat, nor could water be found. In spite of all this, we persisted. They still tried to excuse themselves in every manner possible. At this we became offended, and one night I went out to sleep in the woods apart from them; but they immediately came to me and remained all night, telling me how terrified they were, and beseeching us not to be angry. They said that they would lead us in the direction we wished to go, though they knew they should die on the way.

While we still feigned to be displeased lest their fright should leave them, a remarkable circumstance happened. On that day many of the Indians became ill, and on the next day eight men died. Wherever this became known, there was such dread that it seemed as if the inhabitants would die of fright at the sight of us. They begged us not to remain angry nor require that more of them should die. They believed we caused their death by only willing it, when in truth it gave us the greatest pain. For beyond their loss we feared they might all die or abandon us of fright, and that other people from then on would do the same, seeing what had happened to these. We prayed to God our Lord to relieve them; and from that time the sick began to get better.

Three days later the women whom we sent away returned and said they had found very few people as nearly all had gone for cattle. We ordered the convalescent to remain and the well to go with us. After three days' travel we stopped, and the next day Alonzo del Castillo set out with Estevanico, the Negro, taking the two women as guides. The one who was a captive led them to the town in which her father lived. These houses were the first we saw with the appearance and structure of houses.

After talking with the Indians, Castillo returned to where he had left us and brought five or six of the people. He told us he had found fixed dwellings of civilization, that the inhabitants lived on beans and pumpkins, and that he had seen maize. This news delighted us the most, and for it we gave infinite thanks to our Lord. Castillo told us the Negro was coming with all the population to wait for us in the road not far off. We left and soon met the Negro and the people coming to receive us. They gave us beans, many pumpkins, calabashes, blankets of cowhide, and other things. As this people and those who came with us were enemies and did not speak each other's language, we sent the latter home, giving them what we received, and we departed with the others. Six leagues from there, as night set in, we arrived at the houses, where great festivities were made over us. We remained one day, and the next set out with these Indians. They took us to the settled habitations of others, who lived upon the same food.

From that place onward our status changed. Those who knew of our approach did not come out to receive us on the road as the others had done, but we found them in the houses, and others had been made for our reception. They were all seated with their faces turned to the wall, their heads down, the hair brought before their eyes, and their property placed in a heap in the middle of the house. From this place they began to give us many blankets of skin; and there was nothing they did not give. They were the finest Indians we saw, of the greatest activity and strength. They understood us best, and answered our inquiries intelligently. We called them the Cow nation, because most of the cattle killed are slaughtered in their neighborhood, and along up that river for over fifty leagues they destroy great numbers.

We asked where they got the maize, and they told us from where the sun goes down. Since they did not wish to go there, we asked by what direction we might best proceed. They said that the path was up that river toward the north, that it was a journey of seventeen days, and that we should find nothing to eat except a fruit they call *chacan*, that is ground between stones and even then can be eaten only with difficulty because of its dryness and pungency—which was true. They showed it to us there, but we could not eat it. They informed us also that we would pass through a people that were their enemies, who spoke their tongue; and though they had nothing to give us to eat, they would receive us with the best good will and present us with many mantles of cotton, hides and other articles of their wealth.

And so we traveled all across the country until we came out at the South Sea. Nor was the dread we had of the sharp hunger sufficient to hinder us. Our sustenance each day was a handful of deer suet, which we had been used to saving for such trials. We made the entire journey in seventeen days, and at the close we crossed the river and traveled another seventeen days.

Upon some plains that lie between chains of very great mountains, we found a people who for the third part of the year eat nothing but the powder of straw. That being the season when we passed, we also had to eat of it until we reached permanent habitations where there was an abundance of maize. They gave us a large quantity of grain and flour, pumpkins, beans, and shawls of cotton. We loaded our guides with all these, and they went back the happiest creatures on earth. We gave thanks to God for having brought us where we had found so much food.

From this point we marched through more than a hundred leagues of country, and continually found settled homes with plenty of maize and beans. The people gave us many deer and cotton shawls better than those of New Spain, many beads and certain corals found on the South Sea, and fine turquoises that come from the north. Indeed they gave us everything they had. To me they gave five emeralds made into arrowheads, which they use at their singing and dancing. They appeared to be very precious. I asked where they got these; and they said the stones were brought from some lofty mountains toward the north where there were populous towns and very large houses.

The people all came to us to touch and bless them, which we could accomplish only with great labor, for sick and well all wished to go with a benediction. Many times it happened that some of the women who accompanied us gave birth; and as soon as the children were born the mothers would bring them to us that we should touch and bless them.

These Indians always accompanied us until they delivered us to others; and all held full faith in our coming from heaven. While traveling, we went without food until night, and we ate so little as to astonish them. We never felt exhaustion, neither were we in fact at all weary, so inured were we to hardship. We possessed great influence and authority: to preserve both, we seldom talked with them. The Negro was in constant conversation; he informed himself about the ways we wished to take, of the towns there were, and the matters we desired to know.

We passed through many and dissimilar tongues. Our Lord granted us favor with the people who spoke them, for they always understood us, and we them. We questioned them and received their answers by signs, just as if they spoke our language and we theirs; for although we knew six languages we could not everywhere avail ourselves of them, there being a thousand differences.

Throughout all these countries the people who were at war immediately made friends, that they might come to meet us and bring what they possessed. In this way we left all the land at peace and we taught all the inhabitants by signs, which they understood, that in heaven was a Man whom we called God, Who had created the sky and the earth; Him we worshiped and had for our master; that we did what He commanded and from His hand came all good; and if they would do as we did, all would be well with them. We found them so ready of apprehension that if we had had the use of language by which to make ourselves perfectly understood, we should have left them all Christians.

In the town where the emeralds were presented to us, the people gave Dorantes over six hundred open hearts of deer. They always keep a good supply of them for food, and we called the place Pueblo de los Corazones. It is the entrance into many provinces on the South Sea. Those who go to look for them, and do not enter there, will be lost.

We think that near the coast, by way of those towns through which we came, are more than a thousand leagues of inhabited country. Three times a year the land is planted with maize and beans. There are three kinds of deer, one the size of the young steer of Spain. There are innumerable houses, such as are called *bahios*. They get poison from the fruit of a certain tree the size of the apple. For effect no more is necessary than to pluck the fruit and moisten the arrow with it, or if there is no fruit they break a twig and use the milk. The tree is abundant and so deadly that if the leaves are bruised and steeped in some neighboring water, the deer and the other animals drinking it soon die.

We were in this town three days. A day's journey beyond was another town, at which the rain fell heavily while we were there, and the river became so swollen we could not cross it, which delayed us for fifteen days. During this time Castillo saw the buckle of a sword belt on the neck of an Indian, and stitched to it the nail of a horseshoe. He took them, and we asked the native what they were. He answered that they came from heaven. We questioned him further as to who had brought them there. They all responded that certain men who wore beards like us had come from heaven and arrived at that river, bringing horses, lances, and swords, and that they had lanced two Indians. With the utmost indifference we could feign, we asked them what had become of those men. They answered us that they had gone to sea, putting their lances beneath the water and going themselves under the water; that afterward they were seen on the surface going toward the sunset. For this we gave many thanks to God. We had despaired of ever hearing of Christians again. Even yet we were left in great doubt and anxiety, thinking they might be persons who had come by sea on discoveries. However, as we now had such exact information, we made greater speed. As we advanced on our way, the news of the Christians continually grew. We told the natives we were going in search of that people, to order them not to kill nor make slaves of them, nor take them from their lands, nor do other injustice. The Indians were very glad of this.

We passed through many territories and found them all vacant: their inhabitants wandered, fleeing among the mountains, without daring to have houses or till the earth for fear of Christians. The sight was one of infinite pain to us: a land very fertile and beautiful, abounding in springs and streams, the hamlets deserted and burned, the people thin and weak, all fleeing or in concealment. As they did not plant, they appeased their keen hunger by eating roots and the bark of trees. They related how the Christians had come through the land, destroying and burning the towns, carrying away half the men, and all the women and boys, while those who had been able to escape were wandering about as fugitives, preferring to die rather than live in dread of such cruel usage. Although these Indians were greatly delighted with us, we feared that those who held the frontier and fought against the Christians would treat us badly and revenge upon us the conduct of their enemies. But when God was pleased to bring us there, they began to dread and respect us as the others had done, and even somewhat more. And so it is clear that to bring all these people to be Christians and to the obedience of the Imperial Majesty, they must be won by kindness and in no other way.

The Indians took us to a town on the edge of a range of mountains, where the ascent is over difficult crags. We found many people collected there out of fear of the Christians. They received us well and presented us with all they had. They gave us more than two thousand back-loads of maize, which we gave to the distressed and hungry beings who guided us to that place. The next day we dispatched four messengers through the country, as we were accustomed to do, that they should call together all the rest of the Indians at a town three days' march away. We set out the day after with all the people. The tracks of the Christians and marks where they slept were continually seen. At mid-day we met our messengers who told us they had found no Indians, that they were roving and hiding in the forests. The night before they had observed the Christians from behind trees and discovered they were carrying away many people in chains.

Those who came with us were alarmed at this intelligence; some returned to spread the news over the land that the Christians were coming; and many more would have followed had we not forbidden it and told them to cast aside their fear. The following day those we had sent forward as messengers guided us to the place where they had seen the Christians. We arrived in the afternoon and saw at once that they told the truth. Because of the stakes to which horses had been tied we perceived that the persons were mounted.

When we saw sure signs of Christians and heard how near we were to them, we gave thanks to God our Lord for having chosen to bring us out of a captivity so melancholy and wretched. That night I pleaded with my companions that one of them should go back three days' journey after the Christians who were moving about the country, where we had given assurance of protection. Neither of them received this proposal well, excusing themselves because of weariness and exhaustion. Although either might have done better than I, being more youthful and athletic, the next morning I took the Negro with eleven Indians, and following the Christians by their trail I traveled ten leagues, passing three villages at which they had slept.

The day after, I overtook four of them on horseback. They were astonished at the sight of me, because I looked so strange and was in the company of Indians. They stood staring at me a length of time, so confounded that they neither hailed me nor drew near. I bade them take me to their captain, Diego de Alcaraz.

After we had conversed, he told me he was completely undone; he had not been able to take any Indians in a long time; he knew not which way to turn, and his men had begun to experience hunger and fatigue. I told him of Castillo and Dorantes, who were behind, ten leagues off, with a multitude that conducted us. He thereupon sent three cavalry to them, with fifty of the Indians who accompanied him. The Negro returned to guide them, while I remained. I asked the Christians to give me a certificate of the year, month, and day I arrived there, and of the manner of my coming. This they did. From this river to the town of the Christians, named San Miguel, within the government of the province called New Galicia, are thirty leagues.

After five days, Andres Dorantes and Alonzo del Castillo arrived with those who had been sent after them. They brought more than six hundred persons of that community whom the Christians had driven into the forests. Alcaraz begged us to summon the people of the towns on the margin of the river, who straggled about under cover of the woods, and order them to fetch us something to eat. This last was unnecessary because the Indians were very diligent, bringing us all they could. As soon as we sent our messengers to call them, six hundred souls came, bringing us all the maize they had. They fetched it in closed pots which they had concealed in the earth. They brought us whatever else they had; but wishing only to have the food, we gave the rest to the Christians to divide among themselves. After this, we had many strong words with the Christians; for they wished to make slaves of the Indians we had brought.

We found it difficult to induce the Indians to return to their dwellings, to feel no apprehension and plant maize. They were willing to do nothing until they had gone with us and delivered us into the hands of other Indians, as had been the custom; for if they returned without doing so, they were afraid they would die. Going with us, they feared neither Christians nor lances. Our countrymen became jealous at this, and through their interpreter told the Indians we were the same as they, and for a long time we had been lost; that they were the lords of the land who must be obeyed and served, while we were persons of mean condition and small force.

The Indians cared little or nothing for what was told them. They said the Christians lied; that we had come from where the sun rises, and they from where it goes down; we healed the sick, they killed the sound; we had come naked and barefooted, while they had arrived in clothing and on horses with lances; we were not covetous of anything, but all that was given to us we directly turned to give, remaining with nothing; the others only wished to rob whomever they found, bestowing nothing on any one.

Even to the last, I could not convince the Indians that we were

Christians; and we got them to go back to their residences only with great effort and solicitation. We ordered them to put away apprehension, establish their towns, plant and cultivate the soil.

From abandonment, the country had already grown up thickly in trees. It is, no doubt, the best in all the Indies, the most prolific and plentiful in provisions. It is planted three times in the year. It produces a great variety of fruit and has many beautiful rivers. There are ores with clear traces of gold and silver. The people are well disposed: they serve such Christians as are their friends with great good will. They are comely, much more so than the Mexicans. Indeed, the land needs no circumstance to make it blessed.

The Indians, at taking their leave, told us they would do what we commanded and would build their towns, if the Christians would allow them; and this I say most positively, that if they have not done so it is the fault of the Christians.

After we had dismissed the Indians in peace and thanked them for all the toil with which they had supported us, the Christians, with subtlety, sent us on our way under charge of Zebreros, an alcalde, attended by two men. They took us through forests and solitudes to hinder us from intercourse with the natives, so that we might neither witness nor have knowledge of the act they would commit. It is but an instance of how frequently men are mistaken in their aims. We set about to preserve the liberty of the Indians and thought we had secured it, but the Christians had arranged to go and spring upon those we had sent away in peace and confidence. They executed their plan, taking us through the woods where we were lost for two days, and without water. Seven of our men died of thirst, and we all believed we would die. We traveled twenty-five leagues and reached a town of friendly Indians. The alcalde left us there and went on three leagues farther to a town called Culiacan, where Melchior Diaz was principal alcalde and captain of the province.

The alcalde mayor knew of the expedition and, hearing of our return, he immediately came to us. He wept with us, giving praises to God for having extended over us such great care. He comforted and entertained us hospitably. In behalf of the governor, Nuño de Guzman, and himself, he offered us all the service in his power. He showed much regret for the seizure and the injustice we had received from Alcaraz and others. We were sure that had he been present, what was done to the Indians and to us would never have occurred.

We set out the next day for Anhacan. The chief alcalde begged us to stay, since by so doing we could be of eminent service to God and your Majesty. The deserted land was without tillage and badly wasted. The Indians were fleeing and concealing themselves in the thickets, unwilling to occupy their towns. He wanted us to send for them and command them in behalf of God and the King to return to live in the valleys and cultivate the soil.

This appeared difficult to us. We had no native with us who was intelligent in these affairs. At last we made the attempt with two captives, brought from that country, who were with the Christians we first overtook. They had seen the people who conducted us, and learned from them the great authority we exercised, the wonders we had worked, the sick we had cured, and the many other things we had done. We ordered them to summon the hostile natives. For the protection of the messengers and as a token to the others of our will, we gave them a gourd of a kind we had carried in our hands, which had been our principal insignia and evidence of rank, and with this they went away.

The Indians were gone seven days. They returned with three chiefs, who brought with them fifteen men and presented us beads, turquoises and feathers. The messengers said they had not found the people of the river where we appeared, the Christians having again made them run away to the mountains. Melchior Diaz told the interpreter to speak to the natives for us; to say to them that we came in the name of God, Who is in heaven; that we had traveled about the world many years, telling all the people we found that they should believe in God and serve Him; for He was the Master of all things on earth, benefiting and rewarding the virtuous and giving perpetual punishment of fire to the bad; that when the good die He takes them to heaven, where none ever die or feel cold or hunger or thirst, or any inconvenience whatsoever, but the greatest enjoyment possible to conceive; that those who will not believe in Him or obey His commands, He casts beneath the earth into the company of demons, and into a great fire, which is never to go out, but always torment; that, over this, if they desired to be Christians and serve God in the way we required, the Christians would cherish them as brothers and behave toward them very kindly; that we would command the Christians to give no offense nor take them from their territories but be their great friends. If the Indians did not do this, the Christians would treat them very harshly, carrying them away as slaves into other lands.

They answered through the interpreter that they would be true

Christians and serve God. We ordered them to come down from the mountains in confidence and peace, to inhabit the whole country, and to construct their houses. Among these we told them they should build one for God, with a cross like the one we had at its entrance place; and when Christians came among them, they should go out to receive them with crosses in their hands, without bows or any arms, and take them to their dwellings, giving of what they had to eat, and the Christians would do them no injury but be their friends. The Indians told us they would do as we had commanded.

After the captain had given them shawls and entertained them, they returned, taking the two captives who had been used as emissaries. All of this took place before the notary, in the presence of many witnesses.

As soon as these Indians went back, all those of that province who were friendly to the Christians, and had heard of us, came to visit us, bringing beads and feathers. We commanded them to build churches and put crosses in them; and we made them bring their principal men to be baptized.

Then the captain made a covenant with God not to invade nor consent to invasion, nor to enslave any of that country and people to whom we had guaranteed safety; that this he would enforce and defend until your Majesty and the Governor Nuño de Guzman, or the viceroy in your name, should direct what would be most for the service of God and your Highness.

When the children had been baptized, we departed for the town of San Miguel, arriving on April 1, 1536.

Fifteen days later, Alcaraz returned with the Christians from the incursion, and they told the captain how the Indians had come down and peopled the plain; that the towns were now inhabited and the residents had received them with crosses in their hands and taken them to their houses, giving of what they had, and the Christians had slept among them over night. They were surprised at a thing so novel; but, as the natives had said they had been assured of safety, it was ordered that they should not be harmed, and the Christians took friendly leave of them.

God in His infinite mercy is pleased that in the days of your Majesty, under your might and dominion, these nations should come to be thoroughly and voluntarily subject to the Lord, Who has created and redeemed us. We regard this as certain, that your Majesty is he who is destined to do so much, not difficult to accomplish; for in the two thousand leagues we journeyed on land, and in boats on water, and in the ten months we traveled after coming out of captivity, we found neither sacrifices nor idolatry.

In all that time, we crossed the land from sea to sea; and from information gathered with great diligence, there may be a distance from one to another at the widest part, of two thousand leagues; and we learned that on the coast of the South Sea there are pearls and great riches, and the best and all the most opulent countries are near there.

We were in San Miguel until the fifteenth day of May, when we left for Compostela, where the Governor entertained us graciously, and gave us clothing. I could not wear any for some time, nor could we sleep anywhere else but on the ground. After ten or twelve days we left for Mexico, and all along the way we were well entertained by Christians. We arrived at Mexico on Sunday, the day before the vespers of Saint Iago, and we were welcomed with joy by the Viceroy and the Marquis del Valle.

We rested two months in Mexico, and prepared to embark in October for Spain, but our ship was capsized in a storm and lost, and I decided to remain through the winter, this being a boisterous season for navigation in these parts.

On the tenth day of April, 1537, we embarked again. Many adventures befell us before we reached the Azores—our ships were separated in terrible storms and we were almost taken by French pirates. Finally we reached the island of Terceira, where we rested fifteen days, and left for Portugal. We arrived at the port of Lisbon on the ninth of August, in the year one thousand five hundred and thirty-seven.

That what I have stated in my foregoing narrative is true, I subscribe with my name.

CABEZA DE VACA

Since giving this account of the events attending the voyage to Florida, the invasion, and our going out from there, until the arrival in these realms, I wish to state what became of the ships and of the people who remained with them. I have not touched on this before, as we were uninformed until coming to New Spain, where we found many of the persons, and others here in Castile, from whom we learned everything to the latest particular.

At the time we left, one of the ships had already been lost on the breakers, and the three others were in considerable danger, having nearly a hundred souls on board and few stores. Among them were ten married women, one of whom had told the Governor many things that afterward befell him on the voyage. She cautioned him before he went inland not to go for she was certain few or none would return. The Governor said that he and his followers were going to fight and conquer nations and countries wholly unknown, and in subduing them he knew that many would be slain; nevertheless, that those who survived would be fortunate, since from what he had understood of the opulence of that land, they must become very rich. And further he begged her to inform him where she learned those things that she spoke of. She replied that a Moorish woman of Hornachos had told them to her in Castile, which she had stated to us also before we left Spain. While on the passage many things happened in the way she foretold.

After the Governor had made Caravallo his lieutenant and commander of the vessels and people, he departed, leaving orders that they should take the direct course to Panuco, keeping closely along the shore and looking for the harbor. Having found it, the vessels should enter there and await our arrival. And the people state that when they had boarded the ships, they distinctly heard that woman say to the females that since their husbands had gone inland, putting their persons in so great jeopardy, their wives should in no way take more account of them, but ought soon to be looking for other men to marry, and that she would do so. She and others married or became the concubines of those who remained in the ships.

After we left, the vessels made sail, taking their course onward; but not finding the harbor, they returned. Five leagues below the place at which we debarked, they found the port where we saw the Spanish cases containing dead bodies. The three ships, with the other ship that came from Cuba, and the brigantine, looked for us along the coast for nearly a year. Not finding us, they went to New Spain.

As I have given an account of the vessels, I wish to state who are, and from what parts of these kingdoms come, the persons whom our Lord has been pleased to release from these troubles. The first is Alonzo del Castillo Maldonado, native of Salamanca, son of Doctor Castillo and Doña Aldonca Maldonado. The second is Andres Dorantes, son of Pablo Dorantes, native of Bejar, and citizen of Gibraleon. The third is Alvar Núñez Cabeza de Vaca, son of Francisco de Vera, and grandson of Pedro de Vera who conquered the

Canaries, and his mother was Doña Teresa Cabeza de Vaca, native of Xerez de la Frontera. The fourth, called Estevanico, is an Arabian black, native of Acamor.

When Cabeza de Vaca arrived in Mexico, the understanding he had gained of the Indians set him apart from his fellow Christians. He met with Nuño de Guzman, the governor of New Galicia, the successor and enemy of Cortés. Guzman received the wanderers well, gave them a good reception and tried to learn about their long journey. But Cabeza de Vaca had no intention of letting the slave traders he had met go unpunished. He would have protested to Guzman, but he learned on good authority that the slave traders operated under the Governor's protection and even had documents with his signature approving of their activities. Cabeza de Vaca, with an innocence that was always to mark his career, faced the governor with a copy of the documents and was hurried off to Mexico City while a courier went ahead with correspondence to Viceroy Mendoza discrediting the sun-addled Cabeza de Vaca and his companions.

In Mexico City, the wanderers met with Mendoza. The Viceroy assured them that he already had a case being prepared against Guzman and quickly changed the subject to the treasures they could tell him about. There was an emerald necklace with a story attached to it. There were tales of vague great cities beyond a remote desert. But as to actual treasure and gold, the travelers were never specific, and gold-hungry men were able to read more into the lack of detail than Cabeza de Vaca intended. Mendoza asked the men to prepare a map of the area they had crossed and this proved more a tease than a confirmation of his desires. He pressed for Dorantes and Cabeza de Vaca to head another expedition northward, but both men were reluctant. They spent almost a year in Mexico City, preparing a detailed report, since lost, of their activities and then set out for Vera Cruz, arriving during Lent, 1537. On April 10 they sailed for Spain. The ship on which Diego Dorantes departed turned back. The vessel on which Cabeza de Vaca sailed was almost captured by a French corsair off the Azores and finally reached Lisbon under the protection of a Portuguese fleet convoying home three spice ships from the Orient.

After four months of travel, Cabeza de Vaca reached a Spain gone gold crazy with the news of Pizarro in Peru and the arrival of the glittering Hernando De Soto. The one person who knew Florida well and was anxious to return as its governor arrived home too late, however. The prize, a territory almost half as large as Europe, went to De Soto, and though the new governor asked Cabeza de Vaca to join him, the only survivor of the Narváez expedition ever to return to Spain refused. He had a meeting with the king and disappeared from history for two years.

Then in September 1539, Cabeza de Vaca became involved in a second adventure that was to take him to a different continent and even more strangely than his first, a second adventure in which the one conquistador who knew the Indians as human beings was to suffer for his compassion.

6

Coronado
Seeks the Seven Cities
of Cíbola

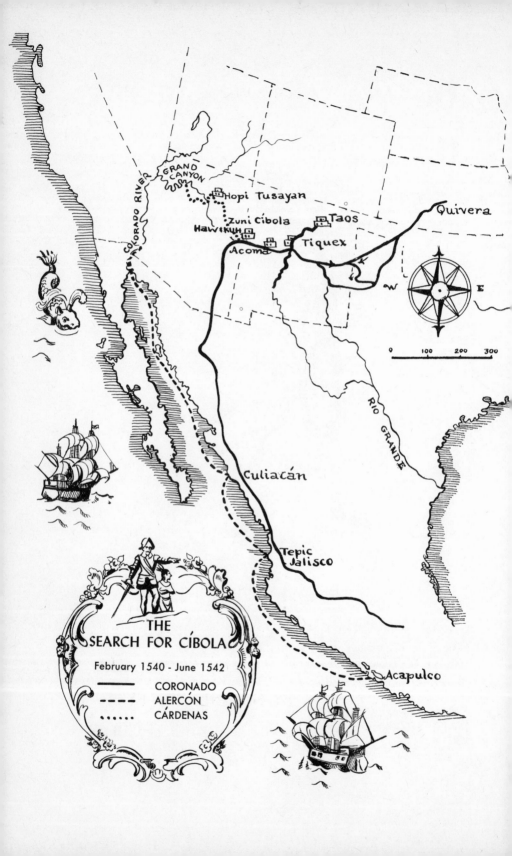

GRAND CANYON

COLORADO RIVER

Hopi Tusayan

Zuni Cíbola

Taos

Hawikuh

Tiquex

Acoma

Quivera

W

E

0   100   200   300

RIO GRANDE

Culiacán

Tepic
Jalisco

Acapulco

THE
SEARCH FOR CÍBOLA

February 1540 - June 1542

———   CORONADO
- - -   ALERCÓN
· · · ·   CÁRDENAS

6

Coronado Seeks the Seven Cities of Cíbola

THE TRAGIC expedition of Narváez and the safe return of Cabeza de Vaca started a chain of events that was to embroil Spain and the New World for years to come. In the *Relación,* written by Cabeza de Vaca, as well as in his lengthy discussions with the viceroy in Mexico City, he created in the minds of the eager administrator a strange picture of the country through which he had traveled. There is no question that Viceroy Mendoza and the men about him were already half deluded before they listened to Cabeza de Vaca's reports of "many signs of gold, antimony, iron, copper and other metals." They had come to the west with the dream of the Seven Cities as part of a long national heritage.

Sometime in the vague Middle Ages, the Moors were supposed to have driven seven Portuguese bishops westward with their people. Crossing the Ocean Sea, these clerics founded the Seven Cities of Antilia. Columbus, the Admiral of the Ocean Seas, was so confident that he had located Antilia that the name was given to the islands of the Caribbean. The viceroy and his friends knew that locating the cities themselves was only a matter of time. They knew also that the sailors who had sailed the ships of Cortés to California had come back with reports of a warrior tribe of Negro women who scorned men and were very wealthy. The Amazon legend was even older than that of the Seven Cities; and if one legend was fact, they thought the other to be. The conquistador Orellana, who sailed the length of the great river of South America, had heard of the tribe of women in that region and in time the name of the tribe—Amazon— was to be given to the river.

The world of the west was the only possible place where the tales could have foundation, and to the hungry and unsophisticated Spaniards, the Seven Cities and the Amazons were to be found in any unknown place. In addition, there was another legend blowing through the colonies like a warm wind—El Dorado. Somewhere on the plateau of Bogotá there was supposed to be a tribe of Indians who anointed their chief in oil then sprinkled him with gold dust until he was a gilded man—El Dorado. The Spaniards had not found him in Colombia, nor anywhere else they had looked. But they knew that legends and tales have a base in fact, and they were certain that somewhere they would find El Dorado—as certain as they were that they had already found the Seven Cities of Antilia.

Mendoza was new to his post, having held it less than a year when Cabeza de Vaca emerged from the country to the north. But he had already begun to hem in Cortés and block any success the conquistador might have in further explorations. The way was already cleared for Mendoza and his friends to take over what would be found in the north. At first he tried to convince Cabeza de Vaca to join him, but the wanderer wanted to return to Spain. Then Mendoza turned to the other survivors of the Narváez expedition, but for one reason or another they were not prepared to go back. They had married well and settled down.

Finally making arrangements with the master, Mendoza obtained the slave variously called Estaban, Estevanico or Estevan. The viceroy then requested that Fray Marcos de Niza begin a preliminary incursion into the land to the north. Fray Marcos de Niza had come well recommended by the bishop and was an experienced traveler. The padre, who received his name from a stay in Nice, had come to the New World in 1531, stopping at Santo Domingo before moving on to Guatemala. He was with Alvarado on the expedition to Peru, was present at the death of the Inca emperor and when Alvarado sold out his rights of Peruvian conquest to Almagro. By September 1536 he was again in Guatemala, where he wrote the bishop of Mexico about his travels. He was summoned to Mexico City and is said to have walked the distance barefooted. Once closeted with the bishop, Fray Marcos told of the inhumanities against the Indians he had witnessed. Details of this were passed on to Las Casas, who may have used them in his *Destruction of the Indies*. The missionary-explorer was recommended to the viceroy as a man who was "skilled in cosmography and the arts of the sea as well as in theology."

With the Negro slave, a fellow padre and an escort of Indians and soldiers, Fray Marcos set out to locate the Seven Cities of Antilia. His small expedition came under the supervision of the acting governor of New Galicia, Francisco Vásquez de Coronado. Leaving the capital, Fray Marcos walked northwest, and on March 1539 he left Culiacán, the small village where Cabeza de Vaca had returned to civilization.

The padre carried with him gold, silver, pearls and precious stones which he planned to show the Indians as samples of what he was looking for. As the small group walked north, Fray Marcos' fellow padre fell ill and was sent home on a stretcher. Then Estaban, the slave, was sent ahead to scout the country and make friends with the Indians. He had orders to leave a cross on the route he took, and by the size of the cross Fray Marcos would be able to determine how close they were to success and the Seven Cities.

For two months Fray Marcos followed a trail of crosses that were larger than a man, clear signs that the Seven Cities were just ahead. He paused once to send messengers to the California coast and waited for their return, and then he pushed on again. Word came back by messenger from Estaban, now far ahead, that he had found seven large cities—the Seven Cities of Cíbola. And so the course of the legend changed and Cíbola replaced Antilia, but so long as the cities were there, the name was not important.

Then an Indian came staggering back down the trail Estaban had taken: the Negro had been killed by the Indians of Cíbola. Soon afterward two wounded Indians joined Fray Marcos with a more complete report. The Negro had angered the Indians of one of the pueblos and they had killed him. The expeditions which came in later years heard tales of the Negro who had asked about precious stones and women and had been killed because of this. The legends still exist in the Zuñi tradition even though the locale of the killing has been changed.

Fray Marcos pressed on, talking with the Indians, seeking advice and information as he went. Then in the distance he claims to have seen a city "which is situated on a plain at the foot of a round hill. The settlement is larger than the city of Mexico, and it is the least of the seven cities." From the Indians who were with him he learned also that there was another set of pueblos—the Hopi—and each town was larger than the one he had already seen. There was no reason to wait any longer. He had found "seven cities in a valley with very good land."

History has never been able to make up its mind about the padre called Fray Marcos. He was certainly a magnificent spinner of tales. He certainly knew how to create an image of himself. He certainly knew what Mendoza and all of the bright young hidalgos sitting back in Mexico City wanted to hear. It is also quite possible he believed he saw the cities. He never said that he entered them. From a hill-top he had seen off in the distance a shimmering city. If he was in Zuñi country—and no one is convinced he was not—then he may have seen the old pueblo with the sun reflecting off the white adobe. But there is enough of the charlatan in the personality of Fray Marcos that no one reading the account is ever quite certain.

At any rate, he fulfilled the instructions of the viceroy.

INSTRUCTIONS OF THE VICEROY TO FRAY MARCOS DE NIZA, NOVEMBER, 1538

First: Upon arriving at the province of Culiacán, you are to exhort and urge the Spaniards residing in the town of San Miguel to treat the peaceful Indians well and not to employ them in excessive tasks, assuring them that by so doing they will be granted favors and re-warded by his Majesty for the hardships they have endured there, and that they will find in me a good supporter for their claims. If they do the opposite they will incur punishment and disfavor.

You shall make clear to the Indians that I am sending you in the name of his Majesty to tell them that the Spaniards shall treat them well, to let them know that he regrets the abuses and harm they have suffered, and that from now on they shall be well treated and those who may mistreat them shall be punished.

Likewise you are to assure them that no more slaves shall be taken from among them and that they are not to be taken away from their lands; on the contrary, they shall be left alone as free people, without suffering any harm. Tell them that they should not be afraid, but acknowledge God, our Lord, Who is in heaven, and the emperor, as he has been placed on earth by His hand to rule and govern it.

Since Francisco Vásquez de Coronado, whom his Majesty has ap-pointed governor of that province, will go with you as far as the town of San Miguel de Culiacán, you shall inform me of how he provides for the affairs of that town in matters pertaining to the service of God, our Lord, and the conversion and good treatment of the natives of that province.

If with the aid of God our Lord and the grace of the Holy Spirit you should find a way to go on and penetrate the land in the interior, you shall take along Estaban de Dorantes as guide. I command him to obey you in whatever you may order him, as he would obey me in person. If he should not do so, he will be at fault and incur the penalties falling on those who disobey the persons empowered by his Majesty to command them.

Likewise the said governor Francisco Vásquez is taking along the Indians who came with Dorantes and others from those regions who could be brought together, so that if he and you consider it advisable that some of them should go along, you may employ them in the service of our Lord as you deem fitting.

You are always to endeavor to travel the safest way possible, informing yourself first as to whether the Indians are at peace or at war among themselves, so that they may not do any violence to your person that would give cause to taking up arms against them and punishing them, because, in this case, instead of helping and enlightening them, this would do just the opposite.

You shall be very careful to observe the number of people that there are, whether they are few or many, and whether they are scattered or living together. Note also the nature, fertility and climate of the land; the trees, plants and domestic and wild animals there may be; the character of the country, whether it is broken or flat; the rivers, whether they are large or small; the stones and metals which there are; and of all things that can be sent or brought, send or bring samples of them in order that his Majesty may be informed of everything.

Endeavor always to learn if there is any information about the seacoast, both of the North and South Seas, for it may be that the land narrows and that a sea inlet reaches the interior of the land. If you should reach the coast of the South Sea, leave letters buried at the headlands, at the foot of some tree outstanding for its size, telling of what you think should be known. Mark the tree with a cross where the letters are left, so that they may be found. Likewise, at the mouths of rivers and suitable harbors, on prominent trees near the water, make the same sign, a cross, and leave letters. Thus if I send ships they will be advised to look for this sign.

Try always to send reports through Indians, telling how you are faring, how you are received, and particularly what you may find.

If God our Lord should will it that you find some large settlement which you think would be a good place for establishing a monastery and for sending friars who would devote themselves to conversions, you are to send a report by Indians, or return, yourself, to Culiacán. Send back reports with the utmost secrecy so that appropriate steps may be taken without disturbing anything, because in the pacification of what is discovered the services of our Lord and the welfare of the natives shall be taken into consideration.

Although the whole land belongs to the emperor, our lord, you shall take possession of it for his Majesty in my name and draw up the documents and set up the markers that you feel are required for this purpose. You must explain to the natives of the land that there is only one God in heaven, and the emperor on earth to rule and govern it, whose subjects they must all become, and whom they must serve.

DON ANTONIO DE MENDOZA

When the padre returned to Mexico City he prepared a detailed report of what he had seen, and Viceroy Mendoza rushed it with a covering letter to the king.

LETTER WRITTEN BY HIS EXCELLENCY, DON ANTONIO DE MENDOZA, VICEROY OF NEW SPAIN, TO HIS MAJESTY, THE EMPEROR, 1539. [THE PLACE IS PRESUMABLY TEMIXTITAN; NO OTHER DATE IS GIVEN.]

In the last fleet in which Miguel de Venago sailed, I sent a letter to your Majesty relating how I had sent two friars of the order of St. Francis to discover the limits of this mainland in the region across the mountains. And since their trip is an event of greater importance than was thought, I shall relate this matter from the beginning.

Your Majesty must recall that whenever I wrote to you I expressed my eagerness to learn where the limits of this province in New Spain were, for it is an extensive land, and there exists no information as to its limits. I have not been the only one who expressed this desire, for Nuño de Guzmán left this city with four hundred mounted men and fourteen thousand footmen, natives of these Indies, the best people and the best organized expedition that had ever been seen in these parts. He accomplished so little that most of them were consumed in the undertaking, and he was not able to go beyond the territory already explored. Later, while this governor was at New Galicia, he sent out some captains with mounted men, but they did not obtain better results than he had got.

Likewise the Marqués del Valle, Hernando Cortés, sent a captain with two ships to explore the coast. The ships and the captain himself were lost. Later Cortés again sent two other ships, one of which became separated from the other. The pilot, with a few sailors, took control of the ship and murdered the captain. Then they sailed into an island where, upon landing, the pilot and some sailors were killed by the native Indians, who took the landing boat. The ship, with the men who had remained on board, returned to the coast of New Galicia, where it foundered. The Marqués obtained information of the land they had discovered from the men on this ship. Immediately, either because of some disaffection with the Bishop of Santo Domingo and the judges of this royal audencia, or, likely, because everything in New Spain had turned out so well for him, without waiting to obtain further verification of what was to be found on that island, he sailed in that direction with three ships and some footmen and horsemen, and none too well provided with the necessary things. The whole affair turned out so different from what he expected that most of the men he had with him starved to death. And even though he had ships and the land was very suitable, with an abundance of provisions, he had no means of conquering it. It seemed as if God drew it away from him supernaturally. And he returned home without accomplishing anything.

After this, having here with me Andres Dorantes, one of those who went in the expedition of Pánfilo de Narváez, I consulted with him many times. It seemed to me that he could render great service to Your Majesty if he were sent with forty or fifty horsemen to lay bare the mysteries of that region. On that account I spent considerable money in providing what was necessary for his journey, and I do not know how it was that the plan fell through and the undertaking was abandoned.

Of the arrangements made for this plan, I retained a Negro who had come with Dorantes, some slaves whom I bought, and a few native Indians of that region whom I had gathered. I sent them with Fray Marcos de Niza and a companion of his, a friar of the order of Saint Francis, men long trained in the hardships of this region, experienced in the affairs of the Indies, earnest persons of exemplary lives, whom I obtained from their provincial. They accompanied Francisco Vásquez de Coronado, governor of New Galicia, to the town of San Miguel de· Culiacán, the last outpost of the Spaniards in that region, two hundred leagues from this city.

When the governor arrived with the friars at this place, he asked some Indians I had given him to return to their land and tell the people there that your Majesty had ordered no more slaves to be taken from among them, that they should lose all fear and return to their homes and live peacefully in them, and that since they had been greatly abused in the past by the treatment they had been accorded, his Majesty would punish those who were responsible for this. After twenty days some four hundred came back with these Indians. Appearing before the governor, they told him that they came on behalf of all the natives to tell him they wanted to see and know the person who had done them so much good by allowing them to return to their homes and plant maize so that they would have food. They had been wandering and hiding in the mountains like wild beasts for years, they said, for fear of being made slaves, and now they and all the others were ready to do what was ordered of them. The governor reassured them with kind words and ordered them fed, keeping them with him for three or four days.

During these days the friars taught them to make the sign of the cross and say the name of Jesus Christ our Lord, which they did in earnest. At the end of this time the governor sent them back to their homes, telling them not to be afraid and to remain calm. He gave them clothes, paternosters, knives, and other things of this nature which I had given him for such purposes. They went away very happy, saying that whenever he sent for them again they and many others would come to do what he commanded them.

When the entry was prepared, Fray Marcos and his companion, before setting out, spent ten or twelve days with the Negro and the other slaves and Indians that I had given him.

And as I had also received information of a province called Topira, situated back of the mountains, and had arranged with the governor that he should find means of learning about it, considering this of primary importance, he decided to go in person to explore it. He arranged with Fray Marcos as to what part of the mountain he would turn at in order to meet him at a town called Corazones, one hundred and twenty leagues from Culiacán. He traveled through this province and found it to conform to what I have written in my letters. There is a great scarcity of provisions, and the mountain range was so rough that he could not find anywhere a way of proceeding ahead, and he was forced to return to San Miguel.

Consequently, because of the poor choice of the route and the inability to find a way, everyone thought that God our Lord wanted to close the door to all those who wished to carry out this undertaking by human force, and open it to a poor barefooted friar. In this manner Fray Marcos began to march inland. Since the way had been so well prepared, he was well received. As he has written all about what befell him on the whole trip, following the instructions I gave him for this journey, I shall not extend myself further, but simply transcribe for your Majesty all that has been related by him.

REPORT OF FRAY MARCOS DE NIZA, SUBMITTED AND NOTARIZED IN TEMIXTITAN ON SEPTEMBER 2, 1539

With the aid and favor of the blessed Virgin Mary our Lady, and our seraphic father Saint Francis, I, Fray Marcos de Niza, a professed friar of the order of Saint Francis, in fulfillment of the above-contained instructions from the illustrious Don Antonio de Mendoza, his Majesty's viceroy and governor of New Spain, set out from the town of San Miguel in the province of Culiacán on Friday, March 7, 1539, taking along Father Fray Onorato as companion. I also took with me Estaban de Dorantes, a Negro, and some Indians the viceroy had liberated and bought for this purpose. They were delivered to me by Francisco Vásquez de Coronado, governor of New Galicia.

I stopped at the pueblo of Petatlan for three days because my companion, Fray Onorato, was taken ill, and I found it advisable to leave him there. I continued on my way for some twenty-five or thirty leagues beyond Petatlan, and did not see anything worth recording here, except that some Indians from the island visited by the Marqués del Valle came to see me. From them I assured myself that it is an island and not the mainland, as some claim.

After four days march over a despoblado, I met other Indians who marveled at seeing me, because they knew nothing of Christians. I tried by all possible means to learn about a country with many settlements and with people more advanced and cultured than those I had met. They told me that four or five days inland, where the cordilleras of the sierras end, there is an open valley in which they said were many very large settlements and people clothed in cotton. When I showed them some metals I had brought with me, they took the gold metal and said that there were vessels of it among the people of the valley, and that they wore round articles of that gold hanging from their noses and ears and that they have some small blades made of it, with which they scrape and remove their sweat.

I turned inland and came to a good-sized settlement named Vacapa. From there I sent Indian messengers to the sea by three different routes, charging them to bring me people from the coast and from some of the islands, in order to obtain information from them. I sent Estaban de Dorantes to the north, with instructions to go fifty or sixty leagues to see whether, by that route, information could be obtained of what we were seeking. I arranged with him that should he learn of some inhabited and rich country—something really important—he should not go any farther but return in person or send me Indians bearing the following sign: If it were something moderate, he should send me a white cross a span in size; if it were of greater importance, he should send one two spans in size; and if it were something greater and better than New Spain, he should send me a large cross.

Four days later messengers from Estaban arrived carrying a very large cross the height of a man. They told me that he had met people who informed him of the greatest thing in the world; that he had Indians with him who had been there, of whom he sent me one. The latter told me so many marvels of the land that I postponed believing them until after seeing them or having further verification. He told me that there was thirty days' travel from the place where Estaban was to the first city of the land, which is called Cíbola.

It seems to me worth recording here what this Indian sent by Estaban says about the country. He says that in the first province there are seven very large cities, all under one ruler, with large houses of stone and lime—all joined in an orderly manner, and the ruler's house is four stories high. The doorways have many decorations of turquoises, of which there is a great abundance, and the people are very well clothed. There are other provinces farther on, each one of which he claims to be much more important than these seven cities. I rendered thanks to our Lord.

On the second day after Easter Sunday, I set out from Vacapa following the road taken by Estaban. I had received other messengers from him, bringing another cross the size of the first one, and urging me to hurry. The messengers told me individually what the previous one had said, without omitting the slightest detail. After three days I met the people who had told him about the seven cities and the country beyond. They advised me that besides these seven cities there are three other kingdoms called Marata, Acus and Totonteac. They gave me some hides of cattle so well tanned and worked that they all looked as if they had been made by men of higher culture. The natives all said that the hides came from Cíbola.

On the next day I continued on my way and came to a settlement where Estaban Dorantes had left a large cross as proof that the information about the good country was always increasing. He left word for me to hurry, that he would wait for me at the edge of the first despoblado. I erected two crosses here and took possession in accordance with the instructions, because this seemed to me a better country than the one we had left behind, and it seemed proper to institute acts of possession from here on.

I traveled for five days, always finding settlements, good lodging, excellent reception, and many turquoises, hides of the cattle, and the same information regarding the country. After traversing the despoblado, I came to a valley well settled with people. They knew as much here about Cíbola as they know in New Spain about Mexico, or in Peru about Cuzco. They described in much detail the construction of the houses and the town's streets and plazas like people who had been there many times and had brought from there the fine things they obtained in exchange for personal service. I told them it was not possible for the houses to be constructed the way they described, so to explain it to me they took dirt and ashes, mixed them with water, and showed me how they set the stone and reared the building. I asked the men of the country if they had wings to ascend to those terraces. They laughed and pictured a ladder for me as clearly as I might do it myself.

At this place I was told of the woolen cloth of Totonteac, where, they said, the houses are like those of Cíbola, but better, and that there are many more of them, and that it is a very extensive place, without limit.

Here I learned that the coast turns west very abruptly, for up to the time of entering the first despoblado, the coast extended always to the north. Since the turning of the coast is very important, I wanted to verify it, and so I went in search of it, and I saw clearly that at a latitude of thirty-five degrees it turns to the west. This brought me no less joy than the good information of the country.

So I returned to proceed on my way through that valley for five days. In each one of the pueblos I obtained very extensive reports of Cíbola, for they go there every year to earn their living. Here I met a man, native of Cíbola, who informed me that there is another very large kingdom and province which is called Acus—there are both Ahacus and Acus. A-ha-cus, with the aspiration, is one of the seven cities; the main one, Acus—Acoma—without the aspiration, is a kingdom and province by itself.

Here in this valley they brought me a hide half as large again as that of a big cow. They told me it came from an animal which has only one horn in the front, and that this horn is curved towards its breast, then turns in a straight point. They say it is so strong that it tears anything it strikes, however strong it may be. They say that there are many of these animals in that country. In color the skin rather resembles that of a buck, and the hair is as long as a finger is thick.

Here I received messengers from Estaban, who told me that he was already in the last despoblado, and very elated, because he was more certain of the riches of the country than before. He sent word to me that since he had taken leave of me he had never caught the Indians in a lie, that thus far he had found everything as it had been described to him, and that he expected to find the rest the same. I believe it to be true, because the fact is that from the very first day when I heard of Cíbola, until now, everything that the Indians told me I have verified. I have traveled one hundred twelve leagues, which makes the veracity of these people quite worth recording.

On the road to Cíbola, I was met by an Indian who arrived very grieved, his face and body covered with sweat. He told me that one day's travel before reaching Cíbola, Estaban sent messengers ahead with his gourd, just as he was in the habit of doing, so that they might know he was coming. The gourd had some strings of jingle bells, and two feathers, one white and the other red. When the messenger arrived at Cíbola, they appeared before the man appointed there by the ruler and gave him the gourd. When he took it in his hands and saw the jingle bells, he at once hurled the gourd to the ground with much wrath. He told the messengers to leave immediately, for he knew what sort of people they represented, and that they should tell them not to enter the city or he would kill them all. The messengers went back and told Estaban what had happened. He told them that it was of no importance, that those who showed anger received him better.

So Estaban continued on his journey until he came to the city of Cíbola. Here the people refused to allow him to enter the city, and put him in a large house located outside of it, taking away from him everything he carried to trade, turquoises and other things he had obtained from the Indians along the way. They kept him there that night without giving him, or those who came with him, any food or water.

The next morning this Indian was thirsty and left the house to get a drink from a near-by river. From that place he shortly afterward saw Estaban fleeing and people from the city pursuing him, and they killed some of those who came with him. Upon seeing this, this Indian, concealing himself, fled up the river and then crossed over it, reaching the road of the despoblado.

On hearing this news, some of the Indians who were with me began to weep. In view of this wretched news I thought I should be lost. I feared not so much to lose my life as not to be able to return and report on the greatness of the country, where God our Lord can be so well served, His holy faith exalted, and the royal patrimony of His Majesty increased. I distributed among the chiefs all the clothing and articles of trade I carried, and told them not to be afraid but to accompany me, which they did.

As we were on our way, one day's journey from Cíbola, we met two other Indians of those who had gone with Estaban. They were bloodstained and had many wounds. They confirmed the unhappy news that Estaban, and all those who were with him, who numbered more than three hundred men, besides many women, had been killed by those of Cíbola, and only they had escaped.

I finally persuaded two of the chiefs to accompany me, and with my own Indians and interpreters, I proceeded on my journey until coming within view of Cíbola, which is situated on a plain, at the base of a round hill.

This pueblo has a fine appearance, the best I have seen in these regions. The houses are as they had been described to me by the Indians, all of stone, with terraces and flat roofs, as it seemed to me from a hill where I stood to view it. The city is larger than the city of Mexico. At times I was tempted to descend to the pueblo, because I knew I was risking only my life, and this I offered to God the day I set out on this journey. In the end, realizing my danger, I feared that if I died no information would be obtained regarding this land, which in my opinion is the greatest and best of all that have been discovered.

When I told the chieftains who were with me how well impressed I was with Cíbola, they told me that it was the smallest of the seven cities, and that Totonteac is much larger and better than all the seven, that it has so many houses and people that there is no end to it.

Observing the nature of the city, I thought it appropriate to name that land the new kingdom of Saint Francis. And so, with the aid of the Indians, I gathered there a pile of stones, and on top of it I erected a small and slender cross, as I had no materials with which to make a larger one. I declared that I was erecting that cross and landmark as a sign of possession, in the name of Don Antonio de Mendoza, viceroy and governor of New Spain for the emperor, our lord, in accordance with my instructions. I stated that I was taking possession there of all the seven cities and of the kingdoms of Totonteac, Acus, and Marata; that I was not going to visit them in order to return to give a report of what had been done and seen.

I turned back with much more fear than food. I traveled with all possible haste until I met the people who had remained behind. I reached them after marching for two days, and together with them I crossed the despoblado, where I was not so well received now as before, because both men and women were weeping bitterly for their people who had been killed at Cíbola. Being afraid, I quickly took leave of the people of that valley and traveled ten leagues on the first day. In this way I traveled from eight to ten leagues each day without a stop until I had crossed the second despoblado.

On my way back, and although I was not lacking in fear, I determined to approach the valley where the sierras end, which, as I have said, I had heard about. There I learned that that valley is inhabited for many days' journey toward the east. I did not dare to enter it for fear of endangering my person and failing to report what I had seen. It seemed to me that the Spaniards would first have to come and settle and dominate this other land of the seven cities and kingdoms I have mentioned, and that this valley could then be more easily explored. I only saw, from the opening of the valley, seven fair-sized settlements, somewhat distant, and below, a very verdant valley with very good soil, from which many smokes rose. I was told that there is much gold there and that the natives make it into vessels, and jewels for the ears, and into little blades with which they wipe away their sweat. These people do not allow those from this region of the valley to trade with them. They could not tell me why.

Here I erected two crosses and took possession of this whole valley. From there I continued my return trip with all possible haste to Compostela, where I found Francisco Vásquez de Coronado, governor of New Galicia. From there I immediately reported my arrival to his Excellency, the viceroy of New Spain, and to our father provincial, Fray Antonio de Ciudad Rodrigo, asking for instructions as to what I should do.

I do not record here many details of the journey because they do not pertain to this case. I tell only of what I saw and was told, of the countries I have traversed, and those of which I have been informed.

FRAY MARCOS DE NIZA, Vice Commissary

By late August Fray Marcos de Niza had returned to New Spain, and Viceroy Mendoza began to organize the expedition which would be charged with the conquest of the Seven Cities. There is no question that he wanted to make the discovery and achieve the victory himself. But there was a scramble for command from the very beginning.

Cortés had not waited for the report of Fray Marcos to send another coasting expedition to the California peninsula. Guzmán, the discredited and detested successor of Cortés, put in his claim for right of conquest. De Soto, Cabeza de Vaca and Alvarado were ready to make their bids to lead the next expedition north.

Mendoza prepared the king for what would come and wrote in detail that he wanted to accomplish a Christian conquest among such civilized peoples as Fray Marcos described. The viceroy would not hear of Cortés becoming involved. Guzmán was already in disgrace and his reputation as a despot was too well known for him to be considered. Cabeza de Vaca was not in a strong enough political position. De Soto and Alvarado were going to be involved elsewhere. If there was "a land rich in gold, silver and other wealth and has great cities," Mendoza wanted it for himself.

He ordered Melchior Díaz, the alcalde mayor of Culiacán, nine hundred miles away and closer to the scene of the future conquest, to take a scouting expedition north without delay to discover if the tales told by the padre were substantially correct. Díaz was an old professional soldier who had lived on the frontier for years and whose word would carry weight.

But no one bothered to wait for a report from Díaz. The news of the padre's great discovery swept through Mexico like a sickness. Everyone wanted to go. Men began to prepare at their own expense. The youthful governor of New Galicia, Francisco Vásquez de Coronado, paid out over fifty thousand gold ducats to help finance the expedition. Mendoza opened his coffers and spilled sixty thousand ducats into the venture. He made arrangements himself to lead the army north, and he withdrew only at the pressure of those about him who believed he was needed in the capital.

Everywhere there was confusion and eagerness as men lined up to submit their names, buy horses, equipment, food and servants to take with them. The city was filled with numerous young men who had been seduced out of Spain with the glimmer of another Mexico City before their eyes, and they were not going to be refused. They had sought no work, had accomplished nothing, had gambled away what little they had brought with them, had gamed and wenched, and now were restless. Nothing suited them better than another Mexico City. In fact, if the good padre was to be believed—and who could doubt him?—there was more than one city. For those who were to remain behind, the forthcoming expedition offered a way to rid the capital of a large number of undesirables. At the same time, there were others who complained the viceroy was stripping the land of its manpower and its horses.

Mendoza had little choice. He had to consider a man to replace him whom everyone would accept, and he turned to the governor of New Galicia. Coronado was already familiar with the country through which the expedition would have to travel in the early stages. He was also wealthy. Born in Salamanca of noble parents in 1510, he had left Spain penniless after years of haggling over a family estate. But he had not remained poor long. Accompanying the viceroy to Mexico City in 1535, the dashing hidalgo soon made himself noticed. Marrying the daughter of the former royal treasurer whose father was reputed to be a natural son of Ferdinand, Coronado moved in the circles of the viceroy's court. He helped Mendoza put down an Indian uprising in 1537. The next year he was the youngest appointee to the newly-formed town council.

The following year he was appointed acting governor of New Galicia to investigate Guzmán's successor in that ravaged province. He had accompanied Fray Marcos on his outward journey and had met him on his return. The youthful Coronado was an obvious choice. One of his brothers was to become an adelantado of Costa Rica and the other, Comendador of the Order of Saint John of Encomienda of Cubillas. From the time of his arrival in the New World, Coronado was destined to greatness. And on January 6, 1540, he was appointed captain-general of Acus—Acoma—which was a city and not a country, Cíbola, the Seven Cities, the Hopi kingdom and anything else he might discover. His second in command, or maestre de campo, was Lope de Samaniago; and García López de Cárdenas, another old soldier and second son, was named a captain. With full pomp and ceremony the expedition marched out of the capital toward New Galicia, accompanied part way by the viceroy and a large number of hidalgos who had elected not to join the expedition. To the older men who had landed twenty years before at Vera Cruz and fought their way west with Cortés, there must have been envy of the magnificent equipment, the youth of the future conquistadores and their numerous horses and mules.

It was written by a contemporary that the expedition was the finest ever launched and it might well have been. Its captain of artillery was Hernando de Alvarado, a relative of the conquistador. No less than three chroniclers accompanied the army. Pedro de Castenada was not always present at many of the more important moments and yet his report is the most complete; Juan Jaramillo was more aware of distance traveled and places visited; and Pedro Mendoza de Soto-mayor, the viceroy's relative, was official historian. His papers have never been found.

In addition Fray Marcos de Niza, Fray Juan Padilla and Fray Luis de Escalona accompanied the expedition. Fray Juan was an old sol-dier who had joined Guzmán in 1529 and had traveled over much of the country. He was to leave his bones and his legend in Kansas, a martyr. Fray Luis was to be martyred near Pecos.

On February 22 the muster roll was taken. Not counting Indians, children and women, they numbered three hundred thirty-six. Two hundred thirty of these possessed horses. There were one thousand Indians and about an equal number of horses. There were nineteen crossbows and twenty-seven arquebuses.

Three women traveled with the army: Francisca de Hozes, the wife of Alonso Sanchez, who was to be a constant problem as well as a witness against Coronado in later years; Maria Maldonado, the wife of Juan de Paradinas, who was remembered because she cared for the sick; and the native wife of Lope Caballero. These soldaderas were not uncommon in Spanish expeditions and there were regulations laid down for the Spanish armies of Europe which authorized four women for common usage to accompany each hundred troops.

A surgeon went with the army. He had no medical equipment, and from the comments made by those who knew him he apparently had no medical training either.

Five Portuguese, two Italians (one of whom had been with Cortés), a Frenchman, a German bugler and a Scot by the name of Thomas Blake or Tomás Blaque as he was called—all are listed on the muster roll.

Mendoza decided to support Coronado by sea and prepared a small fleet under the command of Hernán de Alarcón which sailed north into the Gulf of California with supplies. The two forces never joined, but Alarcón became the first man to sail into the western Colorado River.

Wearing all his gilt armor, Coronado led his expedition northward out of Culiacán toward the Seven Cities of Cíbola. Soon after he left, Coronado met the returning Melchior Díaz. The old soldier had found little to match the report of Fray Marcos. But though word of Díaz' findings reached the column, the padre was able to convince everyone that he had seen the Seven Cities. The column marched on. Coronado's second in command was killed in a skirmish with Indians, and Cárdenas reluctantly accepted the post. Then the young captain-general separated from the main body and went ahead with an advance column of about one hundred men.

For part of the distance they were able to follow a vague trail, but most of the way they had to cut their own road as they went. They passed through Corazones Valley, where Cabeza de Vaca received the animal hearts, through Sonora Valley, Eagle Pass and then they swung west around the Gila Range, crossing Salt River and on until they approached the Cíbola described by Fray Marcos. Along the way the padre had become increasingly unpopular and as the expedition neared the town that was supposed to be larger than Mexico City, they were startled to find a small adobe pueblo—Hawikuh, the most western of the Zuñi towns. Fray Marcos returned to Mexico soon afterward.

Coronado reported his disappointment to Mendoza along with his still undiminished hopes. He was determined to find wealth and greatness. And in his thrashing, he made discoveries far greater than he knew. His men pressed westward toward the South Sea, crossed new rivers, discovered the Grand Canyon of the Colorado, and to the eastward entered the great plains as far as Kansas. Coronado opened up one of the richest and most beautiful areas of the world, and he recorded his reactions himself.

CORONADO TO MENDOZA, AUGUST 3, 1540

The account given by Francisco Vásquez de Coronado, captain-general of the force which was sent in the name of His Majesty to the newly discovered country, of what happened to the expedition after April 22 of the Year 1540, when he started forward from Culiacán, and of what he found in the country through which he passed.

On the 22nd of April last, I set out from the province of Culiacán with a part of the army. Judging by the outcome, it was fortunate that I did not start the whole of the army on this undertaking. The labors have been so very great and the lack of food such that I do not believe this undertaking could have been completed before the end of this year, and not without a great loss of life.

Thirty leagues before reaching the place of which the father provincial, Fray Marcos, spoke so well in his report—the valley into which Fray Marcos did not dare to enter—I sent Melchior Díaz forward with fifteen horsemen, ordering him to make but one day's journey out of two, so that he could examine everything there before I arrived. He traveled through some very rough mountains for four days, and did not find anything to live on, or people, or information about anything except two or three poor villages. From the people here he learned that there was nothing to be found in the country beyond except the mountains, which continued very rough, entirely uninhabited by people. The whole company felt disturbed at this, that a thing so much praised, and about which the father had said so many things, should be found so very different; and they began to think that all the rest would be of the same sort.

I tried to encourage them by telling them that Your Lordship had always thought this part of the trip would be a waste of effort, and that we ought to devote our attention to those Seven Cities and the other provinces about which we had information—that these should be the end of our enterprise. With this resolution, we all marched cheerfully along a very bad way where it was impossible to pass without making a new road or repairing the one that was there. This troubled the soldiers, considering that everything which the friar had said was found to be quite the reverse; because, among other things, the father had said that the way would be plain and good, and that there would be only one small hill of about half a league. The truth is, there are mountains where, however well the path might be fixed, they could not be crossed without great danger of the horses falling over them. It was so bad that many of the animals which Your Lordship sent as provision for the army were lost along this part of the way.

I reached the Valley of Hearts at last, on the 26th of May, and rested there a number of days. Between Culiacán and this place I could sustain myself only by means of a large supply of corn bread, because I had to leave all the corn, as it was not yet ripe. In this Valley of Hearts, we found more people than in any part of the country we had left behind, and a large extent of tilled ground. There was no corn for food among them, but I heard that there was some in another valley called Sonora. As I did not wish to disturb them by force, I sent Melchior Díaz with goods to exchange for it. A little corn was obtained by this trading, which relieved the friendly Indians and some Spaniards.

Ten or twelve of the horses had died of overwork by the time we reached this Valley of Hearts, because they were unable to stand the strain of carrying heavy burdens and eating so little. Some of our Negroes and some of the Indians also died here, which was a great loss for the rest of the expedition. They told me that the Valley of Hearts is a long five days' journey from the western sea. I sent to summon Indians from the coast in order to learn about their condition, and while I was waiting for these, the horses rested. I stayed there four days, during which the Indians came from the sea. They told me that there were seven or eight islands two days' journey from that sea-coast, directly opposite, well populated with people, but poorly supplied with food, and the people were savages. They told me they had seen a ship pass not very far from that land. I do not know whether it was the one which was sent to discover the country, or perhaps some Portuguese.

I set out from the Hearts and kept near the seacoast as well as I could judge. But I found myself continually farther off, so that when I reached Chichilticale I found I was fifteen days' journey from the sea, although the father provincial had said it was only five leagues distant and that he had seen it. We all became very distrustful, and felt great anxiety and dismay to see that everything was the reverse of what he had told Your Lordship. The sea turns toward the west directly opposite the Hearts for ten or twelve leagues. There I learned that the ships had been seen which your Lordship had sent in search of the port of Chichilticale, which Fray Marcos said was on the thirty-fifth degree.

God knows what I have suffered, because I fear that they may have met with some mishap. If they follow the coast, and if they have not been overtaken by some misfortune, I maintain my trust in God that they have already discovered something good for which their delay may be pardoned. I rested for two days at Chichilticale. There was good reason for staying longer, because the horses were becoming so tired; but there was no chance to rest longer, as the food was giving out. I entered the borders of the wilderness region on Saint John's eve. We found no grass during the first days, but a worse way through mountains and more dangerous passages than we had experienced previously. The horses were so tired that they were not equal to it, and in this last desert we lost more horses than before. Some Indian allies, a Spaniard called Spinosa, and two Negroes died from eating some herbs, because the food had given out.

I sent the army-master, Don García López de Cárdenas, with fifteen horsemen, a day's march ahead of me, in order to explore the country and prepare the way, which he accomplished like the man that he is. The way is very bad for at least thirty leagues, through impassable mountains. But when we had passed these thirty leagues, we found fresh rivers and grass like that of Castile. There was a considerable amount of flax near the banks of one river, which was called on this account El Rio del Lino. No Indians were seen during the first day's march, after which four Indians came out with signs of peace. They said they had been sent to say we were welcome, and that on the next day the tribe would provide the whole force with food. The army-master gave them a cross, telling them to say to their people that they need not fear and should stay in their own houses, because I was coming in the name of His Majesty to defend and help them.

After this was done, Hernando de Alvarado came back to tell me that some Indians had met him peaceably, and that two of them were with the army-master waiting for me. I went to them and gave them some paternosters and some little cloaks, telling them to return to their city and say to the people there that they could stay quietly in their houses and that they need not fear. After this I ordered the army-master to go and see if there were any bad passages which the Indians might be able to defend, and to seize any such until the next day, when I would come up. He found a very bad place in our way where we might have received much harm, and immediately established himself there. The Indians came that very night to occupy the place. Finding it taken, they assaulted our men, attacking, I am told, like valiant men. In the end they had to retreat. The Indians sounded a little trumpet as a sign of retreat, and did not do any injury to the Spaniards. The army-master sent me notice of this the same night, and I started on the next day, for we were in such great need of food that I thought we should all die of hunger. The Indians lighted their fires from point to point, and these were answered from a distance with as good understanding as we could have shown. And in this manner notice was given concerning how we went and where we had arrived.

As soon as I came within sight of this city, I sent the army-master, Cárdenas, Fray Daniel and Fray Luis, and Ferrando Vermizzo, with some horsemen, a little distance ahead to tell the Indians that we were not coming to do them any harm, but to defend them in the name of our lord the Emperor. The summons, in the form in which His Majesty commanded in his instructions, was made intelligible by an interpreter. But they, being a proud people, were little affected.

It seemed to them that, as we were few in number, they would not have any difficulty in conquering us. They pierced the gown of Fray Luis with an arrow, which, blessed be God, did him no harm. Meanwhile I arrived with all the rest of the horse and the footmen, and found a large body of the Indians on the plain, who began to shoot with their arrows. In obedience to the orders of Your Lordship, I did not allow my company to attack, telling them that what the enemy was doing was nothing. On the other hand, when the Indians saw that we did not move, they grew so bold that they came up almost to the heels of our horses to shoot their arrows. I saw that it was no longer the time to hesitate, and as the priests approved the action, I charged them. There was little to do because they suddenly took to flight, part running toward the city, which was well fortified, and others toward the plain, wherever chance led them. Some Indians were killed, and others might have been slain if I had allowed them to be pursued. But I saw that there would be little advantage in this, because the Indians who were outside were few, and those who had retired to the city were numerous, besides many who had remained there in the first place.

As that was where the food was, of which we stood in such great need, I assembled my whole force and divided them as seemed best for the attack on the city, and surrounded it. The hunger we suffered would not permit of any delay, and so I dismounted with some of these gentlemen and soldiers. I ordered the musketeers and crossbowmen to begin the attack and drive back the enemy from the defenses. I assaulted the wall on one side, where I was told there was a scaling ladder and also a gate. But the crossbowmen broke all the strings of their crossbows, and the musketeers could do nothing because they had arrived so weak and feeble that they could scarcely stand on their feet. In this way the people who were on top were able to do us great injury. They knocked me down to the ground twice with countless great stones, and if I had not been protected by the very good headpiece I wore, the outcome would have been bad for me. They picked me up from the ground, however, with two small wounds in my face and an arrow in my foot, and with many bruises on my arms and legs, and in this condition I retired from the battle, very weak. The second time they knocked me to the ground, Don García López de Cárdenas had come to my help, like a good cavalier, by placing his own body above mine. Otherwise I should have been in much greater danger than I was. But, by the pleasure of God, these Indians surrendered. Their city was taken, and a sufficient supply of corn was found there to relieve our necessities.

The army-master and Don Pedro de Tovar and Hernando de Alvarado and Pablo de Melgosa, the infantry captain, sustained some bruises, although none of them was wounded. Agoniez Quarez was hit in the arm by an arrow; and one Torres, who lived in Panuco, in the face by another. Two other footmen received slight arrow wounds. They all directed their attack against me because my armor was gilded and glittered. On this account I was hurt more than the rest, and not because I had done more or was farther in advance than the others; all these gentlemen and soldiers bore themselves well, as was expected of them. I praise God that I am now well, although somewhat sore from the stones. Two or three other soldiers were hurt in the battle on the plain. Three horses were killed, and seven or eight others were wounded, but the men and the horses have now recovered and are well.

It now remains for me to tell about this city and kingdom and province of which the father provincial gave Your Lordship an account. In brief, I can assure you that he has not told the truth in a single thing that he said, except the name of the city and the large stone houses. Although they are not decorated with turquoises nor made of lime or of good bricks, nevertheless they are very good houses with three and four and five stories, very good apartments and rooms with corridors. There are some very good rooms under ground and paved, which are made for winter, and are something like hot baths. The ladders which they have for their houses are all movable and portable. The Seven Cities are seven little villages, all having the kind of houses I have described. They are all within a radius of five leagues. Each has its own name and no single one is called Cíbola, but altogether are called Cíbola. This one which I have called a city I have named Granada, partly because it has some similarity to it, as well as out of regard for Your Lordship. In this place where I am now lodged there are perhaps two hundred houses, all surrounded by a wall. With the other houses there might be altogether five hundred families. There is another town near by, which is one of the seven but somewhat larger than this, and the other four are somewhat smaller. I send them all to Your Lordship, painted with the route. The skin on which the painting is made was found here with other skins.

The people of the towns seem to be of ordinary size and intelligent, although I do not think they have the judgment and intelligence to have built these houses. Most of them are entirely naked except the covering of their privy parts, and they have painted mantles like the one which I send to Your Lordship. They do not raise cotton, because the country is very cold. They all have good figures and are well bred. I think they have a quantity of turquoises, which they had removed with the rest of their goods, except the corn, when I arrived. I did not find any women here nor any men under fifteen years of age or over sixty, except two or three old men who remained in command of all the other men and the warriors. Two points of emerald and some little broken stones which approach the color of rather poor garnets were found in a paper, besides other stone crystals. I gave these to one of my servants to keep until they could be sent to Your Lordship, but he has lost them, I am told. We found fowls, but only a few. Yet there are some. The Indians tell me that they do not eat these in any of the seven villages, but that they keep them merely for the sake of the feathers. I do not believe this, because they are very good, and better than those of Mexico.

The climate of this country and the temperature of the air is almost like that of Mexico, because it is sometimes hot and sometimes it rains. I have not yet seen it rain, however, except once when there fell a little shower with wind, such as often falls in Spain. The snow and the cold are usually very great, according to the natives. There are no kinds of fruit or fruit trees. The country is all level, and is nowhere shut in by high mountains, although there are some hills and rough passages. There are not many birds, probably because of the cold and because there are no mountains near. There are no trees fit for firewood here, but they can bring enough for their needs from a clump of very small cedars four leagues distant. Very good grass is found a quarter of a league away, of which we had great need because our horses were so feeble when we arrived.

The food which they eat in this country is corn, of which they have a great abundance, and beans and venison, which they probably eat although they say that they do not, because we found many skins of deer and hares and rabbits. They make the best corn cakes I have ever seen anywhere, and this is what everybody ordinarily eats. They have the very best arrangement and machinery for grinding that was ever seen. One of these Indian women here will grind as much as four of the Mexicans. They have very good salt in crystals, which they bring from a lake a day's journey from here. No information can be obtained among them about the North Sea or that on the west, nor do I know how to tell Your Lordship which we are nearest to. I should judge that it is nearer the western, and 150 leagues at the nearest. The North Sea ought to be much farther away. Your Lordship may thus see how very wide the country is.

They have many animals—bears, tigers, lions, porcupines, and some sheep as big as a horse, with very large horns and little tails. I have seen some of their horns, and the size was something to marvel at. There are also wild goats whose heads I have seen, and the paws of the bears and the skins of the wild boars. For game they have deer, leopards, and very large cows which inhabit some plains eight days' journey to the north. They have some of their skins here very well dressed, and they prepare and paint them when they have killed the cows, according to what they tell me.

These Indians say that the kingdom of Totonteac, which the father provincial praised so much as something marvelous and of such very great size, is a hot lake on the edge of which there are five or six houses. There used to be some others, but these had been destroyed by war. The kingdom of Marata can not be found, nor do these Indians know anything about it. The kingdom of Acus is a single small city where they raise cotton, and this is called Acucu. Acus, with or without the aspiration, is not a word in this region; and because Acucu may be derived from Acus, I say that it is this town which has been converted into the kingdom of Acus. They tell me that there are some other small ones not far from this settlement, which are situated on a river which I have seen and of which the Indians have told me. God knows I wish I had better news to write to Your Lordship, but I must give you the truth.

Three days after I captured this city, some of the Indians who lived here came to offer to make peace. They brought me some turquoises and poor mantles, and I received them in His Majesty's name, making them understand the purpose of my coming to this country. I told them that they and all the others in this province should become Christians and should know the true God for their Lord, and His Majesty for their king and earthly lord. After this they returned to their houses. Suddenly, the next day, they packed up their goods and property, their women and children, and fled to the hills, leaving their towns deserted, with only some few remaining in them.

Seeing this, I went to the town which I said was larger than this. This was eight or ten days later, when I had recovered from my wounds. I found a few of them there. I told them not to feel any fear and to summon their lord to me. By what I can find out or observe, however, none of these towns have any, since I have not seen any principal house by which any superiority over others could be shown. Afterward an old man, who said he was their lord, came with a mantle made of many pieces, with whom I argued as long as he stayed with me. He said that he would come to see me with the rest of the chiefs of the country, three days later, in order to arrange the relations which should exist between us. He did so, and they brought me some ragged little mantles and some turquoises. I said they ought to come down from their strongholds and return to their houses with their wives and children, and that they should become Christians and recognize His Majesty as their king and lord. But they still remain in their strongholds with their wives and all their property.

I commanded them to have a cloth painted for me, with all the animals that they know in that country. Although they are poor painters, they quickly painted two for me, one of the animals and the other of the birds and fishes. They say they will bring their children so that our priests may instruct them, and that they desire to know our law. They declare that it was foretold among them more than fifty years ago that a people such as we are should come, and the direction they should come from, and that the whole country would be conquered. So far as I can find out, the water is what these Indians worship, because they say it makes the corn grow and sustains their life, and that the only other reason they know is that their ancestors did so.

I have tried in every way to find out whether they know of any other peoples or provinces or cities. They tell me about seven cities which are at a considerable distance, which are like these except that the houses there are made of adobe, and small, and that they raise much cotton there. The first of these places is called Tucano. They could not tell me much about the others. I do not believe they tell me the truth, because they think I shall soon have to depart from them and return home. But they will quickly find they are deceived in this. I sent Don Pedro de Tovar there, with his company and some other horsemen, to see it. I have determined to send throughout all the surrounding regions to find out where there is anything, and to suffer every extremity before I give up this enterprise, and to serve His Majesty and Your Lordship, if I can find any way in which to do it.

We have great need of pasture. Also, among all of us there is not one pound of raisins, or sugar, or oil, or wine, except barely half a quart, which is saved to say mass, since everything was consumed, and part was lost on the way. Now, you can provide us with what appears best; but if you are thinking of sending cattle, you should know that it will be necessary for them to spend at least a year on the road.

The death of the Negro [Estevan de Dorantes] is perfectly certain because many of the things which he wore have been found. The Indians say that they killed him because the Indians of Chichilticale said he was a bad man, and not like the Christians, because the Christians never kill women, and he killed them, and because he assaulted their women, whom the Indians love better than themselves.

Some gold and silver has been found in this place, which those who know about minerals say is not bad. I have not yet been able to learn where they got it. They refuse to tell me the truth in everything, because they think that I shall have to depart from here in a short time, as I have said. But I trust in God that they will not be able to avoid answering much longer. I beg Your Lordship to make a report of the success of this expedition to His Majesty, because there is nothing more than I have already said. I shall not do so until it shall please God to grant that we find what we desire. Our Lord God protect and keep your most illustrious Lordship.

From the province of Cíbola, and this city of Granada, the 3rd of August, 1540.

Francisco Vásquez de Coronado kisses the hand of your most illustrious Lordship.

The account of the expedition by the common soldier Pedro de Castañeda, who settled at Culiacán, was written years after the event. It is the document of a simple man, to whom geography meant little, but it is an honest attempt to recall what happened, and it is certainly one of the most important documents in early American history. Sometime in 1554, Castañeda's wife and eight children filed against the government for some recompense for the services the soldier had rendered for the king.

AN ACCOUNT WRITTEN BY PEDRO DE CASTAÑEDA OF NAJERA

After Melchior Díaz and Juan Gallego had arrived in the town of Soñora, it was announced that the army was to depart for Cíbola. Melchior Díaz was to remain in charge of that town with eighty men, and Juan Gallego was going to New Spain with messages for the viceroy. Fray Marcos was going back with him, because he did not think it was safe for him to stay in Cíbola, seeing that his report had turned out to be entirely false. The kingdoms that he had told about had not been found, or the populous cities, or the wealth of gold, or the precious stones which he had reported, or the fine clothes, or other things that had been proclaimed from the pulpits. Those who were to remain were selected and the rest loaded their provisions and set off about the middle of September on the way to Cíbola, following their general.

Don Tristán de Arellano stayed in this new town with the weakest men. From this time on there was nothing but mutinies and strife, because after the army had gone, Captain Melchior Díaz took twenty-five of the most efficient men, leaving in his place one Diego de Alcaraz, a man unfitted for command. The captain went toward the north and west in search of the seacoast. After going about 150 leagues, they came to a province of exceedingly tall and strong men—like giants. They can take a load of three or four hundredweight on their heads. On account of the great cold, they carry a firebrand in the hand when they go from one place to another, shifting it every now and then so that they warm the other hand and the body as well. On this account the large river in that country was called Rio del Tison—[the Colorado River]. Here the captain heard that there had been ships at a point three days down toward the sea. When he reached the place, which was more than fifteen leagues from the mouth of the river, they found written on a tree: "Alarcón reached this place; there are letters at the foot of this tree." He dug up the letters and learned from them how long Alarcón had waited for news of the army and that he had gone back with the ships to New Spain, because he was unable to proceed farther, since the sea was a bay. This bay was formed by the Isle of the Marquis [Cortés], which is called California, and it was explained that California was not an island but a point of the mainland forming the other side of that gulf.

In the meantime, the army was on its way to Cíbola. Everything went along in good shape, since the general had left everything peaceful. In a province called Vacapan there was a large quantity of prickly pears, of which the natives made preserves. The men of the army ate so much of it that they all fell sick with a headache and fever. This lasted twenty-four hours. After this they continued their march until they reached Chichilticalli.

The army proceeded and was about a day's march from Cíbola when a very cold tornado came up in the afternoon, followed by a great fall of snow. The army went on till it reached some caves in a rocky ridge, late in the evening. The Indian allies, who were from New Spain and for the most part from warm countries, were in great danger from the cold. They suffered much pain and had to be carried on the horses, the soldiers walking. Finally the army reached Cíbola, where their general was waiting for them with their quarters all ready.

Here they were reunited, except some captains and men who had gone off to discover other provinces.

The general had sent Don Pedro de Tovar and some men to learn about some villages in a province called Tusayan, some twenty-five leagues from Cíbola. Juan de Padilla, a Franciscan friar who had been a fighting man in his youth, went with them. They entered the country so quietly that nobody observed them. The people do not leave the villages except to go to their farms, especially at this time when they heard that Cíbola had been captured by very fierce people who traveled on animals which ate people. Our men arrived after nightfall and were able to conceal themselves under the edge of the village. But in the morning they were discovered, and the natives came out to meet them with bows and shields and wooden clubs, drawn up in lines without any confusion. The interpreter spoke to them and gave them due warning, for they were very intelligent people. Nevertheless they drew lines and insisted that our men should not go across these lines toward the village.

While they were talking, some men acted as if they would cross the lines, and one of the natives lost control of himself and struck a horse a blow. Fray Juan, fretted by the time that was being wasted in talking to them, said to the captain: "To tell the truth, I do not know why we came here." When the men heard this, they gave the Santiago so suddenly that they ran down many Indians and the others fled to the town in confusion. Some did not even have this chance, so quickly did the people in the village come out with presents, asking for peace. They gave the captain some cotton cloth, although not much, because they do not make it in that district. They also gave him some dressed skins and corn meal, and pine nuts and corn and birds of the country. Afterward they presented a few turquoises. The people of the whole district came together that day, and submitted themselves. They allowed the captain to enter their villages freely to visit, buy, sell and barter with them.

It is governed like Cíbola by an assembly of the oldest men. They have their governors and generals. This was where Don Pedro obtained the information about a large river, and that several days down the river there were some very tall people.

As Don Pedro de Tovar was not commissioned to go farther, he returned and gave his information to the general, who dispatched Don García López de Cárdenas with about twelve companions to go to see this river. He was well received in Tusayan, and was given guides for his journey. They started from there loaded with provisions, for they had to go through a desert country before reaching the inhabited region, which the Indians said was more than twenty days' journey. After they had gone twenty days they came to the banks of the river. It seemed to be more than three or four leagues in an air line across to the other bank of the stream which flowed between them [the Grand Canyon].

This country was elevated and full of low twisted pines, very cold, and lying open toward the north. They spent three days on this bank looking for a passage down to the river. It looked from above as if the water was six feet across, although the Indians said it was half a league wide. It was impossible to descend. Captain Melgosa and one Juan Galeras and another companion, who were the three lightest and most agile men, made an attempt to go down at the least difficult place. They returned without having succeeded in reaching the bottom. They said that they had been down about a third of the way. The river seemed very large from the place which they reached, and from what they saw they thought the Indians had given the width correctly. Those who stayed above had estimated that some huge rocks on the sides of the cliffs seemed to be about as tall as a man, but those who went down swore that when they reached these rocks they were bigger than the great tower of Seville.

This was the Tison [Firebrand] river, much nearer its source than where Melchior Díaz and his company crossed it. These were the same kind of Indians, judging from what was afterward learned. They came back from this point and the expedition did not have any other result.

The villages of that province remained peaceful, since they were never visited again, nor was any attempt made to find other peoples in that direction.

While they were making these discoveries, some Indians came to Cíbola from Cicuye, a village seventy leagues east of this province. Among them was a captain who was called Bigotes [Whiskers] by our men, because he wore a long mustache. He was a tall, well-built young fellow. He told the general that they had come in response to the notice which had been given, to offer themselves as friends, and that if he wanted to go through their country they would consider us as their friends. They brought a present of tanned hides and shields and headpieces, which were very gladly received. The general gave them some glass dishes and a number of pearls and little bells which they prized highly, because these were things they had never seen. They described some animals which, from a picture one of them had painted on his skin, seemed to be cows, although this did not seem possible from the hides, because the hair was woolly and snarled. The general ordered Hernando de Alvarado to take twenty companions and go with them to learn more of this.

Captain Alvarado started on this journey and in five days reached a village called Acuco [Acoma], with a population of about two hundred men. These people were robbers, feared by the whole country round about. The village was very strong, because it was up on a rock out of reach, having steep sides in every direction, and so high that it was a very good musket that could throw a ball as high. The only entrance was by a stairway built by hand, which began at the top of a slope around the foot of the rock. It was a broad stairway for about two hundred steps, then a stretch of about one hundred narrower steps. At the top they had to go up about three times as high as a man by means of holes in the rock, in which they put the points of their feet, holding on at the same time by their hands. There was a wall of large and small stones at the top, which they could roll down without showing themselves, so that no army could possibly be strong enough to capture the village.

On the top they had room to sow and store a large amount of corn, and cisterns to collect snow and water. These people came down to the plain ready to fight, and would not listen to any arguments. They drew lines on the ground and determined to prevent our men from crossing these, but when they saw that they would have to fight, they offered to make peace before any harm had been done. They went through their forms of making peace, which is to touch the horses and take their sweat and rub themselves with it, and to make crosses with the fingers of the hands. But to make the most secure peace they put their hands across each other, and they keep this peace inviolably.

From here they went to a province called Tiguex, three days distant. The people all came out peacefully, seeing that Whiskers was with them. These men are feared throughout all those provinces. Alvarado sent messengers back to advise the general to come and winter in this country. The general was relieved to hear that the country was growing better. Five days from here the captain came to Cicuye [Pecos], a very strong village four stories high. The people came out with signs of joy to welcome Hernando de Alvarado and their captain, and brought them into the town with drums and pipes. They made many presents of cloth and turquoises, of which there are quantities in the region. The Spaniards enjoyed themselves here for several days an talked with an Indian slave, a native of the country toward Florida which is the region Don Hernando de Soto discovered. This fellow said that there were large settlements in the farther part of that coun try. Hernando de Alvarado took him to guide them to the cows; but he told them such great things about the wealth of gold and silver in his country that they did not care about looking for cows, but returned after they had seen a few, to report the rich news to the general. The called the Indian "Turk," because he looked like one.

Meanwhile the general had sent Don García López de Cárdena to Tiguex to get lodgings ready for the army, which had arrived from Sonora about this time. When Hernando de Alvarado reached Tiguex on his way back from Cicuye, he found Don García López de Cár denas there, and so there was no need to go any farther. To give th Spaniards lodging places, the natives in one village had to abandon it and go to others belonging to their friends, and they took with them nothing but the clothes they had on. Information was obtained here about many towns up toward the north, and I believe that it would have been much better to follow this direction than that of the Turk, who was the cause of all the misfortunes which followed.

Everything already related had happened when Don Tristán de Arellano reached Cíbola from Sonora. Soon after he arrived, the general, who had received notice of a province containing eight vil lages, took thirty men and went to see it, going from there directly to Tiguex. He left orders for Don Tristán de Arellano to proceed to Tiguex by the direct road, after the men had rested twenty days In eight days they reached Tutahaco, where they learned that there were other towns down the river.

The general went up the river from here, visiting the whole province until he reached Tiguex, where he found Hernando de Alvarado and the Turk, whose good news gave him great joy. The Turk said that in his country there was a river in the level country which was two leagues wide, in which there were fishes as big as horses, and large numbers of very big canoes, with more than twenty rowers on a side. These canoes carried sails, and their lords sat on the poop under awnings, and on the prow they had a great golden eagle. He said also that the lord of the country took his afternoon nap under a great tree on which were hung many little gold bells, which put him to sleep as they swung in the air. He said also that everyone had their ordinary dishes made of wrought plate, and the jugs and bowls were of gold. He called gold *acochis*. They showed him metal ornaments and he recognized them and said they were not gold; he knew gold and silver very well and did not care anything about other metals. For this reason, and because of the ease with which he told it, he was believed.

The general sent Hernando de Alvarado back to Cicuye to demand some gold bracelets which this Turk said they had taken from him when they captured him. Alvarado was received as a friend at the village. When he demanded the bracelets, they said they knew nothing at all about them, that the Turk was deceiving him and was lying. Seeing that there were no other means, Captain Alvarado got the Captain Whiskers and the governor to come into his tent, and when they had come, he put them in chains. The villagers prepared to fight, denouncing Hernando de Alvarado, and saying that he had no respect for peace and friendship. Captain Alvarado started back to Tiguex, where the general kept Whiskers and the governor prisoners more than six months. This began the want of confidence in the word of the Spaniards whenever there was talk of peace from this time on.

We have already said that when the general started from Cíbola, he left orders for Don Tristán de Arellano to start twenty days later. The men were now rested and provided with food and eager to join their general. He set off with his force toward Tiguex, and the first day they made their camp in the best, largest, and finest village of the [Cíbola] province. This is the only village that has houses with seven stories.

The army continued its march from here. The season had already advanced into December, and it snowed nearly every night. The army passed by the great rock of Acuco, and the natives, who were peaceful, entertained our men well, giving them provisions and birds. Many of the gentlemen went up to the top to see it, and they had great difficulty in going up the steps in the rock, because they were not used to them. The natives go up and down so easily that they carry loads, and the women carry water.

From here they went on to Tiguex, where they were well received and taken care of. The great good news of the Turk gave much joy and helped lighten their hard labors, although when the army arrived we found the whole country in revolt.

The people of Tiguex did not feel well about the seizure of Captain Whiskers and their governor. In addition to this, the general, wishing to obtain some clothing for his soldiers, had summoned one of the chief Indians of Tiguex with whom he was on good terms. He was called Juan Aleman by our men, after a gentleman who lived in Mexico whom he was said to resemble. The general told him that he must furnish about three hundred or more pieces of cloth, which he needed for his people. Juan Aleman said this was a matter for the governors; and that besides, they would have to consult together and divide it among the villages, and that it was necessary to make the demand of each town separately. The general ordered certain of the gentlemen to go and make the demand. They did not give the natives a chance to consult about it, but demanded what they had to give, so that they could proceed at once. Thus these people could do nothing except take off their own cloaks and give them to make up the number demanded of them. Some of the soldiers did not like the blankets or cloaks they received, and if they saw an Indian with a better one on, they exchanged with him without more ado, not stopping to find out the rank of the man they were stripping. This caused much hard feeling.

Besides what I have just said, one whom I will not name out of regard for him, left the village where the camp was and went to another village about a league distant. Seeing a pretty woman there, he called her husband down to hold his horse while he went up. As the village was entered by the upper story, the Indian supposed he was going to some other part of it. While he was there, the Indian heard some slight noise, and then the Spaniard came down, took his horse, and went away. The Indian went up and learned that the Spaniard had violated, or tried to violate, his wife, and so he came with the important men of the town to complain of this.

The general made all the men come together. The Indian did not recognize the man, but he said that he could tell the horse, because he had held his bridle. He was taken to the stables, and found the horse. The master of the horse denied doing it, seeing that he himself had not been recognized, and it may be that the Indian was mistaken in the horse. Anyway, he went off without getting any satisfaction. The next day one of the Indians who was guarding the horses came running in, saying that a companion of his had been killed and that the

Indians of the country were driving off the horses toward their villages. The Spaniards tried to collect the horses again, but many were
lost, besides seven of the general's mules.

The next day Cárdenas went to talk with the natives. He found the
villages closed by palisades and a great noise inside, the horses being
chased as in a bull fight and shot with arrows. The Indians were all
ready for fighting. Nothing could be done, because they would not
come down on to the plain, and the villages are so strong that the
Spaniards could not dislodge them. The general then ordered Cárdenas to surround the village where the greatest injury had been done
and where the affair with the Indian woman occurred. Several captains who had gone on in advance with the general, Juan de Saldivar
and Barrionuevo and Diego López and Melgosa, took the Indians so
much by surprise that they gained the upper story, with great danger,
for they wounded many of our men from within the houses. Our men
were on top of the houses in great danger for a day and a night and
part of the next day, and they made some good shots with their crossbows and muskets. The horsemen on the plain with many of the
Indian allies from New Spain smoked them out from the cellars into
which they had broken, so that they begged for peace.

Pablo de Melgosa and Diego López, the alderman from Seville,
were left on the roof and answered the Indians with the same signs
they were making for peace, which was to make a cross. They then put
down their arms and received pardon. They were taken to the tent of
Cárdenas. According to what he said, he did not know about the
peace and thought they had given themselves up because they had
been conquered. As he had been ordered by the general not to take
them alive but to make an example of them so that the other natives
would fear the Spaniards, he ordered two hundred stakes to be prepared at once to burn them alive. Nobody told him about the peace
that had been granted them, for the soldiers knew as little as he, and
those who should have told him about it remained silent, not thinking
that it was any of their business. When the enemies saw what the
Spaniards were doing, about a hundred men who were in the tent
began to struggle, seizing the stakes to defend themselves.

Our men attacked the tent on all sides, so that there was great confusion around it, and the horsemen chased those who escaped. As the
country was level, not a man of them remained alive. Some who remained hidden in the village escaped that night to spread throughout
the country the news that the strangers did not respect the peace they

had made. This afterward proved a great misfortune. After this was over, it began to snow, and they abandoned the village and returned to the camp just as the army came from Cíbola.

It snowed so much that for the next two months it was impossible to do anything except to go along the roads to advise the natives that if they made peace they would be pardoned and might consider themselves safe. They replied that they did not trust those who did not know how to keep good faith, and that the Spaniards should remember they were keeping Whiskers prisoner and did not keep their word when they burned those who surrendered in the village.

Don García López de Cárdenas was one of those who went to give this notice. He started out with about thirty companions and went to the village of Tiguex to talk with Juan Aleman. Although they were hostile, the Indians said that if he would send away the horsemen and make his men keep away, Juan Aleman and another captain would come out of the village to meet him.

Everything was done as they required, and when they approached they said that they had no arms and that he must take his off. Don García did this in order to give them confidence, on account of his great desire to get them to make peace. Juan Aleman approached and embraced him vigorously, while the other two who had come with him drew mallets which they had hidden behind their backs and gave him two such blows over his helmet that they almost knocked him senseless. Two of the horsemen had been unwilling to go very far off, even when he ordered them. They rode up so quickly that they rescued him from their hands, although they were unable to catch the enemies, the meeting being so near to the village. The horsemen all rode up together and hurriedly carried off their captain, without being able to harm the enemy, while many of our men were dangerously wounded.

They then withdrew, leaving a number of men to continue the attack. Cárdenas went on with a part of the force to another village about half a league distant, because almost all the people in this region had collected into these two villages. As they paid no attention to the demands made on them and would not hear of peace, he returned to his companions whom he had left to keep up the attack of Tiguex. Our men rode off slowly, pretending to flee, so that they drew the enemy on to the plain, and then turned on them and caught several of their leaders. The rest collected on the roofs of the village and the captain returned to his camp.

After this affair the general ordered the army to surround the village.

He set out with his men with several scaling ladders. When he reached the village, he encamped his force nearby, and then the siege began. The enemy had had several days to provide themselves with stores, and they threw down so many rocks that many of our men were laid out. They wounded nearly a hundred with arrows, several of whom afterward died on account of the bad treatment by an unskillful surgeon who was with the army.

The siege lasted fifty days, during which time several assaults were made. The lack of water troubled the Indians most. They dug a very deep well inside the village, but were unable to get water, and while they were digging it, it fell in and killed thirty persons. Two hundred of the besieged died in the fights. During a hard fight, they killed Francisco de Obando, a captain who had been army-master all the time that Cárdenas was away making the discoveries already described, and also Francisco Pobares, a fine gentleman.

One day, before the capture was completed, they asked to speak to us. They said that since they knew we would not harm the women and children, they wished to surrender them, because they were using up their water. It was impossible to persuade them to make peace, as they said that the Spaniards would not keep an agreement with them. So they gave up about a hundred women and boys, who did not want to leave them. Don Lope de Urrea rode up in front of the town without his helmet and received the boys and girls in his arms. When all of these had been surrendered, Don Lope begged them to make peace, giving them the strongest promises for their safety. They told him to go away, as they did not wish to trust themselves to people who had no regard for friendship or their pledged word.

Fifteen days later they decided to leave the village, taking the women in their midst. They started about the fourth watch, in the very early morning, on the side where the cavalry was. The alarm was given by those in the camp of Don Rodrigo Maldonado. The enemy attacked them and killed one Spaniard and a horse and wounded others, but they were driven back with great slaughter until they came to the river, where the water flowed swiftly and very cold. They threw themselves into this, and as the men had come quickly from the whole camp to assist the cavalry, there were few who escaped being killed or wounded. Some men from the camp went across the river next day and found many of them who had been overcome by the great cold. They brought these back, cured them, and made servants of them. This ended that siege, and the town was captured.

In the meantime, Don Diego de Guevara and Juan de Saldivar

had captured the other large village after a siege which ended the last of March, in the year [1541].

About the time the siege ended, messengers reached the army from the city of San Hieronimo with letters from Diego de Alcaraz, who had remained there in place of Melchior Díaz. These contained the news that Melchior Díaz had died while he was conducting his search, and that the force had returned without finding any of the things they were after. The messengers also brought the news that some of the soldiers were ill disposed and had caused several mutinies.

When the general learned this, he sent Don Pedro de Tovar to that city to sift out some of the men. He was accompanied by messengers whom the general sent to Don Antonio de Mendoza, the viceroy, with an account of what had occurred and with the good news given by the Turk. When Don Pedro de Tovar arrived there, he found that the natives had killed a soldier with a poisoned arrow, which had made only a very little wound in one hand. Several soldiers went to the place where this happened, but they were not well received. Don Pedro de Tovar sent Diego de Alcaraz with a force to seize the chiefs and lords of a village in what they called the Valley of Knaves [de los Vellacos], which is in the hills. After getting there and taking these men prisoners, Diego de Alcaraz decided to let them go in exchange for some thread and cloth and other things which the soldiers needed.

Finding themselves free, they renewed the war and attacked them. As they were strong and had poison, they killed several Spaniards and wounded others so that they died on the way back. They retired toward the town, and if they had not had Indian allies from the country of the Hearts, it would have gone worse with them. They got back to the town, leaving seventeen soldiers dead from the poison. They would die in agony from only a small wound, the bodies breaking out with an insupportable pestilential stink. When Don Pedro de Tovar saw the harm done, and that they could not safely stay in that city, he moved forty leagues toward Cíbola into the valley of Suya.

During the siege of Tiguex the general went to Cicuye and promised to give Whiskers his liberty and leave him in the village, as soon as he should start for Quivira. He was received peacefully in Cicuye, and left their governor who was received with much joy and gratitude. Then the general returned, leaving Cicuye at peace and in the hope of getting back their Captain Whiskers.

For almost four months the river had been frozen over so that they crossed the ice on horseback. When it thawed out, orders were given for the start for Quivira, where the Turk said there was some gold and silver, although not so much as in Arche and Guaes. There were already some in the army who suspected the Turk, because a Spaniard named Cervantes solemnly swore that he had seen the Turk talking with the devil in a pitcher of water. He also said that while he had him under lock so that no one could speak to him, the Turk had asked him what Christians had been killed at Tiguex. He told him "nobody," and then the Turk answered: "You lie; five Christians are dead, including a captain."

As Cervantes knew that he told the truth, he confessed it so as to find out who had told him about it. The Turk said he knew it all by himself and that he did not need to have anyone tell him. It was on account of this that he watched him and saw him speaking to the devil in the pitcher.

While preparations were being made to start from Tiguex, people came from Cíbola to see the general, and he charged them to take good care of the Spaniards who were coming from Sonora with Don Pedro de Tovar. He gave them letters for Don Pedro, informing him how to find the army, and that he would find letters under the crosses which the army would put up along the way. The army left Tiguex on the fifth of May and returned to Cicuye, taking Whiskers with them. The general gave them their captain, who already went about freely with a guard. The village was very glad to see him, and the people were peaceful and offered food. The governor and Whiskers gave the general as a guide a young fellow called Xabe, a native of Quivira. This fellow said that there was gold and silver, but not so much of it as the Turk had said.

The army started from Cicuye, leaving the village at peace and under obligation to maintain the friendship because their governor and captain had been restored to them. Proceeding toward the plains, which are all on the other side of the mountains, they came to a river with a large deep current, which flowed down toward Cicuye, and they named this the Cicuye River [the Pecos River]. They had to stop here to make a bridge so as to cross it. It was finished in four days by much diligence and rapid work. As soon as it was done the whole army and the animals crossed. After ten days more they came to some settlements of people who lived like Arabs and who are called Querechos. They had seen the cows for two days. These folks live in tents made of the tanned skins of the cows. They travel around near the cows, killing them for food. They did nothing unusual when they saw our army except to come out of their tents to look at us, after which they came to talk with the advance guard and asked who we were. The general talked with them, but as they had already talked with the Turk, who was with the advance guard, they agreed with what he had said.

These Querechos were very intelligent. Although they conversed by means of signs, they made themselves so well understood that there was no need for an interpreter. They said there was a very large river over toward where the sun came from, and that one could go along this river through an inhabited region for ninety days without a break from settlement to settlement. They said that the first of these settlements was called Haxa, and that the river was more than a league wide and that there were many canoes on it. These folks started off from here next day with a lot of dogs which dragged their possessions.

For two days the army continued to march between north and east, but more toward the north. They saw other roaming Querechos and such great numbers of cows that it seemed incredible. The Turk said it was one or two days to Haxa. The general sent Captain Diego López with ten companions lightly equipped and a guide to go at full speed toward the sunrise for two days and discover Haxa, and then return to meet the army, which set out in the same direction next day.

There was another native of Quivira with the army, a painted Indian named Ysopete. This Indian had always declared that the Turk was lying, and because of this the army paid no attention to him. Even now, although he said that the Querechos had consulted with the Turk, Ysopete was not believed.

The general sent Don Rodrigo Maldonado with his company forward from here. He traveled four days and reached a large ravine like those of Colima, in the bottom of which he found a large settlement of people. Cabeza de Vaca and Dorantes had passed through this place, so that they presented Don Rodrigo with a pile of tanned skins and other things, and a tent as big as a house, which he directed them to keep until the army came up. He sent some of his companions to guide the army to that place so that they should not get lost, although he had been making piles of stones and cow dung for the army to follow.

While the army was resting in this ravine, a tempest came up one afternoon with a very high wind and hail. In a very short space of time a great quantity of hailstones, as big as bowls or bigger, fell as thick as raindrops. All the horses broke away except a few which the Negroes protected by holding large sea nets over them, also helmets and shields. If this storm had struck while they were upon the plain, the army might have been left without its horses, as there were many which they were not able to cover. The hail broke many tents, and battered many helmets, and wounded many of the horses, and broke all the crockery of the army, and the gourds.

From here the general sent out to explore the country, and they found another settlement four days from there. The country was well inhabited. These village settlements extended for three days. This was called Cona. Some Teyas, as these people are called, went with the army from here and traveled as far as the end of the other settlements with their packs of dogs and women and children. Then they gave them guides to proceed to a large ravine where the army was. They did not let these guides speak with the Turk and did not receive the same statements from these as they had from the others. These said that Quivira was toward the north, and that we would not find any good road to there. After this they began to believe Ysopete.

The army rested several days in this ravine and explored the country. Up to this point they had made thirty-seven days' marches, traveling six or seven leagues a day. It had been the duty of one man to measure and count his steps. They found that it was two hundred fifty leagues to the settlements [in the Tiguex country]. When the general realized this, he saw that they had been deceived by the Turk. As the provisions were giving out, and there was no country around here where they could procure more, he called the captains and ensigns together to decide on what ought to be done. They all agreed that the general should go in search of Quivira with thirty horsemen and half a dozen foot soldiers, and that Don Tristán de Arellano should go back to Tiguex with all the army. When the men in the army learned of this decision, they declared that they all wanted to go with him. This did not do any good, although the general agreed to send messengers to them within eight days, saying whether it was best for them to follow him or not. With this he set off with the guides and with Ysopete. The Turk was taken along in chains.

The general started from the ravine with the guides that the Teyas had given him. He appointed the alderman Diego López his army master, and took with him the most efficient men and the best horses. The army still had some hope that the general would send for them, and sent two horsemen, lightly equipped and riding post, to repeat their petition.

The guides ran away during the first few days and Diego López had to return to the army for guides, bringing orders for the army to return to Tiguex to find food and wait there for the general. The Teyas, as before, willingly furnished him with new guides. The army waited for its messengers and spent a fortnight here, preparing jerked beef to take with them. It was estimated that during this fortnight they killed five hundred bulls. The number of these that there were without cows was something incredible. Many fellows who went out hunting were lost at this time, and did not get back to the army for two or three days.

The country there is so level that at midday, after one has wandered about in pursuit of game, the only thing to do is to stay near the game quietly until sunset, so as to see where the sun goes down. Even then they have to be practiced men to do it. Those who are not had to trust themselves to others.

The general followed his guides until he reached Quivira, which took forty-eight days marching, on account of the great detour they had made toward Florida. He was received peacefully on account of the guides he had. They asked the Turk why he had lied and had guided them so far out of their way. He said that his country was in that direction and that, besides this, the people at Cicuye had asked him to lead them off on to the plains and lose them so that the horses would die when their provisions gave out. Then the Spaniards would be so weak that if they ever returned they would be killed without any trouble. And so they could take revenge for what had been done to them. This was the reason he had led them astray, supposing that they did not know how to hunt or to live without corn.

The Turk said all this like one who had given up hope and who found that he was being persecuted, since they had begun to believe Ysopete, who had guided them better than he had. They garroted him, which pleased Ysopete very much, because the Turk had always said that Ysopete was a rascal and that he did not know what he was talking about and had always hindered his talking with anybody. Neither gold nor silver nor any trace of either was found among these people. Their lord wore a copper plate on his neck and prized it highly.

The messengers whom the army had sent to the general returned, as I said. As they brought no news except what the alderman had delivered, the army left the ravine and returned to the Teyas, where they took guides who led them back by a more direct road.

On its return the army reached the Cicuye River more than thirty leagues below the bridge they had made when they crossed it, and they followed it up to that place. The guides said this river joined that of Tiguex more than twenty days from here, and that its course turned toward the east. It is believed that it flows into the mighty river of the Holy Spirit [Espíritu Santo; the Mississippi] which the men of Hernando de Soto discovered in Florida.

A painted Indian woman ran away from Juan de Saldivar and hid in the ravines about this time, because she recognized the country of Tiguex where she had been a slave. She fell into the hands of some Spaniards who had entered this country from Florida. After I got back to New Spain I heard that she told them she had run away from other men like them for nine days, and that she gave the names of some captains. From this it would seem that we were not far from the region they discovered, although they said they were more than two hundred leagues inland. I believe the land at this point is more than six hundred leagues across from sea to sea.

As I said, the army followed the river up as far as Cicuye, which it found ready for war and unwilling to make any advances toward peace or give any food to the army. From there they went on to Tiguex where several villages had been reinhabited, but the people were afraid and left again.

After Don Tristán de Arellano reached Tiguex, about the middle of July, in the year 1541, he had provisions collected for the coming winter. Captain Francisco de Barrionuevo was sent up the river toward the north with several men. He saw two provinces, one called Hemes [Jemez] which had seven villages, and the other Yuque-Yunque. The inhabitants of Hemes came out peacefully and furnished provisions. At Yuque-Yunque the whole nation left entirely vacant two very fine villages, one on either side of the river, and went into the mountains, where they had four very strong villages in a rough country, where it was impossible for horses to go. In the two villages there was a great deal of food and some very beautiful glazed earthenware with many figures and different shapes. Here they also found many bowls full of a carefully selected shining metal with which they glazed the earthenware. This shows that mines of silver would be found in that country if they should hunt for them.

There was a large and powerful village twenty leagues farther up the river, called Braba. Our men called it Valladolid [Taos]. The river flowed through the middle of it. The natives crossed it by wooden bridges made of long, large, squared pines. At this village they saw the largest and finest hot rooms or estufas in the entire country, for they had a dozen pillars, each one of which was twice as large around as one could reach and twice as tall as a man. Hernando de Alvarado visited this village when he discovered Cicuye. The country is very high and very cold. The river is deep and very swift, without any ford. Captain Barrionuevo returned from there, leaving the province at peace.

Another captain went down the river in search of the settlements which the people at Tutahaco had said were several days distant from here. This captain went down eighty leagues and found four large villages which he left at peace. After this captain got back, Don Tristán selected forty companions and, leaving the army to Francisco de Barrionuevo, he started with them in search of the general, since it was past the time set by the general for his return.

When he reached Cicuye the people came out of the village to fight, which detained him four days while he punished them. Just then word was brought that the general was coming, and so Don Tristán had to stay there to keep the road open. Everybody welcomed the general with great joy. The Indian Xabe, who had been given to the general at Cicuye when he started off in search of Quivira, was with Don Tristán. When he learned that the general was coming he acted greatly pleased and said: "Now when the general comes, you will see that there is gold and silver in Quivira, although not so much as the Turk said."

When the general arrived, and Xabe saw that they had not found anything, he was sad and silent, and kept declaring that there was some. He made many believe that it was so, because the general had not dared to enter into the country on account of its being thickly settled and his force not very strong. It took him forty days to return, traveling lightly equipped. The Turk had said when they left Tiguex that they ought not to load the horses with too much provisions, as this would tire them so that they could not afterward carry the gold and silver, from which it is very evident that he was deceiving them.

The general reached Cicuye with his force and at once set off for Tiguex. When he reached Tiguex, he made plans to pass the winter there so as to return with the whole army, because it was said that he brought information regarding large settlements and very large rivers, and that the country was very much like that of Spain in the fruits and vegetation and seasons. The men were not ready to believe there was no gold there. They had suspicions that there was some farther back in the country, because, although this was denied, the natives knew what the thing was and had a name for it among themselves—*acochis*.

Now I wish to give an account of the inhabited region seen and discovered by this expedition, and some of their ceremonies and habits; also the limits within which each province falls, so that hereafter it may be possible to understand in what direction Florida lies and in what direction Greater India. This land of New Spain is part of the mainland with Peru, and with Greater India or China as well, and there is no strait between to separate them. On the other hand, the country is so wide that there is room for these vast deserts and plains which lie between the two seas. The coast of the North Sea [the Atlantic Ocean] beyond Florida stretches toward the Bacallaos [the Newfoundland region] and then turns toward Norway. That of the South Sea [Gulf of Mexico] turns toward the west, making another bend down toward the south almost like a bow and stretches away toward India.

Culiacán is the last place in the New Kingdom of Galicia, and was the first settlement made by Nuño de Guzmán when he conquered this kingdom. It is two hundred ten leagues west of Mexico. There are three chief languages. The first is that of the Tahus, who are the best and most intelligent race. They are now the most settled and have received the most light from the faith. They worship idols and make presents to the devil of their goods and riches, consisting of cloth and turquoises. They do not eat human flesh or sacrifice it. They keep very large snakes which they venerate. Among them are men dressed like women who marry other men and serve as their wives. The women who wish to live unmarried are consecrated at a great festival with much singing and dancing. All the chiefs gather and dance naked. After they dance with a woman, they put her in a hut decorated for this event, and the chiefs adorn her with clothes and bracelets of fine turquoises. Then the chiefs go in one by one to lie with her, and all the others who wish follow them. From this time on these women can not refuse anyone who pays them a certain amount agreed on for this. Even if they take husbands, this does not exempt them from obliging anyone who pays them. The greatest festivals are on market days. The custom is for the husbands to buy the women they marry at a high price, and then to take them to a chief, who is considered to be a priest, to deflower them and see if they are virgins. If one is not, the whole price must be returned, and the husband can keep her for his wife or not, or let her be consecrated, as he chooses. At these times, they all get drunk.

The second language is that of the Pacaxes. These people are more barbarous. Some of them eat human flesh. They are great sodomites, and have many wives, taking even their sisters. They worship painted and sculptured stones, and are much given to sorcery and witchcraft.

The third language is that of the Acaxes, who live in the hilly country and the mountains. They hunt for men just as they hunt animals. They all eat human flesh, and he who has the most human bones and skulls hung up around his house is most feared and respected.

Many rich silver mines have been found in this country. They do not run deep, and soon give out. The gulf of the sea [Gulf of California] begins on the coast of this province, entering the land two hundred fifty leagues toward the north and ending at the mouth of the Firebrand River. This country forms its eastern limit, and California the western. The coast makes a turn toward the south at the Firebrand River, bending down to California, which turns toward the west, forming that peninsula which was formerly held to be an island, because it was a low sandy country. It is inhabited by brutish, bestial, naked people who eat their own offal. The men and women couple like animals, the female openly getting down on all fours.

Petlatlan is so called because the houses are made of petates or palm-leaf mats. Houses of this sort are found for more than two hundred forty leagues in this region, to the beginning of the Cíbola wilderness. The people are of the same race and habits as the Culiacanian Tahues. There is much sodomy among them. In the mountain district there is a large population and more settlements. These people have a somewhat different language from the Tahues, although they understand each other. There are no trees except the pine and no fruits except a few tunas [prickly pear], mesquites and pitahayas.

Petlatlan is twenty leagues from Culiacán, and it is one hundred thirty leagues from here to the valley of Sonora. There are many rivers between the two, with settlements of the same sort of people. There is also the Corazones or Hearts, which is in our possession, down the valley of Sonora.

Sonora is a river and valley thickly settled by able-bodied people. The women wear petticoats of tanned deerskin, and little sanbenitos reaching half way down the body. The chiefs of the villages go up on some little heights they have made for this purpose, like public criers, and make proclamations for the space of an hour, regulating those things they have to attend to. They have some little huts for shrines, all over the outside of which they stick many arrows, like a hedgehog. They do this when they are eager for war.

It is forty leagues from Sonora to the valley of Suya. The town of San Hieronimo was established in this valley, where there was a rebellion later. There are many villages in the neighborhood. The people are the same as those in Sonora and have the same dress and language, habits and customs, like all the rest as far as the desert of Chichilticalli. The women paint their chins and eyes like the Moorish women of Barbary. The people are great sodomites. They drink wine made of the pitahaya, which is the fruit of a great thistle which opens like the pomegranate. The wine makes them stupid.

In this country there were tame eagles, which the chiefs esteemed. No fowls of any sort were seen in any of these villages except in this valley of Suya. Between Suya and Chichilticalli there are many sheep and mountain goats with very large bodies and horns. Some Spaniards declare that they have seen flocks of more than a hundred together, which ran so fast that they disappeared very quickly.

Chichilticalli is so called because the friars found a house there made of colored or reddish earth. The house was large and appeared to have been a fortress. It must have been destroyed by the people of the district, who are the most barbarous yet seen. They live in separate cabins and not in settlements. They live by hunting. The rest of the country is all wilderness, covered with pine forests. The country rises continually from the beginning of the wilderness until Cíbola is reached, which is eighty-five leagues, going north. From Culiacán to the edge of the wilderness the route had kept the north on the left hand.

Cíbola is seven villages. The largest is called Macaque [Matsaki]. The houses are ordinarily three or four stories high, but in Macaque there are some of seven stories. These people are very intelligent. They cover their privy parts and all the immodest parts with cloths made like a sort of table napkin, with fringed edges and a tassel at each corner, which they tie over the hips. They wear long robes of feathers and of the skins of hares, and cotton blankets. The women wear blankets, which they tie or knot over the left shoulder, leaving the right arm out. These serve to cover the body. They wear a neat well-shaped outer garment of skin. They gather their hair over the two ears, making a frame which looks like an old-fashioned headdress.

A man does not have more than one wife. There are estufas or hot rooms in the villages, which are the courtyards or places where they gather for consultation. They do not have chiefs as in New Spain but are ruled by a council of the oldest men. They have priests who preach to them, whom they call papas. These are the elders. They go up on the highest roof of the village and preach from there, like public criers, in the morning while the sun is rising, the whole village being silent and sitting in the galleries to listen. They tell them how they are to live, and I believe that they give certain commandments for them to keep, for there is no drunkenness among them or sodomy or sacrifices, neither do they eat human flesh or steal, but they are usually at work. The estufas belong to the whole village. It is a sacrilege for the women to go into the estufas to sleep. They make the cross as a sign of peace. They burn their dead.

It is twenty leagues to Tusayan, going northwest. This is a province with seven villages, of the same sort, dress, habits and ceremonies as at Cíbola. There may be as many as three thousand or four thousand men in the fourteen villages of these two provinces. It is forty leagues or more to Tiguex, toward the north. The rock of Acoma, which we described in the first part, is between these.

Tiguex is a province with twelve villages on the banks of a large, swift river. It is a spacious valley two leagues wide, and a very high, rough, snow-covered mountain chain lies east of it.

There are seven villages seven leagues to the north at Quirix, and the seven villages of the province of Hemes are forty leagues northeast. Tutahaco, a province with eight villages, is toward the southeast. In general, these villages all have the same habits and customs, although some have certain things which the others have not. They are governed by the opinions of the elders. They all work together to build the villages, the women being engaged in making the mixture for the walls while the men bring the wood and put it in place. They have no lime but they make a mixture of ashes, coals, and dirt which is almost as good as mortar. Before they are married the young men serve the whole village in general, and fetch the wood, putting it in a pile in the courtyard of the villages, from which the women take it to carry to their houses.

The young men live in the estufas, which are underground, square or round, with pine pillars. The top is on a level with the ground.

Some were large enough for a game of ball. When any man wishes
to marry, it has to be arranged by those who govern. The man has
to spin and weave a blanket and place it before the woman, who
covers herself with it and becomes his wife. The houses belong to the
women, the estufas to the men. It is forbidden for the women to sleep
in the estufas, or to enter these for any other reason except to give
their husbands or sons food. The men spin and weave. The women
bring up the children and prepare the food. The country is so fertile
that they do not have to break up the ground the year round, but only
have to sow the seed, which is presently covered by the fall of snow,
and the ears come up under the snow. In one year they gather enough
for seven.

There are a great many native fowl in these provinces, and cocks
with great hanging chins [turkey cocks]. When dead, these keep for
sixty days, and longer in winter, without losing their feathers or opening, and without any bad smell, and the same is true of dead men.

The villages are free from nuisances, because they go outside to
excrete, and they pass their water into clay vessels which they empty
at a distance from the village.

They have their preachers. Sodomy is not found among them. They
do not eat human flesh or make sacrifices of it. The people are not
cruel, for they had Francisco de Ovando in Tiguex about forty days,
after he was dead, and when the village was captured he was found
among their dead, whole and without any wound except the one
which killed him, white as snow, without any bad smell.

I found out several things about them from one of our Indians who
had been a captive among them. I asked him especially why the young
women in that province went entirely naked, however cold it might be.
He told me that the virgins had to go around this way until they took a
husband, and that they covered themselves after they had known man.
The men wear little shirts of tanned deerskin and their long robes
over this. In all these provinces they have earthenware glazed with
antimony and jars of extraordinary labor and workmanship, which
were worth seeing.

Cicuye is a village of nearly five hundred warriors, who are feared
throughout that country. It is square, situated on a rock, with a large
court or yard in the middle, containing the estufas. The houses are all
alike, four stories high. One can go over the top of the whole village
without there being a street to hinder. There are corridors going all
around it at the first two stories, by which one can go around the

whole village. These are like outside balconies, and they are able to protect themselves under these. The houses do not have doors below, but they use ladders which can be lifted up like a drawbridge, and so go up to the corridors which are on the inside of the village. As the doors of the houses open on the corridor of that story, the corridor serves as a street. The houses that open on the plain are right back of those that open on the court, and in time of war they go through those behind them. The village is enclosed by a low wall of stone. There is a spring of water inside, which they are able to divert. The people of this village boast that no one has been able to conquer them and that they conquer whatever villages they wish. The people and their customs are like those of the other villages. Their virgins also go nude until they take husbands, because they say that if they do anything wrong then it will be seen, and so they do not do it. They do not need to be ashamed because they go around as they were born.

There is a village, small and strong, between Cicuye and the province of Quirix, which the Spaniards named Ximena, and another village almost deserted, only one part of which is inhabited. This was a large village, and judging from its condition and newness it appeared to have been destroyed. They called this the village of the granaries or silos, because large underground cellars were found here stored with corn. There was another large village farther on, entirely destroyed, in the yards of which there were many stone balls as big as twelve-quart bowls, which seemed to have been thrown by engines or catapults. All that I was able to find out about them was that sixteen years before, some people called Teyas had come to this country in great numbers and had destroyed these villages. They had besieged Cicuye but had not been able to capture it because it was strong, and when they left the region they had made peace with the whole country. The only thing they could tell about the direction these people came from was by pointing toward the north.

There are seven other villages along this route, toward the snowy mountains, one of which has been destroyed by the people already referred to. These were under the rule of Cicuye. Cicuye is in a little valley between mountain chains and mountains covered with large pine forests. There is a little stream which contains very good trout and otters, and there are very large bears and good falcons hereabouts.

Now we will speak of the plains. This country is spacious and level, and is more than four hundred leagues wide in the part between the two mountain ranges—one, that which Francisco Vásquez de Coronado crossed, and the other that which the force under Don Fernando de Soto crossed, near the North Sea, entering the country from Florida. No settlements were seen anywhere on these plains.

In traversing two hundred fifty leagues, the other mountain range was not seen, nor a hill nor a hillock. Several lakes were found at intervals; they were round as plates, a stone's throw or more across, some fresh and some salt. The grass grows tall near these lakes; away from them it is very short, a span or less. The country is like a bowl, so that when a man sits down, the horizon surrounds him all around at the distance of a musket shot. There are no groves of trees except at the rivers, which flow at the bottom of some ravines where the trees grow so thick that they were not noticed until one was right on the edge of them. There are paths down into these, made by the cows when they go to the water, which is essential throughout these plains.

As I have related in the first part, people follow the cows, hunting them and tanning the skins to take to the settlements in the winter to sell. These people are called Querechos and Teyas. They have better figures, are better warriors, and are more feared. They travel like the Arabs, with their tents and troops of dogs loaded with poles and having Moorish pack saddles with girths. These people eat raw meat and drink blood. They do not eat human flesh. They are a kind people and are faithful friends. They are able to make themselves very well understood by means of signs. They dry the flesh of the cows, cutting it thin like a leaf, and when dry they grind it like meal to keep it and make a sort of sea soup of it to eat. A handful thrown into a pot swells up so as to increase very much. They season pemmican with fat from the cow. They empty a large gut and fill it with blood, and carry this around the neck to drink when they are thirsty. When they open the belly of a cow, they squeeze out the chewed grass and drink the juice that remains behind, because they say that this contains the essence of the stomach. They cut the hide open at the back and pull it off at the joints, using a flint as large as a finger, tied in a little stick, with as much ease as if working with a good iron tool. They give it an edge with their own teeth. The quickness with which they do this is something worth seeing and noting.

There are very great numbers of wolves on these plains, which go around with the cows. They have white skins.

Quivira is to the west of those ravines, in the midst of the country, somewhat nearer the mountains toward the sea, for the country is level as far as Quivira, and there they began to see some mountain chains.

The country is well settled. This country is very similar to Spain in the varieties of vegetation and fruits. The people are of almost the same sort and appearance as the Teyas. They have villages like those in New Spain. The houses are round, without a wall, and they have one story like a loft, under the roof, where they sleep and keep their belongings. The roofs are of straw. There are other thickly settled provinces around it. A friar named Juan de Padilla remained in this province with a Spanish-Portuguese, a Negro, a half-breed, and some Indians from the province of Capothan in New Spain. They killed the friar because he wanted to go to the province of the Guas, who were their enemies. The Spaniard escaped by taking flight on a mare, and afterward reached New Spain, coming out by way of Panuco. This Spaniard was a Portuguese named Campo.

The great river of the Holy Spirit [the Mississippi and Missouri Rivers] which Don Hernando de Soto discovered in Florida flows through this country. It passes through a province called Arache, according to the reliable accounts which were obtained here. It flows across all the level country and breaks through the mountains of the North Sea, and comes out where the people with Don Hernando de Soto navigated it. This is more than three hundred leagues from where it enters the sea. On account of this, and also because it has large tributaries, it is so mighty when it enters the sea that they lost sight of the land before the water ceased to be fresh.

Now it is proper for me to return and speak of the army, which I left in Tiguex, resting for the winter. It never went back to Quivira, because it was God's pleasure that these discoveries should remain for other people and that we who had been there should content ourselves with saying that we were the first who discovered it. May the all-powerful Lord grant that His will be done in everything. It is certain that if this had not been His will Francisco Vásquez would not have returned to New Spain without cause or reason, as he did, and that it would not have been left for those with Don Hernando de Soto to settle such a good country, as they have done, and besides settling it to increase its extent, after obtaining, as they did, information from our army.

At the end of the first part of this book, we told how Francisco Vásquez de Coronado, when he got back from Quivira, gave orders to winter at Tiguex, in order to return, when the winter was over, with his whole army to discover all the settlements in those regions. Don Pedro de Tovar, who had gone to conduct a force from San Hieronimo, arrived in the meantime. He had not selected the rebels and seditious men there, but the most experienced ones and the best soldiers—men whom he could trust—wisely considering that he ought to have good men in order to go in search of his general in the country of the Indian called Turk.

They were not pleased to find the army at Tiguex, because they had come with great expectations, believing that they would find their general in the rich country of the Turk. They consoled themselves with the hope of going back there, and lived in anticipation of the pleasure of undertaking this return expedition to Quivira. Don Pedro de Tovar brought letters from New Spain, both from the viceroy and from individuals. Among these was one for Don García López de Cárdenas, which informed him of the death of his brother, the heir, and summoned him to Spain to receive the inheritance. He was given permission, and left Tiguex with several other persons who received permission to go and settle their affairs. There were many others who would have liked to go, but feared to appear faint-hearted. During this time the general endeavored to pacify several villagers in the neighborhood which were not well disposed, and to make peace with the people at Tiguex. He tried also to procure some of the cloth of the country because the soldiers were almost naked and poorly clothed, and full of lice which they were unable to get rid of or avoid.

The general, Francisco Vásquez Coronado, had been beloved and obeyed by his captains and soldiers as heartily as any of those who have ever started out in the Indies. Necessity knows no law, and the captains who collected the cloth divided it badly, taking the best for themselves and their friends and leaving the rest for the soldiers. This caused some angry murmuring. Others also complained because some favored ones were spared in the work and in the watches and received better portions both of cloth and food. On this account they began to say that there was nothing in the country of Quivira worth returning for.

After the winter was over the return to Quivira was announced, and the men began to prepare the things needed. Since nothing in this life is at the disposition of men, but all is under the ordination of Almighty God, it was His will that we should not accomplish this. So it happened that one feast day the general went out on horseback to amuse himself, as usual, riding with the Captain Don Rodrigo Maldonado. He was on a powerful horse, and his servants had put on a new girth, which must have been rotten. It broke during the race and the general fell. He was hit on the head by a hoof, which laid him at the point of death, and his recovery was slow and doubtful.

While he was in bed, Don García López de Cárdenas, who had started for New Spain, came back in flight from Suya, because he had found that town deserted and the people and horses and cattle all dead. They did not dare to tell the general this news until he had recovered. When he finally got up and learned of it, it affected him so much that he had to go back to bed again. He may have done this in order to bring about what he afterward accomplished, as was believed later.

While he was in this condition, he recollected what a scientific friend of his in Salamanca had told him, that he would become a powerful lord in distant lands, and that he would have a fall from which he would never be able to recover. This expectation of death made him desire to return and die where he had a wife and children.

The physician and surgeon who was doctoring him also acted as talebearer. He treated secretly and underhandedly with several gentlemen who set the soldiers to talking in little knots and gatherings about going back to New Spain. They had him send papers to the general, signed by all the soldiers, through their ensigns, asking for this. Not much time was needed, since many desired it already. When they asked him, the general acted as if he did not want to do it, but all the gentlemen and captains supported them, giving him their signed opinions.

Thus they made it seem as if they ought to return to New Spain, because they had not found any riches, any settled country out of which estates could be formed for all the army. When the general obtained their signatures, the return to New Spain was announced at once. Since nothing can ever be concealed, the double dealing began to be understood, and many of the gentlemen found that they had been deceived. They tried in every way to get their signatures back again. But the general guarded them so carefully that he did not go out of his room, making his sickness seem very much worse, and putting guards about his person and room. In spite of all this, they stole his chest, but it is not known whether they recovered the signatures. They asked the general to give them sixty picked men, with whom they would remain and hold the country until the viceroy could send them support, or recall them, or else that the general would leave them the army and pick out sixty men to go back with him. But the soldiers did not want to remain either way, some because they had turned their prow toward New Spain, and others because they saw clearly the trouble that would arise over who should have the command. As for the gentlemen, I do not know whether it was because they had sworn fidelity or because they feared the soldiers would not support them, but they did what had been decided on, although with ill will. From this time on they did not obey the general as readily as formerly, and they did not show any affection for him. He made much of the soldiers and humored them, with the result that he did what he desired and secured the return of the whole army.

We have already stated that Don García López de Cárdenas came back from Suya in flight, having found that country risen in rebellion. Besides a few who were honored with the charge of public affairs, only the entirely worthless fellows were left in that town. These mutinous and seditious men declared that they had been betrayed and were not going to be rescued, since the others had been directed to go through another part of the country where there was a more convenient route to New Spain. This was not so, because they were still almost on the direct road. This talk led some of them to revolt, and they chose one Pedro de Ávila as their captain.

They went back to Culiacán, leaving the captain, Diego de Alcaraz, sick in the town of San Hieronimo, with only a small force. He did not have anyone to send after them to compel them to return. They killed a number of people at several villages along the way. Finally they reached Culiacán, where Hernandarias de Saabedra was waiting for Juan Gallego to come back from New Spain with a force. He detained them by means of promises, so that Gallego could take them back. Some who feared what might happen to them ran away one night to New Spain.

When the natives at Suya noticed how weak the Spaniards were, they did not continue to trade with them as they had formerly done. Veins of gold had already been discovered before this, but they were unable to work these because the country was at war. The disturbance was so great that they kept constant watch.

The town was situated on a little river. One night they saw fires and they doubled the watches. Not having noticed anything during the night, they grew careless along toward morning. The enemy entered the village so silently that they were not seen until they began to kill and plunder. A number of men reached the plain, but while they were getting out, the captain was mortally wounded. Several Spaniards came back on horses after they had recovered themselves and attacked the enemy, rescuing some, though only a few. The enemy went off with the booty, having killed three Spaniards, many of the servants and more than twenty horses.

The Spaniards who survived started off the same day on foot. They went toward Culiacán, keeping away from the roads, and did not find any food until they reached Corazones, where the Indians, like the good friends they have always been, provided them with food. From here they continued to Culiacán, undergoing great hardships. Hernandarias de Saabedra, the mayor, received them and entertained them as well as he could until Juan Gallego arrived with the reinforcements which he was conducting, on his way to find the army. He was troubled at finding that post deserted when he expected that the army would be in the rich country described by the Turk.

When the general saw that everything was now quiet, and that his schemes had gone as he wished, he ordered that everything be ready to start on the return to New Spain by the beginning of April, in the year 1542.

Seeing this, Friar Juan de Padilla, a regular brother of the lesser order [Franciscan], and another, Friar Luis, a lay brother, told the general that they wanted to remain in that country—Friar Juan de Padilla in Quivira because his teachings seemed to promise fruit there, and Friar Luis at Cicuye. The general sent a company to escort them as far as Cicuye, where Friar Luis stopped, while Friar Juan went on back to Quivira with the guides who had conducted the general, taking with him the Portuguese, as we related, the half-breed, and the Indians from New Spain. He was martyred a short time after he arrived there. We may be sure that he died a martyr, because his zeal was holy and earnest.

Friar Luis remained at Cicuye. Nothing more has been heard about him since. Before the army left Tiguex, some men who went to take him a number of sheep met him as he was on his way to visit some other villages, which were fifteen or twenty leagues from Cicuye, accompanied by some followers. He felt very hopeful that he was liked at the village and that his teaching would bear fruit, although he complained that the old men were falling away from him.

I, for my part, believe that as he was a man of good and holy life, Our Lord will protect him and give him grace to convert many of these peoples, and end his days in guiding them in the faith.

After the friars had gone, the general, fearing danger if people were carried away from that country to New Spain, ordered the soldiers to let any natives held as servants go free to their villages whenever they might wish. In my opinion, though I am not sure, it would have been better if they had been kept and taught among Christians.

The general was very happy when the army started from Tiguex on its way to Cíbola. One thing of note happened during this part of the trip. The horses were in good condition for their work when they started, fat and sleek, but more than thirty died during the ten days it took to reach Cíbola. A large number of them also died afterward before reaching Culiacán, a thing that did not happen during all the rest of the journey.

At Cíbola the army rested before starting across the wilderness, because this was the last of the settlements in that country. The whole country was left well disposed and at peace, and several of our Indian allies remained there.

Leaving behind the settlements that had been discovered in the new land, of which the seven villages of Cíbola were the first to be seen and the last that were left, the army started off across the wilderness. On the second day before reaching Chichilticalli they met Juan Gallego. He was coming from New Spain with reinforcements of men and necessary supplies, expecting that he would find the army in the country of the Turk. When he saw that the army was returning, he did not like it, even after he had talked with the general. There was quite a little movement among the gentlemen toward going back with the new force which had made no slight exertions in coming this far, having encounters every day with the Indians who had risen in revolt. There was talk of making a settlement somewhere in that region until the viceroy could receive an account of what had occurred. Those soldiers who had come from the new lands would not agree to anything except the return to New Spain, so that nothing came of the proposals. Several of the mutineers who had deserted the town of Corazones came with Juan Gallego, who had given them his word as surety for their safety. Even if the general had wanted to punish them, his power was slight, for he had been disobeyed already and was not much respected. He began to be afraid again after this, and made himself sick, and kept a guard.

In several places yells were heard and Indians seen, and some of the horses were wounded and killed before Batuco was reached. There the friendly Indians from Corazones came to meet the army and see the general. They were always friendly and had treated all the

Spaniards who passed through their country well, furnishing them with what food they needed, and men when necessary. Our men had always treated them well and repaid them for these things.

During this journey the juice of the quince was proved to be a good protection against the poison of the natives. At one place, several days before reaching Sonora, the hostile Indians wounded a Spaniard called Mesa. He did not die, although the wound of the fresh poison is fatal, and there was a delay of over two hours before curing him with the juice. The poison, however, left its mark upon him. The skin rotted and fell off until it left the bones and sinews bare, with a horrible smell. The wound was in the wrist, and the poison had reached as far as the shoulder before he was cured. The skin on all this fell off.

The army proceeded without taking any rest, because the provisions had begun to fail. These districts were in rebellion, and so there were not any victuals until they reached Petlatlan, although they made several forays in search of provisions. Petlatlan is in the province of Culiacán, and on this account was at peace, although they had several surprises after this. The army rested here several days to get provisions. After leaving here they were able to travel more quickly than before for the thirty leagues of the valley of Culiacán, where they were welcomed back again as people who came with their governor and who had suffered ill treatment.

It seemed indeed as if the arrival in the valley of Culiacán had ended the labors of the journey, partly because the general was governor there and partly because it was inhabited by Christians. On this account some began to disregard their superiors and the authority which their captains had over them.

Some captains even forgot the obedience due to their general. Each one played his own game, so that while the general was marching toward the town, which was still ten leagues away, many of the men, or most of them, left him in order to rest in the valley, and some even proposed not to follow him. The general understood that he was not strong enough to compel them, although his position as governor gave him fresh authority. He determined to accomplish it by a better method, which was to order all the captains to provide food and meat from the stores of several villages that were under his control as governor.

He pretended to be sick, keeping his bed, so that those who had any business with him could speak to him or he with them more freely, without hindrance or observation. He kept sending for his particular friends to ask them to be sure to speak to the soldiers and encourage them to accompany him back to New Spain, and to tell them that he would request the viceroy, Don Antonio de Mendoza, to show them special favor, and that he would do so himself for those who might wish to remain in his government. After this, he started with his army at a very bad time, when the rains were beginning.

In the uninhabited country which they passed through as far as Compostela there are numerous very dangerous rivers, full of large and fierce alligators. While the army was halting at one of these rivers, a soldier crossing from one side to the other was seized, in sight of everybody, and carried off by an alligator without it being possible to help him. The general proceeded, leaving the men who did not want to follow him all along the way, and reached Mexico with less than one hundred men. He made his report to the viceroy, who did not receive him very graciously although he gave him his discharge. His reputation was gone from this time on. He kept the government of New Galicia for only a short time, when the viceroy took it himself, until the arrival of the court, or audencia, which still governs it. And this was the end of those discoveries and of the expedition which was made to these new lands.

One might well have complained when I passed in silence over the exploits of Captain Juan Gallego with his twenty companions. I will relate them now, so that in times to come those who read about it or tell of it may have an authority on whom to rely. I am not writing fables, like some of the things we read about nowadays in the books of chivalry. There are some things which our Spaniards have done in our own day in these parts, in their conquests and encounters with the Indians, which for deeds worthy of admiration surpass not only the books already mentioned but also those which have been written about the twelve peers of France. If the deadly strength which the authors of those times attributed to their heroes and the brilliant and resplendent arms with which they adorned them are fully considered and compared with the small stature of the men of our time and the few, poor weapons they have in these parts, the remarkable things which our people have undertaken and accomplished with such weapons are more to be wondered at today than those of which the ancients write. I have said all this in order to show that some things which we consider fables may be true, because we see greater things every day in our own times, just as in future times people will greatly wonder at the deeds of Don Hernando Cortés, who dared to go into the midst of New Spain with three hundred men against the vast number of people in Mexico, and who with five hundred Spaniards succeeded in subduing it, and made himself lord over it in two years.

The deeds of Don Pedro de Alvarado in the conquest of Guatemala and those of Montejo in Tabasco, the conquests of the mainland and of Peru, were all such as to make me remain silent concerning what I now wish to relate. However, since I have promised to give an account of what happened on this journey, I want the things I am now going to relate to be known as well as those others of which I have spoken.

The captain Juan Gallego, then, reached the town of Culiacán with a very small force. There he collected as many as he could of those who had escaped from the town of Hearts, or, more correctly, from Suya, which made in all twenty-two men. With these he marched through all of the settled country, some two hundred leagues, with the country in a state of war and the people in rebellion, having encounters with the enemy almost every day. He always marched with the advance guard, leaving two-thirds of his force behind with the baggage. With six or seven Spaniards, and without any of the Indian allies, he forced his way into their villages, killing and destroying and setting them on fire, coming upon the enemy so suddenly and with such boldness that they did not have a chance to collect or even to do anything at all. They became so afraid of him that there was not a town which dared wait for him, but they fled before him as from a powerful army.

He did all this with his seven companions, so that when the rest of the force came up with the baggage, there was nothing for them to do except to pillage, since the others had already killed and captured all the people they could lay their hands on and the rest had fled. They did not pause anywhere, so that although the villages ahead of him received some warning, they were upon them so quickly that they did not have a chance to collect. Especially in the region where the town of Hearts had been, he killed and hanged a large number of people to punish them for their rebellion. He did not lose a companion during all this, nor was anyone wounded except one soldier who was wounded in the eyelid by an Indian who was almost dead and whom he was stripping. The weapon broke the skin, and as it was poisoned he would have had to die if he had not been saved by the quince juice; he lost his eye as it was.

Those people will remember these deeds of theirs as long as they live, and especially four or five friendly Indians who went with them from Corazones, who thought they were so wonderful that they held them to be divine rather than human. If he had not fallen in with our army as he did, they would have reached the country of the Indian called Turk, which they expected to march to, and they would have arrived there without danger because of their good order and the skill with which they were led, and their knowledge and ample practice in war. Several of these men are still in this town of Culiacán, where I am now writing this account and narrative, where they as well as I and the others who have remained in this province have never lacked for labor in keeping this country quiet, in capturing rebels, and increasing in poverty and need, and more than ever at the present hour, because the country is poorer and more in debt than ever before.

I dare to write of the remarkable things I saw on the plains because many men are still living who saw them and who will vouch for my account. Who could believe that one thousand horses and five hundred of our cows and more than five thousand rams and ewes and more than one thousand five hundred Indians and servants, in traveling over those plains, would leave no more trace where they had passed than if nothing had been there—nothing—so that it was necessary to make piles of bones and cow dung now and then so that the rear guard could follow the army. The grass never failed to become erect after it had been trodden down and, although it was short, it was as fresh and straight as before.

Another thing was a heap of cow bones, a crossbow shot long, almost twice a man's height in places, and some eighteen feet or more wide, which was found on the edge of a salt lake in the southern part, and this in a region where there are no people who could have made it. The only explanation of this which could be suggested was that the waves which the north winds must make in the lake had piled up the bones of the cattle which had died in the lake, when the old and weak ones who went into the water were unable to get out. The noticeable thing is the number of cattle that would be necessary to make such a pile of bones.

All the horses took flight when they first saw the bulls. They have a narrow, short face, the eyes sticking out at the side so that when they are running they can see who is following them. They have very long beards, like goats, and when they are running they throw their heads back with the beard dragging on the ground. There is a sort of girdle round the middle of the body. The hair is very woolly, like a sheep's, very fine, and in front of the girdle the hair is very long and rough like a lion's. They have a great hump, larger than a camel's. The horns are short and thick, so that they are not seen much above the hair. In May they change the hair in the middle of the body for a down, which makes perfect lions of them. They rub against the small trees in the little ravines to shed their hair, and they continue this until only the down is left, as a snake changes his skin. They have a short tail, with a bunch of hair at the end. When they run, they carry it erect like a scorpion. It is worth noticing that the little calves are red and just like ours, but they change their appearance and color with time and age.

Another strange thing was that all the bulls that were killed had their left ears slit, although these were whole when young. The reason for this was a puzzle that could not be guessed. The wool ought to make good cloth because of its fineness, although the color is not good.

Another thing worth noticing is that the bulls traveled without cows in such large numbers that nobody could have counted them, and so far away from the cows that it was more than forty leagues from where we saw the bulls to where we began to see the cows.

It does not seem right for me to remain silent about the fact that they venerate the sign of the cross in the region where the settlements have high houses. At a spring in the plain near Acuco they had a cross two palms high and as thick as a finger, made of wood with a square twig for its crosspiece, and many little sticks decorated with feathers around it, and numerous withered flowers, which were the offerings. In a graveyard outside the village at Tutahaco there appeared to have been a recent burial. Near the head there was another cross made of two little sticks tied with cotton thread, and dry withered flowers. It certainly seems to me that in some way they must have received some light from the cross of Our Redeemer, Christ, and it may have come by way of India, from whence they proceeded.

I very much wish that I possessed some knowledge of cosmography or geography so that I could measure the advantage those people who might go in search of that country would have if they went directly through the center of the country, instead of following the road the army took.

It is, I think, already understood that the Portuguese Campo, was the soldier who escaped when Friar Juan de Padilla was killed at Quivira. He finally reached New Spain from Panuco, having traveled across the plains country until he came to cross the North Sea mountain chain, keeping the country that Don Hernando de Soto discovered all the time on his left hand, since he did not see the river of the Holy Spirit at all. After he had crossed the North Sea mountains, he found that he was in Panuco, so that if he had not tried to go to the North Sea, he would have come out in the neighborhood of the border land, or the country of the Sacatecas, of which we now have some knowledge.

This way would be somewhat better and more direct for anyone going back there in search of Quivira, since some of those who came with the Portuguese are still in New Spain to serve as guides. Nevertheless, I think it would be best to go through the country of the Guachichules, keeping near the South Sea mountains all the time, for there are more settlements and a food supply. It would be suicide to launch out on to the plains country, because it is so vast and is barren of anything to eat, although, it is true, there would not be much need of this after coming to the cows.

This is only when one goes in search of Quivira and of the villages described by the Indian called Turk. The army of Francisco Vásquez Coronado went the very farthest way round to get there. They started from Mexico and went one hundred ten leagues to the west, and then one hundred leagues to the northeast, and two hundred fifty to the north. All this brought them as far as the ravines where the cows were, and after traveling eight hundred fifty leagues they were not more than four hundred leagues distant from Mexico by a direct route. If one desires to go to the country of Tiguex, so as to turn from there toward the west in search of the country of India, he ought to follow the road taken by the army, for there is no other, because the arm of the sea which reaches into this coast toward the north does not leave room for any. But what might be done is to have a fleet and cross this gulf and disembark in the neighborhood of the Island of Negroes and enter the country from there, crossing the mountain chains in search of the country from which the people of Tiguex came, or other peoples of the same sort.

As for entering from the country of Florida and the North Sea, it has already been observed that the many expeditions which have been undertaken from that side have been unfortunate and not very successful, because that part of the country is full of bogs and poisonous fruits, barren, and the very worst country that is warmed by the sun. But they might disembark after passing the river of the Holy Spirit, as Don Hernando de Soto did. Nevertheless, despite the fact that I underwent much labor, I still think that the way I went to that country is the best. There ought to be river courses, because the necessary supplies can be carried on these more easily in large quantities. Horses are the most necessary things in the new countries, and they frighten the enemy the most. Artillery is also much feared by those who do not know how to use it. A piece of heavy artillery would be very good for settlements like those which Francisco Vásquez de Coronado discovered, in order to knock them down, because he had nothing but some small machines for slinging and nobody skillful enough to make a catapult or some other machine which would frighten them, which is very necessary.

I say, then, that with what we now know about the trend of the coast of the South Sea, which has been followed by ships which explored the western part, and what is known of the North Sea toward Norway, the coast of which extends up from Florida, those who now go to discover the country which Francisco Vásquez entered, and reach the country of Cíbola or of Tiguex, will know the direction in which they ought to go in order to discover the true direction of the country which the Marquis of the Valley, Don Hernando Cortés, tried to find, following the direction of the gulf of the Firebrand River. This will suffice for the conclusion of our narrative. Everything else rests on the powerful Lord of all things, God Omnipotent, who knows how and when these lands will be discovered and for whom He has guarded this good fortune.

"We who have been there should content ourselves with saying that we were the first who discovered it." So Castañeda summed up the results of the lengthy and expensive expedition.

Quivira had proved to be only a tent village of nomadic Indians. The Seven Cities was little more than dross in the mouths of the men who had come so far to conquer it. The Tiguex country of the Rio Grande had yielded no more. The long journey of Díaz to find the letters Alarcón had left at the base of a tree was only communication. The Grand Canyon of the Rio Grande was just a vast hole in the earth where a thirsty man could not even climb down to the running river below. The humped cows were only good for a meal. The Staked Plains and the land beyond were just more empty space. And the Rio Grande River was a place where the poor Indians built of adobe. The entire venture was a disappointment for the would-be conquistadores. They had only the satisfaction of having been there first.

The expedition had left Culiacán for Cíbola on April 22, 1540.

Back in Culiacán in spring 1542 it began to disband. Those men to whom Culiacán was home rejoined their families. Others decided to remain rather than return to Mexico City. They had traveled far enough. And besides there was the element of failure about what they had done which made them ashamed. Coronado had made the last part of the journey to Culiacán on a stretcher. He had fallen from his horse in December and was still unwell, though he was able to ride to Mexico City, where his reception was cool. Too much money and too many dreams had been spent for nothing. His wife stood by him as did many of his friends. The viceroy after a time seems to have forgiven him the failure. Then the investigations began.

From August 1544 to February 1546, Coronado was under investigation or sentence. Both his residencia as governor of New Galicia and the official investigation of the Cíbola expedition took place at the same time. His old companions in arms stood by him in most instances. There were some who complained of his treatment of the Indians, some who complained of his having accepted horses as gifts or bribes, others who protested that he had drawn his salary as the governor of New Galicia while he was on the expedition.

Probably the worst witness at the hearings was Coronado himself. He was not well. His thoughts were confused, his memory faulty. The judge who had been sent to hear the cases wrote the king in March 1545 that "he is more fit to be governed inside his home than to govern outside it. He is lacking in many of his former fine qualities. And he is not the same man he was when your Majesty appointed him to the governorship. They say that this change was caused by a fall from a horse which he suffered in the exploration and pacification of Tierra Nueva." The judge was understanding and so was the reviewing court of which the judge was a member. Coronado was eventually cleared.

His companion at arms and maestre de campo, Don García López de Cárdenas, was not so fortunate. The man who discovered the Grand Canyon and served as second in command was tried relentlessly for seven years before being convicted, fined, banned from the New World for a decade and sentenced to exile. He had committed two major crimes: he had brought home no gold and the expedition of which he was a part took place when legality and civilization had already caught up with the conquistadores.

To his contemporaries, Coronado was a failure. But he did open a world as vast as any of the men who had found gold. He was as great a figure in the American Southwest as Cortés was in Mexico,

Pizzaro in Peru, Alvarado in Guatemala and Quesada in Columbia. He was not as brutal as Alvarado, Pedrárias or Pizarro, though those with him were tried for brutality and inhumanity.

Only history recalls the favorable about Coronado. His companions went unrewarded in most instances, though their old captain-general gave them food and clothing and horses from what little he was left with. The Council of Mexico City seated him again in time. Though he never recovered the costs of the expedition, he was given an encomienda for his services. This grant came in 1551. He died after a long illness in September 1554 and was buried in the Church of Santo Domingo in Mexico City.

DeSoto

Tries to Establish a Colony

and Opens a Continent

DE SOTO
EXPLORES
THE SOUTHEAST

May 1539 — September 1543

Mabila

De Soto
Died

Apalachen

Ocale

Ocita

Moscoco

Rio Panuco

CUBA

W E

7

De Soto Tries to Establish a Colony and

Opens a Continent

THE NAME of Hernando de Soto is popularly linked with Florida and the discovery of the Mississippi River. But this is a limited view of a young man who probably traveled more widely in the New World than anyone before him. He was the first European to journey into the interior of Florida, Georgia, the Carolinas, Tennessee, Alabama, Mississippi, Arkansas, Texas and Oklahoma. Expeditions under his command may also have penetrated Missouri and Louisiana.

But as far as De Soto and his contemporaries were concerned, he had explored only Florida because the name "Florida" in the first half of the sixteenth century was vaguely applied to the area which stretches from Labrador to the northern area of the Gulf of Mexico.

Hernando de Soto was not the discoverer of the North American coast, and he was not the first to land in Florida. The coastal area of the peninsula had already had a long and bloody history before he arrived on the scene.

No one knows exactly who was the first European to sight the coast, but Juan Ponce de León is generally credited with the first attempts to land on the Island of Bimini—variously Binnini, Binini, Bynimi, etc.—which has since become known as the peninsula of Florida. And the name of Juan Ponce has become incongruously entwined with a romantic legend.

When Juan Ponce arrived in Hispaniola on the second voyage of Columbus, he was already a mature soldier. Little is known of his early life. Like most of those who left their names on the new land, he came from noble but poor parents. He emerges from the fog of

331

history in 1502 when he helped Governor Ovando put down an Indian rebellion. For this assistance, he was made the governor's lieutenant in the town of Salvaleon where he first heard about the island of San Juan, now called Puerto Rico.

In 1508 Juan Ponce visited the island, and in 1509 he received an appointment as governor on the condition he conquer Puerto Rico. The middle-aged governor established his power, and in the process he was probably more vicious in his treatment of the Indians than any of the other conquistadores. The word *aparrear*—to cast to the dogs—was coined at this time. With his dog, Bezerillo, he made Indian hunting a popular sport. His beast fathered the one which accompanied Balboa to Darien, and like Balboa's dog, Juan Ponce's also received a crossbowman's pay. The conquest of Puerto Rico was so successful that within a few years there were almost no natives left alive on the island. And the governor could turn his attention elsewhere.

The legend of the fountain of youth had already come to his ears, and he applied for the right to discover and conquer the Island of Binnini. On February 23, 1512, he received permission from the king. However, the hard-headed Spanish court, in a detailed document, makes no mention about anything as fanciful as a fountain of youth.

The contract is lengthy, but shows better than anything else how closely the crown watched out for its interests and expanded the empire at the least possible cost.

The permission is granted at Juan Ponce's expense, and in such a way that it does not interfere with Portugal's rights, which were still being considered at this time. Permission is also granted for the purchase of ships and supplies through the Royal Casa de Contratación—House of Trade. In fact, it is made clear that anything not costing money will be granted.

THE DISCOVERY OF THE ISLE OF BENNINY

AGREEMENT WITH JUAN PONCE DE LEÓN

Juan Ponce de León: Inasmuch as you commissioned me to entreat and beseech in your behalf that I grant you the right and the power to go in search of and populate the Benniny Islands with certain stipulations which will be stated shortly, therefore in granting your request

I confer to you the right and the power so that you may be able to discover and settle said isle, provided that it—the island—is not one of those which have already been discovered, and according as it comprises the stipulations which are included below in the following manner:

FIRSTLY: that you may choose the ships which you desire, the expense of the mission to be borne by you so that you may fulfil your objective; that is, to discover the aforementioned island. The term allotted you for this exploration is three years, to be reckoned from the day on which this agreement was presented to you, or when you have set yourself up on the island, on the condition that you be required to discover it within the first year of the stipulated three years and that on your return you may go ashore on any of the islands and mainlands surrounding the sea, whether they include those already discovered or to be discovered, with the further condition that they do not include those islands or mainland possessions which belong to the most serene King of Portugal, our very dearly beloved brother. And let those geographical limits which are marked out be respected by you; nor with respect to these possessions may you establish any interest except for those items which you require for your well-being and for the outfitting of your ships and personnel, for which you are to pay a just price.

Article: that you can acquire and may acquire, as far as you are concerned, the warships, items of subsistence, officers and sailors and other personnel which you may need from the kings of Castille, paying for them according to the customary manner and in view of our officers who at present are living or will live at headquarters of the Casa de Contratación. And when in Spain, said purchases are to be witnessed by our officials at the headquarters of the trading house in Seville.

Article: I order that during the period of three years no one else may set out to discover the island of Benniny, and if some one were to discover it, or by chance did discover it, the conditions contained in this agreement shall be considered complied with on your part and not by the person who might discover it. And if it be discovered by another, you would lose nothing of the right which you have with respect to it, provided, as is stated, you set sail for the discovery of the island within the agreed upon first year, and that otherwise the conditions are not valid, and provided the other discoverer does not have any information and certain knowledge of it.

Article: that upon finding and discovering the island under discussion in the manner described, I entrust the governorship and the administration of justice for all the days of your life, and for this I grant you full power and jurisdiction with regard to civil and criminal matters with all its incidents and accessories, appurtenances and rights annexed to the principal.

Article: that on finding the said island, as expressed, that you be obligated to populate it at your expense in the areas and sites which you can best afford to do, and that you take possession of the houses and lands and settlements and farms which you will bring about on the island according to what is outlined in this agreement.

Article: that should you construct fortresses on the island, the expenses will be incurred by us, and we shall set over them in command our governors, as we regard this as an obligation resting with us alone; and if while you are constructing these fortresses, you should build a house or houses for residential purposes and for your defense against the Indians, then these will belong to you; and if there is a necessity for us to use them, you are to turn them over to us, for which an adequate payment will be made.

Article: that I will grant to you, and for the present I do so grant you, for a period of twelve years figuring from the day in which you will discover the island, a tenth of all the incomes and profits which belong to us on the island, the one-tenth not to be counted from our gain.

Article: that the apportionment of the Indians who may be on the island be left to the person or persons whom I named, and not in any other way.

Article: that I shall order, and for the present do order, that the Indians on that island be apportioned by those first there, and that this be done first, and that the first discoverers be provided with their apportionment before any others, and that these first discoverers receive all the advantage there is.

Article: that I grant for a period of ten years that those who went to discover the said island and populate it from that expedition, enjoy the benefits of gold and other metals which might exist on that island without paying us any taxes other than a tithe for the first year, and 9 per cent the second, and 8 per cent the third, and 7 per cent the fourth, and 6 per cent the fifth year, and 5 per cent for the five remaining years, according to the norm by which payment is made in the other possessions; and that with respect to the other colonizers who went afterwards, namely not those who were involved in the initial discovery, these shall pay from the first year a fifth—20 per cent duty.

Article: As a further recompense and in gratitude to you, Juan Ponce de León, it is my pleasure and will that all the islands which are close to the said Benniny Island, which you may discover personally at your expense and not being any for which there has been previous knowledge, you may govern them as well as their inhabitants with the stipulations which are contained in this agreement; and in virtue of it, you are to possess them.

Article: that I grant you the use of the title of Our Governor of said islands and of others which you may discover in the above cited manner.

Article: that you may obtain gold, if there is any, in the same way in which it is presently taken in our possessions or in the manner in which I will prescribe.

Article: that for security which you, Juan Ponce, and the persons who are to go with you, will make and carry out and pay, and thus there will be fulfilled and paid and your word kept, which as respects these declarations in this agreement; it is incumbent upon you to keep and to comply with, and that before you undertake this trip, you give as deposit or security a reliable and clear surety to the satisfaction of our officials.

Article: that the said Juan Ponce and the other persons who are to go with you will all make and comply with and pay all that which is expressed by the declarations in this agreement of mine and each section and part of it; and further you will commit no fraud or deception of any sort nor give favor to, nor help or acquiesce to it; and if such action is known by you, you are to notify us and our officials in our name under penalty that you, or any persons who act to the contrary or carry out the same act, he then who does not comply with the provisions as stated above will have lost any benefice or office which he had been given by the crown and will pay in his own behalf for all the penalties which we would be disposed to order carried out against his person and against his properties of those who did this deed, consented to it or concealed it.

Article: that after having arrived at the island and having ascertained what value there is on it, you are to send me news of it and another notice of it dispatched to our officials who reside at the present seat of government so that we may know what has been done and to decide what further action is necessary on our part.

THEREFORE, Juan Ponce, complying with all the expressed intentions and every aspect of them and having given the mentioned security or leaving and paying for the above-mentioned things, I promise and assure you with the present writing to order that all contained in this agreement be complied with and every portion thereof be met, and I order our officials who reside in Hispaniola in our name to accede to the above-mentioned, to respect the agreement and receive the said security; and for your expedition I order Don Diego Colón, our Admiral and Governor of said Hispaniola Island, and our judges of appeal and the officials of our treasury who reside on the island, and all the authorities of the island to lend you all the support and help which you may need without any part of the agreement being impeded in any way or manner.

EXECUTED in Burgos on the 23 of February in the year 1512. I the King. By order of his Highness, Lope Conchillos. Signed by the Bishop of Palencia.

The new governor of Binniny sailed from Puerto Rico on March 3, 1513. On Easter Sunday, March 27, the expedition passed a small island, and in the first week of April, Juan Ponce de León and his men landed somewhere in the vicinity of what is now St. Augustine. Because of the day—the Spanish Easter of Flowers—the governor gave the name Florida to the country.

During the next several months he tried to make peace with the Indians, but in every instance he and his men were attacked and driven off. Finally he coasted west as far as Pensacola Bay, and after continued trouble with the Indians, he returned to Puerto Rico on September 21, 1513. A year later, with a new contract for Florida, he sailed from Seville with three vessels, but he had a task to accomplish before he established his colony: namely, the conquest or destruction of the troublesome Carib Indians. This war was to continue for several years without much success; and in the years between, others tried their luck in Florida.

Several uneventful expeditions visited the Peninsula. Alonso Alvarez de Pineda coasted the gulf from the Peninsula to Mexico. Lucas Vásquez de Ayllón first sent a slaving ship into the area and then followed in an attempt to set up a colony. He failed tragically and withdrew, as did Francisco de Garay, who had financed Pineda.

Finally, feeling himself free to try again, Juan Ponce wrote the king:

Among my services, I discovered at my own cost and charge the island of Florida and others in its district, and now I return to that island, if it please God's will, to settle it. I shall set out to pursue my voyage in five or six days.

It seems incredible, after so many others had been in the area, that Juan Ponce should stubbornly stick to the idea that Florida was an island.

He attempted his landing in 1521 with two hundred fifty men and fifty horses. Again the Indians were able to drive back the Spanish incursion. They almost destroyed Juan Ponce somewhere near Charlotte Harbor, attacking so vigorously that they killed many of the invaders and seriously wounded the aging conquistador. In disgust, he withdrew to Cuba, along the way losing a ship that eventually fell into the hands of Cortés. Several days after his arrival in Cuba, Juan Ponce died. His body was sent to Puerto Rico for burial, and the way was open for the appointment of a new governor to Florida.

The man who was eventually named to the post never sought it, though there were many who did. The king made a popular selection when he appointed Hernando de Soto to be governor.

About thirty-seven years old, De Soto was a veteran conquistador. He had sailed for Darien with Pedrarias when only nineteen. Once on the Isthmus, he fought as a protégé of the old tyrant, and he earned a reputation of boldness, stubbornness and bravery. He blocked the spread of other Spaniards through the Isthmus, and represented Pedrarias in his dealings with his lieutenants. He fought in a battle that probably saved the life of the future conquistador, Francisco Pizarro, and was jailed in Granada in an attempt to put down a rebellion against the governor. His friends broke him out, and he marched back to Granada with Pedrarias, and together they put the rebel officer's head on a pike.

In 1530 he signed an agreement with Pizarro: De Soto's money for a captaincy on the Inca expedition. And for the next several years De Soto was in the forefront of the action in Peru. He was the first European to meet the ill-fated Atahualpa and the first to protest the attempt to try the Inca emperor. Pizarro and his friends sent the youthful captain elsewhere so that he would not be around when they held their mock trial and very real execution. But De Soto's bravery was never ignored, though there were times when those with him reported his foolhardiness and their fears to Pizarro. Finally, disgusted by the Almagro-Pizarro feud, De Soto left the Indian princess who had become his mistress and their children, and set out for Spain with over one hundred thousand gold pesos—a sum equal to a million American dollars.

De Soto had not been home for sixteen years, and he was given a great reception in keeping with his colorful exploits. The king showed his fondness for the rash youth by permitting him to loan the crown a large sum of money, and Pedrarias' widow showed her approval of the hero by permitting him to marry her daughter, Isabella de Bobadilla. De Soto in this way became the brother-in-law of the late Balboa. The two men had been born in the same town and had been graduates of the same university.

After a restless year in Spain, De Soto requested the governorship of Guatemala and permission to explore the South Seas, envisioning himself after the pattern of Alvarado. Instead, Charles gave him a province that stretched from Rio de las Palmos in Mexico to Florida and the land beyond and in addition he made the conquistador governor of Cuba, which by 1537 was out of the main stream of operations. The grant was clear and typically something Charles would sign.

All expenses were to be paid by De Soto and those who went with him. No lawyers were to be allowed to practice in the area. One hundred Negro slaves could be imported duty free so long as one-third of them were women. De Soto could have for himself twelve square leagues of land on the condition that no piece rested on the sea. In this way Charles made certain the twelve leagues would always be dependent on the crown.

Florida had suddenly become important. Despite the years of failure by Juan Ponce, Narváez, Garay, Ayllón and others, there was the report of Cabeza de Vaca. The wandering conquistador, who had just arrived in Spain from Mexico, never said that there was a great deal of wealth in Florida. His written account stresses, if anything, the poverty of the country, but the word spread quickly through Spain that he was talking to the king and others and that he was saying things which were quite different from what he had recorded.

With the rumors spreading over the country, De Soto had no trouble recruiting men. A number even crossed the frontier from Portugal and asked to join his expedition. Cabeza de Vaca himself refused to go, though some of his relatives signed on. On November 6, the same day that Pizarro defeated Almagro to end the bloody feud with an execution, De Soto sailed from San Lúcar.

The small fleet put in at Cuba and readied for the final journey to the mainland. But during the short time that he stayed in Cuba, De Soto made a command decision that may have changed the course of the expedition's future.

For personal reasons, he removed his maestre de campo, a most able professional soldier by the name of Nuño Tobar. De Soto's wife, Isabella de Bobadilla, had brought along a young niece as a maid-in-waiting, and Tobar had got the young girl pregnant. De Soto, who had left children in Central America and Peru, was angered by the insult to his wife's family and replaced one of the best men he had with him for one who was to prove a continuing failure.

Leaving his wife as his deputy in Cuba, De Soto landed in Florida on May 30, 1539.

What happened to De Soto and his companions in Florida and the land beyond has been carefully recorded by several persons. Not long after the landing, De Soto himself wrote one letter that still exists. The most complete account of the expedition was written some years afterward by a "Gentleman from Elvas." No other name is given us; and as Elvas is in Portugal it is assumed the Gentleman or Hidalgo or Fidalgo was one of those who crossed the border to join the expedition. Richard Hakluyt included the account in a collection of English voyages that was printed in 1609. The Gentleman was not always clear on locations but he was usually accurate on events as he was able to recall them. As a historian, he does stretch credulity by putting in set speeches which no one could have remembered.

What appears to be the official account of the expedition was signed by Luis Hernández de Biedma, who was the factor. Shorter than the Gentleman's report, Biedma's shows little concern with personalities and barely mentions the death of the governor. Another report has been found buried in the history of the Indies written by Oviedo y Valdes, the chronicler-official, who knew many of the conquistadores. This account appears to have been prepared by De Soto's own secretary, Rodrigo Rangel. Oviedo, in accordance with the custom of the time, did not hesitate to take the report and add his own comments to it. Here we find the great cleavage that had already appeared in Indies policy. The death of De Soto brings forth one reaction concerning the governor from the Gentleman of Elvas, and the Rangel-Oviedo account presents a completely different view of the man. On the one side we read admiration and respect for a great captain who by his ability and personality carried the group forward, and on the other side we see contempt and distaste for a ruthless conqueror.

De Soto's surviving letter from Florida is confusing in structure and, while it is difficult to follow, it shows a sensitivity rare among these men.

LETTER OF HERNANDO DE SOTO AT TAMPA BAY TO THE JUSTICE AND
BOARD OF MAGISTRATES IN SANTIAGO DE CUBA

Very Noble Gentlemen:

The being in a new country, not very distant indeed from that where you are, still with some sea between, a thousand years appears to me to have gone by since anything has been heard from you; and although I left some letters written at Havana, to go off in three ways, it is indeed long since I have received one. However, since opportunity offers by which I may send an account of what it is always my duty to give, I will relate what passes, and I believe will be welcome to persons I know favorably, and are earnest for my success.

I took my departure from Havana with all my armament on Sunday, the 18th of May, although I wrote that I should leave on the 25th of the month. I anticipated the day, not to lose a favorable wind, which changed nevertheless for calms upon our getting into the Gulf. Still these were not so continuous as to prevent our casting anchor on this coast, as we did at the end of eight days, which was on Sunday, the festival of Espiritu Santo.

Having fallen four or five leagues below the port, without any one of my pilots being able to tell where we were, it became necessary that I should go in the brigantines and look for it. In doing so, and in entering the mouth of the port, we were detained three days. And likewise because we had no knowledge of the passage—a bay that runs up a dozen leagues or more from the sea—we were so long delayed that I was obliged to send my Lieutenant-General, Vasco Porcallo de Figueroa, in the brigantines to take possession of a town at the end of the bay. I ordered all the men and horses to be landed on a beach, whence with great difficulty we went on Trinity Sunday to join Vasco Porcallo. The Indians of the coast, because of some fears of us, have abandoned all the country so that for thirty leagues not a man of them has halted.

At my arrival here I received news of there being a Christian in possession of a cacique, and I sent Baltazar de Gallegos, with forty men of the horse and as many of the foot, to endeavor to get him. He found the man a day's journey from this place, with eight or ten Indians whom he brought into my power. We rejoiced no little over him for he speaks the language; and although he had forgotten his own, it directly returned to him. His name in Juan Ortiz, an hidalgo, native of Seville.

In consequence of this occurrence, I went myself for the cacique and came back with him in peace. I then sent Baltazar de Gallegos, with eighty lancers and a hundred foot soldiers, to enter the country. He has found fields of maize, beans and pumpkins, with other fruits, and provision in such quantity as would suffice to subsist a very large army without its knowing a want. Having been allowed without interruption to reach the town of a cacique named Urripacoxit, master of the town we are in and also of many other towns, some Indians were sent to him to treat for peace. This, he writes, having been accomplished, the cacique failed to keep certain promises, whereupon the captain seized about seventeen persons, among whom are some of the principal men; for in this way, it appears to him, he can best secure a performance. Among those he detains are some old men of authority, as great as can be among such people, who have information of the country farther on.

They say that three days' journey from where they are, going by some towns and huts, all well inhabited and having many maize fields, is a large town called Acuera where with much convenience we might winter; and that farther on, at the distance of two days' journey, there is another town called Ocale. It is so large, and they so extol it, that I dare not repeat all that is said. There is to be found in it a great plenty of all the things mentioned; also fowls, a multitude of turkeys kept in pens, and herds of tame deer that are tended. What this means I do not understand, unless it be the cattle, of which we brought the knowledge with us. They say there are many trades among that people, and much intercourse, an abundance of gold and silver, and many pearls. May it please God that this may be so; for of what these Indians say I believe nothing but what I see, and must well see; although they know that if they lie to me it will cost them their lives.

This interpreter puts a new life into us by affording the means of our understanding these people, for without him I know not what would become of us. Glory be to God, who by His goodness has directed all, so that it appears as if He had taken this enterprise in

His especial keeping, that it may be for His service, as I have supplicated, and do dedicate it to Him.

I sent eighty soldiers by sea in boats, and my general by land with forty horsemen, to fall upon a throng of some thousand Indians or more whom Juan de Añaso had discovered. The general got back last night and states that they fled from him; and although he pursued them, they could not be overtaken for the many obstructions in the way. On our coming together we will march to join Baltazar de Gallegos, that we may go thence to pass the winter at the Ocale, where, if what is said is true, we shall have nothing to desire. Heaven be pleased that something may come of this that shall be for the service of our Divine Master, and whereby I may be enabled to serve Your Worships, and each of you as I desire and is your due.

Notwithstanding my continual occupation here, I am not forgetful of the love I owe to objects at a distance; and since I may not be there in person, I believe that where you gentlemen are there is little in which my presence can be necessary. This duty weighs upon me more than every other, and for the attentions you will bestow as befits your goodness I shall be under great obligations. I enjoin it upon you to make the utmost exertions to maintain the repose and well-being of the public and the proper administration of justice, always reposing in the licentiate; that every thing may be so done in accordance with law that God and the King may be served, myself gratified, and every one be content and pleased with the performance of his trust, in such a manner as you, gentlemen, have ever considered for my honor not less than your own, although I still feel that I have the weight thereof and bear the responsibility.

As respects the bastion which I left begun, if laboring on it have been neglected or perhaps discontinued, with the idea that the fabric is not now needed, you, gentlemen, will favor me by having it finished, since every day brings change. And although no occasion should arise for its employment, the erection is provident for the well-being and safety of the town: an act that will yield me increased satisfaction, through your very noble personages.

That our Lord may guard and increase your prosperity is my wish and your deserving.

In this town and port of Espiritu Santo, in the Province of Florida, July the 9, in the year 1539.

The servant of you, Gentlemen,

EL ADELANTADO DON HERNANDO DE SOTO

THE EXPEDITION OF HERNANDO DE SOTO
THE NARRATIVE BY THE GENTLEMAN OF ELVAS

True relation of the vicissitudes that attended the Governor Don Hernando de Soto and some nobles of Portugal in the discovery of the Province of Florida now just given by an Hidalgo of Elvas. Viewed by the Lord Inquisitor.

Hernando de Soto was the son of an esquire of Xerez de Badajoz, and went to the Indias of the Ocean Sea, belonging to Castile, at the time Pedrarias Dávila was the governor. He had nothing more than blade and buckler; for his courage and good qualities Pedrarias appointed him to be captain of a troop of horse, and he went with Hernando Pizarro to conquer Peru. According to many reports he distinguished himself wherever he went. Apart from his share in the treasure of Atabalipa, he brought back to Spain, from portions falling to his lot, one hundred eighty thousand cruzados.

In Seville, Soto employed a superintendent of household, an usher, pages, equerry, chamberlain, footmen, and all the other servants requisite for the establishment of a gentleman. From there he went to court, accompanied by Juan de Añasco of Seville, Luis Moscoso de Alvarado, Nuño de Tobar, and Juan Rodriguez Lobillo. All except Añasco came with him from Peru; and each brought fourteen or fifteen thousand cruzados. As it was the first time he was to show himself at Court, Soto, although not profuse by nature, spent largely. He married Doña Isabel de Bobadilla, daughter of Pedrarias Dávila, Count of Puñonrostro. The emperor made him governor of the island of Cuba and adelantado of Florida, with title of Marquis to a certain part of the territory he should conquer.

After Don Hernando had obtained the concession, there arrived at court from the Indias an hidalgo named Cabeza de Vaca, who had been in Florida with Narváez. He told how he and four others had escaped, making their way to New Spain; that the governor had been lost in the sea and the rest were all dead. He brought with him a written account of adventures, which said in some places: Here I have seen this; and the rest which I saw I leave to confer with His Majesty. Generally, however, he described the poverty of the country and spoke of the hardships he had undergone. Some of his kinfolk, wishing to go to the Indias, strongly urged him to tell whether or not he had seen any rich country in Florida. He told them, however, that he and another—one Dorantes, who had remained in New Spain with the purpose of returning into Florida—had sworn not to divulge certain things which they had seen lest someone might beg the government in advance of them. Nevertheless, he gave them to understand that it was the richest country in the world.

Don Hernando de Soto wished Cabeza de Vaca to go with him, and made him favorable proposals; but after they had come to terms, they disagreed because the adelantado would not pay for a ship that the other had bought. Baltazar de Gallegos and Cristóbal de Espindola told Cabeza de Vaca, their kinsman, that they had made up their minds to go to Florida because of what he had told them, and they pleaded with him to counsel them. He replied that he hoped to receive another government, being reluctant to march under the standard of another. He himself had come to solicit the conquest of Florida; and though he had found it had already been granted to Don Hernando de Soto, yet, on account of his oath, he could not divulge what they desired to know. He did advise them, however, to sell their estates and go—that in so doing they would act wisely.

As soon as Cabeza de Vaca had an opportunity , he spoke with the emperor and gave him an account of all that he had gone through, seen, and learned. The Marquis of Astorga was informed of this, and decided at once to send his brother, Don Antonio Osorio; and with him Francisco and Garcia Osorio, two of his kinsmen. They joined the adelantado at Seville, as did Nuño de Tobar, Luis de Moscoso, and Juan Rodriguez Lobillo. Moscoso took two brothers; Don Carlos, who had married the governor's niece, also went and took her with him. From Badajoz went Pedro Calderon and three kinsmen of the adelantado: Arias Tinoco, Alonso Romo, and Diego Tinoco.

From Elvas went André de Vasconcelos, Fernán Pegado, Antonio Martinez Segurado, Men Royz Pereyra, Joam Cordeiro, Estevan Pegado, Bento Fernandez, Alvaro Fernandez; and from Salamanca, Jaen, Valencia, Albuquerque and other parts of Spain, many persons of noble extraction assembled in Seville. Many who had sold their land remained behind in San Lúcar for want of shipping, whereas for countries of known riches it was usual to lack men: and the cause of this was what Cabeza de Vaca told the emperor and given people to understand. De Vaca went as governor to Rio de la Plata, but his kinsmen followed Soto.

Baltazar de Gallegos received the appointment of chief castellan and took with him his wife. The offices were sought by many, and through powerful influence. The place of factor was held by Antonio de Biedma, that of comptroller by Juan de Añasco, and that of treasurer by Juan Gaytan, nephew of the Cardinal of Ciguenza.

From Seville the governor went to San Lúcar with all the people that were to go. He ordered a muster, to which the Portuguese turned out in polished armor, and the Castilians very showily, in silk over silk, pinked and slashed. To the governor such luxury did not appear becoming on such an occasion, and he ordered a review to be called for the next day, when every man should appear with his arms. The Portuguese came as at first; and the governor set them near the standard borne by his ensign. Most of the Castilians wore rusty shirts of mail; all had steel caps or helmets but very poor lances. Some of them tried to get among the Portuguese. Those that Soto liked and accepted were passed, counted, and enlisted. Six hundred men in all followed him to Florida. He had bought seven ships, and the necessary subsistence was already on board.

In the month of April of the year 1538 of the Christian era, when the adelantado had delivered the vessels to their several captains, he took for himself a new ship, fast of sail, and gave another to André de Vasconcelos, in which the Portuguese were to go. He passed over the bar of San Lúcar on Sunday, the morning of Saint Lazarus, with great festivity, commanding the trumpets to be sounded and artillery to be fired.

On Pentecost we came into the harbor of Santiago, in Cuba of the Antillas. The governor sent Don Carlos with the ships, in company with Doña Isabel, to wait for him at Havana, one hundred and eighty leagues from Santiago. He and those that remained, having bought horses, set out on their journey overland.

From Puerto Principe the governor went by canoe to the estate of Vasco Porcallo near the coast to get news of Doña Isabel who, although it was not then known, was in a situation of distress. The ships had parted company, two of them being driven in sight of the coast of Florida. It was forty days from the time of leaving Santiago that the ships arrived at Havana. When the governor received the news, he hastened to meet Doña Isabel.

When he arrived in Havana, he sent Juan de Añasco in a caravel with two pinnaces and fifty men, to explore the harbor in Florida. Añasco brought back two Indians taken on the coast. This caused much rejoicing, not only because they were needed as guides and interpreters but because they said by signs that there was much gold in Florida. The governor and all the company longed for the hour of departure, for the land appeared to them to be the richest of any which until then had been discovered.

Before our departure, the governor deprived Nuño de Tobar of the rank of captain-general and conferred it on a resident of Cuba, Vasco Porcallo de Figueroa, who provisioned the vessels well with hogs and cassava bread. This change was made because Nuño de Tobar had made love to Doña Isabel's waiting-maid, daughter of the governor of Gomera. Though he had lost his place, yet, to return to Soto's favor, he took her to wife, for she was with child by him, and went to Florida. Doña Isabel remained, and with her the wives of Don Carlos, of Baltazar de Gallegos, and of Nuño de Tobar. The governor left as his lieutenant over the island Juan de Rojas, an hidalgo of Havana.

On Sunday, the 18th day of May, in the year 1539, the adelantado sailed from Havana with a fleet of nine vessels—five ships, two caravels and two pinnaces—and ran seven days with favorable weather. On the twenty-fifth of the month land was seen and anchor cast a league from shore, because of the shoals. On Friday, May 30, the army landed in Florida, two leagues from the town of an Indian chief named Ucita.

At night the governor, with a hundred men in the pinnaces, came upon the deserted town; for as soon as the Christians appeared in sight of land, all along the coast were seen smokes, which the Indians make to warn one another.

From the town of Ucita the governor sent the chief castellan Baltazar de Gallegos into the country, with forty horsemen and eighty footmen, to procure an Indian if possible. In another direction he sent Juan Rodriguez Lobillo. The command of Lobillo marched over a swampy land where horses could not travel, and half a league from camp came upon some huts near a river. The natives plunged into the water; nevertheless, four women were secured. Twenty warriors attacked our people and pressed us so hard that we were forced to retire into our camp.

The Indians are exceedingly skillful with their weapons, and so warlike and nimble that they have no fear of footmen. They never remain quiet but are continually running from place to place, so that neither crossbow nor arquebus can be aimed at them. Before a Christian can make a single shot with either, an Indian will discharge three or four arrows; and he seldom misses his object.

Juan Rodriguez Lobillo got back to camp with six men wounded, of whom one died, and he brought with him the four women taken in the huts. When Baltazar de Gallegos came into the open field, he discovered ten or eleven Indians, among whom was a Christian, naked and sun-burnt, his arms tattooed after their manner, and in no respect differing from them. As soon as the horsemen came in sight, they ran upon the Indians, who fled, hiding themselves in a thicket, though not before two or three were overtaken and wounded. The Christian, seeing a horseman coming upon him with a lance, cried out: "Do not kill me, cavalier; I am a Christian! Do not slay these people; they have given me my life!" He immediately called to the Indians, who left the wood and came to him. The horsemen took up the Christian and Indians behind them on their beasts and, greatly rejoicing, got back to the governor at nightfall. When he and the rest heard the news, they were no less pleased than the others.

The name of the Christian was Juan Ortiz, a native of Seville and of noble parentage. He had been twelve years among the Indians, having gone into the country with Pánfilo de Narváez, and returned to the island of Cuba, where the wife of the governor remained. By her command, he went back to Florida in a pinnace with some twenty or thirty others. Coming to the port, they saw a cane sticking upright in the ground, with a split in the top, holding a letter which they supposed the governor had left there to give information of himself before marching into the interior. No sooner had they got on shore than many natives came out of the houses and captured them. The people in the pinnace, unwilling to land, kept along the coast and returned to Cuba.

By command of Ucita, Juan Ortiz was bound hand and foot to four stakes and laid upon scaffolding, beneath which a fire was kindled. But a daughter of the chief begged that he be spared. Though one Christian, she said, might do no good, certainly he could do no harm, and it would be an honor to have one for a captive. The father consented, directing the injuries to be healed.

Three years after falling into the hands of this chief, another chief named Mococo, living two days' journey distant, came and burnt the town. Ucita fled to another of his cities, taking Ortiz with him. He planned to sacrifice Ortiz, for these Indians are worshipers of the Devil and are accustomed to make sacrifices of the blood and bodies of their people, or of any others they can come by. Again Ortiz was saved by the girl, who warned him and told him to flee to Mococo, who she said would receive him with regard.

The cacique Mococo was much gratified. He immediately made the Christian swear to him, according to the custom of the country, that he would not leave him for any other master. In return, he promised to show him much honor, and if at any time Christians should come to that land, he would give him permission to return to them.

Three years later, some people fishing three leagues from land brought news of having seen ships. Mococo gave Ortiz permission to depart. The Spaniard made all possible haste to the shore, but finding no vessels, he supposed the story to be only a device of the cacique to test his inclination. He remained with him nine years, having little hope of ever seeing Christians again. But no sooner had the governor arrived in Florida than it was known to Mococo, who directly told Ortiz that Christians were in the town of Ucita. The captive thinking himself jested with, said that his thoughts no longer dwelt on his people and that his only wish now was to serve him. Still the cacique assured him that it was true and gave him leave to go, telling him that if he did not, and the Christians should depart, he must not blame him, for he had fulfilled his promise.

Great was the joy of Ortiz at this news, though he still doubted its truth. However, he thanked Mococo and went his way. A dozen principal Indians were sent to accompany him, and on their way to the port they met Baltazar de Gallegos in the manner that has been related.

Arrived at the camp, the governor ordered apparel given him, good armor and a fine horse. When asked if he knew of any country where there was either gold or silver, he said that he had not been ten leagues in any direction from where he lived. However, more than thirty leagues distant was a chief named Paracoxi, to whom Mococo, Ucita and all that dwelt along the coast paid tribute. Perhaps he had knowledge of some good country, as his land was better than theirs, being more fertile and abounding in maize. The governor was well pleased and said he desired only to find subsistence so that he could go inland with safety; for Florida was so wide that in some part or other of it, there could not fail to be a rich country. The cacique of Mococo came to port, and calling on the governor, he spoke as follows:

"Most High and Powerful Chief: Though less able to serve you than the least of these under your control, but with the wish to do more than even the greatest of them, I appear before you in the full confidence of receiving your favor, as much so as though I deserved it, not in requital of the trifling service I rendered in setting free the Christian while he was in my power, which I did not do for the sake of my honor and of my promise, but because I hold that great men should be liberal. As much as in your bodily perfections you exceed all, and in your command over fine men are you superior to others, so in your nature are you equal to the full enjoyment of earthly things. The favor I hope for, great Lord, is that you will hold me to be your own, calling on me freely to do whatever may be your wish."

The governor answered him that although it was true that in freeing and sending him the Christian, he had done no more than to keep his word and preserve his honor, nevertheless he thanked him for an act so valuable, and that, holding him henceforth to be a brother, he should in all and through all favor him. Then a shirt and some other articles of clothing were given to the chief, who, thankfully receiving them, took leave and went to his town.

The principal object of Vasco Porcallo de Figueroa in coming to Florida had been to get slaves for his plantations and mines. After some incursions he found that no seizures could be made because of dense forest and extensive bogs, and he determined to go back to Cuba. As a consequence, there grew up such a difference between him and De Soto that neither of them treated or spoke to the other kindly. Still, with words of courtesy, he asked permission to return, and took his leave.

THE RELATION OF THE CONQUEST OF FLORIDA PRESENTED BY
LUYS HERNÁNDEZ DE BIEDMA IN THE YEAR 1544
TO THE KING OF SPAIN IN COUNCIL

We left Baya Honda—Espiritu Santo—to explore inland, leaving behind twenty-six cavalry and sixty infantry in charge of the port until the governor should be heard from, or should send orders to join him. We went west, then northwest, seeking a cacique named Hurripacuxi, who lived twenty leagues from the coast and to whom the Indians said they all paid tribute. From there we went, through swamps and over rivers, fifteen or twenty leagues, to a town which the Indians represented to us as very wonderful, and where the inhabitants, by shouting, caused birds on the wing to drop.

On arrival there, we found it to be a small town called Etocale. We got some maize, beans and little dogs, which were no small relief to people who came perishing with hunger. We remained seven or eight days, and in that time made several forays to catch Indians for guides to the Province of Apalachen, which had great fame wherever we went. We captured three or four, but the best informed of them knew nothing of the country two leagues in advance. We kept on, still in the direction of New Spain, always some ten or twelve leagues from the coast.

In five days' march we passed through several towns and came to a moderately large one called Aguacalecuen. The inhabitants, frightened, had all gone off into the woods. We remained six days to hunt some Indians for guides, and caught ten or twelve women, one of whom was declared to be the daughter of the cacique. The consequence was that her father came to us in peace. He promised us interpreters and guides; but as he did not give them, we had to take him along with us. After seven days' march, we were attacked by more than three hundred warriors, intent on wresting the cacique from us. We killed some and captured the remainder. Among them were Indians who had knowledge of the country farther inland, but they told us very false stories.

We crossed another river, and found towns on the farther bank which the inhabitants had left. However, we were able to find some food there, which we needed. We set out for another town which is on the border of Apalachen, a river dividing the one province from another. Across this stream we made a bridge by lashing many pines together, crossing over with much danger as there were Indians on the opposite side who disputed our passage. When they found, however, that we had landed, they went to the nearest town and remained there until we came in sight, whereupon they set fire to the place and took to flight.

There are many towns in this province of Apalachen, and it is a land abundant in subsistence.

We went to another town called Iniahico. There it appeared to us to be time we should know of those who remained at the port, and that they should hear from us; for we proposed to travel so far inland that we might not be able to hear of them again. The distance we had now marched from them was one hundred ten leagues, and the governor sent orders with Juan de Añasco that they should come to where we then were.

From that town we went to look for the sea, which was about nine leagues off, and we found on the shore the place where Pánfilo de Narváez had built his boats. We found the spot where the forge had stood, and many bones of horses. The Indians told us through the intepreter what others like us had done there.

Juan de Añasco sent the people on by land, while he came by sea in the two brigantines and the boat that were left, as the governor had ordered. On his way to join us in Apalachen, he encountered much danger and suffered much fatigue, for he could not find the coast. He had observed it from the land before leaving, but he could discover no marks from the sea, as these were in shallow inlets that had water in them with the rise of the tide, and with the ebb were bare. We made a piragua, which went out every day two leagues to sea, looking for the brigantines, to show them where to stop. I was thankful when the people arrived, not less for those that came by land than those by water.

On the arrival of the brigantines, the governor directed that they should sail westward to discover a harbor, if one were near, from which to explore the coast to see if anything could be found inland. Francisco Maldonado had the command. He coasted along the country and entered all the coves, creeks and rivers he discovered, until he arrived at a river having a good entrance and harbor, with an Indian town on the seaboard. Some inhabitants approached to traffic, and he took one of them and directly turned back with him to join us. On this voyage he was absent two months, which appeared to us all like a thousand years inasmuch as it detained us so long from advancing to what we understood was to be found in the interior.

After Maldonado got back, the governor told him that we were about to set off in quest of the country which that Indian stated to be on another sea. Therefore Maldonado must return with the brigantines to Cuba, where the Doña Isabel de Bobadilla, his wife, remained; and if within six months' time he should hear nothing of us, he should come with the brigantines and run the shore as far as the River Espiritu Santo, to which we should have to resort. The vessels went to the island, and we took our way northward again, seeking what the Indians had told us about.

We marched five days through an uninhabited country, and came to a great river. The current was so stiff that we could not build a bridge over it, and we made a piragua. With this we reached the opposite shore, where we found a province called Acapachiqui, very abundant in the food to which the Indians are accustomed. We saw some towns but did not visit many because the country was one of very large swamps. There was a change in the habitations, which were now in the earth, like caves; heretofore, they were covered with palm leaves and with grass.

We continued on and came to two other rivers over which we had to make bridges in our usual manner by tying pine trees together. Arrived at another province called Otoa, we found a town rather larger than any we had seen before. From there we went to towns of another province, where we took some unwary persons. The people agreed to come and serve us peacefully for the return of the captives, to which the governor assented, keeping only a part as interpreters and guides.

We were five or six days going through this province, and were well supplied by the Indians from their slender stores. Three days later we came to the province of Altapaha. Here we found a river that ran, not southward like the rest we had passed, but eastward to the sea, where the licentiate Lucas de Ayllón had come years before. Because of this we gave still more credit to what the Indian said, and we came to believe as true all the stories that he had told us.

This province was thickly peopled, and the inhabitants all desired to serve us. The governor inquired of them for that province, Cofitachique, which we were seeking. They said it was not possible to go there, for there was no road, and on the journey we should famish, there being no food. We went on to other caciques, named Ocuti and Cafaqui, who gave us food. They said that if we were going to make war on the Lady of Cofitachique, they would give us all we should desire for the way; but we should understand that there was no road over which to pass; that because of their enmity they had no intercourse, except when they made war upon each other, which was carried on through obscure and difficult places, out of which no one would be expected to issue, and that they were on the journey from twenty to twenty-two days, eating only the plants and the parched maize they took with them. Seeing our determination, they gave us eight hundred Indians to carry our loads of clothing and provisions, and also others as guides.

We were taken directly eastward, and thus traveled three days. The Indian who deceitfully led us had said that he would place us where we were going in that time. Despite the fact that toward the end we began to discover his perfidy, the governor continued on the course, commanding us to husband our provisions as much as possible, since he suspected we should find ourselves in embarrassment and want—as did actually come to pass.

We went on through this wilderness and at the end of thirteen days arrived at some cottages. The Indians had now become so bewildered that they knew not in what direction to turn. The road had given out, and the governor went around to regain it, but failing to find it he came back to us desperate. He directed that the people should return some half a league to a great river, and there he began to give out rations of fresh pork from the hogs we drive with us, a pound to each man, which we ate boiled, without salt or other seasoning.

The governor sent in two directions to find a path, or any mark indicating inhabitants—one person up the river to the north and northeast, and the other down along it to the south and southeast. He allowed to each ten days in which to go and return. The man who went to the south and southeast returned after four days with the news that he had come upon a little town that had some provisions. He brought three or four people from it. Our perfidious Indian spoke with them and he understood them. This was a great relief to us, because of the difficulty there is everywhere in the country of being understood.

Once more the guide repeated the falsehoods he had told us before, which we believed because we heard him talk the language with those Indians. We directly set out with all our people for that little village to await the return of those who had gone in other directions to seek for paths. We tarried four or five days, until all had come together. About fifty fanegas of maize were found in this place, and some parched meal; there were many mulberry trees loaded with fruit, and likewise some other fruits.

From there we proceeded to the town of Cofitachique, two days' journey from the village and situated on the banks of a river which we believed to be the Santa Elena, where the licentiate Ayllón had been. When we arrived at the stream, the Lady of this town sent to us her niece, borne in a litter, with a message. The Indians showed her much respect.

The message said she was pleased we had arrived in her territory, and that she would give us all she might possess. She likewise sent the governor a necklace of five strings of pearls. We were furnished with canoes in which to pass over the river, and the Lady gave us one-half of the town; but after staying three or four days, she suddenly went off into the woods.

The governor sent to search for her. Not finding her, he opened a mosque in which were interred the bodies of the chief personages of that country. We took from it a quantity of pearls weighing as much as six arrobas and a half, or seven [350 pounds], though they were injured from lying in the earth and in the substance of the dead. We found two buried wood axes, of Castilian make, a rosary of jet beads, and some false pearls, such as are taken from Spain to traffic with the Indians, all of which we supposed they got in exchange with the followers of the licentiate Ayllón. From the information given by the Indians, the sea should be about thirty leagues distant.

We knew that the people who came with Ayllón hardly entered the country at all, but remained continually on the coast until his sickness and death. In strife for command, they then commenced to kill each other, while others of them died of hunger. One of those who had been among them told us that of the six hundred men who landed, only fifty-seven escaped—a loss caused to a great extent by the wreck of a big ship they had brought, laden with stores.

We remained in the town of this Lady some ten days. It then became necessary to leave to find a country which might furnish food, as the quantity where we were was sufficient only for the necessities of the Indians, and we, our horses and followers, consumed it very fast.

Again we took the direction of the north. We traveled for eight days through a poor country, scarce of food, until we arrived at one called Xuala, where we still found some Indian houses, though a thin population, for the country was broken. Among those ridges we discovered the source of the great river from which we had taken our departure, believed to be the Espiritu Santo. We went to a town called Guasuli, where the inhabitants gave us a number of dogs, and some maize, of which they had but little. From there we marched four days and arrived at a town called Chiha, which is very plentiful in food. It is secluded on an island of this river of Espiritu Santo, which, all the way from the place of its rise, forms very large islands. In this province, where we began to find the towns set about with fence, the Indians get a large quantity of oil from walnuts. We were detained twenty-seven days to refresh the horses, which arrived greatly fatigued, having worked hard and eaten little.

We left, following along the banks of the river, and came to another province, Costehe, the towns of which are likewise on islands in the river, and from there we went to Coca, one of the finest we discovered in Florida. The cacique came out in a hurdle to receive us with great festivity and many people, numerous towns being subject to him. The next morning we saw all the inhabitants, and detained the cacique so that he might give us persons to carry our loads. We waited seven days to get them. We found plums like those here in Castile, and great quantities of vines on which were very good grapes.

From here we went to the west and southwest, passing through the towns of the cacique for five or six days, until we came to another province called Italisi. The people were gone, and we went to look for them. Some Indians came to us, and the governor sent them to call the cacique, who came bringing to us a present of twenty-six women, skins of deer, and whatever else they had.

From this point we went south toward the coast of New Spain. We passed through several towns before coming to another province called Taszaluza. Its chief was of such size that we all considered him a giant. He awaited us quietly at his town, and on our arrival we made much ado for him with joust at reeds and great running of horses, although he appeared to regard it all as a small matter. Afterward we asked him for Indians to carry our burdens. He answered that he was not accustomed to serving any one, but it was rather for all others to serve him. The governor ordered that he should not be allowed to return to his house but be kept where he was. He felt this detention among us, and from this sprang the ruin that he later worked upon us. He told us he could give us nothing there, and that we must go to another town of his, called Mavila, where he would bestow on us whatever we might ask.

We took up our march in that direction and came to a river, a copious flood which we considered to be that which empties into the Bay of Chuse. Here we learned how the boats of Narváez had arrived in want of water, and how a Christian named Don Teodoro had stopped among these Indians with a Negro, and we were shown a dagger that he had worn. We were here two days, making rafts for crossing the river. During this time the Indians killed one of the guard of the governor, who became angry and threatened the cacique, telling him he would burn him if he did not give up to him those who had slain the Christian. He replied that he would deliver them to us in that town of his, Mavila. The cacique had many in attendance. An Indian was always behind him with a flybrush of plumes, so large as to afford his person shelter from the sun.

At nine o'clock one morning we arrived at Mavila, a small town very strongly stockaded and situated on a plain. We found the Indians had demolished some habitations about it to present a clear field. A number of the chiefs came out to receive us as soon as we were in sight. They asked the governor, through the interpreter, if he would like to stop on that plain, or preferred to enter the town, saying that in the evening they would give us the Indians to carry burdens. It appeared to our chief better to go there with them, and he commanded all to go to the town, which we did.

Having come within the enclosure, we walked about and talked with the Indians, supposing them to be friendly. There were not over three or four hundred in sight, though full five thousand were in the town, whom we did not see. Apparently rejoicing, they began their customary songs and dances. Some women performed for us a little while, for dissimulation, and then the cacique got up and withdrew into one of the houses. The governor sent to tell him that he must come out, to which he answered that he would not; and the captain of the bodyguard entered the door to bring him forth. Seeing so many Indians present, fully prepared for battle, he thought it best to withdraw and leave him. He reported that the houses were filled with men, ready with bows and arrows, bent on some mischief. The governor called to an Indian passing by, who also refused to come. A gentleman near by took the Indian by the arm to bring him, and received a push such as to make him let go his hold. He drew his sword and dealt a stroke in return that cleaved away an arm.

With the blow they all began to shoot arrows at us, some from within the houses, through the many loopholes they had arranged, and some from without. We were wholly unprepared, having considered ourselves on a footing of peace, and we were obliged from the great injuries we were sustaining to flee from the town, leaving behind all that the carriers had brought for us. When the Indians saw that we had gone out, they closed the gates and, beating their drums, they raised flags with great shouting. Then emptying our knapsacks and bundles, they displayed above the palisades all we had brought, as much as to say that they had those things in their possession.

As soon as we retired we mounted our horses and completely encircled the town so that none might escape. The governor directed that sixty of us should dismount and that eighty of the best accoutered should form into four parties to assail the place on as many sides. The first of us getting in should set fire to the houses. Accordingly, we handed over our horses to other soldiers, who were not in armor, so that if any of the Indians should come running out of the town, they might overtake them.

We entered the town and set it on fire, whereby a number of Indians were burned. All that we had was consumed. We fought that day until nightfall. Not a single Indian surrendered to us, all fighting bravely on like lions. We killed them all, either with fire or the sword, or, such of them as came out, with the lance, so that when it was nearly dark there remained only three alive. These placed themselves behind the women who had been brought to dance and who, crossing their hands, made signs to us that we should come for them. When the Christians advanced toward the women, these turned aside and the three men behind them shot their arrows at us. We killed two of them. The last Indian, in order not to surrender, climbed a tree that was in the fence, and taking the cord from his bow, tied it about his neck and hanged himself from a limb.

This day the Indians slew more than twenty of our men. Those of us who escaped only hurt were two hundred fifty, bearing upon our bodies seven hundred sixty injuries from their shafts. At night we dressed our wounds with the fat of the dead Indians, as there was no medicine left, all that belonged to us having been burned. We remained almost a month to take care of ourselves, and God be praised that we were all relieved. The women were divided as servants among those who were suffering most.

We learned from the Indians that we were as many as forty leagues from the sea. We wished the governor to go to the coast, for we had tidings of the brigantines; but he dared not venture there. As it was already the middle of November, the season was very cold and he found it necessary to seek a country where subsistence might be had for the winter. Here there was none, the region being one of little food.

We resumed our direction northward and traveled ten or twelve days, suffering greatly from the cold and rain, in which we marched afoot, until we arrived at a fertile province, plentiful of provisions, where we could stop during the rigor of the season. The snows fall more heavily there than in Castile.

In the province of Chicaza the warriors came out to interrupt the passage of a river we had to cross, and detained us three days. Finally, we went over in a piragua we built, the Indians fleeing to the woods. After seven or eight days messengers came from their cacique, saying that he and all his people desired to come and serve us. The governor received the message well and sent word to him to do so without fail, and that he would present him with many things. The cacique came, bringing a number of persons who bore him upon their shoulders. He gave us some deer-skins and little dogs. The people returned, and every day Indians came and went, bringing us many hares and whatever else the country supplied.

One night we captured some Indians who, on a footing of peace, came to observe how we slept and guarded. Unaware of the perfidy that was intended, we told the cacique that we wished to continue our march the next day. He left, and that night he fell upon us. As the enemy knew where our sentinels were set, more than three hundred men got into the town among us by twos and fours without being observed. They brought fire in little pots, not to be seen.

When the sentinels discovered that more were coming in troop, they beat to arms; but the others had already set fire to the town. The Indians did us very great injury, killing fifty-seven horses, more than three hundred hogs, and fourteen men. It was a great mysterious providence of God that though we were not giving them any cause to do so, they turned and fled. Had they followed us up, not a man of all our number could have escaped. Immediately we moved to a cottage about a mile off.

We knew that the Indians had agreed to return upon us that night; but, God be praised, because of a light rain they did not come. We were in such bad condition that although some horses still remained, we had no saddles, lances or targets, all having been consumed. We hastened to make them, and at the end of five days the Indians came back upon us with their squadrons in order and attacked us at three points. This time we were prepared and aware of their approach. We met them at the onset, beat them back, and did them such injury that, thank God, they returned no more. We remained here perhaps two months, getting ready the necessary saddles, lances and targets, and then left, taking the direction to the northwest toward a province called Alibamo.

At this time there befell us what is said never to have occurred in the Indias. Without there being either women to protect or provisions to secure, and only to try our valor with theirs, the Indians put up a very strong stockade directly across the road over which we had to pass. About three hundred of them stood behind it, resolved to die rather than go back. As soon as they observed our approach, some came out to shoot their arrows, threatening that not one of us should remain alive. When we had surveyed that work we supposed they guarded something—provision perhaps—of which we stood greatly in need; for we had calculated to cross a desert of twelve days' journey where we could have nothing to eat but what we carried. Some forty or fifty of us alighted and put ourselves on two sides, arranging that at the sound of the trumpet we should all enter the barricade at one time. We did accordingly and carried it, although at some cost, seven or eight men and twenty-five wounded. We killed some Indians and took others, from whom we learned that they had done this to measure themselves with us, and nothing else. We looked about for food, although at great hazard, so that we might begin our journey in the wilderness.

We traveled eight days with great care, in tenderness of the wounded and the sick we carried. On mid-day we came upon a town called Quizquiz so suddenly that the inhabitants did not notice us, the men being away at work in the maize fields. We took more than three hundred women and the few skins and shawls they had in their houses. There we first found a little walnut of the country, which is much better than here in Spain. The town was near the banks of the River Espiritu Santo. They told us that, with many other towns near there, it was tributary to a lord of Pacaha, famed throughout the land.

When the men heard that we had taken their women, they came to us peacefully, requesting the governor to restore them. He did so, and asked them for canoes in which to pass that great river. These they promised, but never gave. On the contrary, they collected to give us battle, coming in sight of the town where we were; but in the end they turned and retired.

We left that place and went to encamp by the riverside, to put ourselves in order for crossing. On the other shore we saw numbers of people with many canoes collected to oppose our landing. We set about building four large piraguas, each capable of taking sixty or seventy men and five or six horses. We were engaged in the work for a month. Every day at three o'clock in the afternoon the Indians would get into two hundred fifty very large canoes, well shielded, and approach the shore where we were. With loud cries they would exhaust their arrows upon us, and then return to the other bank. When they saw that our boats were ready for crossing, they all went off, leaving the passage free.

We crossed the river, which was nearly a league in width and some twenty fathoms deep, and found some good towns on the other side. Once more following up the stream on the way to that province of Pacaha, we came first to the province of another lord against whom Pacaha waged severe war. The cacique came out peacefully to meet us, saying that he had heard of us for a long time and that he knew we were men from heaven, whom their arrows could not harm. Therefore he wished to have no strife, only to serve us. The governor received him kindly. We permitted no one to enter the town, in order to avoid mischief, and we encamped on a plain, where we lay two days.

On the day of our arrival the cacique said that inasmuch as he knew the governor to be a man from the sky who must necessarily go away, he asked him to leave a sign, of which he might ask support in his wars, and which his people might call upon for rain, which their fields needed, as their children were dying of hunger.

The governor commanded that a very tall cross be made of two pines, and told him to return the next day, when he would give him the sign from Heaven for which he asked; but that the Chief must believe that he would lack for nothing if he had true faith in the cross.

He returned the next day, complaining because we delayed so long in giving him the sign he asked. He set up such a loud wailing because the compliance was not immediate that he caused us all to weep at the devotion and earnestness in his entreaties.

The governor told him to bring all his people back in the evening, and that he would go with him to his town and bring the sign he asked. He came in the afternoon with them, and we went in procession to the town, while they followed us. It is the custom of the caciques to have near their houses a high hill made by hand, some having the houses placed thereon. We set up the cross on the summit of such a mount, and we all went on bended knees, with great humility, to kiss the foot of that cross. The Indians did the same as they saw us do. Then they brought a great quantity of cane and made a fence about the cross; and we returned that night to our camp.

In the morning we took up our course for Pacaha, which was up the river. We traveled two days and then discovered the town on a plain, well fenced about and surrounded by a water ditch made by hand. We came near and halted, not daring to enter there. Discovering that many people were escaping, we assailed and entered the town, meeting no opposition. We took only a few people, for nearly all had fled, without, however, being able to carry off the little they possessed.

While we were still halted in sight of the town, before venturing to enter it, we saw coming behind us a large body of Indians, whom we supposed to be advancing to the assistance of the place. We found they were those we had left behind, among whom we had raised the cross, who were following us to lend succor should we need any. We took the cacique to the town, where he gave the governor many thanks for the sign we had left him, telling us the rain had fallen heavily in his country the day before, and his people were so glad of it that they wished to follow us and not leave us.

The governor put him into the town and gave him every thing found there, which was great riches for those people—some beads made of sea-snails, the skins of cats and of deer, and a little maize. He returned home much gratified. We remained in this town twenty-seven or twenty-eight days, to discover if we could take a path to the north, whereby to come out on the South Sea.

Some incursions were made to capture Indians who might give us the information; particularly to the northwest, where we were told there were large settlements through which we might go. We went in that direction eight days, through a wilderness which had large swamps where we did not find even trees. There were only some wide plains on which grew a plant so rank and high that even on horseback we could not break our way through. Finally we came to some collections of huts, covered with rush sewed together. When the owner of one moves away, he will roll up the entire covering and carry it, the wife taking the frame of poles over which it is stretched. They take these poles down and put them up so readily that though they should move anew every hour, they can carry their house on their backs conveniently enough. We learned from this people that there were some hamlets of the sort about the country, the inhabitants of which employed themselves in finding places for their dwellings wherever many deer were accustomed to range, and a swamp where there were many fish. When they had frightened the game and the fish from one place, they would all move off with their dwellings to some other part where the animals were not yet shy. This province, called Calua, had a people who care little to plant, finding support in meat and fish.

We returned to Pacaha, where the governor had remained, and found that the cacique had come in peacefully, living with him in the town. There also arrived the cacique from the place behind at which we had put up the cross. The efforts of these two chiefs who were enemies, each to place himself on the right hand when the governor commanded that they should sit at his sides, was a sight worth witnessing.

THE RELATION OF RANGEL AS FOUND IN OVIEDO

Casqui had brought a daughter, a fine young girl, to the governor. Pacaha gave him one of his wives, blooming and very worthy; and he gave him a sister and another Indian woman of rank. The governor made the two caciques friends and embraced them and ordered that there should be merchandising and business between one country and the other, and they agreed to it. And after this the governor departed thence the 29th of July.

But I could wish that along with the excellencies of the cross and of the faith that this governor explained to these chiefs, he had told them that he was married, and that the Christians ought not to have more than one wife, or to have intercourse with another, or to commit adultery; that he had not taken the daughter whom Casqui gave him, nor the wife and sister and the other woman of rank whom Pacaha gave him; and that they had not got the idea that the Christians, like the Indians, could have as many wives and concubines as they desired, and thus, like the Indians, live as adulterers.

THE REPORT OF BIEDMA CONTINUES

Finding that there was no way by which to march to the other sea, we returned toward the south and went with the cacique to where was the cross, and from there took the direction to the southwest, to another province called Quiquate. This was the largest town we found in Florida, and was on the arm of the Rio Grande. We remained there eight or nine days to find guides and interpreters, still with the intention of coming out if possible on the other sea. For the Indians told us that eleven days' travel from there was a province where they subsisted on certain cattle, and there we could find interpreters for the whole distance to that sea.

We departed with guides for the province called Coligua, without any road, going at night to the swamps, where we drank from our hands and found abundance of fish. We went over much even country and some of broken hills, coming straight upon the town as though we had been taken there by a royal highway, instead of which not a man in all time had passed there. The subsistence in this land is very plentiful, and we found a large quantity of dressed cows' tails, and others already cured. We inquired of the inhabitants for a path in the direction we held, or a town on it, near or far. They could give us no sort of information, only that if we wished to go in the direction where there were people, we should have to return upon a west-southwestern course.

We continued to pursue the course chosen by our guides, and went to some scattered settlements called Tatil Coya. Here we found a copious river which we afterward discovered empties into the Rio Grande, and we were told that up the stream was a great province called Cayas. We went there and found it to be a population that, though large, was entirely scattered. It is a very rough country of hills. Several incursions were made, in one of which the cacique and a large number of people were taken. On asking him about the particulars of the country, he told us that in following up the river we should come upon a fertile province called Tula. The governor wished to see if it were a place in which he could winter the people, and he set off with twenty men on horseback, leaving the remainder in the province of Cayas.

Before coming to the province of Tula we passed over some rough hills and arrived at the town before the inhabitants had any notice of us. We attempted to seize some Indians, who began to yell and show battle. They wounded eight of our men and nine or ten horses; and such was their courage that they came upon us in packs, by eights and tens, like worried dogs. We killed some thirty or forty of them. The governor thought it not well to stay there that night with his small force, and returned on the way we had come, going through a bad passage of the ridge, where it was feared the natives would beset us, to a plain in the valley made by the river. The next day we got back to where the people lay, but none of our Indians could speak the language of those we brought nor could any be found in the province.

Orders were given that all should make ready to go to that province, and we marched there at once. The next morning after our arrival, at daybreak, three very large squadrons of Indians came upon us by as many directions. We met them and beat them, doing some injury, and they returned upon us no more.

In two or three days they sent us messengers of peace, although we did not understand a thing they said for want of an interpreter. By signs we told them to bring persons who could understand the people living back of us; and they brought five Indians who understood our interpreters. They asked who we were and what we sought. We asked them for some great provinces where there should be much provision, for the cold of the winter had begun to threaten us sharply, and they said that on the route we were taking they knew of no great town. But they pointed out that if we wished to return to the east and southeast, or go northwest, we should find large towns.

Discovering that we could not prevail against the difficulty, we returned to the southeast and went to a province called Quipana at the base of some very steep ridges. From there we journeyed to the east and, having crossed those mountains, went down upon some plains. There we found a population suited to our purpose, for there was a town near by in which was much food. It was seated by a copious river emptying into the Rio Grande, from which we had come. The province was called Viranque. We stopped there to pass the winter, and suffered so much cold we thought we would perish. At this town the Christian—Ortiz—died whom we had found in the country belonging to the people of Narváez and who was our interpreter.

We left there in the beginning of March, when it appeared that the severity of the winter had passed, and followed down the course of the river. We found other provinces well peopled and having a quantity of food. Finally we came to a province called Anicoyanque, which appeared to us to be one of the best we had found in all the country. Here another cacique, called Guachoyanque, came to us in peace. His town is upon the River Grande, and he is in continual war with the other chief with whom we were.

The governor directly set out for the town of Guachoyanque and took its cacique with him. The town was good, well and strongly fenced. It contained little provision, the Indians having carried that off. The governor had determined, if he should find the sea, to build brigantines by which to make it known in Cuba that we were alive, so that we might be supplied with horses and things of which we stood in need. He sent a captain southward to see if some road could be discovered by which we might go to look for the sea, because nothing could be learned from the account given by the Indians. He got back and reported that he found no road, nor any way by which to pass the great bogs that extend out from the Rio Grande. The governor, at seeing himself thus surrounded, and nothing coming about according to his expectations, sickened and died. He left us, recommending Luis de Moscoso to be our governor.

FROM THE ACCOUNT OF A GENTLEMAN OF ELVAS

The governor, conscious that the hour approached in which he should depart this life, commanded that all the king's officers should be called before him, to whom he made a speech. He said that he was about to go into the presence of God, to give account of all his past life; and since He had been pleased to take him away at such a time, and when he could recognize the moment of his death, he, His most unworthy servant, rendered Him hearty thanks. He confessed his deep obligations to them all, whether present or absent, for their great qualities, their love and loyalty to his person, well tried in the sufferance of hardship, which he ever wished to honor, and had designed to reward, when the Almighty should be pleased to give him repose from labor with greater prosperity to his fortune. He begged that they would pray for him, that through mercy he might be pardoned his sins, and his soul be received in glory: he asked that they would relieve him of the charge he held over them, as well of the indebtedness he was under to them all, and to forgive him any wrongs they might have received at his hands. To prevent any divisions that might arise as to who should command, he asked that they would be pleased to elect a principal and able person to be governor, one with whom they should all be satisfied, and, being chosen, they would swear before him to obey: that this would greatly satisfy him, abate somewhat the pains he suffered, and moderate the anxiety of leaving them in a country, they knew not where.

Baltazar de Gallegos responded in behalf of all, consoling him with remarks on the shortness of the life of this world, attended as it was by so many toils and afflictions, saying that whom God earliest called away, He showed particular favor; with many other things appropriate to such an occasion. And finally, since it pleased the Almighty to take him to Himself, amid the deep sorrow they not unreasonably felt, it was necessary and becoming in him as in them to conform to the Divine Will; that as respected the election of a governor, which he ordered, whomsoever his Excellency should name to the command, him would they obey. Thereupon the governor nominated Luis Moscoso de Alvarado to be his captain-general; when by all those present was he straightway chosen and sworn governor.

The next day, the twenty-first of May, departed this life the magnanimous, the virtuous, the intrepid Captain, Don Hernando de Soto, Governor of Cuba and Adelantado of Florida. He was advanced by fortune, in the way she is wont to lead others, that he might fall the greater depth. He died in a land and at a time that could afford him little comfort in his illness, when the danger of being no more heard from stared his companions in the face, each one himself having need of sympathy, which was the cause why they neither gave him their companionship nor visited him, as otherwise they would have done.

Luis de Moscoso determined to conceal what had happened from the Indians, for Soto had given them to understand that the Christians were immortal. Besides, they held him to be vigilant, sagacious, brave; and although they were at peace, should they know him to be dead, they, being of their nature inconstant, might venture on making an attack. And they were credulous of all that he had told them,

who made them believe that some things which went on among them
privately, and he had come at without their being able to see how,
or by what means, that the figure which appeared in a mirror he
showed, told him whatsoever they might be about, or desired to do;
whence neither by word nor deed did they dare undertake any thing
to his injury.

So soon as the death had taken place, Luis de Moscoso directed
the body to be put secretly into a house, where it remained three days;
and thence it was taken at night by his order to a gate of the town
and buried within. The Indians, who had seen him ill, finding him
no longer, suspected the reason; and passing by where he lay, they
observed the ground loose, and looking about, talked among themselves. This coming to the knowledge of Luis de Moscoso, he ordered
the corpse to be taken up at night, and after an abundance of sand
was cast among the shawls that enshrouded it, the body of Soto was
taken out in a canoe and committed to the middle of the stream.

The cacique of Guachoya asked for him, saying: "What has been
done with my brother and lord, the governor?" Luis de Moscoso told
him that he had ascended into the skies, as he had done on many other
occasions; but as he would have to be detained there some time, he
had left him in his stead. The chief, thinking within himself that he
was dead, ordered two well-proportioned young men to be brought,
saying that it was the usage of the country when any lord died to
kill some persons who should accompany and serve him on the way,
on which account they were brought. And he told them to command
their heads to be struck off, that they might go accordingly to attend
his friend and master. Luis de Moscoso replied to him that the governor was not dead but only gone into the heavens, having taken with
him of his soldiers sufficient number for his need, and he besought
him to let those Indians go and from that time forward not to follow
so evil a practice. They were presently ordered to be let loose that
they might return to their houses; but one of them refused to leave,
alleging that he did not wish to remain in the power of one who, without cause, condemned him to die, and that he who had saved his life
he desired to serve so long as he should live.

Luis de Moscoso ordered the property of the governor to be sold at
public outcry. It consisted of two male and three female slaves, three
horses, and seven hundred swine. For each slave, or horse, was given
two or three thousand cruzados, to be paid at the first melting up of
gold or silver, or division of vassals and territory, with the obligation
that should there be nothing found in the country, the payment

should be made at the end of a year, those having no property to pledge to give their bond. A hog brought in the same way, trusted, two hundred cruzados. Those who had left any thing at home bought more sparingly, and took less than others. From that time forward most of the people owned and raised hogs; they lived on pork, observed Fridays and Saturdays, and the vespers of holidays, which they had not done before; for at times they had passed two or three months without tasting any meat, and on the day they got any, it had been their custom to eat it.

FROM THE RELATION OF RANGEL AS FOUND IN OVIEDO

Give ear, then, Catholic reader, and do not lament the conquered Indians less than their Christian conquerors or slayers of themselves, as well as others, and follow the adventures of the governor, ill governed, taught in the School of Pedrarias de Ávila, in the scattering and wasting of the Indians of Castilla del Oro; a graduate in the killing of the natives of Nicaragua and canonized in Peru as a member of the order of the Pizarros; and then, after being delivered from all those paths of Hell and having come to Spain loaded with gold, neither a bachelor nor married, knew not how nor was able to rest without returning to the Indies to shed human blood, not content with what he had spilled; and to leave life as shall be narrated, and providing the opportunity for so many sinners deluded with his vain words to perish after him.

THE REPORT OF BIEDMA CONTINUES

Since we could find no way to the sea, we agreed to take our course to the west, on which we might come out by land to Mexico, should we be unable to find anything, or a place whereon to settle. We traveled seventeen days, until we came to the province of Chavite, where the Indians made much salt; but we could learn nothing of them concerning the west. Then we went to another province called Aquacay, and were there three days on the way, still going directly westward. After leaving this place, the Indians told us we should see no more settlements unless we went down in a southwest-by-south direction, where we should find large towns and food; that in the course we asked about, there were some large sandy wastes without any people or subsistence whatsoever.

We were obliged to go where the Indians directed us, and went through several provinces. Each time we went through lands that became more sterile and afforded less subsistence. We continually asked for a province which they told us was large, called Xuacatino. The cacique of Nondacao, where we were, gave us an Indian to put us purposely somewhere where we could never come out. The guide took us over a rough country, and off the road, until he told us at last he did not know where he was leading us, but that his master had ordered him to take us where we should die of hunger. We took another guide, who led us to a province called Hais, where, in season, cattle are wont to herd. When the Indians saw us entering their country, they began to cry out: "Kill the cows—they are coming": and they sallied forth and shot their arrows at us, doing us some injury.

Continuing our march, we came to the land of Xuacatino, which was among some close forests and was scant of food. From here the Indians guided us eastward to other small towns, poorly off for food. They said they would take us to where there were other Christians like us, which afterward proved false. They could not have had knowledge of any others than ourselves, although since we had made so many turns they might have observed our passing in some of them. We returned to go southward, with the resolution of either reaching New Spain or dying. We traveled about six days in a direction south and southwest and then stopped.

From there we sent ten men on swift horses to travel eight or nine days as far as possible, and see if any town could be found where we might re-supply ourselves with maize, to enable us to pursue our journey. They went as far as they could go, and came upon some poor people without houses, having wretched huts into which they withdrew. They neither planted nor gathered anything, but lived entirely upon flesh and fish. Three or four of them, whose tongue no one could understand, were brought back. Reflecting that we had lost our interpreter, that we found nothing to eat, that the maize we brought upon our backs was failing, and it seemed impossible that so many people should be able to cross a country so poor, we determined to return to the town where the Governor Soto died. There it appeared to us there was convenience for building vessels with which we might leave the country.

We returned by the same road we had taken until we came to the town; but we did not discover such good outfit as we had thought to find. There were no provisions in the town, the Indians having taken them away, so we had to seek another town where we might pass the winter and build the vessels. I thank God that we found two towns very much to our purpose, standing upon the Rio Grande, which were fenced around, having also a large quantity of maize. Here we stopped and with great labor built seven brigantines, which were finished in about six months. We threw them out into the water, and it was a mystery that, calked as they were with the bark of mulberry trees, and without any pitch, we should find them stanch and very safe. We also took with us some canoes, into which were put twenty-six horses, in the event we found any large town on the shore of the sea that could sustain us with food. We thought also to send a couple of brigantines to the Viceroy of New Spain, with a message to provide us with vessels in which we could get away from the country.

The second day, descending the stream, there came out against us about forty or fifty very large and swift canoes, in some of which were as many as eighty warriors, who assailed us with their arrows. Some of our men in the vessels thought it trifling not to attack them; so, taking some of the small canoes we had, they went after them. The Indians surrounded them so that they could not get away, and upset the canoes. Twelve very worthy men were drowned, beyond the reach of our succor, because of the great power of the stream and the few oars in our vessels.

The Indians were encouraged by this success to follow us to the sea, which we were nineteen days in reaching, doing us much damage and wounding many people. They had found we had no arms that could reach them from a distance, not an arquebuse nor a cross-bow having remained, but only some swords and targets. In consequence, they lost their fears and would draw very near to let drive at us with their arrows.

We came out by the mouth of the river and entered into a very large bay. It was so extensive that we passed along it three days and three nights, with fair weather, in all the time not seeing land, so that it appeared to us we were at sea, although we found the water still so fresh that it could well be drunk, like that of the river. Some small islets were seen westward, to which we went. From there we kept close along the coast, where we took shell-fish and looked for other things to eat, until we entered the River of Panuco, where we came and were well received by the Christians.

LUIS HERNÁNDEZ DE BIEDMA

The survivors of De Soto's expedition came ashore at Panuco on September 10, after three years of misery. They had traveled far, had seen much and had known great disappointment and hardship. Their reception at Mexico City was described by Juan Coles, a member of the expedition:

A gentleman of importance, a citizen of Mexico named Xaramillo, took into his house eighteen men, all from Estremadura, and he clothed them with fine broadcloth of Segovia, and to each one of them he gave a bed with mattresses, sheets, and blankets and pillows, a comb and brush, and everything else needful for a soldier, and all the city was greatly pained to see them clothed with deer skins and cow [buffalo] skins, and that they did them this honor and kindness for the many labors they knew that they had undergone in Florida. On the other hand, they did not care to show any favors to those that had been with Captain Juan Vásquez Coronado, a resident of Mexico, to discover the Seven Cities, because, without necessity, they had returned to Mexico without daring to make a settlement. These had returned shortly before we did.

Juan Coles makes the mistakes historians have made over the years, confusing Francisco Vásquez de Coronado with his brother who became Governor of Costa Rica. But the temper of the two receptions may have been explainable by the additional fact that Coronado's had been financed out of Mexico City and that it had been a disappointment, where the De Soto expedition had begun in Spain and Cuba.

About a month after the stragglers landed in Panuco, Maldonado, whom De Soto had avoided meeting, landed at Vera Cruz. He tried several times in the preceding two years to locate the lost army and may even have carried his search as far as Canada. With the tragic report in hand, he set sail for Cuba to inform the governor's widow. Doña Isabella barely survived the news of her husband's death, dying only a few days after meeting with Maldonado.

The well-equipped and well-financed expedition had started with about six hundred men. Only three hundred twenty were with Luis Moscoso de Alvarado when they stopped in January to build the small fleet on the Mississippi. Fewer still were in the party that arrived at Panuco. But as soon as Viceroy Mendoza received Moscoso's report, he began to plan another expedition to Florida. De Soto's men had had enough. Some went on to Peru, some went home to Spain while others remained in Mexico City, too defeated or too ill to try again.

The exact route of the De Soto expedition has always been in doubt. Like that of Cabeza de Vaca and Coronado, there is enough information in the chronicles to indicate direction, rivers crossed and physical landmarks. But specific details are usually lacking. It is commonly accepted that De Soto followed the coast from Tampa Bay to about Tallahassee, and from there turned northeast to the Savannah River, which he followed generally through the Blue Ridge country down to the Alabama River to Mobile Bay, and then turned northwest toward Memphis, from which place the expedition cut westward to Arkansas above the Canadian River, and eastward back to the Mississippi. The governor's successor, Luis Moscoso de Alvarado, continued west again, crossing the Sabine and Trinity Rivers until he reached the Red River. From this point he seems to have doubled back on his own trail to the Mississippi. Here he stopped to build his ships and then made the seven-hundred-mile journey down river under constant Indian attack. The survivors coasted Texas southwest and on to Panuco, Mexico.

Postscript

WHEN THE last of De Soto's men came ashore at Panuco, the great age of the conquistadores in North and Central America came to an end. Others were to follow the trails they cut. Colonies were to be established in Florida and Alta California. Juan de Onate was to lead families into the Coronado country. The Seven Cities of Cíbola were joined to the Rio Grande pueblos, and the province of New Mexico was formed. Cattle was raised and crops planted. Onate himself wasted one of the largest fortunes in the New World chasing the vague dream of sudden wealth which he believed lay somewhere above el Paso del Norte. A century later Diego de Vargas was spurred to reconquer the province from the rebellious natives by a wispy report that there were mines to the west. The Spaniards never found them.

The tremendous energies that were expended to win the continent for God and Spain gave way to sloth. The Elizabethan sea dogs under Drake and Hawkins slashed at the wealth of the empire, and in retaliation Charles' son, Philip II, spent the fortunes won by the conquistadores on the ill-fated armadas. Spain in half a century became the greatest empire the world has ever known. But it was easier to conquer the New World than to hold it.

With careful planning and organization, Balboa established a colony and discovered an ocean. Though the captains from Cuba probed the edges of Yucatan and Mexico with caution, they discovered a new civilization and brought home word of yet another ruled from the city in the lake beyond the mountains. Where these men had been timid, Cortés was bold. Few commanders have ever moved so swiftly, so cunningly, and against such odds. However history may judge his excesses, it must take into account his singleness of purpose and his military genius.

Though most people have failed to understand the importance of Alvarado in the gallery of conquistadores, the man whom the Indians compared to the sun itself had the rash qualities of his companions and their fantastic courage to such a degree that he stands as a symbol of the best and the worst of all of them.

No reader can easily forget the strange figure of the slave-conquistador who crossed the continent trying his hand at medicine and prayer. Cabeza de Vaca was possessed of an understanding beyond that of his contemporaries, and for this he suffered. But his journal reveals that he never claimed the miracles which others believed he performed and that he never killed an Indian. He appears a tragic figure at the end, but an honorable one, while others who won great victories committed great crimes. The tragedy of Cabeza de Vaca is the tragedy of a man who was misunderstood, whose talents for dealing with the natives were unwanted by his countrymen.

The tragedy of Coronado is simpler and not one of his own making. He commanded the strongest and best supplied expedition ever to set out for conquest in the New World, and it came to nothing. There was no Mexico City waiting to be conquered. There were only adobe villages and a small cluster of skin tents. The prize was not worthy of the efforts to win it, and so he came home injured and in disgrace. His contemporaries, who were eager for wealth, were disappointed in what he had accomplished. But as time has passed, the records of his travels have become important, and those who in later years followed him through the plains country, the adobe kingdoms and the mountains to the sea, became aware just how sweeping his expeditions were. The same slow recognition of achievement has come to the man who was buried by his fellows in the Mississippi. De Soto wandered through the eastern half of the United States and westward beyond the river. The stories brought back by his companions were not of wealth of gold and silver, but of land, and in the end it was the land that mattered.

This was the great achievement of the conquistadores—that in half a century they opened up half the world. The treasure they found brought ruin to Spain. The empire they created was impossible to hold. But the land they found, the places where they left the names and the bodies of companions became the monuments to their courage and their faith.

Chronology

1501

October. Rodrigo de Bastidas discovers Gulf of Darien; Vasco Núñez de Balboa with expedition.

1502

May. Admiral Christopher Columbus sails from Cadiz on last of four voyages.

1503

Leonardo da Vinci paints "Mona Lisa."

1504

November 26. Queen Isabella dies.

1505

Christ's College in Cambridge founded.

July 17. Martin Luther enters Augustine monastery at Erfurt.

1506

May 20. The Admiral dies.

1508

Juan Ponce de León begins conquest of Puerto Rico.

Luther becomes Professor of Divinity at Wittenberg.

Michelangelo begins painting ceiling of Sistine Chapel in Rome.

1509

Diego de Colón comes to Santo Domingo as governor.

November. Alonzo de Ojeda sails from Spain to settle New Andalusia; Francisco Pizarro in party.

November. Diego de Nicuesa sails from Spain to settle Urába.

1510

September. Balboa stows away aboard one of relief vessels of Martín Fernández de Enciso; Pascual de Andagoya with expedition.

Diego de Velásquez sent by Colón to conquer Cuba; his lieutenant, Pánfilo de Narváez.

1512

De Ratione Studii et Instituendi Pueros of Erasmus published.

1513

April. Juan Ponce, seeking "island of Bimini," discovers, names Florida.

September 25. Balboa crosses Isthmus of Panama, discovers Southern Sea.

Machiavelli begins writing *The Prince.*

September 9. Scots, allied with France, defeated at Flodden.

1515

April. Pedrarias Dávila sent to Darien as governor.

January 1. Louis XII of France dies, and succeeded by Francis I.

1516

January. Bartolemé de Las Casas heads commission of Hieronymite fathers to study means of alleviating wrongs suffered by Indians.

January 23. Ferdinand of Aragon dies, succeeded by Charles, his grandson.

1517

Balboa arrested by Pizarro on orders of Pedrarias; tried, executed.

February. Francisco Hernández de Córdoba discovers eastern coast of Yucatan; Bernal Díaz del Castillo with expedition.

Turks conquer Egypt, intercept traffic en route to India.

1518

May. Juan de Grijalva sent by Velásquez to Yucatan to follow up discoveries of Córdoba; Pedro de Alvarado with expedition.

Royal College of Physicians founded by Linacre.

"Assumption of the Virgin" painted by Titian.

1519

Hernando de Soto sails for Darien.

February 10. Hernán Cortés leaves Cuba for Yucatan and Mexico.

August 16. Cortés begins march inland from Vera Cruz to Mexico.

November 8. Montezuma welcomes Cortés to Mexico.

November 14. Cortés takes Montezuma prisoner.

June 28. Charles of Spain elected Holy Roman Emperor to succeed Maximilian I.

August 10. Magellan begins first circumnavigation of globe.

1520

April 23. Narváez arrives at San Juan de Ulua with orders from Velásquez to punish Cortés.

May 29. Cortés captures Narváez at Cempoala.

June 24. Cortés re-enters Mexico to relieve Pedro de Alvarado.

June 29. Montezuma dies.

June 30. The Noche Triste. Spaniards leave Tenochtitlan, Mexico.

December 28. Cortés leaves Tlascala to begin reconquest of Mexico.

Machiavelli publishes *Arte della Guerra.*

June 15. The Pope declares Luther heretic.

July 14. Charles V, Henry VIII sign secret treaty at Calais.

1521

April 28. Thirteen brigantines built in Tlascala by Cortés launched on the lake at Texcoco.

August 13. Reconquest of Mexico complete.

April 27. Magellan killed in Philippine Islands.

1522

October 15. The Emperor appoints Cortés governor, captain-general and chief justice of New Spain.

February 2. Pope Leo X bestows title of *Fidei Defensor* on Henry VIII.

September. First edition of Luther's New Testament; Zwingli begins Reformation in Zurich.

1523

November. Pedro de Alvarado sent by Cortés to conquer Guatemala.

Europeans expelled from China.

1524

July. Pedro de Alvarado founds Spanish city of Guatemala.

Holbein paints "Dance of Death."

1527

May 6. Rome sacked by Germans, Spaniards.

1528

April 15. Narváez lands in Florida; Álvar Núñez Cabez de Vaca treasurer of expedition.

September 22. Remnants of the Narváez expedition gather on Galveston Island under Cabeza de Vaca.

January 21. England declares war on Charles V.

1529

November 19. Antonio de Mendoza appointed viceroy of New Spain.

June 29. Treaty of Barcelona reconciles Charles V and the Pope.

September 21. Turks begin first siege of Vienna.

1532

De Soto joins Pizarro in Peru.

First edition of Chaucer's complete works published; also *Pantagruel* by Rabelais.

1534

March. Pedro de Alvarado lands in Peru.

August 26. Diego de Almagro "buys out" Alvarado in Peru for 100,000 pesos de oro.

April 20. Cartier reaches Labrador.

August 15. Jesuit Order founded in Paris.

1536

July 24. Cabeza de Vaca, three other survivors of Narváez expedition reach Mexico.

1537

April 20. De Soto is named governor and adelantado of Florida and Cuba.

1539

March 7. Fray Marcos de Niza, Estaban set out from Culiacán to find Seven Cities of Cíbola.

April 18. Francisco Vásquez Coronado confirmed as governor of New Galicia.

May 21. Fray Marcos learns of death of Estaban.

May 30. De Soto lands at Tampa Bay on coast of Florida.

July 8. Ulloa, sent by Cortés, sails from Acapulco, explores Gulf of California.

September 2. Fray Marcos reports fabulous Seven Cities of Cíbola to Mendoza, Coronado.

November. De Soto finds remains of camp of Narváez at Bahia de las Cavallos.

March. Venice and Turkey sign truce.

April. Great English monasteries are dissolved.

May. Saxony, Brandenburg become Protestant.

1540

February 5. Cortés stops at Havana on way to Spain.

February 23. Coronado sets out from Compostela to find Cíbola.

March. De Soto breaks camp in Florida, goes northeast across what is now Georgia.

March 28. Coronado arrives in Culiacán.

Michael Servetus discovers circulation of blood.

Cardinal Contarini tries to reconcile Protestants, Roman Catholics.

May 9. Hernando de Alarcón sails from Acapulco to co-operate with Coronado, who starts from Culiacán to march toward Corazones valley.

July 7. Coronado reaches Cíbola, captures pueblo of Hawikuh, which he calls Granada.

August. García López Cárdenas discovers Grand Canyon.

August 3. Friar Marcos returns to Mexico with Juan Gallego.

August 26. Alarcón enters mouth of Colorado River.

August 29. Hernando de Alvarado goes eastward to buffalo plains.

October. De Soto reaches head of Mobile Bay.

November 29. Mendoza, Pedro de Alvarado sign agreement on common exploration and conquests.

1541

January. The Turk tells Coronado about Quivira.

April 23. Coronado starts from Tiguex to cross buffalo plains to Quivira.

May 8. De Soto reaches Mississippi River.

June 29. Pedro de Alvarado dies in Nochistlan in New Galicia.

July. Coronado and thirty horsemen arrive in Quivira.

December. Coronado falls from horse, injured severely.

Expedition of Charles V to Algeria fails.

August 26. Turks conquer Buda; Hungary becomes Turkish province.

1542

Cabeza de Vaca appointed governor of Paraguay.

Spring. Coronado and men begin return to Mexico.

May 21. De Soto dies, is buried in Mississippi River.

1543

September 10. Survivors of De Soto expedition reach Panuco.

De Revolutione Orbium Celestium by Copernicus published; also *De Humani Corporis Fabrica* by Vesalius.

1544

November 30. The New Laws for Indies, abolishing Indian slavery, promulgated.

1547

December 2. Cortés dies.

January 28. Henry VIII dies.

1549

Mendoza leaves Mexico; appointed viceroy of Peru.

1554

November 1. Coronado dies.

1556

January 16. Charles V resigns Spain to Philip II.

Glossary

adelantado   a title similar to a governor or president; frequently hereditary

alcalde   a mayor and magistrate of a town; chairman of a town council

alguacil   a police official or constable

arroba   a weight of about twenty-five pounds

audiencia   a royal tribunal or court of justice, or the hearing given by authorities to a proposal

cacique   a Caribbean word for the head of a tribe which became the general term for an Indian chief

castellano   a Castilian, or the Spanish language, but most frequently used as the name of a small coin of about one-fifth ounce of gold

clérigo   a cleric, Roman Catholic clergyman, padre

despoblado   a desert or uninhabited place

encomienda   a grant of a specified number of Indians, which included protection and exploitation (see General Preface)

ensenada   a creek, cove, inlet or small bay

entrada   the entry or ingress into a territory, but used to describe a military or reconnoitering expedition

fanega   a Spanish bushel, about 1.6 U.S. bushels

hidalgo   a nobleman

licentiate   one who holds a high college degree, a lawyer

maestre de campo   a military rank about equal to a colonel, a commander serving under a captain-general

oro   gold

palmitos   dwarf fan palms

piragua   a small vessel

regidor   alderman or magistrate, a councilman

repartimiento   a division or allotment of land made to an individual, the forced labor of natives (see General Preface)

residencia   the judicial hearing which took place at the close of a term of office to inquire into the honesty of service, hear charges against the administrator and see that justice was done

Acknowledgments

We would like to acknowledge the co-operation of the librarians of the Union Theological Seminary of New York City and of the Newberry Library in Chicago. In addition, we want to express our thanks to Ethel Blacker, Irma Rosen and Andrée Coers for both their help and suggestions.

Our thanks is extended to the University of New Mexico Press for permission to use materials from pages 42-44, 50-53, 58-62, 63-82 and 159-185 of the book *Narratives of the Coronado Expedition 1450-1542*, by George P. Hammond and Agapito Rey, copyright 1940 by the University of New Mexico Press.

Thanks is also due the Cortés Society for permission to use Bartolomé de Las Casas' account of the Grijalva expedition and S. J. Mackie's translation of the Pedro de Alvarado letters.

Other sources used in the writing of *The Golden Conquistadores* are as follows:

The Hakluyt Society publications: report of Pascual de Andagoya, publication number 34, 1865; account of Bernal Diáz del Castillo concerning the Córdoba expedition, the publication of 1890.

Letters to Cortés, 2 vols., translated and edited by Francis Augustus MacNutt, April 1908: the Cortés letters.

George P. Winship, *14th Annual Report of the U. S. Bureau of Ethnology*, 1896 (reprint 1904): the account of the 1540 expedition to Cíbola, written by Pedro de Castañeda of Najera.

The Narratives of Álvar Núñez Cabeza de Vaca, translated and edited by Buckingham Smith, privately printed, Washington, D. C., 1851: the relation of Cabeza de Vaca.

The Narrative of the Career of Hernando de Soto, translated by Buckingham Smith, privately printed, Washington, D. C., 1857; quoted material in the book on Hernando de Soto.

I. R. B.

H. M. R.